Perilous Power

Updated with a new preface by Gilbert Achcar, covering events since 2007 including the late-2023 renewal of military conflict between Israel and Hamas, this new edition provides readers with an essential critical perspective on the U.S. role in the Middle East.

The volatile Middle East is the site of vast resources, profound passions, frequent crises, and long-standing conflicts, as well as a major source of international tensions and a key site of direct U.S. intervention. Two of the most astute analysts of this part of the world are Noam Chomsky, the preeminent critic of U.S. foreign policy, and Gilbert Achcar, a leading specialist of the Middle East who has lived in that region for many years. In this book, Chomsky and Achcar bring a keen understanding of the internal dynamics of the Middle East and of the role of the United States, taking up all the key questions of interest to concerned citizens, including such topics as terrorism, fundamentalism, conspiracies, oil, democracy, self-determination, anti-Semitism, anti-Arab racism, the Israeli-Palestinian conflict, and the sources of U.S. foreign policy.

This book provides the best readable introduction for all who wish to understand the complex issues related to the Middle East from a perspective dedicated to peace and justice.

Noam Chomsky is one of the most cited scholars in history and has profoundly shaped contemporary understanding of American politics. He has authored numerous books on linguistics, history, and politics. He is Institute Professor (Emeritus) in the Department of Linguistics and Philosophy at MIT, and Laureate Professor of Linguistics and Agnese Nelms Haury Chair in the Program in Environment and Social Justice at the University of Arizona.

Gilbert Achcar teaches at the School of Oriental and African Studies, University of London.

Stephen R. Shalom, author of the preface, is a Professor at William Paterson University.

Chomsky from Routledge

Titles in the Series

Perilous Power
The Middle East and U.S. Foreign Policy
Noam Chomsky and Gilbert Achcar

Letters from Lexington
Reflections on Propaganda

A New Generation Draws the Line
Humanitarian Intervention and the 'Responsibility to Protect' Today

Power and Terror
Conflict, Hegemony, and the Rule of Force

Internationalism or Extinction
Noam Chomsky
Edited by Charles Derber, Suren Moodliar, and Paul Shannon

Chomsky for Activists
Noam Chomsky, Charles Derber, Suren Moodliar, and Paul Shannon

Perilous Power
The Middle East and U.S. Foreign Policy

Noam Chomsky and Gilbert Achcar

Edited with a preface by Stephen
R. Shalom

Routledge
Taylor & Francis Group

NEW YORK AND LONDON

Designed cover image: © Getty Images

Third edition published 2024
by Routledge
605 Third Avenue, New York, NY 10158

and by Routledge
4 Park Square, Milton Park, Abingdon, Oxon, OX14 4RN

Routledge is an imprint of the Taylor & Francis Group, an informa business

© 2024 Noam Chomsky and Gilbert Achcar

Preface to the 2007 Edition © 2007 and 2024 Stephen R. Shalom

The right of Noam Chomsky and Gilbert Achcar to be identified
as authors of this work has been asserted in accordance with
sections 77 and 78 of the Copyright, Designs and Patents Act 1988.

First edition published by Paradigm Publishers 2007
Second edition published by Routledge 2016

ISBN: 978-1-032-87266-7 (hbk)
ISBN: 978-1-032-87267-4 (pbk)
ISBN: 978-1-003-53175-3 (ebk)

DOI: 10.4324/9781003531753

Typeset in Sabon
by Apex CoVantage, LLC

Contents

Preface to the 2024 Edition
Fifteen Years Later

The last postscript to this book was completed in March 2008. The United States was then in the midst of a presidential election year, its troops were still stationed in Iraq and Afghanistan, and its Middle East policy was in a shambles, heavily affected by the already evident massive failure of its occupation of Iraq. Israel, Washington's key regional ally, was still reeling from the fiasco of its 2006 onslaught on Lebanon. Overall, the peak in Washington's regional hegemony attained in the 1990s, in the wake of the first U.S.-led war against Iraq, had clearly become a thing of the past.

Iraq's invasion of Kuwait in 1990 had offered President George H. W. Bush a golden opportunity to considerably enhance U.S. domination over the Middle East along with a massive increase of U.S. military deployment in the region. This was done with a green light at the UN Security Council from an ailing USSR. The principal challenger to U.S. hegemony in the region was in the final throes of agony, on its way to dissolution by the end of the next year. Even Syria, that long-term regional ally of Moscow, had spectacularly changed sides, joining the U.S.-led coalition in its onslaught on Iraq, a country ruled by a rival faction of the same Arab nationalist Baath party ruling Syria. Those who remained recalcitrant—Yemen's government and the Palestine Liberation Organization (PLO)—were severely punished economically by the Saudi kingdom.

That was the decade during which Washington sought to set up a "new Arab order" as part of the "new world order" announced by George H. W. Bush in a famous speech pronounced on September 11, 1990.[1] In one of history's biting ironies, it is on that exact same day, eleven years later, that the U.S. witnessed the "mother of all" terrorist attacks on its soil. Iraq's Saddam Hussein had failed to deliver in 1991 the "mother of all" battles that he had promised in the face of the U.S.-led coalition. Ten years later, Osama bin Laden succeeded spectacularly in his own endeavor to inflict upon the United States "the mother of all terrorist attacks."

Bush's son, George W. Bush, and his administration believed that they could seize upon this tremendous shock to dramatically enhance U.S.

hegemony over the Middle East by invading Iraq and changing its regime to their liking. They got entangled in the many contradictions of a highly complex Iraqi situation, failing to control the country, and eventually losing credibility in the eyes of friends and foes alike. By 2008, it had become clear that the U.S. occupation of Iraq was no longer sustainable, especially since the majority of U.S. public opinion had finally awakened from the fantasies that had led it to support the invasion. Whereas Bush senior, by launching on Iraq the first massive attack by U.S. forces since Vietnam, had managed to somewhat "bury" the so-called Vietnam Syndrome—in other words, the U.S. public's distaste of their country's involvement in wars—his son unearthed that same "syndrome" and brought it to a higher degree yet, thanks to the additional effect of the Abu Ghraib scandal and Wikileaks.

Barack Obama moved into the White House in 2009. His Middle East policy was the direct consequence of his predecessor's colossal failure. As a member of the Illinois Senate, Obama had opposed the Bush administration's war drive: he had even addressed an antiwar rally in Chicago in October 2002. He could therefore proudly boast about his political wisdom during his 2008 presidential campaign, at a time when the Iraqi débâcle had become obvious to all. Thus, once in the White House, Obama could only fulfill the U.S.–Iraq Status of Forces Agreement (SOFA) that the Bush administration had negotiated with Iraq's government prior to leaving office. The agreement stipulated that all U.S. forces would leave Iraq by the end of 2011.

The Obama administration initially showed limited interest in the Middle East, a region that had become very frustrating for the previous president, George W. Bush, who had witnessed hawkish general Ariel Sharon become Israel's prime minister in March 2001, soon after Bush's own inauguration. In 2002, Israel launched an onslaught on the Palestinian territories parallel to the post-9/11 U.S.-led "war on terror" that started in Afghanistan in October 2001. Unlike that congruence between Washington and its Israeli ally, it was a yet more extreme Israeli right-winger that the Obama administration had to contend with after Benjamin Netanyahu's rise in March 2009 to become Israel's prime minister for the second time. Netanyahu would remain in office until June 2021, as the longest-lasting in office of all prime ministers in Israel's history. After eighteen months in opposition, he would return to office in December 2022. Obama, during the eight years of his presidency (2009–2017), was thus confronted with an Israeli prime minister in cahoots with his Republican opponents, at a time when the latter's right-wing drift had already gone quite far, and hostility between the two U.S. ruling parties had reached a historical peak. Having pompously launched his Middle East policy with a resounding speech in Cairo in June 2009, in which he projected himself as an advocate of democratic freedoms to the annoyance of his host, Egyptian president Husni

Mubarak, and that of most other Arab rulers, Obama announced what he would actually be doing during his two terms. He committed to withdrawing all U.S. troops from Iraq; acknowledged the Palestinian people's long-lasting tragedy; rejected Israel's expansion of its settlements in the Palestinian West Bank; indicated a relatively open attitude toward Hamas; acknowledged Iran's right to develop nuclear energy within the boundaries of the Nuclear Non-Proliferation Treaty; and expressed his willingness to talk to the Iranian government, without preconditions.[2]

Obama would deliver on all these counts, but that is precisely what alienated even more Washington's traditional allies in the region, starting with the Saudi kingdom. The waning influence of the United States in the region was quite striking in 2011, the year of the Arab Spring. U.S. forces completed their withdrawal from Iraq in that same year, leaving a country where Tehran's influence had become significantly greater than that of Washington. History will retain that the United States invaded Iraq, paying a high human, moral, and economic price (let alone the much higher price paid by Iraq, of course), only to hand the country over to its worst regional enemy.

Faced with a wave of uprisings that engulfed Egypt, its biggest ally in the region, as well as four other Western-friendly Arab states (Tunisia, Bahrain, Yemen, and Libya, the last of these having started collaboration with Washington in the wake of the U.S. invasion of Iraq), the Obama administration appeared rather impotent. It advocated an "orderly transition" for fear of a generalization of the kind of chaos that prevailed in Iraq after the dismantlement of the Baathist state. Washington delegated the task of achieving that type of transition to tiny, very rich, Qatar, the sponsor of the Muslim Brotherhood—the most important regional network of dissident political movements.

In alliance with Turkey, Qatar would back the Muslim Brotherhood's bid to seize the reins of the uprisings in the above-mentioned countries—except Bahrain where the opposition belonged predominantly to the Shiite branch of Islam (the Brotherhood is Sunni)—as well as in Syria, the only country among the six theaters of uprisings in 2011 that was at odds with Washington. (Syria had gone from support, under Hafez al-Assad's leadership, for the first 1991 U.S.-led war on Iraq for the "liberation" of Kuwait, to opposition, under Assad's son Bashar, to the 2003 U.S. invasion that aimed to overthrow the neighboring rival Baathist rule.) For the regional transition to be "orderly," Washington hoped that the old regimes' statal backbones would find a compromise with the Brotherhood.[3]

This policy appeared to be working for a while in Tunisia, Egypt, and Yemen. In Libya and Syria, the regimes chose to bloodily confront the popular uprisings, thus provoking a civil war. Under pressure from its European allies, the Obama administration was reluctantly brought to intervene militarily in

Libya, albeit with some caution and expressly excluding the deployment of troops on the ground. Washington's intervention, along with NATO powers and other allies, was greenlighted by the UN Security Council, like the first U.S.-led war on Iraq and unlike the second. Both Moscow and Beijing abstained, instead of blocking the resolution by veto. However, Washington's drift away from the UN-authorized mission of protecting civilians, to thereafter providing bombing support to the insurgency against Muammar al-Qaddafi's regime, while trying to remote control this insurgency, ended in the even larger collapse of the Libyan state in the fall of 2011.

This important fiasco increased Obama's reluctance to militarily intervene in the Middle East—and his general hopelessness about the region. His Secretary of State, Hillary Clinton, soon published an article heralding the administration's "pivot to Asia," which was widely interpreted as an announcement of relative disengagement from the Middle East.[4] The Libyan fiasco opened the way to the collapse of the "orderly transition" and the return to power of old regime forces in Egypt and Tunisia. The administration's policy of benign neglect of the Syrian civil war, delegating to the Gulf monarchies the role of sponsors of the armed insurgency against the Assad regime, led to the control of that insurgency by Islamic fundamentalist forces, including an avatar of Al-Qaeda that would prove much worse still: the so-called Islamic State (IS), which was established in Syria by survivors of the defeated Iraqi branch of Al-Qaeda.

When IS moved back from Syria into Iraq in the summer of 2014, managing to sweep a vast stretch of Iraqi territory in the face of a collapsing national army (a forerunner of the Afghan débâcle of August 2021), the Obama administration was forced back into the conflict. As in Libya, it did not engage U.S. troops in direct fighting, but brought bombing support to local forces fighting IS: left-wing Kurdish guerillas in north-east Syria and a combination of right-wing Kurdish guerillas and pro-Iran Shiite militias in Iraq. Remote warfare would indeed become the hallmark of the Obama administration, which offset its reluctance to commit troops on the ground with an unrestrained use of drones in various theaters of conflict.

The Obama administration's timorous attitude emboldened both Iran and Russia to directly intervene in Syria: Iran starting from 2013—first through its Lebanese proxy, Hezbollah, then directly as well—and Russia starting from 2015. These interventions would eventually enable the Syrian regime to secure control of nearly 70% of Syria's territory, while other chunks of the country remain under Israel's or Turkey's control, or ruled by a mutated branch of Al-Qaeda or by a Kurdish left-wing movement backed by a limited contingent of U.S. troops.[5] Syria fell into enormous and very tragic mayhem, one result of which has been a massive wave of Syrian refugees into Europe, reaching a peak in 2015 and feeding the rise of xenophobic far-right currents throughout the continent.

The Saudi monarchy was extremely unhappy with the priority that the Obama administration gave to cutting a deal with Iran with a view to limiting the country's accession to nuclear capabilities. Signed in 2015, this deal was perceived by the Saudis as an appeasement of Iran's regime, which indeed expanded its regional involvement afterward. That same year, 2015, the Arab oil monarchies, led by the Saudi kingdom and much to the annoyance of the Obama administration, launched a destructive intervention in the civil war that had begun in Yemen the year before. The Saudi monarchy feared that Iran would gain a crucial foothold in that strategically located country of the Arabian Peninsula through its support of the Houthis, a fundamentalist movement that had become hegemonic among Yemeni followers of a branch of Shiism.

The rise of the far right had been ongoing worldwide, boosted by the destabilizing effects of the Great Recession of 2008. In the United States, the rightward drift would eventually bring Donald Trump into the White House. Unlike his predecessor, Trump was in full harmony with the reactionary forces in the Middle East: with Netanyahu as well as the governments of the United Arab Emirates (UAE) and the Saudi kingdom. His first visit abroad as president was to the Saudi kingdom where he met the heads of state of the United States' reactionary Arab allies. He backed their war in Yemen and focused his administration's efforts on fostering the establishment of official relations between the Arab Gulf monarchies and Israel to the detriment of the Palestinian cause, managing to sponsor accords between Israel and the UAE, along with Bahrain.

Of all U.S. presidents since the Israeli state was born in 1948, none has gone so far as Donald Trump in taking up the cause of the Israeli far right, headed by Netanyahu. When Trump left the White House in January 2021, boasting about the "peace" that he had brokered between Israel and two Arab reactionary governments, the situation in the Palestinian Occupied Territories as well as within Israel's pre-1967 borders had reached a peak of tension. The whole Middle East was on the cusp of implosion. A second wave of regional uprisings in 2019 had been subdued thanks in large part to the Covid-19 pandemic, but the fire was still burning under the ashes in all four countries that were involved: Sudan, Algeria, Iraq, and Lebanon.

The Biden administration would miserably fail in redressing the situation. The débâcle over which it presided in Afghanistan a few months after Biden's inauguration hugely contributed to its discredit. During his presidential campaign, Joe Biden had pledged to boycott the Saudi crown prince and de facto ruler, to whom he attributed the responsibility of the assassination abroad of a Saudi dissident and U.S. resident. When Vladimir Putin launched his invasion of Ukraine in February 2022, it became the Saudi prince's turn to shun the U.S. president. The latter now needed the cooperation of the Saudis whose importance had been hugely enhanced by the Ukraine war and its impact on global oil and gas markets. Joe Biden had to swallow his words and pay a visit to the Saudi kingdom to meet the young prince.

Meanwhile, his administration had failed in securing a resumption of the deal with Iran that Trump had single-handedly discarded. It has been witnessing with anxiety China's increasing influence in the Middle East and its developing relations with all key regional actors, including those, like the Saudis, who were regarded until recently as Washington's closest Arab allies. Since then, the Biden administration's priority in the Middle East has been to complete what Donald Trump had started, striving to foster an accord between the Saudi kingdom and Israel. In this regard, therefore, as in that of U.S. relations with China, Joe Biden has been more of a continuator of his immediate predecessor and present major rival for the 2024 presidential race than a continuator of Barack Obama, whom he accompanied in the White House as vice-president.

The Biden administration's benign neglect of the Palestinian issue is one of the factors that allowed the situation to deteriorate to the point of exploding on October 7, 2023. On that day, the Palestinian Hamas movement launched a spectacular violent attack on the Israeli periphery of the Gaza Strip, prompting Israel to prepare a huge offensive to reconquer that territory which its forces had evacuated in 2005. At the time of writing, there is much fear among the Palestinians that this will become a second instance of the displacement and dispossession of the Palestinians that happened in 1948 and that they call the Nakba (catastrophe, in Arabic). Whatever the outcome, it is beyond doubt that this new tragic episode in the Israel-Palestine conflict is going to tremendously aggravate regional destabilization.

The ever more "dysfunctional superpower"—as Robert Gates, former Secretary of Defense under George W. Bush and Barack Obama, aptly called the United States[6]—has been inexorably losing influence in the Middle East since the ill-conceived invasion of Iraq launched by George W. Bush's administration in 2003, over twenty years ago. Washington is very unlikely to ever recover the degree of regional hegemony that it enjoyed in the last decade of the past century. In this respect, as well as more generally, the twenty-first century has already failed the project of a "new American century" that those who lobbied for Iraq's invasion and populated the second Bush administration were foolishly pursuing.

Gilbert Achcar
October 15, 2023

Preface to the 2007 Edition

There's a well-known college admissions interview question that asks, "If you could have dinner with any two people in history, whom would you choose?" Opinions will no doubt vary when considering the range of historical figures over all the domains of human knowledge, but if one were interested in learning about the modern-day Middle East from contemporary analysts, I can't imagine more engaging and informative dinner companions than Noam Chomsky and Gilbert Achcar.

I first met Noam Chomsky in 1966, when I was a student at MIT. He was at this time already renowned for revolutionizing the field of linguistics and had recently become an outspoken critic of the U.S. war in Vietnam. For four decades since, I have read and learned immensely from his analysis of foreign policy, the media, and the role of intellectuals in society. But even more impressive than his prodigious intelligence has been his extraordinary commitment to social change. As an undergraduate, I was struck that such a distinguished scholar would join with students at sit-ins and demonstrations. In the early 1970s when I was working on a small newsletter challenging martial law in the Philippines, the first subscription renewal we'd receive in the mail each year would be from Noam Chomsky. This has been a consistent pattern as long as I've known him. He has helped innumerable political organizations and publications, answered countless letters from around the globe, and taken the time to talk to, advise, and inspire all those struggling for a better world.

In the early 1970s Chomsky began writing about the Middle East, returning to a topic that had concerned him since his involvement as a youth in the left-wing Zionist movement. In the early 1950s, he and his wife had considered living on an Israeli kibbutz, and though they ultimately decided not to, he has always had an intense interest in the region and in questions of peace and justice there. In 1974, his book *Peace in the Middle East? Reflections on Justice and Nationhood*[1] was published. His next book-length study of the Middle East was written in the aftermath of the 1982 Israeli invasion of Lebanon: *The Fateful Triangle: The United States, Israel, and the Palestinians.*[2] Many of Chomsky's other books include sections or essays on the Middle East—as any consideration of U.S. foreign policy must, given the importance and volatility of the region—but this current volume is his first entirely new book since *The Fateful Triangle* to focus exclusively on that part of the world.

Gilbert Achcar has shared Chomsky's strong commitment to international peace and justice and his keen interest in understanding U.S. foreign policy. In addition, Achcar has a deep firsthand as well as scholarly knowledge of the Middle East. Having grown up and lived in Lebanon for many years, Achcar was intimately involved in the politics of the region and well acquainted with left circles in the Arab world. After moving to France, he continued to carefully follow Middle East events, both as an academic and as an antiwar activist.

I first met Gilbert in February 2003, shortly before the U.S.-led invasion of Iraq, when he spoke as part of a book tour at William Paterson University in New Jersey, where I teach. Over the next few years, I found his analyses of Iraq and of the wider Middle East extremely valuable, based on his expertise and his close reading of the Arabic-language press. I frequently posted his articles and translations on ZNet, a progressive website on which I work, hoping to bring his insights to a wider English-speaking audience.[3] Though most of our communication has been by trans-Atlantic e-mail, we have become friends, and in late 2005 Gilbert and I coauthored an article assessing various plans being put forward for the "redeployment" of U.S. troops from Iraq.[4]

Achcar's writings are informed by an appreciation of the broader considerations of international relations, especially the strategic triad among the United States, China, and Russia, elaborated in his *La Nouvelle Guerre Froide (The New Cold War)*.[5] In his volume *The Clash of Barbarisms: September 11 and the Making of the New World Disorder*,[6] he established himself as a perceptive analyst and uncompromising critic both of Washington's quest for global domination and of Islamic fundamentalism. At the same time, he has always shown a sensitive understanding of some of the emotions ignited by the Israel-Palestine conflict, even among progressive circles, as he demonstrated in his editing of an exchange of letters between two Jewish leftists.[7] Achcar's numerous articles—some of which are collected in his book *Eastern Cauldron: Islam, Afghanistan, Palestine, and Iraq in a Marxist Mirror*[8]—have provided hard-headed yet passionate analysis and practical advice to those seeking global justice. His April 2003 essay, "Letter to a Slightly Depressed Antiwar Activist," has rightly become a classic.[9]

This current book is not two writers' separate essays strung together. It is based on a dialogue between them—sometimes agreeing, sometimes complementing one another's analysis based on their own perspectives and information, and sometimes disagreeing—and as such it represents more than the sum of its parts. Through their conversation, a richer understanding emerges from their shared commitments and their varied expertise and experiences.

Chomsky and Achcar decided from the outset that it would be useful to have a third person present to moderate their face-to-face conversation. This project was to be a two-way conversation, but a third party would pose the questions, keep the discussion on track, and take care of the technical process of recording, enabling the two discussants to concentrate on their analyses and arguments. I was invited to serve in this role. As much as possible, I tried to keep out of the conversation, just moving it along as necessary.

The procedure we followed involved several steps. We began by developing a list of questions to be addressed. The aim here was to generate questions that could not be answered by resorting to an encyclopedia, but that sought to reveal the underlying factors and dynamics at work. Events in the Middle East are so fast moving that any attempt to provide a factual description would soon be outdated, but an analysis of the major forces at play and of the way to approach the critical issues would enable readers to make sense of the past and understand current and future developments. Though this was to be a book about the Middle East, the region cannot be understood apart from the interests and interventions of outside powers, especially in recent years the United States. So we tried to include broad themes relating to the Middle East and U.S. foreign policy as well as to particular areas of conflict. The themes included terrorism (what it is, the extent of the threat, and how it should be dealt with), conspiracies (to what extent do they help us understand political developments), fundamentalism (what drives it, where it is strongest), democracy (its state in the Middle East, how it has been affected by the Iraq war), and the roots of U.S. foreign policy in the region (especially the role of oil and the significance of the "Israel lobby"). The specific conflicts we focused on were Afghanistan following September 11, Iraq in all its dimensions—the U.S. role, political developments, the situation of the Kurdish people (in Iraq and also in Turkey)—as well as potential conflicts in Iran and Syria. And, of course, we wanted to devote considerable attention to the Palestinian-Israeli conflict: its historical roots, current dynamics, and potential solutions, taking up as well the nature of Israeli society, the various Palestinian political forces, and the issues of anti-Semitism, Islamophobia, and anti-Arab racism.

With the questions finalized, the three of us got together in Noam's office at MIT in Cambridge, Massachusetts, for three days of conversation from January 4 to 6, 2006. Squeezing in three days with Noam is never an easy task, given his incredibly busy schedule—and indeed, we had to pause once for a previously arranged interview with a foreign journalist. Nevertheless, we were able to get in about fourteen hours of conversation. Our sessions were genial and lively, yet when there were disagreements, neither Noam nor Gilbert held back from stating his opinion strongly. (The discussion was sufficiently intense that twice we neglected to eat lunch.)

The fourteen hours of recordings that we generated were then ably transcribed by Melissa Jameson. From the transcription, I prepared a rough edit, eliminating redundancy and tangents, reordering some of the sections, and improving readability. Then Gilbert and Noam each went through and edited their remarks. The goal here was not to produce a faithful verbatim transcript of the conversation. Rather the idea was to allow each of them to clarify or expand on their remarks (though not to change a major argument to which the other had already responded). We took the view that oral comments made without access to sources should not serve as the last word. So we verified facts and checked and filled in quotations as necessary. And, because we believe that readers should not be expected to take what authors say on faith, we felt it important to add in documentation for all nonobvious or controversial claims.

In any work of this sort, the question of updating the material invariably arises. We thought it would be misleading and confusing to bring the conversations up to date by means of the editing process. There is no doubt that as you are reading this preface, important new events will have already taken place in the Middle East. So we decided to let the main text remain as a record of Chomsky's and Achcar's assessments as of January 2006, but to include a separate Epilogue, prepared six months later, in which each of the authors could comment on significant new developments. Then, for the paperback edition, we added a new postscript, completed on March 24, 2008, in which the authors were asked to address some of the developments of the previous two years.

I hope that this book, bringing you Noam Chomsky and Gilbert Achcar as dinner companions to discuss the Middle East, will provide much food for thought.

Stephen R. Shalom

1 Terrorism and Conspiracies

Defining Terrorism

SHALOM: What do you think is a reasonable way to define terrorism?

CHOMSKY: I've been writing about terrorism since 1981. That's the year the Reagan administration came into office, and they declared very quickly that a focus of the administration was going to be a war on terrorism—in particular, state-directed international terrorism. President Ronald Reagan, Secretary of State George P. Shultz, and other officials of the administration spouted elaborate rhetoric about "the plague of the modern age," a return to "barbarism in our times," the "scourge of terrorism," and so on.

Anyone with even a minimal acquaintance with history knew what was going to happen. It was going to turn into a terrorist war. You don't declare a war on terrorism unless you're planning yourself to undertake massive international terrorism, which is indeed what happened. And I expected that, as did my friend Ed Herman,[1] and together and separately we began writing about terrorism. Since this was in the context of the Reagan administration's declaration of the war on terror, the natural thing to do seemed to be to take the official definitions of the U.S. government. So I took the definition that's in the U.S. Code, the official system of laws, which is pretty reasonable; and shorter versions are in army manuals and so on. That's the definition I've been using ever since. It is pretty much a commonsense definition. It says that terrorism is "the calculated use of violence or threat of violence to attain goals that are political, religious, or ideological in nature . . . through intimidation, coercion, or instilling fear."[2] It's also essentially the same as the official British definition, at present.

However, the U.S. definition was rescinded in practice, presumably because of its obvious implications. If you take it literally, it turns out, almost trivially, that the United States is a leading terrorist state, and that the Reagan administration in fact was engaging in extensive international terrorism. So it had to change the definition, obviously, because it

DOI: 10.4324/9781003531753-1

couldn't allow that consequence. And since that time there have been other problems.

For example, under Reagan administration pressure, the United Nations passed resolutions on terrorism; the first major one was in December 1987, a resolution condemning the crime of terrorism in the strongest terms, calling on all states to work together to eradicate the plague and so on—a long, detailed resolution. It passed, but not unanimously. It passed 153 to 2 with 1 abstention. Honduras abstained. The two who voted against it were the usual two, the United States and Israel.[3] In the General Assembly proceedings, the U.S. and Israeli ambassadors explained their votes, pointing out that there was an offending passage in the resolution that said: "Nothing in the present resolution could in any way prejudice the right to self-determination, freedom and independence, as derived from the Charter of the United Nations, of peoples forcibly deprived of that right . . . particularly peoples under colonial and racist regimes and foreign occupation or other forms of colonial domination, nor, in accordance with the principles of the Charter and in conformity with the above-mentioned Declaration, the right of these peoples to struggle to this end and to seek and receive support."[4] The United States and Israel couldn't accept that, obviously. The phrase "colonial and racist regimes" meant South Africa, which was still an ally under the apartheid regime. Technically, the United States had joined the embargo against South Africa—but in fact it had not. Trade with South Africa increased, and methods were found for getting around the embargo so Washington could continue to support the Pretoria regime—and the same with Israel, which was in fact one of the conduits for getting around the South Africa embargo. And "foreign occupation" was obviously referring to the West Bank, Gaza, and the Golan Heights, so neither the United States nor Israel could permit resistance against that occupation—even legitimate resistance, which of course does not include terrorist attacks against civilians. So, although it's not technically a veto in the General Assembly, the United States and Israel *effectively* vetoed the resolution.[5]

And when the United States vetoes something, it's a double veto: For one thing, it's blocked; and for another thing, it's erased from history. And so this U.S. action wasn't reported, right in the midst of the furor about terrorism, and it's out of history. You can barely find it in scholarly studies, since it leads to the wrong conclusions. And the same is true of the official definitions—they are down the memory hole. I continue to use them, and they continue to be the official definitions. But since then, since the mid-1980s, a scholarly industry has developed, with conferences, and ponderous tomes and meetings of the United Nations and so on, to see if someone can solve this "very difficult problem" of defining terrorism. There are dozens of different definitions and analyses in the legal journals, and nobody can quite do it. It's perfectly obvious why, but no one will say so. You have to find a definition that excludes the terror *we* carry out against *them*, and includes the terror that *they* carry out against *us*. And that's rather difficult. People have tried to restrict it to subnational groups. But that doesn't work because they want to talk about terrorist states. In fact, it's extremely hard, probably impossible, to formulate a definition that would have the right consequences, unless you define it just in terms of those consequences.

The operative definition of terror ought to be, from the point of view of U.S. policymakers: Terror is terror in the standard sense if you do it to us; but if we do it to you, it's benign, it's humanitarian intervention, it's with benign intent. That's the definition that's actually used. If the educated sectors were honest, that's what they'd say. Then the whole problem of defining would be over. But short of that, we have only two choices: either to use the official definitions, which I do; or to say, well, it's an impossible problem, very deep, and so on. And so it will remain unless we're able to recognize the operative significance.

ACHCAR: One might point also to attempts at expanding the concept: for instance, the European Union's definition of terrorism in June 2002,[6] which included "causing extensive destruction to a Government or public facility . . . a public place or private property likely to . . . result in major economic loss," or even "threatening to commit" any such destruction. This could encompass acts of the kind that global justice or environmentalist or peasant protestors have committed against, say, a McDonald's restaurant or an experimental agricultural field with genetically modified organisms or the like, and these would fall therefore under the category of terrorism. This is a serious and dangerous expansion of the definition.

CHOMSKY: It's part of the expansion, and in a way it makes sense. What you should do is simply define terrorism as acts we don't like. And acts we do like, they are not terrorism.

It's the same dishonesty we see in discussions of aggression or intervention. Aren't there perfectly straightforward definitions of aggression? Robert Jackson, the chief counsel for the prosecution at the post-1945 International Military Tribunal for Nazi war criminals at Nuremberg, gave a careful, clear definition of aggression.[7] And that was reaffirmed in 1974 by a General Assembly resolution that passed in a voice vote with no objections, so there is an authoritative General Assembly resolution that says approximately the same thing.[8] But it's useless, because according to that definition probably every American president could be charged as a war criminal. Not only are things like the war in Vietnam or Iraq, of course, aggression; but even the Contra war waged by the Reagan administration against Nicaragua counts not as international terrorism but as aggression under the Jackson and General Assembly definitions. Part of one of the subcases of the definition of aggression is about supporting armed groups on the territory of a state to carry out violent acts in the state under attack without the agreement of that state.[9] That's the Contra war by definition. So that's aggression. Thus, all of the members of the Reagan administration and of course the Democrats who pretty much supported them are guilty of war crimes. But you can't have that. So, therefore, the definition of aggression is also held to be very complex and obscure.

ACHCAR: We've been talking about the official definitions of terrorism, but what then would we agree among ourselves to be the definition of terrorism? In the public mind, I would say that terrorism is seen as basically that which targets civilian populations or democratic governments. That's the most common view of terrorism, the targeting of civilians for goals that are linked to attempts to get governments or other collectivities to act in a certain way. Actions against an occupying army are not labeled terrorism by most people. The irony is that even in the final statement of the conference of the Iraqi political forces held in Cairo, Egypt, in November 2005, a distinction was made between the right to resist foreign occupation, deemed legitimate—which, although it was not stated explicitly, meant that actions against U.S. occupying troops in Iraq are an exercise of the right of resistance—and reprehensible terrorism, which was restricted to attacks on fellow Iraqis. And that's quite ironic, because this was a conference involving representatives of the supposedly U.S.-allied Iraqi government, including the president and the prime minister.

I would think that the definition of terrorism that is least problematic is that which points to acts against unarmed innocent civilians. Taking innocent civilians as targets or hostages is definitely terrorism, even in the fight against a foreign occupation.

CHOMSKY: Then you do get into a definitional problem, because shooting somebody on the street isn't necessarily an act of terrorism. So it has to be the threat or use of force, primarily against civilian targets, for ideological, religious, political, or other purposes, perhaps aimed at influencing a government. (ACHCAR: Or a collectivity.) Or a collectivity.

ACHCAR: Not acts targeting individuals as such, but trying to impose something on a collectivity or a government. (CHOMSKY: Exactly. That's correct.) That would be, I think, a rounded definition of terrorism, though not exhaustive.

CHOMSKY: And that's very close to the official U.S. definition, though it's not used in practice because this would make the United States a leading terrorist state.

SHALOM: And then there are tough cases about whether low-level government officials count as innocent civilians.

CHOMSKY: That's true. Look, this isn't physics. There are no terms of political or social discussion that have clear definitions.

ACHCAR: No. On the fringes, it becomes a legal matter. Then you have to discuss it case by case. It gets to the courts.

CHOMSKY: Even in the hard sciences, there weren't clear definitions until the sciences became advanced. Even in mathematics: terms like "limit," for example. Definitions don't come until much later. So what you really want isn't to find a sharp definition but to identify a concept. And this one's easily identifiable; it's just not acceptable. Because if you agree to this characterization, it's going to turn out that the acts of the powerful fall under the definition of terrorism, and that's not allowed.

ACHCAR: And then we might add to the definition the same distinction that you get in an International Relations 101 course, regarding the "actors": the distinction between governmental, intergovernmental, and nongovernmental actors. The same distinction, the same categories, can be applied to terrorism. There is nongovernmental terrorism, which has been very prominent in the news these last few years, and there is governmental terrorism, and also intergovernmental terrorism, when you have NATO or such intergovernmental institutions conducting acts that we understand from our definition of terrorism to be terroristic. And the U.S. government itself cannot reject the idea that there is such a thing as governmental terrorism since it accuses many other states of being terroristic.

CHOMSKY: There have been efforts to restrict terrorism to subnational groups, but that runs against policy, because, exactly as you say, then you can't label certain states as terrorist. But then you're back to the same dilemma—how do you exclude yourself? (ACHCAR: Right.)

The Terrorist Threat

SHALOM: Is there actually a terrorist threat to Europe or the United States, or is that all concoction?

CHOMSKY: No, there's a very serious threat. In fact, the threat is being escalated, consciously. It didn't start on 9/11. If you go through the 1990s— first of all, there was an attempt to blow up the World Trade Center in 1993, which came pretty close to succeeding; with a little better planning— I think you, Gilbert, wrote this in your *Clash of Barbarisms*[10]—it would have killed tens of thousands. Then they were going to blow up the tunnels and the UN building, the FBI buildings, and so on. They were stopped just in time. They were essentially jihadis, trained by the United States in

Afghanistan, led by an Egyptian cleric who was brought into the United States under CIA protection. That was a serious act of terror.

Throughout the 1990s, there was a whole literature of technical books, published for example by MIT Press—what amount to cookbooks on terrorism, saying that terrorism is very likely.[11] And of course, since 9/11, there have been a lot more. And it's a major terrorist threat. Former defense secretaries Robert McNamara and William Perry offer a subjective estimate of the likelihood of a nuclear detonation on a U.S. target in the next ten years at more than 50 percent. That's pretty high, and U.S. intelligence regards such an attack as inevitable if the current course is pursued.[12] And other kinds of terrorism—bioterror and others—are also very possible. But this is a very low priority for the government; they don't care very much, so they are acting very consciously in ways that actually increase the threat. And it's not even secret, it's just not a high priority for them. The clearest example is the invasion of Iraq. The invasion was undertaken with the expectation that it probably would increase the threat of terror. That was the advice given by the government's own intelligence agencies and by others, by lots of specialists on terror, who said it was very likely to increase terror, for pretty obvious reasons. One reason is that we're telling the world that we're going to invade and attack anyone we feel like. So, therefore, any potential target is going to try to develop a deterrent. Nobody's going to confront the United States on the battlefield. U.S. military expenditures are approximately the same as for the rest of the world combined, and U.S. weaponry is far more advanced technologically. You have to have another form of deterrent, and there are only two: One is nuclear weapons, and the other is terror. So what Washington is doing, in effect, is asking potential adversaries to develop a terrorist system and nuclear weapons.

And quite apart from that, and this I don't think could have been predicted, the invasion of Iraq was such a total military catastrophe that it actually created an insurgency with no outside support. That's almost unheard of. The partisans in Europe during the Nazi occupation couldn't have survived if they didn't have outside support; moreover, Germany was fighting a wider world at the time. But in Iraq, the United States created an insurgency, which is creating trained terrorists; it's training people in terrorism. And it's drawing some outsiders in for training in terrorism, and in fact the postwar assessments of the CIA and others are exactly that—that the war has created training grounds for professionalized terrorists who will spread around the world and carry out terrorism. It was predicted, and it happened to an extent beyond what was predicted, but it's just a low priority in Washington, for which taking control of the energy resources of the Middle East is just a lot more important.

And this shows up in many other ways. There is an agency of the Treasury Department, OFAC, the Office of Foreign Assets Control, which has the task of monitoring suspicious financial transfers around the world. That's a big part of the so-called war on terror. OFAC officials testified to Congress in April 2004 on their operations. It turns out that they had four employees tracing financial transfers that might be attributable to Osama bin Laden or Saddam Hussein, and almost six times that many monitoring possible evasion of the embargo against Cuba. Furthermore, this goes back to 1990, right through the Clinton years. From 1990 to 2003, they had opened 93 investigations related to terrorism and more than 100 times as many—10,683—related to Cuba. Since 1994, they had imposed $9,425 in terrorism-related fines and $8 million, more than 800 times more, in fines for evasion of the Cuba embargo,[13] which embargo has been declared illegal by every relevant international body and which the United States is alone with Israel in backing. But those are the priorities. Punishing Cubans is way more important than cutting back terror. And this runs through case after case.

The current situation with Syria is a perfectly good example. Whatever you think of Syria is another question, but the Syrian government was providing substantial information to the United States on terrorism. They have much better connections and they can infiltrate Islamic terrorist groups in a way the CIA can't. The Syrian regime doesn't like the Islamic terrorists— it's a secular monstrosity instead of a religious monstrosity—so it was providing the United States with valuable intelligence. But the U.S. was willing to give that up in order to make sure that there isn't some part of the region that is not following orders. Not following orders is considered a major crime and that has to be punished. And the logic is understandable; any Mafia don can explain it. You cannot permit what's called "successful defiance." The charge against Cuba, back forty years ago, during the Kennedy-Johnson years, according to the internal records, is that Cuba's "successful defiance" of U.S. domination—a domination that went back 150 years, meaning to the Monroe Doctrine—was intolerable. The problem had nothing to do with the Russians, just with Cuba's successful defiance of policies going back 150 years. It's unacceptable. It's like some storekeeper not paying his protection money. You can't accept that, because then other people would get the same idea, and the system of domination and control would erode. That's far more serious to U.S. policymakers than protecting the country from terror.

A fairly high-level commission was set up to look at what went wrong on 9/11, and it made a whole series of recommendations, most of which were ignored. After the termination of the commission, they set up a private commission to continue monitoring it, and they keep producing reports, and they keep lamenting the fact that the recommendations are not being followed[14]—and the reason is that it's just not a high priority. The Bush administration doesn't care that much. And in fact, instigating terror is okay, too, if it serves some higher goal. This is all quite apart from the kind of terror that we carry out against others. But just limiting ourselves to the terror that fits the operative definition—what they do to us—simply is not a high priority. It never has been.

ACHCAR: Terrorism, as we've defined it, is more than a threat; it's a reality. (CHOMSKY: And it'll get worse.) There is an ongoing war, completely uneven, completely asymmetrical, between a huge, mighty, very powerful state and its allies, on the one hand, and on the other hand, nongovernmental terroristic organizations with limited means, but which can inflict huge damage when they target civilians. First of all, it is impossible to protect any state from terrorism—and Israel is the main illustration of that. No state goes beyond the Israelis' measures for preventing terrorism in security terms, and nevertheless, it's not working. And obviously, at the level of the United States or Europe, this kind of prevention is absolutely impossible—you can't surround the United States with a wall!

CHOMSKY: The U.S. government is reported to be planning to build a wall now along the Canadian border.

ACHCAR: Even that wouldn't be effective.

CHOMSKY: No, if you look at the technical books on this, or the government studies, for example—like I said, they're kind of cookbooks. One of the things they point out is that most U.S. import trade involves containers. There are huge numbers of containers coming in, which are almost impossible to inspect. They could hold radioactive materials, for example. You can't inspect them at the point of origin. There were some calculations in one of these studies. If you tried to inspect the containers in, say, Rotterdam, which is one of the main shipping points from Europe, you would have gridlock all over Europe, literally.

ACHCAR: Aside from that, even if we supposed theoretically that there was a way to protect a country from foreign nongovernmental terrorism, you would still have the problem of local terrorism. After all, in the United States before 9/11, you had Oklahoma City, and then the anthrax episode after 9/11, which mysteriously has been forgotten.

CHOMSKY: The anthrax was apparently traced to a federal lab.

Responding to Terrorism

SHALOM: So, what do we do? What can be done about terrorism?

CHOMSKY: Reduce the reasons for it. Take, say, al-Qaeda. They were carrying out terrorist acts in the Soviet Union, from Afghanistan, in the 1980s. These were pretty serious. In fact, at one point, they almost led to a war between the Soviet Union and Pakistan. After the Russians pulled out of Afghanistan, the terrorism stopped. Of course, they're still carrying out terrorist acts from Chechnya, but not from Afghanistan. Whatever you think of these people—Osama bin Laden and the rest—their positions are pretty straightforward. And their words and their deeds are pretty much in accord. As far as I know, the specialists on the topic agree with this; bin Laden and others see themselves as defending Muslim lands from attack. So, if you stop attacking Muslim lands, you'll reduce the threat of terror. Same with other kinds of terror.

ACHCAR: And there's an economic aspect to this as well, because there is a very obvious correlation between the neoliberal turn of the last quarter-century and the increase in those forms of violence labeled as terrorism, or even urban violence in general. Neoliberal globalization has brought the disintegration of the social fabric and of social safety nets. People are more and more experiencing a state of disarray and social anxiety, and this leads to forms of violent assertions of "identity," extremism or fanaticism, whether religious or political or whatever.

CHOMSKY: There are regular projections of the National Intelligence Council, the collective of U.S. intelligence agencies, that say the process of what they call globalization "will be rocky, marked by chronic financial volatility and a widening economic divide. . . . Regions, countries, and groups feeling left behind will face deepening economic stagnation, political instability, and cultural alienation. They will foster political, ethnic, ideological, and religious extremism, along with the violence that often accompanies it."[15] The military projections say the same thing. Likewise, if you look at the Clinton-era studies of the space command,[16] they say we're going to need to militarize space because—same thing—the economic processes around the world, globalization, are creating a sharper and sharper divide between the haves and the have-nots. And the have-nots may even be able to develop nuclear weapons and other such means, and we're going to need new weapons to protect ourselves from the predictable effects of the international measures that are being taken. So, again, you undertake the measures knowing what the consequences are going to be, and then you develop more brutal and violent means to suppress them. But if you actually want to suppress terrorism, then don't carry out measures that are going to devastate societies.

ACHCAR: And more generally, I would say the antidote to terrorism is definitely not the so-called war on terror. Rather, it is justice: political justice, the rule of law, social justice, economic justice. This is the only real antidote to terrorism.

CHOMSKY: And ending repression. (ACHCAR: Of course.) In the case of Islamic terrorism, a lot of it is just—you're attacking us, so we're going to defend ourselves.

SHALOM: Some of the grievances pointed to by al-Qaeda are clearly instances of aggression. But their list of grievances includes, for example, East Timor as a case of an attack on Islam. Presumably, there you don't agree.

CHOMSKY: One doesn't have to agree with what they think they have a right to. They supported Indonesia's invasion of East Timor because a Muslim state invaded an animist, Christian state. It doesn't mean we have to go along with that. It's outright aggression.

ACHCAR: This has never been a major concern for al-Qaeda or bin Laden; this is really a very marginal issue for them.

CHOMSKY: The point is, they have a point of view. You can try to understand the point of view. As a matter of fact, the Pentagon understands it, as when Paul Wolfowitz announced, when he was still the deputy secretary of defense, that the United States was going to try and shift military bases out of Saudi Arabia—this was one of the reasons for invading Iraq. He said straight out: This will undercut some of al-Qaeda's propaganda. We've occupied a holy, Muslim land.[17]

ACHCAR: Because U.S. officials knew that the origin of bin Laden's turn against the United States was the deployment of U.S. troops in the Saudi kingdom. And they knew perfectly well all the dangers this implied, even though from a military point of view it made no sense: They could have deployed these troops in Kuwait. There were what—5,000 troops? That's just nothing, you could put them anywhere in the area, in safer spaces, but they wanted to keep them in the Saudi kingdom for obvious reasons related to the importance of this huge oil reserve for the United States, in terms of global strategy. They were thus willing to pay the price for that, in a sense. Hardly anyone mentioned that fact in the 1990s. U.S. officials do things knowing they will breed terrorism, but they do them nevertheless, because they obey other considerations, which for them are far more significant than the lives of civilians.

9/11 Conspiracies

SHALOM: So, this then raises the question: How do you assess the claims that 9/11 was plotted by the Bush administration, or by Mossad, etc?

CHOMSKY: I'm deluged with stuff about this. I don't read a lot of it, because I generally don't think it's worth looking at. But I've looked at some of it, just out of curiosity, and it seems to me that those who make such claims just do not understand the nature of evidence. After all, why do scientists do experiments? Why not just take videotapes of what's happening outside? Things that are going on in the phenomenal world are just too complicated to study. You're not going to get sharp results from studying them; you're going to get all kinds of confusion, strange things happening you can't understand, and so on. So what you do are controlled experiments. But even in carefully controlled experiments, there are all sorts of anomalies—unexplained coincidences, apparent contradictions, and so forth. If you read the letters column of a technical scientific journal, such as *Science,* the letters consist very substantially of people raising points like this about carefully controlled experiments, talking about this coincidence that you didn't notice, or this went wrong and you didn't notice. When you try to do the same thing for real-world phenomena, when you try to apply those standards to it, yes, you're going to find all sorts of odd things. With the kind of evidence that is being used, you could prove that the White House was bombed yesterday.

Plus there is the style of the presentation of the evidence. People who know nothing about civil engineering, except what they picked up on the Internet somewhere, are giving learned treatises on what must have happened: How could a building do this, that, and the other thing? These are not trivial matters. You can't just look up on the Internet and say, "I'm an accomplished civil engineer." So those who make such claims just don't understand the nature of evidence.

The second point is that the idea that the Bush administration would undertake something like this is almost beyond comprehension. First of all, it was very unclear what was going to happen—you could not predict the outcome. In fact, notice what happened when one of the airplanes was stopped in Pennsylvania: Suppose that had happened to all of them? Anything could have happened. So you're carrying out a very chancy operation. A lot of people would have been involved in the planning. There are almost certain to be leaks. (ACHCAR: Of course.) If there was any leak at all, they'd all be lined up in front of firing squads without a trial, and that would be the end of the Republican Party forever. To gain what? Well, there's the "who gains" argument; but that, too, is meaningless. Every power system in the world gained from 9/11. You could prove that the Chinese did it, because it gave them an opportunity to crush the Uighurs in western China. In the first interview I gave after 9/11, a couple of hours afterward, one of the first things I said was that every power system in the world is going to use this as an opportunity to increase violence and repression. This is exactly what happened everywhere—the Russians in Chechnya, Israel in the West Bank, Indonesia in Aceh, China in western China; half the governments in the world instituted protection against terrorist acts to try and control their own populations better. By the "who gained" argument, you could say that every power system did.

But the final point, and the most important, I think, is that these claims about 9/11 are diversions. Even if it were true that the Bush administration had planned and implemented the attacks, that would be a minor point compared with the crimes that they're committing against the American people and the world. Just their instigation of terror is a far more serious danger to the people of the United States than destroying the World Trade Center. They're increasing the danger of nuclear war, significantly. That's very important. It's not talked about much except in technical literature, but it's very serious, and could lead to incredibly more tragic consequences than the destruction of the World Trade Center. So all of this focus on this highly unlikely, implausible scenario is simply diverting attention from the real crimes and the real threats, and I think that's the reason why this theorizing is rarely criticized by the government or commentators. I think it's welcomed by the administration. If you try to say anything about the fact that the United States invaded Iraq to get its oil, or anything serious, there's a torrent of vilification and lies that is elicited immediately. The very striking fact about the 9/11 conspiracy theories is that there is very little criticism of them. Some people may make a joke or something, but they don't come under any serious criticism. And the reason is, I think, that they're welcomed as a diversion.

I recently came across a document that is relevant to this. It offered suggestions about declassification written for the Pentagon—and one suggestion was that DOD officials should periodically release information on the Kennedy assassination to keep the JFK assassination industry alive and focused on trying to figure out plots about the Kennedy assassination; as long as they're on that wild-goose chase, they won't be asking serious questions.[18] And I expect much the same is true here.

ACHCAR: And then you have those who tell you: You say this is a "conspiracy theory" and doesn't hold water, but the government's version is also a conspiracy theory—a conspiracy by the al-Qaeda organization and the nineteen hijackers. This is putting a purely phantasmagoric kind of construction on the same level as something that has gone through an investigation in which many countries and many agencies were involved. It's preposterous.

On the other hand, however, there's the so-called weak version, which says that although the Bush administration didn't plan 9/11, nor did they work seriously on preventing it, they had some hints, which they didn't want to take into consideration.

CHOMSKY: But we have a much stronger case than that. They have more than hints on further terrorist acts. For example, as I quoted before, very credible sources regard a terrorist nuclear attack as very likely. That's serious. Are they doing anything about it? They're only increasing the likelihood of it.

ACHCAR: Exactly. This way of putting things is something that one could accept.

CHOMSKY: It's not a conspiracy theory; it's just a ranking of priorities.

ACHCAR: There are actually two very clear cases where attacks against U.S. interests functioned in a way crucial for U.S. imperial designs: Iraq's invasion of Kuwait in 1990, which led to the reshaping of the world order after the Cold War, and 9/11, which led to the implementation of a whole set of policies aimed at furthering U.S. control of the Middle East's oil-producing areas and other strategic spots. The World Trade Center attack was very crucial in the latter. Whether consciously or unconsciously or semiconsciously, U.S. policymakers were in need of a certain type of event, and they didn't do anything really serious to prevent that type of event from happening. So there is a range of interpretation that I think is legitimate for people to have in mind, which is much more legitimate than conspiracy theories claiming that the Bush administration organized 9/11.

CHOMSKY: I'm still skeptical about that. I just don't think planners are ever that smart. I mean, in the cases where I've looked, they mostly don't know what's going on. When you look in detail at planners, they don't have a grasp of what is going on in the world. The idea that they could make meticulous plans—

ACHCAR: I didn't say that. There is a very big difference between making meticulous plans and being conscious about the fact that you are not doing—

CHOMSKY: Something that you could do.

ACHCAR: Exactly. You are not doing what you should do to prevent an event because the occurrence of that event actually would serve you. It's not at all meticulous planning.

CHOMSKY: This reminds me of the one time I ever testified at a Senate committee; it was the Foreign Relations Committee, headed by J. William Fulbright. Fulbright, a very conservative senator, was pretty sick of the Vietnam War, and thought the United States should pull out. And he turned his Foreign Relations Committee hearings into a kind of academic seminar about the war. I was invited to talk and the person who was testifying with me was Arthur Schlesinger Jr., who had served in the White House in the early 1960s. So the two of us were there. This was around 1970. I talked mostly about the Kennedy administration, which I think was the main culprit, and he disagreed with what I was saying, but then at one point he turned to me and said something like, "You know, the problem

with your analysis is that you're underestimating the stupidity of planners." I was inclined to say, "Well, you were there." But I think his point
is not wrong. They mostly don't know what they're doing. When you read
through the internal documentary record, it's mind-boggling what they
don't understand. (ACHCAR: Of course.) I just am not inclined to attribute
to them the ability to make complicated plans.

ACHCAR: No, I agree. That's precisely the point. It has nothing to do with
complicated plans; it's behaving in such a way as to allow an event that you
wish for to happen. Not preventing it is not the same as planning for it.

CHOMSKY: They would have been taking really huge risks. Not stopping
9/11 could have meant destroying the White House. It came pretty close
to that.

ACHCAR: Right, I don't think they knew anything about the details of what
would happen. Of course.

CHOMSKY: If you had any idea that this was going on, you'd have to try to
stop it because the consequences would be too unpredictable.

ACHCAR: But then, let me point to a contradiction. You said repeatedly that
they are not seriously fighting terrorism, and now you say they would be
taking big risks if they had hints and did not act. But actually they were
taking big risks in the sense that they were not seriously fighting terrorism,
as you said, because a nuclear device or a dirty bomb or a biological plot
could happen and that could have been far more serious than 9/11.

CHOMSKY: Notice the difference in targets. They are not making serious
efforts to protect civilians, but they are making serious efforts to protect
power systems. (ACHCAR: Absolutely.) Well, that's a crucial difference. The
kind of attack that was taking place on 9/11 could have involved power
systems (ACHCAR: Sure.) and in a sense, it did: the Pentagon, and the World
Trade Center. I don't think they wanted those things to happen. That's
attacking the center of power.

ACHCAR: The point is, they surely were not aware of what exactly was
being prepared. Of course, they took all possible measures to protect what
you call "power systems," but, as you yourself pointed out, they cared
much less about the population at large.

CHOMSKY: If they had evidence that a dirty bomb was going to be smuggled
into the United States, I don't think they'd let it happen. The sense in which
they're not taking precautions against the dirty bomb is much more global.
They are not carrying out the global policy that would prevent the rise of
terror that can lead to this—all right, that's a big thing. But knowing that
there's going to be an airplane attack against major centers, or knowing

that there's a dirty bomb being smuggled into New York—that, I'm convinced, they would try to stop. It's just too dangerous.

ACHCAR: Yes, but there are many considerations lending support to the thesis that they wished some terrorist action happened that they could seize as a pretext: One can make a whole list of the benefits of 9/11 for the Bush administration. Huge benefits. This administration was kind of illegitimate before that, due to the very way Bush acceded to the presidency, and then suddenly after 9/11 there was a very broad national and international consensus backing it. And it felt suddenly empowered to implement policies that were considered impossible before 9/11, such as establishing a military presence in the heart of the former Soviet Union, in Central Asia, seizing the pretext of the Afghanistan war, then invading Iraq, and so on. On the other hand, consider the very important bunch of people who are in the administration and who were among the twenty-five founders of the Project for the New American Century (PNAC) whose agenda was implemented after 9/11—people like Dick Cheney, Donald Rumsfeld, Paul Wolfowitz, Zalmay Khalilzad, and many other lesser members of the current Bush administration, to whom one should add George W.'s brother, Jeb Bush—

CHOMSKY: As a matter of fact, the policies that they are pursuing are not very different from those of the Clinton administration.

ACHCAR: What made the difference is precisely 9/11. In the PNAC literature, there is a much-quoted reference to this idea that we are in need of something like a new Pearl Harbor to pursue the policies that are necessary for our project.[19]

Saddam Hussein's Invasion of Kuwait

SHALOM: Gilbert, you raised the case of the Iraqi invasion of Kuwait in 1990. What do you think the U.S. role was there?

ACHCAR: The United States didn't do anything serious to prevent Saddam Hussein from invading Kuwait in 1990. Now, if one wants to jump from that to the conclusion that the United States actually wanted Saddam Hussein to invade Kuwait, there are serious grounds for believing that, but you will never be able to prove it because it's a matter of intention—unless Bush Sr. writes in his memoirs at some point that he wanted that to happen. It's obvious to me that it was in the interest of U.S. imperial policy for Saddam Hussein to invade Kuwait at that point. That was a windfall for the first Bush administration, in the same way that it was a kind of blessing for the Bush Jr. administration to have 9/11. Therefore, you have some serious grounds for inferring—from the fact that they did not seriously try to prevent it, although they knew something was hatching—the suspicion that they were actually wishing that it occurred.

CHOMSKY: I'm dubious. We have to look at these cases really carefully. I did to some extent look at that one. We have some documents. I actually spent a fair amount of time talking afterward to April Glaspie, who was the American ambassador to Iraq in 1989–90. She was a kind of embarrassment to the U.S. government after the invasion of Kuwait, so they sent her off to where I ran into her, in San Diego, and I talked to her for a while. And then I read the documents. My impression is—this is a surmise—that they really didn't know. For example, the United States was providing aid to Saddam Hussein up to practically the day of the invasion, and Britain as well; I think they regarded Saddam Hussein as their friend. A couple of months before the invasion, you remember, the Bush administration sent a senatorial delegation. The transcript is kind of comical.[20] These senators were actually expressing their admiration for Saddam Hussein, their love for him. They were releasing more aid; Bush was overruling the Treasury Department to offer further aid to Saddam Hussein. And this goes right up to just about the day of the invasion. It is true that Glaspie transferred to Saddam Hussein instructions, if you like, that were fairly ambiguous. They indicated that the United States would not object if he did something to rectify boundaries, which means take the Rumeilah oil fields from Kuwait and maybe gain some access to the sea or something. Or to raise oil prices. The U.S. had no objection to raising oil prices. And my suspicion is that Saddam Hussein just misinterpreted. I mean, he was a dictator. Dictators are in a very bad position to make judgments: Nobody talks to them, nobody tells them anything, and they think they understand everything. He got this expression of attitude or instructions from the White House, and he said, okay, they're not going to care if we take Kuwait. In fact, as soon as Iraq saw that there was this huge reaction, within days they began to offer to pull out. From August 8 or 9, 1990, there were negotiations, proposals, and they just kept coming. Within days, as soon as they saw what the reaction was. And here I think you can suggest more persuasively that the United States wanted them to stay. In fact, there is even evidence for that.

ACHCAR: Yes, but what you are saying, Noam, doesn't contradict what I said. Because if the U.S. government truly wanted Saddam Hussein to do what he did—and I repeat, no one can prove it—they would behave normally toward him, of course, until the very last minute. They wouldn't give him any impression that they were seriously worried. That's what I mean. (CHOMSKY: That's possible.) Do you think for one second that if the United States government really wanted to prevent this guy . . .? (CHOMSKY: They could have prevented it.) They could have just told him that if you ever invade Kuwait, we will consider it an act of war against us. Period. Then, even a crazy dictator like him would have thought twice about it.

CHOMSKY: Like I say, I think he was surprised by the U.S. reaction. But this still leaves open a question that isn't going to be answered until we get internal documents, and maybe not even then. There are grounds for believing that it was a double misinterpretation. Glaspie seemed very sincere in describing it, as far as I could tell; she indicated to me that they actually intended to tell him exactly what was permissible: You can rectify borders, you can raise prices, but don't do anything more. And he interpreted that as saying you can invade.

ACHCAR: But come on. The U.S. government knew exactly who Saddam Hussein was, a man crazy enough to invade part of Iran.

CHOMSKY: But that was ten years before, and he'd been weakened by then. And now he was the United States' friend. I don't know. It's going to be an open question until there is some better evidence than we have. What we do know—and here we have evidence—is that right after the invasion, Colin Powell (then the chair of the Joint Chiefs of Staff), for example, is described in internal meetings as saying that the worst outcome would be if Saddam Hussein withdrew from Kuwait and left a puppet government in place. That we can prevent. That's why we're not going to accept any negotiation or any kind of arrangements.

SHALOM: Tariq Aziz, Iraq's foreign minister, has stated that the plan among the Iraqi leadership had been only to force a border rectification. And then at the last minute, Saddam Hussein decided on a full invasion.[21]

CHOMSKY: That could be. That's more consistent with my sense of it, in terms of the way a crazed dictator would operate. I mean, these guys are operating alone. We know that the mistakes dictators make are astonishing. Look at Stalin and the invasion of the Soviet Union. He had overwhelming evidence from all over the place that Hitler was going to invade. But he just trusted his own instinct, and didn't do anything.

ACHCAR: I tend to think that, even had the Iraqi army stopped at the level of so-called rectification of borders, U.S. intervention would have resulted.[22] (CHOMSKY: You think so?) I think so because that was a defining moment in world history, actually, for the post–Cold War period. The Gulf War was a crucially decisive event for the United States, to bury the Vietnam Syndrome, as Bush Sr. said at the time; to demonstrate the capability of U.S. armaments accumulated under Reagan; to show that although the Soviet Union was crumbling, there was a great need for the United States in the world, especially where the partners were concerned—the partners being Western Europe and Japan, who are much more dependent on Middle Eastern oil than the United States is, and unable of course to thwart Saddam Hussein's ambitions and repel his army on their own. They needed the United States for that, the only country in the Western world that could do so. Moreover, it was an excellent opportunity for the United States to reverse something that it had wanted to reverse since it happened in 1962, and that is the withdrawal of U.S. troops from the Saudi kingdom. At the time, they had been compelled to withdraw by the pressure of Arab nationalism on the Saudi kingdom, and ever since then, the United States had wanted to go back there militarily, to reestablish a direct military presence in that part of the world.

You take the sum of all that and you understand why they had to find a suitable pretext. If Saddam Hussein did not exist at the time, they would have had to invent him. They needed a pretext like the one he purveyed, in order to implement their designs. I agree about Hussein's stupidity and all that, but we should remember that the United States, after the end of the Cold War, was faced with all kinds of people saying there should be a drastic reduction in military spending, the so-called peace dividend. If we were indeed entering into an era when economic competition was replacing wars, one of the major advantages of the United States in the global system—which is its military might—would have lost much of its value.

CHOMSKY: The Bush Sr. administration was composed of more or less traditional conservatives. (ACHCAR: True.) They had no social goal of creating a major international confrontation; in fact, they were kind of afraid of it. To show that they wanted Iraq to rectify borders, that's not very difficult. Because they said so. Glaspie, in her conversation with Saddam Hussein, pretty much said, We don't mind if you rectify borders. And if that had been all that happened, they would never have been able to mobilize Saudi Arabia to allow troops. They got the Saudi rulers to agree because they convinced them that the Iraqis were massing on the border and going to invade their country. If they had stopped near the Iraq-Kuwait border, they could never have carried that out. I can't prove it, but my suspicion is U.S. officials were caught by surprise.

SHALOM: In the transcript of Glaspie's conversation with Saddam Hussein, she says, "We have no opinion on the Arab-Arab conflicts, like your border disagreement with Kuwait." But she also says the dispute should be settled peacefully. (CHOMSKY: Right.) And he replies that he hopes it can be, but if they are unable to find a solution, "Iraq will not accept death." And she says, she had thought to postpone her trip "because of the difficulties we are facing. But now I will fly on Monday." And she leaves.[23]

CHOMSKY: That says you can rectify borders. And I think he took it to mean, you can invade Kuwait. The United States said we're not going to do anything if you rectify borders.

ACHCAR: After the end of the war with Iran, Saddam Hussein had assumed an increasingly aggressive stance toward his Arab neighbors. (CHOMSKY:

Especially to try and get the price of oil raised.) And the Saudi kingdom was very much worried. Contrary to what you say, I think the Saudi rulers would definitely have welcomed U.S. intervention, even if the Iraqi army had stopped at a certain limit within Kuwaiti territory, because they knew that Saddam Hussein was trying to lay his hands on some further source of income in order to sustain the huge, hypertrophied army that he had built up during the war against Iran. After that war, he was faced with two options: One was to drastically reduce this whole apparatus that he had built for war purposes and to concentrate on reconstruction and civilian concerns. And the other was to maintain his military and look for some additional source of income for that purpose. He was already blackmailing his rich neighbors with threats because of the financial debt he owed them.

CHOMSKY: The point is, there was a straightforward way to do that, and the United States wasn't objecting to it: Raise the price of oil, and get the Arab countries to cancel his debts. His argument was, Look, we fought the war with Iran to defend you, and now you've got to pay us, and forgive our debt to you. And you have to raise the price of oil. In fact, he accused the Kuwaiti government of keeping the price of oil down in order to strangle Iraq.

ACHCAR: But Washington would not want that, and was not going along with that.

CHOMSKY: That's not true; they told him they didn't mind that. In fact, I don't think the U.S. government did mind. The United States does not necessarily want low oil prices. It wants them within a range. When prices are too low, it's not good for the United States.

ACHCAR: Neither too low nor too high; they want to keep it at what they call the optimum level, that's well-known. But at that point, I think they didn't want that to happen in that way, with Saddam Hussein dictating the level of the oil market.

CHOMSKY: Well, in that Glaspie interchange, there's no indication that they're opposed to his doing something like shaking a fist to raise oil prices—which is perfectly tolerable to the United States and all the profit-seeking corporations.

SHALOM: Glaspie even says there are many Americans (such as the president) who want to see oil prices go up because they come from oil-producing states.[24]

CHOMSKY: It's just that she was talking for the State Department and saying we don't mind—which is probably correct: They didn't mind. When the prices rise, profits for energy corporations rise. The United States and Britain, which develop high-cost oil, are able to bring onto the market their oil from the North Sea and Alaska; and the funding that goes to Saudi

Arabia pretty much recycles back to the United States in one fashion or another: Treasury securities, Bechtel construction contracts, and so on.

ACHCAR: Yes, yes, but Washington could not have been happy if Saddam Hussein—through his military blackmail—got the other Arab states to agree to a rise in oil price and to forgive his debts to them, allowing him to carry on building up his military power. Add to it the fact that for Israel, Iraq was a major concern after the Iran-Iraq war: As long as the two countries were destroying each other, everyone was happy—Israel was happy, the United States was happy. And former secretary of state Henry Kissinger, among others, said it blatantly: Our interest is that they continue destroying each other for the longest time possible. But after the war Israel and the United States had a real reason to be concerned with this huge military power that Saddam Hussein had built. To be sure, they used the Iraqi military threat as a propaganda device to justify the war. It was going to be a war against the "fourth largest army in the world," as they labeled it, which of course we know was a pure propaganda lie, as usual, overblowing the significance of that army, especially with regard to the technology it possessed at the time. But I am convinced that Iraqi military power was nevertheless a real concern for the United States, and that the Bush Sr. administration was in need of a pretext to do what they did at the time.

CHOMSKY: They were supporting Saddam Hussein almost right up until the day of the invasion—and in fact, after the war they returned to supporting him. He probably could have been overthrown by the Shiite rebellion in March 1991. And they authorized him to crush the rebellion (ACHCAR: Certainly.) because they didn't regard him as that much of a threat.

ACHCAR: But they had achieved what they wanted by then. They had reduced Iraqi military power to one-third of what it was.

CHOMSKY: Why was that even a goal? Look, they were providing Saddam Hussein with the means to develop weapons of mass destruction right up until practically the day of the invasion. If they wanted to weaken the army, why do that? This was long after the war with Iran. I don't think they regarded him as a danger. They regarded him as somebody they could incorporate into the American system. (ACHCAR: I don't believe so.) But why were they continuing to provide him with extensive armaments?

ACHCAR: Who provided Saddam Hussein with extensive armaments after the Iran-Iraq war?

CHOMSKY: The United States and Britain—Russia probably, too, Germany, France, others—were continuing to provide him with means to develop advanced weaponry. In fact, even the agricultural aid was doing that. The agricultural aid was crucial. After Saddam Hussein's campaign of repression against the Kurds in 1986–89, all kinds of agricultural areas had been heavily damaged, so they started providing him with agricultural aid. This was strengthening the country.

ACHCAR: You could say so in a sense, but that was not changing any real component of Iraqi military power after 1988, which was a real problem for the United States. Before the recent U.S. invasion, the neocons had a blueprint for an Iraqi army very much reduced in size, something the United States tried to implement and then abandoned early in the current occupation of Iraq. (CHOMSKY: That's 2003.) Yes, but this addressed the issue that they don't want a powerful, unreliable Arab state, and I am sure that they never took Saddam Hussein as a reliable ally. I disagreed with all those who, at the beginning of the Iran-Iraq war, presented Saddam Hussein as some kind of U.S. agent. I never believed that the United States considered this man as a strategic ally—like Israel, for example.

CHOMSKY: No, of course not. It's not a client state.

There's another element there. Remember Iran, Washington's main enemy. They want a counter to Iran in the region. That's Iraq.

ACHCAR: They used here the very classical Machiavellian policy of getting two of your enemies to fight each other. That's a very clever policy.

CHOMSKY: But that continues after the end of the Iran-Iraq war in 1988. Iran is still there. It's not destroyed, it's still a powerful state, but they want a local counter to it. And I think that's a sufficient reason for explaining why they were giving limited but real support to Saddam Hussein.

ACHCAR: I think that Iran was very much weakened militarily, and the best proof of that is that Iran had to accept the UN resolution on ending the war. As Iranian leader Ayatollah Ruhollah Khomeini himself said in 1988, it was a poisoned chalice that he was drinking.

CHOMSKY: But notice when they did it. They did it when the United States got directly involved in the war. When Washington made it clear that it was going to get involved by reflagging Kuwaiti ships and destroying the Iranian airliner, at that point Iran said, Well, we can't fight the United States. But it was still left there as a major, big, powerful state. There would be no counter to it, unless Iraq were there. We don't have the documents, but a rational position for the Bush Sr.-style, Scowcroft-style planners would have been to maintain Iraq as a militarized and functioning society on a reasonable scale. Not one that's capable of threatening anyone, but one that's capable of holding off Iran. It seems to me that that's a conservative interpretation, but a sufficient reason for explaining why U.S. officials were giving, not huge, but substantial military and other support to Saddam Hussein, right up to the invasion.

ACHCAR: My disagreement would be that in order to counter Iran, Washington didn't want Iraq to do it, but wanted instead a direct U.S. presence in the area. They wanted the Saudis and other oil monarchies to feel that they needed direct U.S. protection more than ever. They wanted badly to get back to that area, to the Saudi kingdom, where, in Dhahran after World War II, they had built one of the most important military bases in the world outside of the United States. And the United States deeply resented—as a real problem and a defeat—the fact that it had to evacuate that base. This is, in fact, what raised the strategic importance of Israel, a subject we'll discuss later. But ever since being ejected from its Saudi base, Washington has longed to reverse that. And Saddam Hussein provided it with just the golden opportunity to do so.

I think you are really belittling the total lack of confidence the United States had in Saddam Hussein. They knew the guy was completely unpredictable. He had several times used very harsh anti-American rhetoric; he continuously used anti-Israeli rhetoric. And he was upping the ante against his Arab neighbors, including the Saudi kingdom.

CHOMSKY: The U.S. military presence in the area is mainly to control what happens to the oil production. The United States didn't gain anything by having 5,000 troops there. In fact, that probably harmed U.S. interests. It harmed U.S. interests in exactly the way we saw; it helped give rise to a jihadi movement that the United States is now fighting.

ACHCAR: That's your assessment, and it's correct. But that's not the way U.S policymakers saw it. The way they saw it is that they reestablished their ability to intervene directly in that part of the world, as they had been planning since the presidency of Jimmy Carter. And that was tremendously important.

CHOMSKY: We agree that the 1990 invasion of Kuwait was used for that purpose, but it's a long step between that and saying they wanted it for that purpose. They had other ways of doing it. The other ways to do it were in fact what they were doing, a kind of conservative approach, which was giving limited but significant support to Saddam Hussein, keeping him as a counter to Iran, maintaining their own highly dominant relation over and very close relation with Saudi Arabia and the emirates. And that's a pretty good arrangement for them; there was no particular reason to stir it up, with all the uncertainties and complexities that could follow. They knew it was a volatile region; once you start mixing in it, anything could happen.

ACHCAR: Then why did they impose an embargo on Iraq, after 1991?

CHOMSKY: Once Iraq conquered Kuwait, then of course it's going to be the end. (ACHCAR: Then Saddam Hussein turned suddenly into a bad guy?)

He broke the rules. It's like Cuba's successful defiance. You're allowed to act up to a point, but if you break the rules, you're going to be punished. Why are they punishing Iran? Because in 1979 Iran broke the rules, so it's going to be punished forever. And Iraq's going to be punished forever. Like Serbia. Anyone who does not accept the orders is going to pay for it. That's the way you run a well-ordered system. But as long as they more or less keep to the orders, there's no particular reason to smash them. That's imperial management!

ACHCAR: We have a different reading of the scenario.

2 Fundamentalism and Democracy

Fundamentalism

SHALOM: How important is Islamic fundamentalism as a source of unrest in today's world?

CHOMSKY: Islamic fundamentalism is mainly *a reaction* to forces of unrest in the world. For many years there was strong secular nationalism all over the Arab and Muslim world. Egypt's Gamal Abdel-Nasser was a secular nationalist. Iraq has a long tradition of secular nationalism that goes back a century, with democratizing efforts and so on. Iran had a secular nationalist program over a half-century ago, at the time the government of Mohammed Mossadegh was overthrown in 1953. The failure of secular nationalism, which was both internal and external, and was strongly attacked from the outside, left a vacuum, and I think to an extent the vacuum was filled by Islamic fundamentalism. I guess that's the way you see it too, Gilbert?

ACHCAR: Sure, but let me just stress, first of all, the fact that the Islamic fundamentalist brand of nongovernmental terrorism is only the most visible nowadays. Nongovernmental terrorism is but a tiny fraction of global terrorism, which is mainly governmental terrorism and mostly practiced by the United States. In terms of what is the main source of unrest in today's world, we have both emphasized the fact that it's the behavior of the U.S. government, at all levels.

CHOMSKY: Do we agree that the power, the rise of Islamic fundamentalism, is a reflection of the decline, both internal and external, of secular nationalism?

ACHCAR: I would be even more straightforward than that. The present strength of Islamic fundamentalism is a direct product of very direct U.S. policies. What you've said is perfectly correct, but with the proviso added

DOI: 10.4324/9781003531753-2

that secular nationalism has been weakened and destroyed by the United States as its main enemy. In the 1960s, the dominant trend in the Muslim world in general was secular nationalism and, in the Arab world, Arab nationalism as embodied by Egyptian president Gamal Abdel-Nasser. The United States fought this brand of nationalism, basing itself on the most reactionary brand of Islamic fundamentalism implemented and propagated by the Saudi kingdom. That's something of which I keep reminding my audiences in my public talks: The main and oldest ally of the United States in the Middle East is not Israel, it's the Saudi kingdom, which existed long before the state of Israel was even born. And the United States very deliberately used Islamic fundamentalism through the Saudi kingdom in countering secular nationalism, communism, or whatever kinds of secular left-wing or progressive currents there were all over the area. And this policy continued through the Soviet war in Afghanistan. The United States backed Islamic fundamentalism in that war—the Mujahideen. Who were the Mujahideen? They were Islamic fundamentalist groups, some of them very fanatic, used against the Soviet Union.

CHOMSKY: That's exactly how it looks to me. In fact, again, we can go on. U.S. backing of General Muhammad Zia-ul-Haq in Pakistan through the 1980s was another case of support to an Islamic fundamentalist regime against secular nationalism.

ACHCAR: The United States even supported the Taliban at the beginning, when they came to power in Afghanistan in 1996.

CHOMSKY: Nasser of course was the main Arab enemy in the 1950s and 1960s, but the same policy extended to Abdul-Karim Qassem after he overthrew the monarchy in Iraq in 1958 because the United States assumed it was a nationalist coup, on behalf of a secular nationalist movement, that (we now know from U.S. government internal records) President Dwight D. Eisenhower and Secretary of State John Foster Dulles greatly feared was going to take over the oil of the Middle East and use for regional purposes—which would have been a horrendous disaster for the United States. The U.S. didn't use Middle East oil at that time, but it wanted the oil to be there for its allies, Europe and Japan. If under Nasser's and then, they thought, Qassem's influence in Iraq, the region might use the oil for its own population, and its own development, this would greatly weaken the strong U.S. control over its supply in Europe and Japan. So, yes, secular nationalism had to be destroyed. And Saudi Arabia, the most extreme fundamentalist state, was the way to do it, and later in the Reagan years the United States helped Pakistan move toward fundamentalism. They even allowed it to develop nuclear weapons and pretended they didn't know.

Israel did pretty much the same. Israel wanted to destroy the Palestine Liberation Organization, the PLO, which was secular nationalist, and, in the course of this, helped develop Islamic fundamentalist groups up to the late 1980s. (ACHCAR: That's right.) Israel was in fact explicitly supporting such groups to counter the PLO in the Occupied Territories. They pretty much did the same in Lebanon. I don't think they intended it there, but that's what happened. They invaded Lebanon to demolish the secular PLO, and they ended up with Hezbollah.

ACHCAR: Actually, they very deliberately disarmed all groups that were based on secular ideologies with a multireligious membership—communist or nationalist or other. And they didn't disarm communalist groups, whether Shiite or Druze, not to mention their Christian allies.

CHOMSKY: Was there a source for Hezbollah prior to the Israeli invasion? Did Hezbollah grow out of something indigenous in Lebanon that was already there?

ACHCAR: Yes, it grew out of the Amal movement, a Shiite communalist movement that was not disarmed by the Israelis, just as they did not disarm the Druze militias, or the Christian right-wing militias. But they disarmed of course the PLO and the Lebanese left.

CHOMSKY: Was Amal fundamentalist?

ACHCAR: No. They were founded by a religious figure, but were always more a Shiite communalist organization than a religious one, let alone a fundamentalist one.

CHOMSKY: So how did the transition go from Amal to Hezbollah?

ACHCAR: By a radicalization that was catalyzed by the 1982 Israeli invasion of Lebanon.

CHOMSKY: And that catalyzed fundamentalists?

ACHCAR: Yes. And so you had a splinter group that developed into Hezbollah, and that was backed by Iran. That's the classic tale of the Sorcerer's Apprentice—you'd find tens of such cases in the area, more specifically related to the issue of Islamic fundamentalism. It's actually because, as a general pattern in the region, when Arab nationalism, Nasserism, and similar trends began to crumble in the 1970s, most governments used Islamic fundamentalism as a tool to counter whatever remnants there were of the left or of secular nationalism. Another striking illustration of the same phenomenon is Egyptian president Anwar al-Sadat. He fostered Islamic fundamentalism to counter the remnants of Nasserism after he took over in 1970 and ended up being assassinated by Islamic fundamentalists in

1981. It's the same story all over again: The U.S. government let some kind of genie out of the bottle, but they can't control it and after a while, it turns against them. The combination of their own repression of progressive or secular ideologies and the subjective failure—the bankruptcy—of these ideologies, aggravated by the collapse of the Soviet Union, left the ground open to the only ideological channel of anti-Western protest available, which was Islamic fundamentalism. Islamic fundamentalism was a religious ideology that was tolerated and even used and encouraged by the local regimes and by the United States, and that became the channel to which the resentment against the United States and the regimes themselves finally transferred.

CHOMSKY: Without trying to draw the analogy too closely, I think there is something partially similar in the U.S. Christian fundamentalist situation. "Fundamentalism" is a Protestant term; it comes from Princeton in the early part of the last century. But what we call fundamentalism had very deep roots in the United States from the early colonists, and it's always been there. There's always been an extreme, ultrareligious element, more or less fundamentalist with several revivals repeating over and over; there was another one in the 1950s. That's why we have "In God We Trust" and "One Nation Under God" and all this stuff.[1] But in the last twenty-five years it has been turned for the first time into a major political force. And that I think is conscious exploitation, similar to what you're describing, to try to undermine, in this case, progressive social policies. Not very radical policies but, rather, the mild social democratic policies of the preceding period are under serious attack—under neoliberal attack, under neoconservative attack. The Christian fundamentalists who were always there were mobilized into a political force for the first time to provide a base for this, and also—to the extent that the political system functions, which is not much—to shift the focus of many voters from the issues that really affect their interests (such as health, education, economic issues, wages) over to religious crusades to block the teaching of evolution, gay rights, and abortion rights. These are all issues, for example, about which CEOs just don't care very much. They care a lot about the other issues. And if you can shift the focus of debate and attention and presidential politics and so on to questions that are quite marginal for the wealthy—questions of, say, gay rights—that's wonderful for people who want to destroy the labor unions, construct a social/political system for the benefit of the ultrarich, while everyone else barely survives.

This fundamentalist mobilization has occurred during a unique period of American economic history—there's never been anything like it—where, for about twenty-five years, real wages have either stagnated or declined for the majority. Real median family incomes for the majority are steady or maybe declining. That's never happened before. There were things like the Great Depression, but never twenty-five years of stagnation for the majority through a period with no serious economic disruptions. Working hours have been going way up, social benefits way down, indebtedness growing enormously. These are real social and economic crises. And the way it's been dealt with, to a large extent, is by mobilizing what's always been there, the Christian fundamentalist sectors, and turning them into an active political force. And in the same period, shifting the discourse, and the focus and so on, to those issues that are of concern to the fundamentalists, but of only marginal concern to the people who own and run the society. In fact, you could take a look at the attitudes of CEOs: They're what are called liberal. They're not very different from college professors. And if the population can become obsessed with "evolution theory" and gay rights and so on, fine with them, as long as they're running the social and economic policies. So, for example, after the last election, the business press was describing the "euphoria," as they called it, in boardrooms; and it wasn't because they were against gay marriage. Some were, some weren't; many of them or their children are gay anyway—no, what they knew is that it was a free run for business. And if you can manage that, that's an achievement; it's one of the ways the population can be kept under control. Plus inducing fear, which is a standard device.

It's kind of striking, but my impression is that there was a real shift with the administration of Jimmy Carter. Pre-Carter, nobody really cared very much whether the president was religious—did anyone care whether Lyndon Johnson went to church every Sunday? But Carter, who was probably sincere, somehow taught party managers that if you put on a pious face—and you talk about how you're lusting in your heart and feel guilty and you saw Jesus and so on—that's a way of appealing to a big voting bloc. Now, since Carter, I think every presidential candidate has pretended to religious experience. Even Bill Clinton, who's probably about as religious as I am, made sure to be seen every week singing in the Baptist church. It has been in some ways parallel to what you describe about the rise and use, in fact, of Islamic fundamentalism.

ACHCAR: You are making a very important remark here, actually, because one has to ask: Why, starting from Carter, did this become profitable politically?

CHOMSKY: The Carter years also saw the initiation of the neoliberal policies; that's the same period.

ACHCAR: And here we have precisely the coincidence I mentioned previously. We have the crisis of the mid-1970s—global economic crisis, a major synchronized economic crisis, which created a state of disarray, the loss of familiar points of reference, the spread of what sociologists call "anomie" for all kinds of people. And this made the ground very fertile for religious revivalism or fundamentalism, because in such situations people tend to seek refuge in identity markers. Thus we've seen all over the world, since the shift of the last quarter of the twentieth century, a huge rise in all kinds of identity or tribal politics, whether ethnic, nationalist, religious, sectarian, fundamentalist, or whatever, and this applies to U.S. society, too. Hence the kind of Carter appeal, as you said. The reason the same religious decoy was not used before in the same way was that it wouldn't have been effective before. Actually at some points in modern history, it was even counterproductive for politicians to show too much religious face.

SHALOM: Perhaps we should clarify terms here. There are some very traditional, religious Muslims who say that "fundamentalism" is an attitude toward religion and that it doesn't imply that you want to impose this on somebody else. So, for example, in the United States we have the Amish, who are religious traditionalists, but they don't go around trying to blow up people of other religions and so on. So according to this view one shouldn't use "fundamentalism" as a politically derogatory term; what we are calling fundamentalism should be called something else, like extremist fundamentalism or something of that sort. Do you buy that distinction?

CHOMSKY: I think religious Muslims would make that distinction, just as, when some Jewish fundamentalists were stopped just before they blew up a mosque, religious Jews dissociated themselves from them. That makes sense. But I think Gilbert is talking about something else, the general phenomenon of the rise of the fundamentalist appeal along with the collapse of secular nationalism and the real problems that people are facing. They have to have some way of identifying among themselves in order to confront these problems. The method of secular nationalism, communism, and so on, which had been partially smashed from the outside, partially deteriorated from within, left a vacuum. And there was something comparable in the United States. The 1970s saw the onset of a severe reaction against the social and economic programs enacted under President Franklin Roosevelt's New Deal and continuing through Lyndon Johnson's Great Society that benefited the majority of the population. Starting with the breakdown of the international economic order, known as the Bretton Woods system, capital became increasingly deregulated and neoliberal programs were instituted that caused for much of the population not massive suffering, not disaster, but difficult social and economic conditions; in fact, that had never happened before in American history. It became possible—I think maybe Carter initiated it, unintentionally—to mobilize religious sentiment, which had always been there, and to turn it into a major political force, into the focus of political discourse, to the limited extent to which it exists, displacing social and economic issues. Take right now. For most of the population, the major issues are things like exploding health care costs. But neither political party wants to deal with that; they're too much in the pocket of the insurance companies and the financial institutions and so on. So instead they have battles about evolution theory and intelligent design, and they'll argue about that. Meanwhile, the rich go on their way, running the country. The correlation between these social and economic programs of the roughly neoliberal kind that have led to serious conditions for most of the population, on the one hand, and, on the other hand, revivalism, and exploitation and magnification of religious fundamentalism as a political phenomenon for the first time, and as a core of political debate—that correlation is too close to be disregarded, I think.

ACHCAR: To address your question, Steve, one must enter into a semantic discussion about terms and their meanings, as one might choose different terms. For instance, one might speak of "orthodoxy" to label a narrow interpretation or literal interpretation of religion, as long as it is practiced at just the personal or familial level. The term "fundamentalism" generally points not only to the literal interpretation of religious scriptures but also to the desire of imposing it on society and government, and having everyone abide by these rules. That's what is usually meant by "fundamentalism." And in that meaning, we can see, for the reasons that we've just mentioned, that it's a global phenomenon, not something related to Islam alone. Jewish fundamentalism, Hindu fundamentalism, Catholic, Protestant, etc.—all brands of religious fundamentalism arose in the last quarter-century. It's a remarkable phenomenon, synchronized worldwide.

CHOMSKY: I think Hindu fundamentalism is a good example. Because, again, it existed since the 1920s, but it became a powerful and extremely dangerous phenomenon in just the last two decades or so.

ACHCAR: Exactly, and for the same reasons, the same basic ingredients. The social and economic conditions created by the major shift in the world economy after the 1970s, on the one hand, and, on the other, the bankruptcy of all kinds of progressive ideologies, because of the social and political failure of the states that embodied these ideologies, whether nationalist or communist or whatever: All that combined led to the vacuum being filled by the only ideological tool remaining for the expression of mass resentment, which was religion. That's also because the nonrational, the faith dimension of religion, makes religious ideologies much more difficult to refute than ideologies embodied in state models and political experiments that reached their limits. So, yes, this is a global historical phenomenon that of course is not limited to Islam.

CHOMSKY: Jewish fundamentalism is a little different. It is associated, in part, with the occupation of the West Bank and Gaza Strip and, in part, here in the United States, with developments in the 1960s. It's interesting that the extremist Jewish groups took off in the late 1960s, sometimes in conscious imitation of things like Black nationalism, and some of them became the Jewish Defense League, which modeled themselves on Black nationalists. But there was also a very sharp rise in the number wanting to live according to some image of the seventeenth century. So where you had some young people in the late 1960s going off to a Hindu ashram, others were joining the Lubavitcher Rebbe[2]—and this just exploded. And it was worked into ways of justifying the Israeli occupation of Palestinian territory.

ACHCAR: And it was used for expansionist purposes as in the case of Gush Emunim, the religious settler movement in the Occupied Territories. Simha Flapan, a former leader of Israel's Mapam Party, made the point in his book *The Birth of Israel: Myths and Realities*[3] that it was the Labor Party's Yigal Allon who encouraged them to establish the first settlement in Hebron.

The Saudi Kingdom

ACHCAR: In the case of Islamic fundamentalism, by any criterion one wants to use, it's obvious that by far the most fundamentalist Islamic state on earth is the Saudi kingdom. It is the most obscurantist, the most reactionary, and the most oppressive of women. The treatment of women there is absolutely appalling. When you compare the Saudi kingdom to the Islamic Republic of Iran, Iran looks like a beacon of women's emancipation. I am not kidding. That is in relative terms, of course. By the standard of women's emancipation, democracy, or whatever social value of modernity you want to take into consideration, Iran would rank much higher than the Saudi kingdom. And yet, the country that the United States vilifies as fanatically religious is Iran, whereas the Saudi dynasty are "our friends." And courted friends, at that.

SHALOM: What are the origins of Saudi fundamentalism?

ACHCAR: Saudi fundamentalism is an outgrowth of the alliance between an eighteenth-century Islamic preacher, Muhammad bin Abdel-Wahhab (a very fundamentalist preacher, whose name is used to label the Saudi brand of Islamic fundamentalism, "Wahhabism"), and Muhammad bin Saud, the head of a tribe that became the Saudi ruling dynasty. And this Saudi tribe conquered the major chunk of the Arabian Peninsula that was turned into the Saudi kingdom in the early 1930s. Since then, the Saudi kingdom has been based on a compromise between the ruling dynasty—to an important part of which one could apply what Noam was saying about people like Clinton, namely the skepticism about the sincerity of any religious belief they pretend to have—and the religious "Wahhabi" establishment. The Saudi kingdom has always rested on these two pillars. And the United States has very consciously fostered and supported this combination as an excellent formula for the stability of this very, very important piece of real estate for the United States.

One cannot exaggerate the degree of supervision and control that the United States exerts on the Saudi kingdom. They are now even discussing the education curriculum of the kingdom in the U.S. Congress! I sent Noam recently a link to a resolution passed by the House of Representatives about this issue.[4] There are not many examples in U.S. history of the U.S. Congress interfering in such a way in the education curriculum of another country. But this is just a mockery, actually: Washington in fact wants the Saudi family to enforce only cosmetic changes, simply in order to save face after having come under assault because of the contradiction between its tight links with the Saudis and its pretension that it is democratizing the Middle East— a pretension that has become the main ideological pretext of its war drive in the region, after the collapse of the "weapons of mass destruction" fable.

The Saudi kingdom is a fairly backward society that has ossified into a tribal structure and is subject to very obscurantist religious fundamentalist control. That's something that the United States would not like to change, really, because doing so would introduce intolerable uncertainty or unpredictability regarding the future of that country.

CHOMSKY: Do you think there are progressive forces pressing for substantial change inside the Saudi kingdom?

ACHCAR: Nothing significant, for the reasons we've already noted. When you suppress all kinds of ideological expressions but one, then nature abhorring a vacuum, this one will be used as the main channel. The irony is that the phenomenon that led to Islamic fundamentalism becoming the main channel for popular resentment in the Middle East over the last few decades applies even to the Saudi kingdom, where resentment against the monarchy has taken the form of Islamic fundamentalism. Anti-House of Saud fundamentalists, like bin Laden himself, condemn the ruling dynasty for being hypocrites, allied with a morally corrupt state, an enemy of Islam: the United States. The two major rebellions against the Saudi monarchy in recent history have been the 1979 insurrection in Mecca, which was led by a fundamentalist, and then al-Qaeda.

CHOMSKY: What about the Saudi bourgeoisie?

ACHCAR: The Saudi bourgeoisie is very much under state control and very much intermingled with the dynasty for the sake of its business. You have there thousands of princes and princesses of the ruling family, and a big business layer associated with them and making such huge profits out of the exploitation of the oil income that it is definitely not interested in taking the risk of removing the monarchy—if ever that were possible in any case. Osama bin Laden's family is a good case in point. They are extremely wealthy entrepreneurs, getting into all kinds of building projects, taking advantage of the spending craze that the Saudi kingdom has known since the 1970s, after the first major increase in oil prices. True, this same family has got one of its members mainly and truly motivated by the fanatical interpretation of Islam that is prevalent in the kingdom, who went fighting the Soviet Union in Afghanistan for years, and enjoyed the experience so much that he continued against the United States. But al-Qaeda rank and file in the Saudi kingdom are certainly not bin Ladens in that they are definitely not the sons of wealthy families. Most of them are people from relatively downtrodden segments of Saudi society. And here we have the same phenomenon at play as elsewhere: There is a massive, socially rooted resentment against the monarchy and against the sponsor of the monarchy—that is, the United States. And it takes the form of Islamic fundamentalism as the only kind of ideological channel that is open to these people—even culturally speaking: Their education system is so heavily religious that, except for wealthy people who pay for their kids to get a different kind of education by sending them abroad, or those selected by the system to get a scholarship for pursuing their studies abroad (a few thousand altogether), all the rest are prisoners of that ideological framework.

CHOMSKY: What about the sectors that have come back from abroad? Do they return with secular, more modern ideas and aspirations?

ACHCAR: No, very rarely with regard to aspirations. Most of them come back with just the happiness of being "Saudis," of enjoying a society where they can afford to have a lot of privileges that their Western counterparts could not afford to have—several servants, for instance. Also, it's such a patriarchal society, and since those who study abroad are male by an overwhelming majority, most of them are not interested in shaking off the prevailing structure. This is a very hypocritical society indeed, because it allows segments of society to enjoy some kinds of prohibited pleasures—as long as it is hidden, and not ostentatious. Moreover, the wealthy can afford every now and then to take vacations in more liberal countries. Saudi princes and the rich have flats or villas or palaces, depending on the level of wealth, in various places where they can go and enjoy a different kind of life at will, while the Saudi kingdom is their business base. Such people have a vested interest in keeping the structure as it is.

CHOMSKY: There's nothing like a labor movement?

ACHCAR: Oh, it's unimaginable in the Saudi kingdom. It's the most repressive kind of state; if "totalitarianism" has any meaning, that's totalitarianism there. Any attempt at organizing anything challenging the powers that be is repressed in the most terrible way. In the Saudi kingdom, people risk their lives or physical integrity for things that you would consider as trivial. It's a country where you have special police whipping people found in the street at the time of prayer. It's a society under total control; it's difficult to imagine worse than that. And that is a major ally of the United States and the single Muslim state that is courted by all the Western states, because of its oil wealth. The United States knows that this very oppressive structure is the only guarantee that exists for the stability of the Saudi kingdom, and it also guarantees that the kingdom needs U.S. protection. The United States is the Lord Protector, the overlord of the Saudi kingdom, which in turn is a "protected kingdom," as in medieval history, and has been so from its inception in the sense that it built relations with the United States almost from the start, to counter Britain and then the Soviet Union, or whichever threat it faced. And I think that Western public opinion, U.S. public opinion in particular, remains in a state of ignorance about that. People don't realize who the staunchest ally of the United States in the Middle East really is and what it means. And whenever there is some critical attention being paid to the Saudis, it is for a rather dubious agenda, as is the case with the criticism by some of the neocons and other supporters of Israel, as part of the Saudi-Israeli competition in the United States.

CHOMSKY: Those neocons are not important people—you know, people make a big fuss about them, but among the policies that they're proposing, only those that fit general policy are accepted; those that oppose general policy are simply dismissed. (ACHCAR: I agree.) Like the proposals of Richard Perle, Douglas Feith, and the rest, to impose a Hashemite kingdom on Iraq[5] and so on—they just throw them out.

ACHCAR: This neocon discourse hostile to the Saudi kingdom is the kind that this administration, or any other for that matter, would never buy into. That is quite obvious: I agree with Noam entirely on this issue, and I never accepted the view that the neocons were ruling the country.

Democracy in the Middle East

SHALOM: How would you assess the state of democracy in the Middle East?

CHOMSKY: There have been over the last century quite important developments. There were movements toward democracy all over the region.

Iran didn't have a marvelous democracy, but it had a parliamentary system, which goes way back, until the United States and Britain overthrew it in 1953.

Iraq, even under effective British rule, was developing the basis for parliamentary democracy. Britain tried to block it; the United States didn't like it, but it was developing. And that included things like developing a very strong labor movement. In American political science, that's not supposed to be part of democracy, but it is if you're serious. It's a way for a large part of the population to become involved effectively in political decisionmaking. And Iraq had quite a strong labor movement, a lot of which was crushed by the Baath coup in 1963. The 1963 coup, which was certainly supported by the United States and *may* have been instigated by the United States—there's reason to believe that, but anyhow, certainly supported[6]—was followed by a massacre, which involved, as in Indonesia, CIA lists of opposition figures to be murdered, so-called communists, meaning a term of broad application. And it did undermine significantly the Iraqi Communist Party, which was a force for democracy, given the way it was organized in the labor movement and so on, in that period. The Baath party and Saddam Hussein severely repressed the labor movement, and now the United States is doing the same. In fact, they're still imposing Saddam Hussein's antilabor laws. The unions are reconstructing; they're quite courageous, but a lot of them are getting killed.

And the same has been true in other parts of the Arab world; there have been continuing efforts, which have been aborted both by outside forces and by internal problems. And it still continues.

In Egypt there's a resurgence of long-existing democratic forces, the Kifaya movement, which wants to get rid of the dictatorship of Hosni Mubarak. According to their own account, they describe the movement as having originated primarily in a protest movement against Israeli repression of the second Intifada. That's what set it off. It didn't mean much in the West, but that repression was very brutal right away, in October 2000. The movement then expanded to include other Palestine solidarity groups, and then was joined by the opposition to the Iraq war and so on. It's a movement for democracy that is being repressed pretty brutally by the Mubarak dictatorship, but it's there.

And there are many other such developments, and anybody who travels in the region can see it. Beirut, Lebanon, for example, is a very lively city. In fact, we just saw a comical example of that. The Bush administration a short while ago sent around a specialist in public relations, Karen P. Hughes, the undersecretary of state for public diplomacy, on a tour through the Middle East. She was going to explain to the backward people of the Middle East that they don't really understand us, that we really love them. Some people were calling it the "I'm a mom" tour: She started her talk in every place she went by saying, "I'm a mom, I love children"; then she told her audiences how they really didn't understand how much we loved them and so on. Not surprisingly, it fell completely flat everywhere. She was accompanied by the chief diplomatic correspondent for the *New York Times,* Steven R. Weisman, who wrote a follow-up report on it.[7] I don't know if it was tongue-in-cheek: I hope it was; I'm never sure. But what he said was her speeches didn't work because she kept to "concise sound bites, rather than sustained arguments." Weisman explained that "[i]n American campaigns, such messages repeated over and over can have an effect because a presidential candidate dominates the news with every statement he makes, and if that fails to work, money can be poured into saturation advertising." But then he said: "By contrast, in the lively and percussive environment of this region," it didn't work. So we have a long way to go in democracy promotion to teach them how to become real democrats.

Shortly after that came another revealing incident, which wasn't reported in the United States, but was reported in the English-language Lebanese press.[8] There was a debate in Beirut between the public affairs officer at the American embassy, Juliet Wurr, and an American Fulbright scholar, Joshua Landis, about bringing democracy to Lebanon. They described the public affairs officer as starting her talk with what she called "the 4 E's of exchange, engagement, education and empowerment"—like a Power-Point demonstration for corporate executives.[9] That's not democracy. If any place in the Middle East has a lively and percussive atmosphere, it's probably Beirut. These are lively societies, which are just going to laugh at this kind of nonsense.

ACHCAR: Noam described the potential for democracy, and the potential is there, of course, as he says, and quite strong, much stronger than what people usually tend to believe. Think of an event like the 1979 Iranian revolution: A major aspiration of those masses revolting, even though they rose under the leadership of Ayatollah Ruhollah Khomeini, was democracy. That's why Khomeini felt the need to include democracy as a key demand in his platform and called for a constituent assembly, one of the traditional democratic demands against absolutist rule. He confronted the Iranian dictator, the shah, Mohammad Reza Pahlavi, in the name of democracy. Of course, after taking power, Khomeini totally perverted this democratic aspiration and, instead of the constituent assembly, set up an Islamic "Assembly of Experts," and imposed a theocratic government. But the fact remains that there was a strong aspiration toward democracy in the Iranian revolution. And in a sense, relatively speaking, there still exists, despite everything, some real degree of democratic life in Iran, where you have elections with surprises—like the recent presidential election in June 2005, which saw the victory of Mahmoud Ahmadinejad. To be sure, the contest is limited to factions of the regime, and it's definitely not a full or real or free democracy. But there's a certain amount of popular participation in official politics, and it so happens that this occurs in the state that is considered to be the quintessence of evil by the Bush administration.

On the other hand, as I've already emphasized, the oldest and dearest Muslim ally of the United States, the Saudi kingdom, is the most extreme antithesis of democracy—you can't imagine worse. And the fact that the Saudi kingdom is the linchpin of U.S. regional hegemony has had a very strong impact on the whole region, and is one reason why, when Arab secular nationalism and the progressive currents collapsed, this did not lead to some kind of democratic change like you had in Eastern Europe. The only exception to the "third wave" of democratic changes, as Huntington would call it[10]—that is, the global democratization process that kicked off in the 1980s—has been the Middle East. I've called that the "Arab despotic exception."[11] You have had changes all over the world—Latin America, Eastern Europe, sub-Saharan Africa, Eastern Asia—but nothing comparable in the Middle East. There are two reasons for this exception: oil, of course, and the fact that if you implement democracy there, the "bad guys" would win. That's what Huntington calls the "democracy paradox":[12] that in some countries, democracy leads to the victory of forces hostile to the West. For him, that's a paradox, because he believes that if you are a real democrat, you should be a client of Western powers.

So you had a situation in the Middle East where authoritarian rule prevailed, with the exception of Lebanon, among Arab countries, and Turkey, within certain limits and because of European pressure. (In Turkey there is a *controlled* democracy; as a Turkish judge put it not long ago, Turkey is a state with a constitution, not a constitutional state—a very accurate formula.) Aside from these two cases and, of course, the very special Israeli one, what you have are more or less autocratic or despotic regimes, absolute monarchs, some of them granting a degree of parliamentary representation, but with no popular sovereignty whatsoever, or dictators originating in the military—or in the police, like the Tunisian president who is considered a good guy by Western governments because of his zeal in repressing Islamic fundamentalists to prevent contagion from neighboring Algeria. So, democracy in the Middle East is still very much a demand on the agenda, a demand that needs to be fulfilled; it is quite far from being an accomplished fact.

After 9/11, the Bush administration acknowledged this situation. The commitment to uphold human rights, "human dignity" as they put it, was prominent in Bush's January 2002 State of the Union speech as well as in the National Security Strategy of September 2002. Bush later recognized in his famous speech at the National Endowment for Democracy in November 2003 that, in the past, until now, the United States had been privileging stability over democracy, and in the name of stability it had been allowing and supporting authoritarian regimes. But now, he declared, his administration had come to the conclusion that this ought to be changed because—and the influence of neocon ideology was very clear here—we must understand that our interests are best served with democracy flowering all over the area.[13] But that remained mostly, as it always has, at the level of discourse.

CHOMSKY: Others, though, are pretty frank about what U.S. policy *actually* is. So, for example, the most prominent scholar-advocate of what's called democracy promotion, the head of the Democracy and Rule of Law Project of the Carnegie Endowment for International Peace in Washington, D.C., Thomas Carothers, who calls himself a neo-Reaganite, has written very honestly about all these things.[14] He was part of the State Department in the 1980s, part of what they call the "democracy enhancement" programs under Reagan. He describes these programs as very sincere—we really wanted to do it—but there was a problem: The wrong people might win. So therefore, in El Salvador, which was their prize example, he said the United States had two policies. One was to run technically credible elections, and the other was to make sure our candidate wins. He says it virtually in those words. And if anybody looks at what has happened, they'll find that that's exactly what was done. True, that meant having to massacre 70,000 people, and blowing the brains out of the leading intellectuals, but that's what had to be done. Yet still, says Carothers, it's sincere. In fact, he says if you look at it you'll find what he calls a strong line of continuity that runs through every U.S. administration through George W. Bush. Every administration is schizophrenic, beset with some kind of strange malady. They support democracy if and only if it conforms to U.S. economic and strategic objectives.[15]

ACHCAR: When we look at the facts, we find indeed that what Carothers characterizes as "split presidential personality," to use his formula, is a disease that also affects George W. Bush.[16] He suffers from exactly the same syndrome. On the one hand, there is some type of prodemocracy discourse, and the current administration has taken this further with regard to the Middle East than any previous administration—though of course with regard to Eastern Europe, it is a very old tradition.

But when we consider the facts, on the other hand, as opposed to the words, we find that one of the countries over which the United States has the most leverage in the Middle East is the Saudi kingdom. And the only issue that Karen Hughes thought necessary to impress on the Saudis was the right of women to drive—this, in a country where women don't have the right to vote, not to mention even very basic civil rights, family rights, and so on. In the Saudi kingdom, women are deprived of most rights—rights that in any normal country would be considered very elementary.

When the Bush administration started its military campaign after 9/11, it invaded Afghanistan in alliance with the Pakistani military dictatorship, which had overthrown a democratically elected government. The October 1999 coup d'état in Pakistan was led by General Pervez Musharraf, who regularly gets invited to the White House, posing for pictures with Bush—a great democrat, according to the official propaganda. The United States had supported the Taliban when they came to power backed by the Pakistani military in 1996. In 2001, the United States and Pakistan overthrew the Taliban in alliance with other enemies of democracy, the Northern Alliance Mujahideen warlords. This provided the United States the opportunity to extend its military presence in Central Asia, buying the collaboration of very despotic regimes—those of Uzbekistan, Kyrgyzstan, and others. The Bush administration has boasted a great deal about the 2003 Rose Revolution in Georgia, in the Caucasus. But, in neighboring Azerbaijan, it supports one of the worst, most despotic tyrants you still have on earth, and that's because of oil interests. The current Azeri dictator, Ilham Aliyev, whose father ruled the land for over thirty years before him, was once pronounced an honorary citizen of Texas by then-governor George W. Bush in appreciation of his support for American oil companies.[17] So Bush's democratic credentials are nil. Anyone with an elementary knowledge of the facts wouldn't give the slightest credit to the Bush administration's democratic discourse. We'll discuss later the case of Iraq, but one thing is clear: It is only when the weapons-of-mass-destruction pretext started collapsing a few months after the invasion of Iraq in 2003 that the administration turned up the volume of the democratic pretext. Then, they dashed off their blueprint for reforming what they called the "Greater Middle East" the year after. All the Arab press and all serious observers stressed the fact that this was a completely rhetorical project, more a public relations operation than anything else.[18] It was only meant to create the illusion that the United States was concerned with spreading democracy to this part of the world where the "war on terror" was taking place.

Nevertheless, Washington had to put some pressure then on its traditional clients to get some minimal cosmetic reforms in order to convince the U.S. public that it was serious. Under this pressure, the Saudis organized municipal elections for the first time in thirty years. It wasn't the first time in the history of the kingdom, but the first time in three decades. But what were these elections about? They were restricted to male voters, voting for candidates who themselves were restricted to males and who had to be approved by the authorities—and hence an overwhelming majority of them were fundamentalists, many of them hard-line fundamentalists. In addition, at stake in the elections were only *half* the seats of the kingdom's municipal councils, the other half being designated by the monarchy. And that was praised as a major step toward democracy by the Bush administration. It is completely ridiculous.

In Egypt, also, Washington put some pressure on Mubarak—who has ruled the country since 1981, a quarter-century already!—to introduce some level of apparent competition into the political system, which had been monopolized by his party. Mubarak complied in ways that involved no threat to his control of the government. Whereas previously the Egyptian president was ritually confirmed by plebiscite after having been "elected" by the parliamentary majority, which he controlled completely, now there was a so-called pluralistic election. The other candidates, however, had to be approved by Mubarak's parliamentary majority! So he allowed a few of them to run, even people who didn't like him, who were not under his control, just to please Washington, while taking every kind of measure to rig the election, held in September 2005. Then the parliamentary elections followed in November–December: They were organized by regional rounds, which is a very convenient method for a dictatorship. When you have to organize elections under pressure, you take the precaution of having them by rounds, so that if between the first and second, or second and third, rounds you sense it's not going well, you can still stop them, as the military did in Algeria in January 1992—or you can rig them even more heavily! Anyhow, Mubarak, who is not stupid, saw to it that the Muslim Brotherhood—a fundamentalist group—emerged clearly as the major power to gain from this carefully controlled opening, and this was his way to convince the United States to stop bothering him. His message to the Bush administration was: If you push for democracy, you'll get these guys in power. So, leave me alone! And I think they got the message in Washington loud and clear: They stopped putting pressure on Mubarak and are quite worried about losing Egypt.

Fundamentalism and Democracy

SHALOM: What happens when the force most likely to be elected is in fact some kind of fundamentalist movement, as was the case in Algeria, or a fascist movement, or something like that, that is likely to undermine democracy?

CHOMSKY: As in the United States, for example? The United States is one of the most fundamentalist countries in the world and has long been, and one of the few functioning voting blocs here is the extreme fundamentalists, who out of either cynicism or belief have a big effect on the administration.

You can see it all over the place. Do you know any other countries where there are struggles going on over whether you're allowed to say that humans weren't created 6,000 years ago? I don't know if there's any other country in the world where that goes on.

ACHCAR: The Saudi kingdom is one. There, creationism is the official theory.

SHALOM: Point taken, Noam. But I expect there are going to be elections in the United States in 2008 and probably in 2012.

CHOMSKY: Yes, the United States has a couple of hundred years of tradition, so you can be pretty sure elections are going to go on. Algeria doesn't, it's just emerged from French colonialism recently; it had a series of dictatorships. Nevertheless, there's no reason to think that, if the 1992 Algerian elections had gone on, this would have been the last election. They had a first-round election, and it looked as though it was going to be reasonably fair, and as though people whom the West and the Algerian military leadership didn't like were going to win, so they cancelled the election.

SHALOM: But they were also people that you yourself didn't like.

CHOMSKY: I didn't like them, either. I don't like most of the governments in the world—but what has that got to do with anything? I don't like the Israeli prime minister. Does that mean that Israel for the Jewish population isn't a democracy? It is. But a democracy doesn't mean you elect who I like. In fact, in the United States, I don't even think we have elections in much more than a formal sense. We don't have elections in the sense that other countries do, countries that are themselves hardly models of democracy. Take the second-largest country in the hemisphere, Brazil. Something happened in Brazil that is unimaginable in the United States. Someone was elected president who actually comes out of the general population; he was a union leader who had no higher education. There are actually political parties in Brazil, unlike here—not just candidate-producing organizations. With all of its very serious flaws, the Brazilian Workers' Party is a political party. People participate in it in various ways, it's doing things all the time, it's got social programs and so on. There are mass popular movements, like the landless workers' movement, which is huge. There are professional associations, there are unions, there are all sorts of things. With that kind of mixture of what political scientists call "secondary associations," you have the basis for some degree of democratic functioning, and it's possible for people to elect someone from their own ranks. Compare it with here. In 2004 you had two men, both coming from backgrounds of extreme privilege and political power; both went to the same elite university; both joined the same secret society, which is one of the Ivy League secret societies for training people to be members of the ruling elite. Both of them were able to run because they were supported by pretty much the same corporate interests. They had an election in which issues were almost totally suppressed. The elections were run by the public relations industry. They were more or less on the level of toothpaste ads. You don't look at an advertisement expecting to learn anything. The idea is to delude you by imagery. That's the way this campaign was. Voters were often unaware of the stand of the candidates on the issues. There were serious studies that showed voters to be misinformed about candidates' positions.[19] The election was diverted to topics that the people who really run the country don't care much about, the so-called cultural issues. But most issues of real concern to people were just off the agenda.

Take the issue of national health care. The *New York Times* reported during the election campaign that Democratic presidential candidate John Kerry couldn't suggest a government health program because "there is so little political support for government intervention in the health care market."[20] But take a look at the polls: For a long time, depending on how the question was asked, about two-thirds of the public has said the United States should have a national health care system.[21] That the political system can't mention an issue supported by a large majority of the population is a sign of serious deterioration of democracy; you have the formal institutions, but they're not functioning. So, yes, there are real democratic deficiencies, and you don't have to look at Algeria to find them.

ACHCAR: There are two problems with the Algerian model. One is the internal problem, and the other one is the attitude of outside forces. The internal problem is the absurdity of the idea that you could defend democracy by suppressing democracy. Under the pretext that you want to prevent forces that you suspect of having an antidemocratic agenda from coming to power through democratic means, you just cancel democracy! This means that you deem they have the popular majority, and that you want to block majority power in the country: You thus establish minority power based on force, since minority power against the majority can by definition only be based on coercion. The result is a military dictatorship, and the end result in Algeria was a terrible degradation of the situation, at a huge cost in human lives and social and economic deterioration. Algeria is still suffering from the terror brought by the clash between, on the one hand, those segments of the fundamentalist movement that got radicalized as a result of the coup and resorted to very violent actions and, on the other hand, the military dictatorship perpetrating a great many atrocities through overt or covert means, with the population caught between the hammer and the anvil. It was a truly awful situation. Moreover, the fact is that in any case, power is not decided by the ballot box in Algeria. It's not in most countries on earth, one could say, but in countries like Algeria—or Turkey, for that matter—real power is in the hands of the military. (In other countries, real political power might be in the hands of the holders of economic power, for instance.) If the Islamic fundamentalists had won the election in Algeria, all they could have formed would have been a government like the Turkish one, with only limited power, checked by the military. That actually would have been a much better outcome for the Algerians: These two forces could have neutralized each other, balanced each other peacefully, and that could have helped open a wider democratic space, in a sense. The Algerian case is a very clear illustration of the fact that suppressing democracy in the name of democracy leads to disastrous results.

As for Western attitudes toward that issue, they had strictly nothing to do with any attachment to democracy or hatred of fundamentalism. One more time, the Saudi kingdom is a blatant illustration to the contrary. The reason why Western powers supported the coup in Algeria is related to the 1991 Gulf War.

In the 1991 Gulf War, the whole Sunni Islamic fundamentalist movement underwent a split all over the Muslim world. Major sections of the movement followed their popular base in opposing the war, and only a minority remained faithful allies to the Saudi kingdom and the oil monarchies, and supported the war. Had the Islamic Salvation Front in Algeria supported the U.S. war in Iraq—for instance, claiming that it was concerned for Kuwait's sovereignty—and had it remained a close friend of the Saudi kingdom, you can be sure there would have been no endorsement, at least by Washington, for a coup in Algeria. Here, again, this is quite hypocritical. The same argument is also being used now in Iraq: that the United States is needed to prevent fundamentalism, or rather Iranian-style fundamentalism, from prevailing. Washington considers the Saudi government a great friend, but it would prevent an Iran-style government from taking hold in Iraq for the sake of secularism. This is quite farcical.

CHOMSKY: It has nothing to do with fundamentalism; it's a question of who supports you and who doesn't. And in fact, the United States is actually pretty ecumenical as far as religion goes in terms of whom it supports and whom it opposes and often crushes. Latin America is the most dramatic example, and has the longest history. After all, in the 1980s, the current administration and its mentors basically fought a war against the Catholic Church, because it was moving toward liberation theology, and that was intolerable. And it was brutal.

How anybody can talk about democracy promotion by the United States with a straight face—this is very hard for me to understand. Just in the same period as Bush's pronouncements about democracy promotion, Washington supported a military coup in Venezuela to overthrow the elected government. They had to back down because of the uproar in Latin America, which actually does take democracy more or less seriously. When that failed, the Bush administration just turned to standard subversion, which is going on right now. Whatever one thinks about the Venezuelan government, it leads Latin America by quite a margin in popular support for the elected government. Yet the United States is doing everything it can to subvert it, in exactly the traditional ways: trying to support opposition groups, which are called prodemocracy groups since they oppose a government that Washington opposes, even though these groups had just been involved in a military coup against an elected government.

In the December 2005 elections that took place in Venezuela, the United States was aware that its candidates were going to lose substantially. So it therefore either supported or organized—we don't know which—a boycott. That's a standard way of delegitimizing a government you don't like: Get the opposition to boycott it. Then you can claim that it's not a democracy. Washington did exactly the same thing in Nicaragua in 1984. It was clear that the candidate favored by the United States was going to lose. In fact, it turned out he was a CIA asset; they got him to withdraw, and then they could claim it wasn't a legitimate election. That was a very interesting case, because it was probably the most observed election in history at that time. And all the international observers—the Latin American Studies Association, various European parliamentary delegations, and so on— confirmed that it was a fair election by Latin American standards.[22] But the Reagan administration declared Nicaragua was a dictatorship and the election just disappeared from history. When you can't win, you boycott, delegitimize, and do other things to block democracy. In the Nicaraguan case, of course, it wasn't just subversion: Washington was also carrying out a major terrorist war to overthrow the Sandinista government and finally succeeded in doing so.

The point is, without going through the details, that U.S. democratic rhetoric and undemocratic substance have a long history. Anyone with a gray cell functioning knows that you should just pay no attention to the rhetorical pronouncements of leaders. When the Iraqi elections were held in January 2005, the Iranian minister made a very eloquent speech about how Iran supports democratic elections in Iraq, and was in favor of democracy—did anybody listen? Did every scholarly article start by saying, "We understand that Iran has made it clear that democracy promotion is the leading plank in their foreign policy"? But that's what happened here. Every journal article began with something like "Democracy promotion is the hallmark of the Bush foreign policy." Based on what? Based on rhetorical pronouncements. The massive evidence against it doesn't make any difference. The dear leader spoke. OK, that's what it is. The past evidence and the current evidence are all to the contrary, but what's the difference?

Democracy Since the Iraq Invasion

SHALOM: Some people argue that regardless of what U.S. intentions were, one consequence of the U.S. invasion of Iraq is that there's been an increase in democracy in the Middle East, and, in fact, they use Lebanon as an example.

CHOMSKY: Unless the CIA is taking credit for the bombing that killed former Lebanese prime minister Rafic Hariri, setting off a whole chain of events, the United States had nothing to do with democracy in Lebanon. But yes, it could be true. It's interesting to see the reporting in the West from the Middle East, in the *New York Times,* say. So, the *Times* correspondents in the Middle East have a number of times pointed out that it's a common feeling in the region that Osama bin Laden made a major contribution to democracy in the Middle East by attacking the World Trade Center. It could be true. You could say the same about Japanese fascism. Japanese fascism was grotesque, responsible for horrendous atrocities in Asia. But it made a major contribution to democracy in Asia by triggering a chain of events that kicked out the European invaders. Do we therefore praise Japanese fascism? When you take something as complicated as a society, and you smash it with a bludgeon, all kinds of things can happen. Some of them may be favorable, some may be unfavorable. It has nothing to do with evaluating it. You don't praise Osama bin Laden, you don't praise Japanese fascism, you ask what they were trying to do, and what did they do. Yes, there can be all kinds of consequences. It's conceivable that when you look at the invasion of Iraq twenty-five or thirty years from now, you may say it helped set off democratizing forces in the Middle East. Maybe. Then it will be as good as Japanese fascism, or Osama bin Laden.

ACHCAR: If that is the historical outcome, it would be in the realm of unintended consequences. Given what real democratic choices would lead to in the Middle East—governments hostile to U.S. interests—this is definitely not what Washington wants. What Washington wants, and what it means by democracy, is the installation of governments under U.S. control with democratic façades, and nothing more. That was the project for Iraq.

The Bush administration used to say that a postinvasion Iraq would serve as an attractive model in the region. Now, Iraq has definitely not become an appealing model in the Middle East; on the contrary, it has become an appalling model, because people now associate this democracy with deep insecurity and civil war. It is a negative model as well because the United States has been implementing in Iraq, very consciously, a conception of democracy that is inspired by the Lebanese model of democracy, namely one based on the ethnic and sectarian distribution of offices. This is definitely a very bad recipe for a stable political system, leading to all kinds of problems. I mentioned previously that the Bush administration exerted some pressure on its allies, its traditional client states, for cosmetic "democratic" reforms—limited measures that could be imported into the existing despotic structure, without changing the basic situation, but that could be sold to public opinion in the United States as representing a step forward in democracy promotion. A second reason U.S. officials supported these measures was that they came to the conclusion that some kind of barometer was needed to indicate what's going on at the level of public opinion. Actually, most of the time, that's how they look at elections: as barometers for that purpose. As I've already said, Mubarak, for his part, understood that quite cleverly and made sure that the barometer showed the most worrying possible result to Washington. For that, he opened a real, though limited, space for the Muslim Brotherhood, but he did so on purpose. He opened the space for these people, not for others, because he knew that the outcome would worry Washington. Once the show was over, he took his revenge on Ayman Nour, the relatively young presidential candidate who dared to challenge him, and he sentenced Nour to five years in prison. Though Washington liked Nour, you hardly heard anything about it, because they got the message from Mubarak and stopped "harassing" him.

Historically speaking, the invasion of Iraq has been a major destabilizing factor in the whole Middle East. Some of the craziest of the neocons, however, were somewhat conscious of that; they had their theory about "constructive instability,"[23] and there were echoes of that in administration discourse at some points. When people told them "You are creating instability," they replied, "That's democracy." But that was just defensive argumentation against the fact that they have been actually endangering U.S. interests. This Bush administration has behaved in the most stupid way possible, and will likely go down in history not as the promoter of democracy in the Middle East but as the undertaker of U.S. interests in the region.

3 Sources of U.S. Foreign Policy in the Middle East

Oil

SHALOM: What are the driving dynamics of U.S. policy in the Middle East?

CHOMSKY: If the Middle East didn't have the major energy reserves of the world, then policymakers today wouldn't care much more about it than they do about Antarctica. It has been known since the early twentieth century, when the world economy shifted to oil, that the largest and most easily accessible supply of energy resources is located in the Middle East. Over the years, the assessment of just how rich and how easily accessible they are has escalated. It was certainly clear, however, by the 1920s. In fact, the United States itself did not become a global power until World War II, but one area in which it did exert itself earlier was the Middle East, where it insisted on U.S. oil firms getting a share of the energy resources of present-day Iraq and other former territories of the Ottoman Empire, which originally had been divided among British, Dutch, and French interests after World War I. In the early 1930s, U.S. companies obtained a foothold in Saudi Arabia. Washington recognized immediately that this was an immense prize, and they wanted to keep it for themselves. During World War II, a fight took place between Britain and the United States over control of Saudi Arabia. Undersecretary of the Navy William C. Bullitt warned President Franklin D. Roosevelt in 1943 that the British were trying to "diddle" the United States out of its concessions in Saudi Arabia,[1] and as a result, Roosevelt authorized Saudi Arabia to receive lend-lease aid under the rationale that "the defense of Saudi Arabia is vital to the defense of the United States."[2] So Saudi Arabia got aid mainly in order to keep the British out and to buy off the Saudi ruling class.

There were similar developments elsewhere. Following World War I, it was recognized that Venezuela—dominated by Britain—had major oil resources, and so President Woodrow Wilson essentially kicked the British out of Venezuela in 1920 to take it over.

DOI: 10.4324/9781003531753-3

In the Middle East after World War II, the United States was perfectly happy to have Britain be a kind of partner in controlling the region, but the British were unable to pick it up, so gradually the relationship between Britain and the United States settled into one of total dependency, with Britain becoming almost a client state. In one of the recent issues of the major British foreign policy journal, *International Affairs,* the journal of the Royal Institute, there's a good article where Britain is described as "the spear carrier for the *pax americana.*"[3]

One important thing to bear in mind is that the United States did not at that time want control of these regions in order to use the oil for its own consumption. North America was the major producer in the world until about 1970, or close to it. The United States was not using much Middle Eastern oil, and actually it still does not particularly rely on it. The United States wanted to control it because that's a lever of world domination; its main concerns have been its industrial rivals. Washington has always worried that Europe might become what's called a Third Force, that it might go off in an independent direction. And it could: It's a region roughly comparable to the United States in terms of economy and population, in many ways more advanced. So one way of keeping Europe dependent has been to make sure that it's reliant on oil, and that the United States controls the oil. In fact, a good deal of Marshall Plan aid in the years following World War II was devoted to shifting Europe from internally abundant coal supplies to U.S.-controlled oil supplies. The same was done in Japan. In fact, U.S. policymakers long recognized that this kind of arrangement would give the United States veto power, as George Kennan put it,[4] over what others might do.

That was recently reexpressed by Zbigniew Brzezinski, who's one of the more sensible of the current crop of analysts. He wasn't that enthusiastic about the invasion of Iraq, but he said that controlling Iraq would give the United States "critical leverage" over the other industrial societies, because if you control the oil upon which they rely for survival, they're dependent on your decisions for all sorts of other things; it's geopolitical control.[5] In the year 2000, a National Intelligence Council study, *Global Trends 2015,* projected that by 2015 the United States would itself rely on more stable Atlantic Basin supplies—from the Western Hemisphere and western Africa.[6] But the United States wants to control the major energy reserves of the world in the Middle East, for reasons of global control.

My feeling is that that's been the driving issue all along. Historically, there were sometimes strategic concerns—for the British, say, the Middle East was crucial for maintaining their lines of contact with India. But I think for the United States that's been at most a secondary consideration. The focus has mainly been and continues to be the one huge, incomparable resource of this region. It's kind of striking to see the taboo against mentioning it. For any person of minimal rationality, it's obvious that the United States invaded Iraq because it's right in the midst of the richest oil producing regions in the world. But we're expected to believe that the U.S. would have invaded Iraq even if it was producing just dates and all the oil supplies in the world were in southern Africa. If you suggest otherwise, you are accused of indulging in a conspiracy theory. But in fact oil has been the driving force all along.

The British had a structure for control when they were the main power dominating the region back during the time of World War I, when the importance of oil was first being recognized. British foreign secretary Lord Curzon described how they had to set up what he called an "Arab façade"—self-governing states that would only be façades, behind which the British would rule with various constitutional and other arrangements.[7] In effect, there would be the appearance of an independent state, but the British would rule it, rather like the East European satellites of the Soviet Union or the Central American satellites of the United States. Formally, they rule themselves, but in actuality the big power basically rules. This was the system set up by the British in the Middle East. So Iraq was formally independent in 1932, but they couldn't move much beyond British limits, until 1958, when they threw the British out. The same applied to Egypt and various other Arab states. The United States took this system over and pretty much maintained it, but they added another layer of structure to it: what were called peripheral states. These would be the gendarmes—the local cops on the beat, the Nixon administration once called them—with police headquarters in Washington and a branch office in London. They were preferably non-Arab, so Turkey was the main one. Iran, as long as it was under the shah, was a major one. Pakistan was providing the royal guard for the Saudi kings and so on. And Israel became part of this peripheral system beginning with the June 1967 Arab-Israeli war.

Israel performed a tremendous service to the Saudi kingdom in 1967 by defeating Egypt's Gamal Abdel-Nasser, who was their main threat. And if we ever could get archival information from the Saudi family, I would be willing to bet anything that they were pressing Lyndon Johnson to unleash Israel to crush Nasser. It's hard to imagine that they wouldn't have been. It was a kind of tacit alliance. It was even recognized by U.S. intelligence; the defense intelligence agency did have some public books and so on, probably representing policy, describing the U.S. system in the region as based on a tripartite alliance, a tacit alliance, among Saudi Arabia, where the oil is; Iran, which is a big powerful state; and Israel. Technically, Saudi Arabia was formally at war with Israel, but it was basically allied. And Iran and Israel were very closely allied. There was no mutual recognition, but there was in effect an Israeli embassy in Tehran, with someone serving in effect as ambassador, and leading officials were going up and back.

And this system of control—Arab façades and peripheral gendarmes—has pretty much survived a lot of crises and maintained itself. I think the invasion of Iraq is just another piece of it.

ACHCAR: The centrality of oil for U.S. policy in the Middle East is not speculation. One just has to read every strategic document produced by Washington for decades, which has been stressing oil as the major factor behind the importance of the area. Still, as Noam said, when you bring that in to explain invasions that they justify on other grounds, because oil wouldn't be convincing enough to public opinion, they get mad. But most of the time, the explanation is very explicit. Of course, there are ways of putting it to make it more palatable: The United States supposedly is protecting the global economy and its access to oil. In the strategic documents, the U.S. presents itself consistently as defending not only its own interests but also the interests of its partners and allies against all kinds of threats.

Oil actually represents a combination of economic and strategic interests. No one can downplay the significance of the economic interests, which are immense with regard to the oil industry. U.S. oil companies are now more prosperous than ever, by the way, with the new wave of oil price increases. On the other hand, there is also the huge strategic importance of the control of oil, which gives the United States decisive leverage over its partners and potential rivals. Japan is a partner whose allegiance to the United States is guaranteed by, among other factors, U.S. control over its oil sources in the Middle East. But China, a potential threat to U.S. global hegemony, is checked, too, by the same control. You can't understand what is happening in global politics if you don't pay attention to the maneuvers involving Russia, China, Japan, and the United States around the issue of oil.

CHOMSKY: This is now crystallizing. There is currently an Asian Energy Security Grid forming, based primarily on China and Russia, but India presumably will join in, and South Korea, and maybe Japan—though the latter is ambivalent for the reasons that Gilbert mentioned. This is an attempt to have a big, organized systematic control over energy sources internal to this huge Asian area. It has some substantial resources of its own, particularly in Siberia. However, they would love to get Iran into it. And it's just possible that Iran—if it decides Western Europe is just too much in the pocket of the United States to ever act independently—might just give up on the West and turn to the East, joining the Asian Energy Security Grid and becoming one of its linchpins. This would be nightmarish for the United States.

It's striking that India, though it's trying very hard to maintain its new alliance with the United States, nevertheless seems to have disregarded U.S. orders about a pipeline to Iran. The United States tried very hard to get them not to continue with that pipeline, but they just refused. Again, this is part of a move toward energy independence.

Incidentally, this taboo in the United States and Britain against mentioning the oil in Iraq, almost a religious taboo, is leading to a very curious situation with regard to the whole debate about withdrawal. Across the spectrum, left to right, the talk about withdrawal is avoiding the question of what happens to the oil if the United States withdraws. But for the U.S. planners that has to be central. For them to withdraw from Iraq and not to leave a client state would be an utter catastrophe. They would be losing their position in the world. Just imagine what an independent Iraq is likely to do. Democratic or not, it's going to have a Shiite majority, which will be influential, probably dominant. It already has links to Iran. Ayatollah Ali al-Sistani, the leading Shiite cleric, was born there; the Badr Brigade, the militia that has been pretty much running southern Iraq, was trained there. And they're extending those relationships. Shiite Iraq and Shiite Iran have friendly relations already. There's a substantial Shiite population in Saudi Arabia, right across the border, who have been bitterly oppressed by the monarchy. That happens to be where most of the Saudi oil is. Independent Shiite-dominated Iraq will certainly stimulate autonomy efforts in the Shiite regions in Saudi Arabia, in alliance with Iran. Just think what you've got there: This could end up meaning that the major oil reserves in the world are outside the control of the United States—maybe, even worse, linked up to an Asian Energy Security Grid with China at the center of it. You can't imagine a worse nightmare in Washington. The fact that this isn't even being discussed in connection with all the withdrawal talk is a case of ideologically imposed blindness that is mind-boggling.

ACHCAR: I think it is nevertheless present as a subtext. When you read those statements by Democrats, for instance, on the exit strategy, it's clear that the main concern is the issue of oil. And that's why they say we cannot cut and run.

CHOMSKY: You're right that it's a subtext, but it's unexpressed. They say that we can't cut and run because of our credibility, that Americans don't cut and run, but it's amazing that nobody can come out and say, we can't cut and run because if we do, we get the ultimate nightmare, the oil reserves of the world are out of our control.

SHALOM: Some people make the argument that this would lead to a worldwide depression, which even progressives should be concerned about.

CHOMSKY: But even that's wrong. The issue is not a worldwide depression. It's that the United States becomes a second-class power; it's whether Washington is going to sit by and say, okay, we give up our position of world domination. I have not found a sentence in any of the public discussion of this, from left to right, that is bringing out what just has to be the core issue. The same thing with all these comparisons of Vietnam and Iraq. They're senseless. In the case of Vietnam, the United States could gain its major war aims by destroying Indochina. But you can't destroy Iraq. It's inconceivable. It's far too valuable, you have to control it. Withdrawing from Vietnam meant a minor embarrassment to Washington for a couple of years, nothing else. Withdrawing from Iraq would mean utter catastrophe for American world dominance.

ACHCAR: You have the recognition of that in statements by people like former secretaries of state Henry Kissinger and George Shultz, saying that Iraq is a much more serious case for the United States than Vietnam. And a defeat in Iraq would be a much more serious blow to U.S. interests and credibility.

CHOMSKY: Notice the euphemisms. They always use the word "credibility"— American credibility. What's at stake is not credibility but running the world.

ACHCAR: You have to read between the lines. And they know that the readers they are concerned with read between the lines.

CHOMSKY: Yes, inside planning circles, this is surely understood. But in the entire public discourse, it's missing.

ACHCAR: Some also say that it would be nightmarish to have some fundamentalists getting control over such a major resource as oil.

CHOMSKY: It's all couched in euphemism. (ACHCAR: Hypocrisy.) They don't care about women's rights, they don't care about religion, they don't care about credibility; what they care about is running the world. You lose the major oil resources of the world, and it's finished. And you're not just losing them; you're losing them to a rising, competing power. And one of the reasons they hate China so much is that China, unlike Europe, can't be intimidated. China's been there for 3,000 years, they're going to do what they want, they're not going to be intimidated. And in fact China is starting some inroads into Saudi Arabia: They started trade relations and they even have some limited military relations. And Saudi Arabia, if they see the way things are going, they might join in. The consequences for the United States are just awesome. And it isn't discussed because of the taboo. We're not allowed to imagine that the United States could follow rational interests. In the intellectual world, in the academic world, in the media, we are repeatedly told that the United States does not follow rational interests, but moral instincts. And this is so deeply ingrained that it makes debate almost surreal, pretty much across the spectrum. I can't think of a comparable example for this.

SHALOM: Does the average U.S. citizen or West European citizen have a personal stake, a vested interest, in the U.S. government succeeding in its mission of domination?

CHOMSKY: If they think they do, they have to be talked out of it. The job of the progressive movements is precisely to convince the population of imperial powers that they have no right whatsoever to determine things for anyone else.

I often get invited to conferences in Europe—by fairly progressive groups, not right-wingers, or I wouldn't be invited—which are discussing topics such as: Is it best for the world if the United States and Europe maintain world order? Who in the rest of the world wants that? That's considered a legitimate question among people who are more or less progressive and liberal, not right-wing fanatics. And it has a long tradition: the "civilizing mission" in France; British liberals, such as John Stuart Mill, calling it our responsibility to the barbarians in India to maintain order and give them good civilization. This is called Wilsonian idealism in the United States! Just look what Woodrow Wilson did, in Haiti and the Dominican Republic and every other place he touched. It was monstrous. But nevertheless we speak of Wilsonian idealism, and of our obligation to teach the world the ways of good government. The people of the Third World are like naughty children, as Wilson's secretary of the interior put it, who require a "stiff hand."[8] This is just a deeply embedded imperial conception, all across the intellectual and moral culture. And it is a conception that has to be eradicated.

So, yes, it's undoubtedly right. The ordinary person in Europe and the United States probably thinks it's important for the United States to maintain its dominance. But that's exactly the task of the progressive movements, to dismantle that system of morally grotesque and historically absurd conceptions.

Israel, the Israel Lobby, and U.S. Policy

SHALOM: What role does the pro-Israel lobby play in U.S. policy in the Middle East? The American Israel Public Affairs Committee (AIPAC) often gets 94 out of 100 senators signing on to some of its statements.

CHOMSKY: Senators are happy to sign on to a statement if it will bring them some money and some votes and they know it doesn't mean anything. So, for example, year after year the Senate passes resolutions saying that the United States should recognize Jerusalem as Israel's united and eternal capital, and they know it doesn't have anything to do with policy. So they can sign on to it freely, and they can pick up their checks and get some votes. If you look at the actual influence, in my opinion, the most influential pro-Israel lobby is not AIPAC; it is American liberal intellectuals. I think that is much more significant than AIPAC, and that traces to the June 1967 Arab-Israeli war. Before 1967, Israel was not much of an issue. My friend Norman Finkelstein once reviewed *Dissent,* the journal of democratic socialists, just to see what they had to say about Israel. Pre-1967 there were a handful of articles about Israel, mostly pretty disparaging. After 1967, they became just fanatic Zionists. In fact, I remember in the Israeli press once, in 1982, when there were a lot of protests because of Israel's invasion of Lebanon, there was a kind of ironic article, lamenting how Israeli prime minister Menachem Begin was going to lose Israel all of its support around the world. And they said the last person waving Israel's blue and white flag as the ship went down would be Irving Howe, the coeditor of *Dissent.* Howe had been totally anti-Zionist previously and then turned suddenly after 1967. It didn't have to do with the war, it had to do with Israel's victory. After the victory, many left liberals became super-Zionists. And this is a big segment of articulate American opinion. And they're not necessarily Jewish; many were not.

A lot of this had to do with Vietnam, I think. These people were basically in favor of the Vietnam War. They didn't like the fact that the United States was unable to crush the Vietnamese. It was disturbing and insulting. It was connected to things happening inside the country. A Black-Jewish conflict was beginning to develop along class lines. Many Jews in New York City, for example, by the 1960s had moved into the bureaucracy, become teachers, and so on, and they were often the ones in positions of direct domination over poor Black and Hispanic communities. The 1968 Ocean Hill–Brownsville conflict marked a real downturn in Black-Jewish relations.[9] The feminist movement was beginning—women were starting to stand up for their rights. Young people weren't listening to orders. Everything was falling apart, whether in Vietnam, or New York, or in the family or whatever. All of a sudden Israel came along and showed how you treat Third World upstarts properly. You smash them in the face and crush them, and that's terrific. And they were admired for that. And at that point, you had a real love affair going, which shifted the nature of discourse about the matter. Any minimal criticism of Israeli policy elicited tirades of hysteria; people were silenced. The tone of discussion, even the content of discussion, shifted enormously. And that has been a significant lobby, and it remains. And the whole reporting and commentary on the Occupation period has been completely distorted by it. In my opinion, AIPAC is pretty slight in comparison with that. The liberal intelligentsia is the major Israeli lobby. It's almost never discussed when people talk about lobbies, but I think it's the most important one. And, yes, that's been influential in reshaping and severely distorting the nature of everything that's happened there. And it remains so. AIPAC is also significant, of course.

There's also a huge voting bloc that is significant: Christian evangelicals. They're by far the biggest pro-Israel voting bloc. Many of them are anti-Semitic, particularly the ones who believe in the rapture. Consider what the rapture means: The idea is that after Armageddon all the Jews will either convert to Christianity or go to hell. You can't be more anti-Semitic than that. But they very strongly support Israel, however it fits into their theology. And Israel appreciates it. The *Jerusalem Post*, for example, the English-language newspaper in Israel, just started a new edition directed toward Christian evangelicals. They recognize that this is a big voting bloc they can mobilize—especially now that the Christian right has become politically important for the first time, for other reasons that we've talked about. So all of that is significant, but weigh it all in the balance and I still don't think it competes with U.S. geopolitical planning. If these interests ever come into conflict, geopolitical planners win. We see that on issue after issue.

We saw it recently once again, on an issue that wasn't discussed much here but was very important in Israel. By now Israel's economy is almost a caricature of that of the United States. It's a high-tech, highly militarized economy, and its comparative advantage is advanced military production, linked closely to the United States. And it needs markets. The main market it has been trying to develop is China. And the U.S. government doesn't like that. So there has been a conflict developing, several times already, between Israel and the United States, on sales of advanced military equipment to China. The equipment is produced in Israel, but it's tightly tied to the United States, using a lot of U.S. technology. In 2000 President Bill Clinton forced Israel to cancel a big arms sale to China of its Phalcon airborne early warning system. And notice the lobby didn't do anything; there was not a peep from the lobby.

In 2005 there was another controversy, which got quite serious: Israel had sold anti-aircraft missiles to China, and China wanted to upgrade them, and contracted with Israel to do so. But the Pentagon didn't want Israel to increase Chinese military capacity. So a real conflict developed. It was economically important for Israel, and the United States wouldn't let them do it. It got to the point where the Pentagon refused to have any contact with its Israeli counterparts. There were sanctions imposed. Pentagon officials demanded that Israel pass legislation to block the sales, and also write a letter of apology to the United States, which it did. It finally was patched over, but for Israel this was not a small thing.[10] The lobby knew all about it, but didn't do anything. The lobby knew better than to come into confrontation with U.S. power. As long as they can work with U.S. power, or close to it, they can be very loud and self-congratulatory. But they're not idiots; they're not going to run up against U.S. power, so they backed off. This is one of the most dramatic cases. It's kind of striking, but I don't think it was even reported here, although it was all over the Israeli press for weeks.

ACHCAR: I think that's a very important point to make. That is, the main factor behind U.S. foreign policy is definitely not the pro-Israel lobby. Attributing decisive influence to the pro-Israel lobby is a phantasmagoric view of politics, which is quite widespread. Of course, it is very much believed in the Arab countries, but you can find it all over the world, even in the United States itself. Behind it there is often some degree of anti-Semitism, especially when people refer to a "Jewish lobby" allegedly in control of U.S. foreign policy. Actually, all this amounts to turning things upside down: To believe that Israel is conducting U.S. policy is to believe that the tail wags the dog. It should be rather obvious to any student of U.S. foreign policy over the decades that the oil lobby is far more powerful in orienting U.S. foreign policy, and has been so since the 1930s and 1940s, compared to whatever kind of pro-Israel lobby you can point to. And that is confirmed when one studies the evolution of the relationship between the United States and Israel. As we mentioned earlier, the strategic value of Israel came to the fore since the mid-1960s—of course, the 1967 war was a major turning point, but it was a turning point within a trend that existed already. And what was behind that trend? The main issue was the rise of progressive Arab nationalism, which managed to force the United States out of the Saudi kingdom. Washington lost its direct military presence. And at that time, mind you, logistics were not what they became thirty years after. Moving troops with the rapidity that took place in 1990 was not something they could do then—so for the United States to be out of that area and to dismantle the major military base it had in Dhahran, in the heart of the oil-producing area in the Saudi kingdom, was resented as a really severe blow. By then, the United States was losing ground in the whole Middle East, faced with the rise of Arab nationalism. And it so happened that Arab nationalists took over also in some oil-producing countries—such as Iraq, Algeria, and later Libya. All that tremendously enhanced the importance to Washington of the Israeli state, as a kind of watchdog, or U.S. force by proxy. And of course, in the 1967 war, Israel very consciously played the role of trying to put down two major enemies of the United States in that part of the world—Nasser's government, in Egypt, and the Syrian government, which in 1967 was ruled by the left-wing faction of the Baath Party. Syria was at that time considered in Washington to be some kind of second Cuba, because the Baathist left wing used a lot of Marxist phraseology.

CHOMSKY: What was their connection to Iraq at that point?

ACHCAR: In Syria, the left-wing faction was in power between 1966 and 1970. But Iraq was not ruled by Baathists in 1967. The Baathists came to power in Iraq in February 1963, but were pushed aside after November of that same year; they returned to power only in 1968. When the 1967 war occurred, Syria and Egypt were the two major and priority enemies of the United States in that part of the world. And Israel proved to be a wonderful asset in that regard, defeating these two U.S. enemies.

The 1967 war actually is itself a good illustration of the role Israel came to play as a strategic asset for the United States. Israeli progressives used to refer to Israel as an "aircraft carrier of the United States"—of course, this formula is a caricature, but it says something about the kind of relationship that has existed. Yet Israeli interests have not totally coincided with those of the United States, and we saw this in the 1967 war itself when Israel invaded and conquered the Jordanian-ruled West Bank. There was no specific U.S. interest served by Israel's seizure of the West Bank; on the contrary, the West Bank was part of the Jordanian kingdom, a staunch ally of the Western system and of the United States itself. Thus, the 1967 war already was a good illustration of the pattern of close relationship and convergence of interest, without a total coincidence of interest. From time to time, areas of divergence come to the fore, at any point when Israeli behavior or Israeli demands or requests clash with the overall interests of the United States in the area—and, above all, with the requisites for the stability of U.S. regional allies, which stability is often threatened by Israeli behavior. And that's also what lies behind the sort of competition you have between the Saudis and the Israelis.

What Noam said about the Saudi kingdom being quite happy to see Egypt defeated in 1967 is indisputable, all the more so given that Nasser was engaged in direct war against the Saudi kingdom in Yemen—they were supporting opposite sides in a Yemeni civil war. Egypt's 1967 defeat at the hands of Israel signaled at the same time Egypt's defeat in Yemen: Nasser had to withdraw his troops from there. And shortly thereafter, in the 1970s, the role of the Saudi kingdom was tremendously enhanced. You had first the death of Nasser himself in 1970, finalizing the end of Nasserism and the bankruptcy of Arab nationalism; and then the rise of oil prices after the 1973 Arab-Israeli war, giving much more important weight to the Saudi kingdom. The Saudis and Israelis entered into a kind of competition in order to try to influence the orientation of U.S. policy in one way or another, according to each side's particular agenda. So there is a real degree of competition between the Saudis and the Israeli state, although they are part of a common system. It's similar to the clash of lobbies within the United States; actually, it's part of the same system of lobbying, because the Saudis and Israelis each have considerable internal domestic leverage in the U.S. political system.

Israel and U.S. Interests

SHALOM: Let me give a couple of counterarguments that are often raised against your arguments on the pro-Israel lobby. One counterargument says that the United States has for years blocked the international consensus on Israel/Palestine favoring the establishment of a Palestinian state, but that it is precisely the failure to implement this consensus that causes the instability in the region. So isn't Israel a source of instability rather than an ally of the United States in maintaining stability? Second, you talk about Israel as a proxy force, but in 1991 in the Gulf War, and now in Iraq, the United States knew that to be too closely identified with Israel was in fact a liability. So you could bring in Syrian troops in the Gulf War, you could bring in the Egyptians, you could bring in any Arab or outside force as an ally, but the one country you couldn't bring in as an ally was Israel.

CHOMSKY: I think all that's true, but I think it bears on a different question: What's the *right way* to maintain stability? One way to maintain stability is to try to move toward peace and justice and satisfying people's legitimate needs and so on, and then, yes, you reduce tension. The other way to maintain stability is with a mailed fist. And it's a question of which way you want to do it. You could say the same thing about the slums in the United States. One way to deal with the problems of violence and crime and drugs and so on is to carry out social policies that will make the cities decent places to live. The other way is to throw huge numbers of people in jail and to have a violent police system and so on. Those are just choices about how to maintain stability. The United States has, in general, not just in the Middle East but even domestically, opted for the harsh method. So I think the logic of all those arguments is correct, and it just has to do with the question of the choice of means to maintain stability. Power systems quite often pick the violent approach. For them it's easier. They pay costs when they choose to accommodate people's needs—the taxes, the programs, and so on. Police are pretty cheap. And I think the same holds true on the international scene. So, yes, you can say it's bad judgment or something. But that doesn't mean it's not the judgment.

ACHCAR: Added to that is the fact that Israel's importance has been dependent on other factors of stability or instability for U.S. interests. Israel is not the only factor. For instance, the Palestinian guerilla movement became a major factor of instability and threat to U.S. regional hegemony—first in Jordan, where it was crushed in 1970, and then in Lebanon. And that was a major concern for the United States. It wasn't possible to deal with that by creating a Palestinian state, which either would have been a pure Bantustan that wouldn't have solved anything or would have been handed over to the Palestinian movement, which was considered a terrorist threat and a dangerous enemy. It was not the proper time to put pressure on the Israeli ally.

If you look at things from that last angle, you notice that the most serious pressure brought by the United States on Israel after the mid-1960s was brought by the Bush Sr. administration, in 1991. Why? Well, you had by then the reestablishment of the United States' direct military presence in the Middle East. This was the reversal of the very factor that I mentioned as lying behind the increased importance of Israel from the 1960s on. At that time, you had anxious discussions going on in Israel around one existential question: Are we losing our strategic importance to the United States because it regained its direct military presence in the area and because we were not useful in the Iraq war? In the 1991 war against Iraq, the United States actually pressured Israel not to interfere. And that led to real anxiety in Zionist circles in Israel about the strategic relationship with the United States. The Bush Sr. administration needed to stabilize the area at that time and to make sure that U.S. hegemony was firmly reestablished. "Reestablished" is not the right word actually: U.S. regional hegemony had never before reached the level it attained in 1990–1991; before then, you had several countervailing powers: the Soviet Union, Arab nationalism, and so on. So the United States wanted to stabilize that newly acquired unipolar hegemony.

It was at that point that the Bush Sr. administration really twisted the arm of the Israeli government, led by the right-wing Likud Party, to get on board the so-called Peace Process—the negotiations that started in Madrid, Spain, at the end of October 1991. You had then a period of high tension between Israel and its U.S. godfather.

Twelve years later, Bush Jr. made some remarks reflecting a somewhat similar intention. In the immediate aftermath of the 2003 invasion of Iraq, when the administration thought that controlling Iraq would be an easy task, the president indicated his intention to exert pressure on Israel to support his "Road Map," in order to get Israel to make the necessary concessions for achieving some peace deal, or to restore the dynamics of the Oslo process, which had by then collapsed. But the quagmire that the administration encountered in Iraq prevented it from exerting any pressure on Israel. It couldn't pursue two goals at the same time: putting sharp pressure on Israeli prime minister Ariel Sharon while dealing with the increasing trouble in Iraq. And the Bush administration is now losing its confidence about the strength and stability of its hegemony in the region. The anxiety now is to be found on the part of U.S. policymakers: What is our future in that area? Are we going to suffer a major defeat? And if so, how terrible is it going to be? Now is not the time, in their conception of things, for embarrassing their Israeli ally with any serious pressure. So the degree to which the U.S. government is willing to pressure its Israeli ally into concessions deemed necessary for some kind of stabilizing settlement very much depends on the overall set of conditions, and the overall strategic factors of stability and instability. If you look at the issue only through the narrow prism of Israel, you can't understand Washington's behavior, which is determined by the overall picture.

CHOMSKY: Gilbert, I'm interested in what you think. In the Arab world, this myth of Israeli power has been a kind of defensive mechanism that prevents people from trying to do anything. You constantly hear or read, well, what can we do? Israel is so powerful in the United States that there's no point in our trying to carry out efforts of public diplomacy or anything else; we're just going to lose.

ACHCAR: The myth of Israeli power has an ideological function. It exonerates the United States of responsibility. And it's perfect for the Saudis, in particular, because they can thus explain: "We have to fight the Jews and their nasty influence in Washington, and try to win over our American friends. And we do have allies in the United States, whom we should support." With such an argument, you can't blame them for being closely linked to the United States, since they are competing against the Israelis for U.S. favor; so the ideological function is clear.

CHOMSKY: I was thinking more about Arab intellectuals.

ACHCAR: Not all Arab intellectuals adhere to the view of decisive Israeli power, fortunately. A significant section would point to the United States as being the main source of the problem, or the main enemy. (CHOMSKY: Not just as an agent of Israel?) Yes, although the proportion of intellectuals who believe that the U.S. is the main enemy has been much reduced with the reactionary ideological dynamics of recent years.

SHALOM: In the lead-up to the Iraq war, there were some on the left who said that since oil companies are conservative, and wouldn't want to set the whole region on fire, the war is not being driven by oil interests; so there's no logical reason for the United States to be moving toward war except that it works for Israel. This is a dramatic example of the tail wagging the dog.

ACHCAR: This idea is widespread, but it's obviously off the mark.

CHOMSKY: What Gilbert is saying holds true here in the United States, too. For parts of the left, if you can exonerate the United States and make it look like the problem is the Jews, you don't have to come into direct confrontation with real power. You can be passive. You can say, in reality, the United States is on my side, we just have to go after the Jews. In a way, it's a little bit like what was said in that Pentagon declassification document I referred to earlier [in Chapter One]—if we can get people to focus on something that doesn't matter, they won't raise the really hard problems.

ACHCAR: It's a traditional feature of history, the scapegoat mechanism.

SHALOM: There are some who make the same charge against you, Noam. They argue that the tough battle is to confront the power of the Israel lobby. And by saying that the Israel lobby is irrelevant, you're avoiding the tough fight.

CHOMSKY: But just look at the thinking. There are two powers in the United States: One is the U.S. government, and the other is the Israel lobby. Which one is hard to confront? Can we be serious? Whatever you think of the Israel lobby, it is nothing compared with the power of the U.S. government.

ACHCAR: Noam never said that the pro-Israel lobby is irrelevant, by the way.

CHOMSKY: It is relevant. In fact, as I already said, there is a real pro-Israel lobby, and they're ignoring it, namely the intellectual community. That's a serious one. Of course, it's harder to confront, because that means you're coming up against articulate opinion, which is not going to kill you, but you get the flood of lies and vilification and everything else. But as for what is usually thought of as the Israel lobby—who cares? So the Anti-Defamation League (ADL) writes nasty comments about you—does that matter? What's hard about confronting the ADL or AIPAC? What cost is there to it? Nothing.

ACHCAR: There's also a clear disproportion between the degree of attention focused on this pro-Israel lobby and that focused on the oil majors—even on the left, even the radical left.

CHOMSKY: I've been very high on the ADL hate list for twenty-five years. They have a huge file of slanderous material on me that they circulate. I know this because about twenty years ago I was going to have a debate with Alan Dershowitz[11] and somebody in the ADL office was supposed to deliver the file to him—it had written on it "to Alan Dershowitz"—but a copy of it was leaked to me. It was quite comical. So they have a file on you at the Anti-Defamation League, or they circulate slander about you. But does it matter?

SHALOM: In 1982, during the huge antinuclear demonstration in New York City, there was silence about the most likely cause of nuclear war, namely the fact that Israel was at that time invading Lebanon.

CHOMSKY: That's true, but that's because strong leadership elements of the antinuclear movement are part of the same liberal intellectual community that is in love with Israel. They're part of the pro-Israel lobby, the really powerful part, not AIPAC.

4 Wars in the "Greater Middle East"

Afghanistan

SHALOM: How would you assess the U.S. war against Afghanistan in 2001?

CHOMSKY: In my opinion, the war in Afghanistan was conceived as one of the most atrocious crimes in recent years. The United States went to war in Afghanistan with the expectation that there was a strong likelihood that they would drive 5 million people over the edge of starvation. That was criminal.

On September 16, 2001, five days after 9/11, there was a story in the *New York Times* by John F. Burns, their chief correspondent, which said: Washington has "demanded a cutoff of fuel supplies, . . . and the elimination of truck convoys that provide much of the food and other supplies to Afghanistan's civilian population."[1] When I read that I thought there was going to be a worldwide blowup over it—they're cutting off convoys of food on which 5 million people are relying for survival.[2] But there wasn't a peep. In anticipation of U.S. bombing, all the aid agencies had to take their workers out.[3] The workers were coming out, saying this is hideous. You could read it in the *New York Times:* The Afghan people are on a lifeline, and we're cutting that lifeline, they screamed.[4] Once the bombing began, the number at risk of starvation was raised to 7.5 million,[5] and the aid organizations pleaded for the bombing to stop.[6] Afghans were screaming about it too, some of the leading ones. So, for example, Afghan opposition leader Abdul Haq, who was one of the U.S. favorites, had an interview in the *Guardian* with Anatol Lieven, in which he bitterly condemned the United States for bombing. He said they're just bombing to show off their muscle, they don't care how many Afghans they put at risk, and they're undermining the efforts of anti-Taliban Afghans to overthrow the Taliban from within.[7]

I should say that groups like the Revolutionary Association of Afghan Women (RAWA) were strongly opposed to the war on Afghanistan, but no one paid any attention to them. On October 24–25, 2001, after little more

DOI: 10.4324/9781003531753-4

than two weeks of bombing, there was a meeting in Peshawar, Pakistan, of about 1,500 Afghan notables, tribal leaders, and others—some coming from inside Afghanistan, some from Pakistan. The meeting was actually pretty well covered in the United States, with several major reports in the *New York Times* and other newspapers. And they discussed everything and they had all kinds of disagreements. But there was one thing they agreed about unanimously: Stop the bombing.[8] It was reported, but the bombing continued.

Fortunately the starvation didn't happen. We don't know what did happen, because nobody checks, you don't look at your own crimes. But yes, it didn't end up killing 5 million people. Thankfully. But was that proof that it was a reasonable thing to do? No. That's totally irrelevant. You could just as well say Soviet leader Nikita Khrushchev was right to put missiles in Cuba in 1962—because it didn't lead to a nuclear war. But the fact that it didn't happen didn't make him right to risk nuclear war. You evaluate actions on the basis of the likely consequences, not the actual consequences. That's elementary.

The facts are uncontroversial. For example, Harvard's leading specialist on Afghanistan at that time, Samina Ahmed, had an article in *International Security,* one of the most respectable journals around, saying that "[b]ecause humanitarian assistance was disrupted by U.S. military strikes, millions of Afghans are at grave risk of starvation."[9] But there seems to be no comprehension of the moral implications of undertaking actions that might be putting 5 million, and by their own later estimate, up to 7.5 million, at risk of starvation. That's absolutely shocking.

Apart from the cutoff of food a few days after 9/11, in early October there were various unclear maneuverings. The United States demanded that they hand over Osama bin Laden, and the Taliban made some moves, saying maybe he could be handed over to an Islamic country. There were negotiating options possible.

ACHCAR: The Taliban gave a very sensible argument from the standpoint of international law. They asked the United States to submit a formal extradition request with evidence. Taliban chief Mullah Omar said give us evidence and we will hand him over.

CHOMSKY: That's exactly right—they said give us some evidence and we'll consider it. Asking a government to hand someone over without evidence is unheard of. Suppose Iran says, "Hand over George Bush." Is anybody going to listen? That's outlandish. We know now one reason why Washington didn't hand over evidence. They just didn't have any. In June 2002, about eight months after the bombing of Afghanistan, the head of the FBI, Robert Mueller, informed the press for the first time on who was involved in 9/11. The FBI didn't know. After probably the most intensive investigation in the world, with every intelligence agency working on it, the most he could say is, we believe that the plot may have been hatched in Afghanistan, but that the planning and the implementation were carried out in the United Arab Emirates and in Germany.[10] If they didn't have solid evidence eight months later, then that means they didn't have any in October 2001. Eight months later, they had suspicions—probably the suspicions are correct, I have them too—but that's no basis for handing somebody over. Bush then made his famous statement that countries that harbor terrorists are terrorist states, they have to be treated like terrorists themselves, and so on and so forth. Think of what the implications of that policy would be if applied to others! But that was the sole demand: Hand over Osama bin Laden and his lieutenants, without evidence. And we're not going to ask for extradition because you don't deserve it. That was the sole cause for war.

Three weeks into the bombing of Afghanistan, the chief of the British Defense Staff, Admiral Sir Michael Boyce, declared that "[t]he squeeze will carry on until the people of the country themselves recognize that this is going to go on until they get the leadership changed."[11] Notice, if you don't want to call it international aggression, it is surely terrorism, by exactly the most narrow definition: We're going to keep bombing you until you throw out your government.

Later the story was that the United States always had the humanitarian goal of going after the Taliban. But that wasn't so. It was only three weeks into the bombing that there was the first hint of that. What were the actual reasons for the war? Probably just as Abdul Haq said, to show U.S. muscle, to show that "we're the boss."

ACHCAR: The Bush administration had to react to 9/11 and held discussions among themselves: Iraq first or Iraq later? Afghanistan was given priority because al-Qaeda was based there and it would be better understood by the U.S. public as the arena in which to react against al-Qaeda—since it was designated as the culprit for 9/11. On the face of it, of course, U.S. policymakers had serious reasons for wanting to destroy the al-Qaeda network.

To understand the rest of the story, I think one should start, first of all, by explaining what the reasons for going into Afghanistan *were not*. I don't give any credit to those explanations about U.S. designs for building pipelines across Afghanistan. They don't hold water as a rationale for the war. The fact is that the United States did not plan, and is not planning, for the control of Afghanistan in the same way it is trying to control Iraq. This major distinction can be seen in the very different sizes of the U.S. military deployment in each country. Iraq has ten times the number of U.S. troops as Afghanistan, although for any serious attempt at controlling Afghanistan, you'd need many more troops than are needed to control Iraq, and, needless to say, many more than those actually deployed in Iraq. You'd need more because of the geography of Afghanistan, its size, and all its complexities. In Afghanistan, therefore, the United States delegated to its NATO allies the control of the capital because it is not really interested. Washington is interested in keeping bases in Afghanistan because of the country's strategic location, not because it wants to control Afghanistan per se. It's not an important prize, not an important piece of real estate for its own sake. Actually, the ideological framework created by 9/11 and the Afghanistan war provided an opportunity to establish a direct military presence not only in Afghanistan but in Central Asia, which, strategically speaking, is considerably more important. Countries like Kyrgyzstan and Uzbekistan, where the United States set up air bases after 9/11, lie in the heart of the former Soviet Union. If you add to this the U.S. involvement in the Caucasus, you see that Washington is trying to set a military vice around the Caspian Basin, which is an important source of hydrocarbons, not only oil but especially gas.

Most importantly, there is a non-oil-related, very important strategic consideration, which is the fact that Afghanistan and, even more so, Central Asia, geopolitically speaking, lie in the heart of the landmass extending from European Russia to China; and the increasing military cooperation between China and Russia since the early 1990s has been, and remains, a major concern to U.S. policymakers, although they don't speak much about it. The concern has been increasing actually. In August 2005, joint maneuvers took place between the Russian and Chinese armed forces—an unprecedented phenomenon. So the fact that the United States is militarily present in the middle of that area is, from the strategic point of view, extremely significant. Russian president Vladimir Putin realized that he could not prevent U.S. intervention in the area after 9/11, because the United States was much too assertive in its desire to go there, and had the ideological pretext to sell this endeavor to the U.S. public in the name of the "war on terror," all the more so that local despots welcomed its presence. This put the Bush administration in a very strong position. The Russians could not openly oppose this U.S. move, so Putin put on a brave face and tried to limit the damage and get compensation for it. But he got nothing. Bush did not give Russia any concession, whether on the ABM treaty[12] or whatever. Moscow therefore resumed its efforts against U.S. involvement in its backyard, and the recent turnaround of Uzbekistan on the issue of the U.S. base[13] was truly an important setback for the United States. That was called for by the Shanghai Cooperation Organization, which is presently the main framework for the Chinese-Russian alliance and includes most of the former Soviet republics of Central Asia, with Iran, Pakistan, and India as observers.

CHOMSKY: The Shanghai Cooperation Organization is a parallel to the Asian Energy Security Grid. And it seems to be turning into a sort of NATO-style organization aimed at Central Asia, to confront the United States.

ACHCAR: On the face of it, the starting point of that organization was irreproachable from Washington's perspective—it was part of the war against terrorism. But as a matter of fact, it is a framework through which the Russians and the Chinese are trying to coalesce against U.S. incursions into their domains and threats to their supply lines. Afghanistan's main value, from Washington's point of view, is its strategic location and nothing else really important beyond that—of course, along with the issue of al-Qaeda, on which the Bush administration actually failed, since they still haven't been able to capture any of the most wanted individuals.

CHOMSKY: What they did was spread al-Qaeda all over the world, like a cancer.

ACHCAR: Exactly.

Responding to 9/11

SHALOM: So how should the United States have responded to 9/11?

CHOMSKY: It was a major crime, right? How do you deal with a crime? First you try and find out who the criminals were, then you apprehend them, then you bring them to justice. You cannot apprehend them until you know who they are. So the first step is to try to find out who did it. As I said, they never did that. Eight months later they were saying the plotting and implementation were probably carried out in the UAE and Germany. Therefore, that's where you should have been looking to apprehend them. But in any event, the first step is to find out who did it, and gather some evidence about it. Suppose you had evidence about Osama bin Laden— which I assume is true—then you apprehend him. How? Seek extradition.

Here's a way to do it. We have an example in front of us at this moment. Venezuela is seeking the extradition of Luis Posada Carriles, one of the most notorious international terrorists. He is wanted in Venezuela for his participation in the 1976 blowing up of a Cubana airliner that killed seventy-three people. He's also been involved in numerous other terrorist acts. Nicaragua ought to try him for his participation in the Contra war. After he escaped miraculously from a Venezuelan jail in 1985, the United States sent him off to the Ilopango Air Base in El Salvador where he was working with the Oliver North operation to support the Contra war, a major international terrorist war, which killed many more people than

9/11. So here is a major international terrorist who managed to escape to the United States recently, and Venezuela applies to have him extradited. That's the way to do it. But of course there's a problem—the United States won't extradite him. So they're probably going to send him to live happily in Florida, I imagine alongside his friend Orlando Bosch, who was his presumed co-conspirator in the Cubana bombing, and who is accused by the FBI of involvement in about thirty terrorist acts; the FBI and the Justice Department wanted Bosch deported as a threat to American security. George Bush Sr., in this case, gave him a presidential pardon. Now, remember the George W. Bush doctrine, announced with regard to Afghanistan: States that harbor terrorists are terrorist states and have to be treated as such. OK, then, according to George W. Bush the air force ought to be bombing Washington. But what is the right way to do it? The right way is to do what Venezuela tried to do, and what Cuba has tried to do: Gather solid evidence that they're criminals and then apply for extradition. In the case of bin Laden, nobody would have wanted much evidence, but just present some reasonable grounds for extradition and pressure the Taliban to destroy the al-Qaeda bases. This might well have worked. You don't know unless you try. If it works, fine; if it takes some type of international operation, fine, let's organize some type of international operation.

SHALOM: An international military operation?

CHOMSKY: If it's necessary, but that's a last resort. First you go through the stages of a police investigation and a police operation, as in any criminal act.

ACHCAR: The UN Security Council voted a resolution offering its services to the United States. People were not even asking for evidence, they were ready to act on U.S. request. And they would have: You have a whole gamut of measures in the UN Charter to coerce states into abiding by decisions made by the Security Council.

CHOMSKY: In fact, you might not have had to coerce the Taliban. You can't prove it but they were giving indications that they might have done it. But the United States did not want to explore those indications, because they wanted to bomb.

SHALOM: There were already Security Council sanctions on Afghanistan.

CHOMSKY: Yes, for other reasons. But the Taliban did give indications that they would consider extradition. We don't know exactly how serious they were, or what they would have considered, because the United States wouldn't hear it. But there were plenty of steps to take—not the United States directly, but the Security Council—but you can't do any of that unless you have some evidence. Actually in this case, they probably could have done it without evidence. . . . But the right way to do it is the way Venezuela is currently trying to do it, with Posada Carriles.

ACHCAR: The fact of the matter is that Washington's behavior points to what we were just saying—that the main concern was not really to get Osama bin Laden—

CHOMSKY: Or even to destroy the bases, because the Taliban might have done that, too. They weren't very happy about al-Qaeda. In fact, until 1998, the relations between the Taliban and Osama bin Laden were pretty cool. They didn't want competing influence. It was after Clinton's bombing of Sudan and Afghanistan that relations tightened up. Clinton's bombing is responsible for strengthening the Taliban/al-Qaeda relationship.

ACHCAR: But even then, you still had many reports pointing to the tensions, enmities, and antipathies that existed between the so-called Arab guerillas in Afghanistan—al-Qaeda, that is—and the Afghans, the Taliban in this case.

CHOMSKY: You know, the Afghan opposition leaders—including Abdul Haq—had a plausible case when they said they could overthrow the Taliban from within. We know now what they already knew—that the Taliban had a very thin and weak system of control. And it might have been overturned from within. But the United States didn't want that.

ACHCAR: But actually, in the end that is what happened. The United States did not invade Afghanistan, properly speaking.

CHOMSKY: True, they used the Northern Alliance, a bunch of warlords and terrorists. But Abdul Haq and others were pretty serious guys of whom the West would have approved. They might have been able to defeat the Taliban from within. They thought they could do it, but the United States didn't want them to.

ACHCAR: Exactly, in the same manner that they didn't want someone to overthrow Saddam Hussein from within, unless they could control Iraq.

CHOMSKY: And just like they didn't permit the Shiite rebellion to win in 1991.

ACHCAR: In Iraq, Washington wanted to lay their hands over the whole country. But in the case of Afghanistan, they just wanted to set up a military presence in the country and control the central government.

CHOMSKY: In any event, there were plenty of alternative options for Afghanistan. But the worst thing to do was to put millions of people at risk of starvation. That was horrendous. It's true that 9/11 was a terrible atrocity, but it registered in the West, not because it was a terrible atrocity—there have been plenty of worse atrocities—but because it was against the wrong people. You don't do that to people like *us,* we do that to people like *you.* That's history. There are plenty of cases that illustrate this. One that I've cited that has infuriated people, but I'll repeat it, since it's correct, is the 1998 bombing of the al-Shifa pharmaceutical plant in Sudan, which killed probably ten times as many people as 9/11. This pharmaceutical plant was supplying half the country's needs, and its destruction meant that tens of thousands of desperately poor people didn't get the medicine they needed and died, according to the best estimates available.[14] The United States claimed they thought it was also producing chemical weapons. Maybe it was, maybe it wasn't. That's irrelevant. Suppose that al-Qaeda blows up some huge chemical facility in London because it thinks maybe they're involved in some weapons program, and they kill, to get the right numbers, maybe hundreds of thousands of people. Is that legitimate? It's outlandish.

It's true that 9/11 was a horrible atrocity. However, it was not the horror of the atrocity that caused the reaction but the nature of the victims. When even larger numbers have been killed by us in Sudan or in so many other places over hundreds of years, there has barely been a reaction.

Afghanistan Today

SHALOM: What about Afghanistan today? Is it a positive showcase?

CHOMSKY: It's not a showcase. You could argue that Afghanistan is better off today. That's not really the question. Is Afghanistan better off today than it would have been if the Afghans had been left to overthrow the Taliban themselves, which they probably would have done? There's also another question. Consider India: Is it better off today than it was under the British? Much better off. Since the British were kicked out, it hasn't had any of those huge famines that killed tens of millions of people. But do we therefore celebrate Pearl Harbor every December 7? Because, as I noted before, Pearl Harbor led to a series of events that drove the white man out of Asia.

ACHCAR: In fact, however, it is very much disputable whether Afghanistan is better off now, and it is questioned even by some human rights organizations. You can take several indicators. The fact is that, because the United States did not need to fully control the country, it resorted to proxy forces to topple the Taliban. These were the warlords of the Northern Alliance, who were definitely no better than the Taliban. As a matter of fact, the Taliban were able to seize control of the country so easily in 1996 precisely because of the hatred and resentment of the majority of Afghans against those very warlords of the Northern Alliance. The Taliban provided the Afghans with something they very badly wanted: stability. This stability, of course, was combined with a very obscurantist, very backward, worse-than-medieval kind of fundamentalist ideology and practice. But they brought nevertheless some degree of stability. That's the major explanation for the Taliban's coming to power—it's not because of their superior military means: They were in fact rather poorly armed. To be sure, they were backed by U.S. ally Pakistan and had Washington's blessing—two major sources of strength. But they found acceptance from a plurality of Afghans because of what I pointed to. What the United States has done now is to bring back the very warlords who were the source of all sorts of disasters when they ruled the country after the collapse in 1992 of the Najibullah regime, which had survived the departure of Soviet troops in 1989.

One could only say that the capital, Kabul, where NATO troops are concentrated, is better off than it used to be under the Taliban. But if you look at most of the rest of the country, it is under the control of the warlords, as is the new so-called parliament. It's a total caricature of anything called democracy. If you set up institutions like a parliament, devoid of any real democratic content and controlled by the most backward medieval-like forces, and call that democracy, it's a mockery. The warlords now control the bulk of the country; they leave it to the U.S. stooge Hamid Karzai to play the role of president and to be the façade of the country because the United States wants that. And as for human rights, the country is certainly not much better off now than it used to be under the Taliban. It is still subject to a thoroughly reactionary brand of Islamic fundamentalist rule. Women in most areas still suffer the same kind of intolerable oppression. And for a significant segment of the Afghan population, the situation has gotten even worse, because though the Taliban were completely reactionary people, they were at least abiding by their own rules—very reactionary rules, to be sure—whereas the warlords' exercise of power is totally arbitrary. They do anything that serves their interests. So take drug production, for instance. Under the Taliban, narcotics production and trafficking had been substantially reduced, but Afghanistan has again become what is called a "narco-state." To say that this country is a positive showcase could only be very ironical. The Bush administration very obviously does not care very much about the internal situation in Afghanistan. I think they never even had the intention of changing that poor country. They may have been stupid enough to believe that Iraq would be easy to control, but they could not be so stupid as to think that Afghanistan would be easy to control. They knew that this was an uncontrollable country, and that's why they deployed only 19,000 troops there.

SHALOM: Nineteen thousand U.S. troops. But there are NATO and other foreign troops.

ACHCAR: Yes, they represent a few additional thousands, but this is still nothing compared to what Afghanistan would require if one were to try and assert real control over it.

SHALOM: And so what should be done now? What should those committed to justice be calling for?

CHOMSKY: Reparations. Massive reparations from everybody who's been involved—the United States and the Russians.

SHALOM: To whom do you give the reparations?

CHOMSKY: You try to find local organizations that are functioning, and there are some. Some of them are foreign. For example, there is a foreign clinic there run by Gino Strada, a fantastic Italian doctor who has run clinics and small hospitals all over the world, but the main ones are in Afghanistan. They were there under the Russians, the warlords, the Taliban, and throughout the American war. They're still there. It's a small operation, but that's a worthy recipient of aid. There are also domestic Afghan groups, including women's groups and other local organizations. To the extent something can be done with the Karzai government, do that. But the key is to find modalities to compensate for the atrocities that have been carried out by the Russians and the Americans against these people for the last twenty-five years. The United States didn't organize the Islamic jihadis in Afghanistan in the 1980s to liberate Afghanistan; it did so for its own purposes. And this harmed Afghanistan profoundly. The historical evidence from partially released Russian archives seems to indicate that the Russians would have withdrawn from Afghanistan within a year or two; but when the resistance turned from an Afghan resistance into a foreign-backed terrorist resistance, they held on. None of this was done to help the Afghans; it's harmed them badly, just as the Russian invasion did. That's the kind of thing you ought to pay reparations for.

SHALOM: What about U.S. and allied troops there?

CHOMSKY: U.S. troops shouldn't be there. If anything, there should be forces under UN General Assembly supervision, as a way to avoid the Security Council. The General Assembly is not great, but at least it's less ridiculous than the Security Council, with its thoroughly undemocratic rules for membership and voting. It's going to take funding, however, and the United States doesn't want to fund the United Nations. Incidentally, the U.S. *population* wants to fund it. It's one of those many great gaps between public opinion and public policy. The population wants to give substantially increased U.S. support for UN peacekeeping operations. So this could be done if we could turn the United States into a functioning democracy, so that public opinion mattered. There are certainly plenty of resources for it.

It's not going to be easy to patch it up; it's a hard thing, like Gilbert says. I don't know what you can do for Afghanistan; they're going to have to do it themselves, regardless of what help others can provide. But any outside assistance that is given should be constructive assistance and not done for self-serving reasons, which means not by one of the great powers.

ACHCAR: I agree. The fact is that the United States, by its presence in Afghanistan, is presently fueling the Taliban's comeback—as is the case in Iraq, where its presence fuels the so-called insurgency. U.S. troops are deeply resented and hated by a major section of the Afghan population, with the same ethnic/sectarian complications that exist in Iraq—in Afghanistan, the Pashtun are more or less in the position of Iraqi Arab Sunnis, except that they constitute a plurality. Afghanistan is witnessing—and this is confirmed by many reports—a real resumption and increase of Taliban influence in the country. The only conclusion is that the United States should get out of Afghanistan now.

CHOMSKY: And the U.S. Baghram air base should be dismantled.

ACHCAR: Indeed. As for the presence of UN troops in that country, I'm afraid U.S. military action has created a real dilemma there: Either the country is run by the warlords, with some degree of coexistence among them because of the foreign presence, or, if the foreign presence is removed, there will be a resumption of the internecine warfare between the warlords that brought the Taliban to power. I'm afraid this is one of the tragic situations that we have in some parts of the world now because of irresponsible policies followed by the United States. It's difficult to point to any positive solution. But the one thing in my view that is clear is that the United States should get out of that country. If the Afghan population wants foreign troops to remain deployed in its country, they shouldn't include U.S. troops at any rate or be under U.S. control by proxy through NATO, nor should they include troops from any of the other great powers, as Noam said.

The United States and Iraq, 2003

SHALOM: Turning to Iraq, why did the United States invade that country in 2003?

CHOMSKY: I share the opinion of the people in Baghdad.

In November 2003, the president made the eloquent speech to the National Endowment for Democracy[15] that Gilbert already mentioned about how he was pursuing his messianic mission to bring democracy to the Middle East, and that that's why the United States invaded Iraq. The press fell over itself with awe for this most noble war in history. A couple of days later Gallup released a poll taken in Baghdad shortly before in which there was an open-ended question: "Why do you think the U.S. invaded Iraq?" There were some who agreed that it was the messianic vision: 1 percent. One percent of people in Baghdad said the war was waged to bring democracy; 5 percent said it was to help Iraqis; 4 percent said it was to destroy weapons of mass destruction; but a plurality, 43 percent, said the motive was to "rob Iraq's oil."[16] I think that's approximately correct. Iraq has enormous energy reserves—actually they're unknown, because they're uncharted—but they're generally thought to be the second highest in the world, after Saudi Arabia; also, they're extremely cheap and accessible. You don't have to dig through permafrost or play with tar sands—you just put a pipe in the ground. We've already discussed how policymakers understood that if you control the energy resources of the region, you have tremendous power—what George Kennan referred to sixty years ago as "veto power" over your rivals. Actually we just saw an example of that in Europe with the Russian interruption of gas deliveries to Ukraine. If Russia just turned the spigot off, it would send Europe into a tailspin. Now it's not much of a threat on the part of Russia, because they're not strong enough to implement it, but on the part of the United States it would be a tremendous threat: We don't have to do anything, just say "raise the price of oil." So it puts Washington in an enormous position of power. Plus it means that U.S. and U.K. companies will have the inside track on Iraq's resources rather than, say, the French or the Russians, who had concluded important oil deals with Baghdad. And Iraq will also provide a terrific place for U.S. military bases, given that, as the Pentagon has conceded, they can't keep their military bases in Saudi Arabia.

So there was every possible reason to invade, if you wanted to dominate the world. Also, it looked very easy. My own guess had been that the war would be over in about three days, and that they'd easily be able to reconstruct. It looked like the easiest conquest in history, but it turned into one of the worst military catastrophes in history. I think a reasonable assessment was that it would be a very easy victory. Iraq was held together with Scotch tape; it was devastated by sanctions. It wasn't known at the time, but we now know that the United States and Britain had been bombing Iraq very intensively for at least a year before the invasion to make sure there'd be no possible defense. I think Iraq's military budget was approximately the same as that of Kuwait, which has less than 10 percent of Iraq's population. Furthermore, the United States was in a position easily to reconstruct it. The invasion, if it had been carried out intelligently, would have terminated the sanctions, which were destroying the country, and would have gotten rid of Saddam Hussein, which would be a relief to the overwhelming majority. They could have sent in a class from the MIT Electrical Engineering department to get the electrical system working; they could have invested any amount of money for reconstruction. There was no external support for any insurgency. They had to actually create an insurgency, virtually, by their own brutality and viciousness. It just looked like a walkover. And it's an enormous prize. So I think it's natural that they thought they would carry it off. There thus were very substantial reasons for invading. Of course, this is apart from any question of justification. Germany, of course, had reasons for invading Western Europe, too. But I think the analysis of Baghdad's residents is quite plausible.

ACHCAR: There's another aspect of the question that is interesting: Why did the United States invade Iraq in 2003 and not earlier? And in particular, why didn't the U.S. invade Iraq in 1991? This question directly ties in, I believe, with our previous discussion about U.S. policy and the Iraqi invasion of Kuwait. In my view, the United States had the desire to add Iraq to the Saudi kingdom as countries under full control of the United States. These two countries account for almost two-fifths of global oil reserves: 25 percent, the official figure for the Saudi kingdom, plus 12 percent, the official figure for Iraq. That's 37 percent and that's huge. Then add Kuwait, 8 percent. By controlling these countries and the other Gulf oil monarchies, leaving Iran aside, the United States is controlling half the world's oil reserves. So that's exactly as Noam said—a hugely important prize. But Washington knew quite well that without occupying Iraq, and without exerting direct control by means of military presence, there was no way to have in Baghdad a submissive government of the Saudi type. Now, the problem in 1991 was, as Bush Sr. (in his memoirs coauthored with his national security adviser Brent Scowcroft) himself said—and I think on this we can credit him with telling the truth—the United States did not go on to Baghdad because that would have been "unilaterally exceeding the United Nations' mandate."[17] Remember that in January 1991, it had been very difficult for the Bush administration to get a green light for the war from Congress, even for the limited goal of expelling Iraqi troops from Kuwait. (The U.S. population at that time was still very much affected by the so-called Vietnam syndrome.) In the Senate, a switch of only three votes would have meant defeat for the war resolution. There was no mandate whatsoever for the Bush administration to occupy the whole of Iraq, particularly given that Bush Sr. had needed the UN fig leaf to get domestic approval for the intervention and the UN resolutions were only about liberating Kuwait. Accordingly, absent the possibility of occupying the country, Washington preferred to keep Saddam Hussein in power. And that's why they let him crush the insurgencies in southern Iraq and in the north. They let Saddam Hussein use helicopters, although U.S. forces had total control of the skies, and the U.S. Army executed a maneuver, clearing the way for the Republican Guard, the elite backbone of Saddam Hussein's regime, to go south and crush the insurrection. The population of the south remembers all that perfectly and that's why they have no confidence whatsoever in the U.S. government.

The Bush Sr. administration made the following calculation: We have no valid alternative to Saddam Hussein that suits our interests. The best choice, then, is to keep a weakened Saddam Hussein—we have cut his claws and will take all measures necessary to prevent them from growing again. We keep a weakened Saddam Hussein, checked by an embargo, until the conditions are there for us to invade the country and occupy it, and to be therefore in a position to install a government devoted to us. And they kept seeking this opportunity. There was a bipartisan consensus in U.S. ruling circles on the importance of the prize, the importance of getting hold of Iraq. When Clinton is asked why didn't you invade Iraq? he never says that it was for whatever moral or legal reason; he only explains that he was not in a position to do it. The Lewinsky affair was at its height at the very time that he had a real political opportunity to invade in 1998, around the issue of UN inspections in Iraq, so all he could do was bomb the country, and nothing beyond that.

Even the Bush Jr. administration, although it was from the start full of people obsessed with the invasion of Iraq—like those signatories gathered by the Project for the New American Century for the famous 1998 letter to Clinton urging him to take military action against Iraq and to remove Saddam Hussein's regime[18]—and although Bush Jr. himself in the 2000 presidential campaign said that his father had made a mistake and should have gone all the way to Baghdad, they were not in a position to do it before 9/11. We know now from many sources that the first reaction of the barons of the Bush administration after 9/11 could be summarized as "Great! We've finally got an opportunity to invade Iraq." There were disagreements within the administration, however, with Powell advocating Afghanistan first and Rumsfeld advocating Iraq first; we now know the rest of the story. So we can say, in a sense, that the United States invaded Iraq thanks to 9/11, although there is no connection whatsoever between Iraq and 9/11. The attacks on New York and Washington provided the ideological cover, which allowed the Bush administration to invade.

SHALOM: Policymakers during the administration of Bush Sr. have indicated that they thought that Saddam Hussein would be overthrown internally, so there was no need for an invasion.

ACHCAR: This means that they thought that the CIA, in collaboration with the Saudi and the Jordanian kingdoms, would be able to organize some faction of the army and overthrow a weakened Saddam Hussein with a coup d'état, which would open the way for some kind of tutelage of the United States over the country.

CHOMSKY: In the 1990s, they tried repeatedly. If I can just add to what Gilbert said, it was stated pretty openly in 1991. Take the *New York Times.* They have a position, chief diplomatic correspondent, which is a euphemism for State Department representative, which was Thomas Friedman at the time, and he said it quite frankly. He said the best of all worlds for the United States would be an iron-fisted military junta ruling Iraq much the way Saddam Hussein did, but not *him,* because he's an embarrassment. And if we can't get that, we have to have the second best, namely Saddam Hussein.[19]

Incidentally, in addition to what Gilbert said, the United States even refused to allow rebelling Iraqi generals access to captured materiel. They didn't ask for support, just access to captured materiel. The United States refused, and the rebels were slaughtered. After the massacres—it was pretty clear what had happened—Alan Cowell, who is the *Times*'s longtime Middle East correspondent, wrote that it's sort of unpleasant and we're unhappy about it, but there's a very broad consensus among the United States and its allies, Saudi Arabia and so on, that Saddam Hussein offers more hope for the stability of the region than those who are trying to overthrow him.[20] In other words, if we let Iraqis gain independence, that'll undermine stability. "Stability" is a code word for U.S. dominance. But if we keep Saddam Hussein there, there's a better hope for stability, we can run the region—in part by manufacturing his alleged threat to others. I think that's exactly what happened. They tried throughout the 1990s to organize coups, which would have been the best of all worlds—an iron-fisted military junta without Saddam Hussein's name on it—but they underestimated the degree of his control over the intelligence apparatus, the Mukhabarat, and other security forces, and they couldn't get away with it. But certainly it was intended. And yes, I think 9/11 gave the ideological cover. That sounds exactly right to me.

SHALOM: Did the Saudi kingdom have a different view in 1991 compared to 2003 as to whether it wanted Saddam Hussein in or out of power?

ACHCAR: The Saudi kingdom had the same "vision" that Bush Sr. had: They wanted, of course, to get rid of Saddam Hussein—he was a real nuisance for them. But they did not want to get rid of him at any cost. That is, they wanted to be sure to have a good replacement. And they were in favor of what Bush Sr. opted for—that is, the embargo and checks—while trying to overthrow Saddam Hussein by internal means.

CHOMSKY: Does Saudi intelligence have a good sense of what goes on internally in Iraq? Could they have guessed how powerful the regime was?

ACHCAR: Everyone knew it was a very powerful regime. This was a paranoid dictator, surrounding himself with concentric circles checking each other.

CHOMSKY: Did the Saudis have a sense that the coup efforts might succeed?

ACHCAR: They tried, up to the last minute before the invasion. Actually throughout the 1990s, there were two different types of attempts at over-throwing the regime. I call them the two scenarios: the Chalabi scenario and the Allawi scenario. The one represented and advocated by Ahmed Chalabi, a close collaborator of Rumsfeld's Pentagon and a neocon buddy, bet originally on some insurrectionary action from outside the Baathist apparatus and was dedicated to the goal of dismantling that apparatus. The other scenario, the one represented and advocated by Iyad Allawi, bet on turning the Baathist apparatus against Saddam Hussein, by exploiting dissensions within it and buying off a big chunk of it. Of course, they knew that they wouldn't really be able to break the close circle around Saddam Hussein, but at least they could take over major segments of the apparatus and especially the army, because the army traditionally was never under the same tight control as the other components of the apparatus.

CHOMSKY: Including the Republican Guard?

ACHCAR: The Republican Guard and other special forces were the praetorian guards of the regime, and it would have been difficult, though not impossi-ble, to split them. But the regular army kept some tradition of relative inde-pendence. The Baathists had come to power as a small minority party—they had organized a coup d'état. Saddam Hussein, who was never in the military and held the army in suspicion, relied chiefly on his party militias and his Mukhabarat, his intelligence service. I think the Saudis were very much bet-ting on the army. The Saudis, and the Jordanians, were very much in favor of the Allawi scenario, which was supported by the State Department and the CIA in the Bush Jr. administration: Allawi, a former Baathist, had been a col-laborator of British intelligence and the CIA for many years. He attempted to organize a coup with some officers of the Iraqi army in 1996, but it failed.

CHOMSKY: Did the Saudis and the Jordanians take Chalabi seriously?

ACHCAR: Definitely not. On this issue, the Saudi kingdom clearly had much better relations with the State Department than with the Pentagon in the rift within the Bush administration. As you know, the Pentagon has also been the location of the largest concentration of neocons, and the neocons have the kind of hostile discourse about the Saudi kingdom that I mentioned previously and which is very much irritating to the Saudis. You remember the famous incident in 2002, when the Defense Policy Board, chaired then by neocon "dark prince" Richard Perle, organized a presentation on the Saudi kingdom during which a speaker went to the point of defining targets to bomb within the country. The Saudis became furious and got this man fired from the Rand Corporation. Bush himself, most probably, and the whole Bush family were also quite angry—that was going really too far! So the Saudis were definitely in favor of the Allawi scenario. And now we know—it has been reported by the *New York Times*[21]—that in the last couple of months before the invasion, this debate was not yet settled. On one side were Allawi, the State Department, and the CIA, advocating some deal with the Iraqi military. They had contacts with the Iraqi defense minister to organize some kind of coup when the U.S. forces started walking in, with the result that they would get an interlocutor in power willing to collaborate with them. On the other side was Chalabi, backed by the neocons, who had a lot of influence on Rumsfeld, and then on Vice President Dick Cheney, and then on Bush; Chalabi got the upper hand in this discussion, with his blueprint calling for the total dismantling of the Iraqi military and political apparatus and turning Iraq into a neutral state that would be friendly even to Israel. They envisioned an Iraq with an army of only 40,000, ridiculously small for a country of its size, that would be structurally dependent on U.S. protection and, hence, a permanent U.S. protectorate.

Chalabi's main concern was pushing for the dismantling of the Baathist apparatus. Why? One dimension is certainly his profound hatred of the Baath, which is not for sectarian reasons but, rather, for political reasons. (Both Allawi and Chalabi are Shiites, so the religious factor does not provide an explanation for their differences.) When it all turned sour, Washington ended up believing that Chalabi had been so eager to destroy the Baathist state because of some connection he had with Iran—that's when he was accused of leaking information to Iran. It's true that, especially after his fall from grace with Washington, he tried to act very much as a Shiite sectarian figure, although no one took him very seriously. The fact remains that, before the invasion, he was strongly in favor of dismantling the Baathist power apparatus and was afraid for good reason, I think, that the Allawi scenario would prevail. The neocons leaked to the media, in the months before the invasion, the news that the United States was considering cutting a deal with part of the Baathist apparatus, warning that it would lead to "Saddamism without Saddam."

CHOMSKY: In 1991, this was called "the second best of all possible worlds."

ACHCAR: Indeed. And therefore, as we know, the Chalabi scenario prevailed: There was a full invasion and occupation, the army crumbled, and then the head of the U.S. occupation authority, L. Paul Bremer, dismantled whatever remained of the Baathist apparatus, the party, the armed forces, the secret services, and even the border police, an act that was quite crazy from the angle of security! And they found themselves in the present quagmire.

Other Major Powers and Iraq

SHALOM: Back in February 2003, when prowar forces in the United States were pouring out all their French wine and renaming French fries because France wasn't cooperating in the Security Council, a lot of people in the antiwar movement were sort of cheering on France and Germany and Russia, and other governments that opposed the war. How reliable are these governments in their antiwar stances?

CHOMSKY: Their reliability is approximately zero. Sensible antiwar activists don't ally themselves with governments. There was something important about their position—namely, there was a reason why they were being so bitterly denounced by U.S. elites: They were meeting minimal conditions of democracy. For whatever reason—pure cynicism, in fact—they were acting the way a democratic government is supposed to act. In short, they were responding to the will of the overwhelming majority of their populations. The position of the antiwar movement should have been that it's fine that these governments are paying attention to their populations, whatever their reasons may be, but we certainly don't ally with them, or have any trust in them.

What happened here was quite intriguing, but was basically ignored. I can't recall any display of hatred and contempt for democracy as extreme as what took place in those months in the United States, pretty much across the spectrum. There was what Rumsfeld called "Old Europe" and "New Europe." Under his definition, they are distinguished by a very sharp criterion: Old Europe consists of the countries where the governments took the same position as that of a large majority of the population; New Europe—the "hope for democracy"—is the governments that disregard an even larger percentage of the population. Some of it was almost comical, like Italian prime minister Silvio Berlusconi being invited to the White House as the representative of the hope for democracy. You don't know whether to laugh or cry. But the worst case was José María Aznar, the Spanish prime minister. He was so lauded by Bush and by British prime minister Tony Blair as the hope for democracy that he was brought to their summit in the Azores, where they basically declared the war a couple of days before the invasion. Aznar joined in this war declaration right after polls in Spain showed that the war had the support of 2 percent of the population, so therefore he's the great hope for democracy.[22] He was willing to follow orders from Crawford, Texas, with 2 percent of the population supporting him. What does that tell you about the attitudes toward democracy?

Some of it became surreal. When the Turkish government, to everyone's surprise, including mine, went along with the opinion of 95 percent of its population and refused to allow a U.S. offensive through Turkey, the Turkish government was bitterly condemned for lacking democratic credentials—that was the phrase that was used—because it went along with the opinion of 95 percent of the public. That great dove, Secretary of State Colin Powell, immediately announced we're going to have to have sanctions against Turkey.[23] Most extreme was former undersecretary of defense Paul Wolfowitz. He is the person identified in the United States and, as far as I know, the European media as the leading force in democracy promotion—the "idealist in chief," as he was called in the *Washington Post*.[24] He berated the Turkish military for not intervening to compel the government to overrule 95 percent of the population; he basically ordered them to apologize to the United States, and to say, "Let's figure out how we can be as helpful as possible to the Americans."[25] And this was supposed to be democracy. And this farce went on, without comment. The fact that anyone can talk about democracy promotion, after this display, is astounding.

This is what the antiwar movement should be emphasizing. And if there are a couple of governments that for their own cynical reasons happen to agree with the majority of the population and take the right position, fine, but that's the end of it; there's nothing more to say about them. Tomorrow they'll do the opposite, because they're acting out of pure cynicism—power interests—anyway.

ACHCAR: Noam's quite right to stress the importance of this feature of our times. There's a general trend at the level of the mainstream media to praise those ruling politicians who rule without considering the polls; that is deemed a great virtue. But behind it is the very elitist idea, also embedded in the very concept of "representative democracy," that, once elected, a representative is free to do whatever he or she wants, even against the unanimous will of his or her constituency. But I must also say that in the case of the three governments that we've mentioned—France, Germany, and Russia—it was certainly not out of any consideration for democracy that they were against the war. I don't need to elaborate on the Russian government. But even the French and German governments do not hesitate to pursue the most unpopular neoliberal policies and assaults on social gains. On the issue of Iraq, their motivation was definitely not any democratic principle: There were much more down-to-earth considerations at stake.

Iraq is a country where there was a direct clash of interests, in a very primary economic sense, between the United States and Britain, on the one hand, and France and Russia—one could add China—on the other hand. The Soviet Union and France were the main partners of Saddam Hussein for many years, providing him with arms. France, especially, was his main military backer in the war against Iran. And despite Russian collusion and French participation in the 1991 war on Iraq, Saddam Hussein tried to play his traditional partnership with France and Russia, during the UN embargo years, as a counterweight to the United States and Britain in the Security Council. French and Russian companies were granted important oil concessions that were conditioned on lifting the embargo. That is why at some point Paris and Moscow changed their attitude, trying to find ways to lift the embargo, and were blocked on that by Washington and London. The United States and British refusal to lift the embargo—that is, to allow the lifting of the embargo if and when UN inspectors determined that Iraq had disarmed—was rightly perceived by Paris and Moscow as a refusal to permit them to take advantage of the oil concessions they had been granted. And they very much saw the dedication of Washington and London to invade Iraq as a desire to snatch the prize from them. Actually one of the first proclamations after the invasion was that all contracts granted by Saddam Hussein were to be considered null and void. So that's the main reason why Paris and Moscow opposed that war. Had the Bush administration offered them a substantial slice of the cake, I'm sure they would have joined in. But the Bush administration was so arrogant that it didn't want to grant them much of anything, and that's why they kept opposing the war to the end.

In the German case, there were no direct economic interests at stake. At best, if one were generous with German chancellor Gerhard Schröder, one could grant him some concern over superior geopolitical considerations— for example, to say that he had some concerns about the fact that the United States should not have all the levers over Europe—and one could link that also to the very close relationship he had nurtured with Putin, and the deals being worked out for a new gas pipeline going from Russia to Germany through the Baltic Sea. But that would be a generous assessment of Schröder's motivation. If one wanted to be less generous, one would just stress that there's a big dose, not of democracy but of opportunist electoralism, behind his stance, because the preparation for the invasion of Iraq happened at a time when the German chancellor was projected as the loser in the forthcoming parliamentary elections, because of his neoliberal social program, which caused the traditional constituency of social democracy to be reluctant to support him; and therefore, the only popular issue he could find was opposition to the war, at a time when, indeed, the polls were showing that the overwhelming majority of German public opinion was opposed to the war.

Rulers like Chirac, Putin, or Schröder should definitely not be regarded as allies by the antiwar movement, especially since they are themselves hawkish warmongers when their interests are at stake. Russian forces are waging a terrible quasi-genocidal war in Chechnya. The French government still considers itself a colonial power in Africa, and behaves as such. Not to mention the fact that both France and Germany are involved in Afghanistan, along with the U.S. troops. To that we should add that although Paris and Berlin did not support the invasion of Iraq politically, technically speaking they did everything they could to facilitate it: the Germans, of course, by letting the whole U.S. military infrastructure on their territory be used for that purpose,[26] the French by opening their airspace to U.S. warplanes. So we should not be fooled by such governments. The antiwar movement, at least its most dynamic sectors, is closely linked with the global justice movement, and I believe that's a very good combination because these are two facets of the same reality: opposition to imperial wars and to neoliberalism.

CHOMSKY: I could add an analogous comment about U.S. attitudes. I don't think it's just arrogance; the United States has a real interest in undermining France and Germany, because they are the industrial, commercial, and financial center of Europe. The rest is a kind of periphery. The United States has had a deep concern back through the 1940s that Europe might strike out on an independent path. That's one of the reasons they were so concerned about French president Charles de Gaulle, with his call for a Europe from the Atlantic to the Urals. And the forces that might impel Europe that way today are "Old Europe." That's one of the reasons the United States was so much in favor of expanding the European Union (EU) to include the former Soviet satellites, which it plausibly assumes it can control. And it's one of the reasons also why U.S. policymakers are so supportive of getting Turkey into the EU—not because they love Turkey, but because that's another way of diluting the influence of the powerful sectors in Europe and ensuring, they hope, that Europe will remain under U.S. control. Whatever position Germany and France had taken on the Iraq war, that would remain constant.

It's also what happened in 1990 when Soviet leader Mikhail Gorbachev agreed to allow Germany to be unified, which from the Russian point of view was an enormous threat. Unlike the United States, Russia has real security concerns. Germany alone practically destroyed Russia twice in the first half of the twentieth century. For a unified Germany to be incorporated into a Western military alliance was a tremendous threat. So Gorbachev agreed to German unification, but on one condition: that he get a firm pledge from Bush Sr. that NATO would not expand to the east. Within a couple of years, however, Clinton just reneged on the commitment, and expanded NATO to the east, right to the borders of Russia. Russia responded, as you'd expect, by beginning to increase its offensive military capacity. Russia had been pressing very hard for the elimination of nuclear weapons, and it had declared—as the United States and NATO had not—that it would not be the first to use nuclear weapons. After Clinton's backing down on the NATO pledge, Russia backed down on its moves and moved toward a more militaristic, offensive posture, extended more under Bush Jr. These are really important developments that are part of the background of the hysteria about Old Europe and New Europe. New Europe is important for the United States as a way of undermining European independence.

ACHCAR: I quite agree. But we should also stress the fact that in New Europe public opinion was overwhelmingly against the war, even more so than in Old Europe!

CHOMSKY: The only place prowar sentiment reached 10 percent was Romania.[27]

ACHCAR: So it was in New Europe that governments most disdained the opinions of their own populations.

CHOMSKY: But they are obedient to the United States when they dilute European independence.

The Current Situation in Iraq

SHALOM: What is the current political situation in Iraq? What's going on?

ACHCAR: In a sense, it's a direct continuation of what I was saying previously. The starting point to understand the situation is the Chalabi blueprint, which was a total failure and had to be abandoned after a few months, but which had already led to a state of chaos and complete disintegration of the state apparatus. The blueprint was first implemented by L. Paul Bremer, with a view of the Iraqi situation according to which the United States would find popular support for its protectorate or control over the country, through men like Chalabi; they thought Chalabi enjoyed real popular support. But it became clear, from very early in the occupation, that that was not the case. And Bremer decided therefore to take the time needed to try to create the conditions for such support, while implementing quite stupid attempts to imitate U.S. behavior in post-1945 Germany and Japan. He wanted to put a lock on the political, constitutional, and economic future of the country before organizing any elections. So in a very colonial manner he started issuing decrees aimed at imposing neoliberal reforms on Iraq's economy, which were both inane and ruinous for the country. Bremer wanted to draft the constitution of the country as well. But he found an unexpected obstacle: Grand Ayatollah Ali al-Sistani and the Shiite religious power. Before the invasion, the United States used to deal with the Iraqi opposition in exile, with Chalabi playing the role of intermediary. The only serious forces among the exiles were, on the one hand, the Kurds and, on the other, the Shiite Islamic fundamentalist forces: the Supreme Council for Islamic Revolution in Iraq (SCIRI) and the Islamic Dawa Party. For Washington, it was obvious that it was a provisional marriage of convenience and nothing else—allies to be dispensed with as soon as the goal was achieved.

The United States actually thought that Sistani would rather be a collaborationist—that was one of their bets. And they bet also on Abdul-Majid al-Khoei—the son of a Grand Ayatollah who had been Sistani's teacher and who had died in Iraq under house arrest in 1992—but the son was assassinated at the very beginning of the occupation when he returned to Iraq from Britain. This was actually the first major blow that Washington and London suffered in Iraq. They accused Muqtada al-Sadr of having organized the assassination.

CHOMSKY: Do you think Khoei would have played the same role Sistani has? The same sort of political role in the country?

ACHCAR: No, I think he would have been much closer and much friendlier to the occupation than Sistani, who had never lived in the West. Sistani's instructions to his followers from the start, as reported to me at the time by a well-informed Shiite friend, were: no resistance to the invasion, but no greeting either, only caution. That was quite wise from his point of view: We don't greet the invaders, we already have been through the painful experience of 1991 and saw what they did to us, but we won't defend the Baathist regime, for that matter. Let them topple Saddam Hussein, and then we will see if they are really willing to help us.

It is important to note that, contrary to the prevailing image, the SCIRI was not in favor of the invasion of Iraq. The present head of the SCIRI, Abdul-Aziz al-Hakim, expressed beforehand the view that there were other and better means of getting rid of Saddam Hussein than an invasion. He asked the United States and Britain to just implement UN Security Council Resolution 688 of 1991,[28] which would prevent the regime from using its repressive means, since the U.S. and the U.K. had actual total control over the country militarily through their air dominance. Saddam Hussein couldn't move a single tank without their green light. So, block him from using his heavy weaponry, impose free elections on him—or create conditions whereby we could revolt without getting massacred.

CHOMSKY: Was that an official position of the SCIRI?

ACHCAR: It was expressed in a long interview in the *Tehran Times* a couple of months before the invasion took place, for instance.[29] And there were other factions of the opposition in exile expressing the same position. No one can pretend that the Iraqi people would have wanted the invasion to happen if they were given other means to get rid of the dictatorship. They would certainly have preferred other means, because no one likes to be occupied by the United States, at least in the Middle East, where the United States is so much hated for various reasons that we all know and that we have discussed.

One month after Bremer took over in May 2003, he started concocting his plans about drafting the constitution—like General Douglas MacArthur in post-1945 Japan. As soon as Sistani was told of that, he issued a very official fatwa, rejecting completely the Bremer plan, which consisted of setting up constituent "caucuses" basically designated by the occupation authority. Sistani instead demanded elections—an elected constituent assembly—as the only acceptable way to draft a constitution. Sistani's stand against Bremer essentially said, we have no trust in you or any assembly that you would pick; we want an elected constituent assembly. And the confrontation went on for several months. In November 2003, Bremer tried to force through a kind of halfway concession to Sistani—saying that his procedure would set up only a provisional constitution, and then there would be elections later for a permanent constitution. Sistani, however, was not stupid. He understood that Bremer wanted to create facts on the ground that would become very hard to reverse, and therefore, Sistani kept up the pressure and got convinced of the necessity for mass action. He accordingly called for mass demonstrations, and there were these really huge mass demonstrations in January 2004 against the U.S. occupation authority. Washington at that time was up to its neck in troubles, confronted by several problems, one being the official acknowledgment of the fact that there were no weapons of mass destruction in Iraq, ruining the key pretext for the invasion. That's when Bush gave the 2003 National Endowment speech we've already mentioned, upping the volume on democracy: The subsidiary pretext for the invasion became the only remaining one, and therefore the major one. At the same time, you had the Abu Ghraib torture scandal, and many other problems coming together. So the Bush administration was definitely not in a position to confront a mass movement of the Shiites, a movement that is much more formidable than any violent actions or armed actions by any group.

CHOMSKY: It should be stressed that this was a real triumph of nonviolent resistance.

ACHCAR: Of course.

CHOMSKY: It is kind of surprising that even the Western antiwar groups that are committed to nonviolence and pacifism didn't pick up the story. It is one of the greatest achievements of nonviolence that I can think of. They forced the occupying army to back off, to permit elections, to permit the Iraqis to write the constitution. That's quite an achievement.

ACHCAR: Yes, and one reason for the fact that it wasn't picked up is that the attention devoted to this mass movement by the media was close to zero. (CHOMSKY: That's right.) They weren't confronted with any decapitation or any such niceties that they love to report prominently. You can say the same of the April 9, 2005, demonstration organized by Muqtada al-Sadr. It was a huge demonstration in Baghdad that burned puppets of Bush, Blair, and Saddam Hussein—a very meaningful gesture.

CHOMSKY: Certainly the planners see it; they can't disregard it. The media can keep it quiet here.

ACHCAR: Of course, but public opinion, including the left fringe of public opinion, doesn't see that, and doesn't have its attention focused on this aspect—especially given that a section of the radical left seems to believe that resistance to foreign occupation can only mean armed struggle.

Now, to get back to our story: Bremer feigned a concession to Sistani, but tried nevertheless to push through his own agenda. He delayed the elections as long as possible, under various false pretexts, so they were postponed to January 2005, whereas Sistani had been asking for immediate elections since the very beginning of the occupation. And Bremer promulgated a provisional constitution, the Transitional Administrative Law, which introduced a lot of mechanisms difficult to reverse and which stated that the future constitution would not be ratified if a two-thirds majority in three provinces, out of eighteen, voted against it. This was meant to give veto power to the Kurds, which actually means veto power to the United States using the Kurdish Alliance as its proxy.

In any event, elections did take place finally in January 2005, and the United Iraqi Alliance (UIA), a coalition dominated by the Shiite Islamic fundamentalist organizations, the SCIRI and Dawa, got a majority in the parliament. Washington's new preferred stooge after Chalabi's fall from grace, Iyad Allawi—who had been placed by Bremer at the head of the nominally sovereign Iraqi interim government in June 2004—failed to achieve a significant showing in the election, despite the heavy intrusion and support of the United States and its Arab clients, and despite all the resources that were available to Allawi as head of the interim government. This was a major disappointment and setback for the United States. Though Allawi got less than 15 percent of the votes, Washington tried nevertheless to secure for him key ministries in the new government. But the UIA refused. This is the explanation for why it took so long after the elections to form a new government. For several weeks there was a tug-of-war going on between the UIA, on the one hand, and the United States through the Kurdish Alliance, on the other. Finally a government was formed without Allawi, headed by the UIA's and Dawa's Ibrahim al-Jaafari.

Then the rest of the 2005 political and constitutional timetable that was agreed upon got implemented: the drafting of the constitution, a referendum on the constitution on October 15, 2005, and finally new parliamentary elections on December 15, 2005. In the latter elections the UIA won about half the parliamentary seats. And it seems that Allawi was again a disappointment to the United States, although he once more got plenty of financial support—he even had access to a private plane, not from his own pocket, you can be sure—and strong backing from the Arab mass media. But his second electoral attempt was again a failure.

Nevertheless, sharp debates are taking place again because the Kurdish Alliance—that is, the United States—is trying once more to get Allawi or his group in the new government, particularly for a major "power ministry" such as Interior or Defense. The UIA is at the very least quite reluctant, and the Sadrists—Muqtada al-Sadr's followers within the UIA, whose clout has enormously increased in the country and in the UIA—say they consider that to be a red line. And what is not said is that there is also a red line drawn by Iran against Allawi to counterbalance Washington's effort to push him through. So here we are, with all this arm wrestling, this trial of strength and wheeling-and-dealing going on among the various forces in Iraq, including the occupation authority represented by U.S. Ambassador Zalmay Khalilzad, who acts as though he is an Iraqi politician.

But everything points to the conclusion that 2006 will probably be a very difficult and decisive year in Iraq, at the very least for the United States, because Washington will very likely confront mounting pressure for its withdrawal from the country, and this time coming from the full sectarian spectrum of Arab Iraqis. An indication of that is already perceptible in the last request made by the Jaafari government to the UN Security Council, in November 2005, for the renewal of the UN mandate that serves as the fictitious legal cover to the presence of occupation troops in Iraq. The Jaafari government saw to it that the UN resolution that extended the mandate of the occupation troops until the end of 2006 stipulated that the Iraqi government retains the right to ask at any moment for the termination of the mandate.[30] So the UIA took safeguards to ensure that it has the authority to insist that the United States get out.

To that we should add the fact that the Sadrists have emerged as much more powerful in the new parliament than they had been in the previous one. Although there is considerable enmity between the SCIRI and the Sadrists, the SCIRI could not fail to acknowledge the rising popularity of the Sadrist current, and understood that if they did not get the Sadrists on board, then the latter would get, at the very least, a comparable chunk of the popular vote and the SCIRI would then face a difficult situation, or be beaten electorally. This is because their popularity is rather lower than Sadr's: They are seen as people who were in exile in Iran, whereas Sadr plays the Iraqi and Arab nationalist card, and is thereby able to appeal to the Iraqi Arab Sunnis. So Sadr now has much more leverage in the institutions, not to speak of his leverage on the street. The Sadrists combine the two: They entered the electoral arena and keep organizing mass demonstrations, which are hardly reported in the media.

CHOMSKY: Do they take place outside Baghdad also?

ACHCAR: Oh yes, in the south particularly. They have organized several demonstrations recently, including a mobilization estimated at 100,000 people, to protest the lack of public services and electricity, putting the blame on the occupation.

SHALOM: Where was that demonstration?

ACHCAR: It took place in several towns, in Baghdad, but also in the south and elsewhere. When the Sadrists say, "We will demonstrate this Friday or that other day," they organize demonstrations wherever they are. For reasons probably linked to security and logistics, they have organized only one central national demonstration until now; that was in Baghdad on April 9, 2005, and it was gigantic. You've got very wild variations in the estimates, but the figures were commonly in the many hundreds of thousands. This current is gaining more and more influence among the Shiites, and that in itself is a terrible defeat for the United States: The Sadrist current has become the worst and most feared enemy of the U.S. occupation.

CHOMSKY: Do you think that these efforts of doing some reconstruction work in Sadr City[31] are having an effect on the population—all the attempts to do a little rebuilding, by the occupation authority?

ACHCAR: No, because it's just feeding people's frustration. When they compare the rapidity with which the Baathist government restored basic services after 1991 with what is happening now, the Iraqis conclude that this occupation doesn't really care about the basic needs of the Iraqis and is interested only in oil and that's it.

SHALOM: And they don't blame the resistance, the insurgency, for the slowness of the reconstruction?

ACHCAR: People don't buy it: You can't blame the insurgency in the south because the insurgency is not significantly present in that part of the country. When some people in Western countries praise the "insurgency," at least on the left, or in the antiwar movement, they tend to forget that this is an insurgency limited to one minority of the population. The only constituency of this insurgency is the Arab Sunni population, which means roughly 20 percent of the population—a constituency that has good reasons, reasons of national pride and freedom, to be hostile to the U.S. occupation, and of course, reasons that are very much increased by the brutal and clumsy behavior of U.S. forces. For anyone who knows Iraqi society, the U.S. armed forces in Iraq behaved exactly like an elephant in a china shop. But aside from this very legitimate resentment, a significant section of Iraq's Arab Sunnis also resent the fact that they are no longer the empowered minority—although this is rather phantasmagoric for many of them, because they enjoyed no real privileges. They take, however, the fact that Arab Sunnis were a large majority in the Baathist military and political ruling establishments, in the parliament, the army officer corps, and so on, as a measure of communal privilege. The ruling clique, of course, was not only mostly Arab Sunni, but essentially was restricted to the familial and tribal circles of Saddam Hussein, who very much exploited those aspects of Iraqi society, despite his alleged and very much undeserved "modernist" image.

The Sunni population felt strong resentment against the occupation on these two kinds of grounds, combined to different degrees, and that's also reflected in the fact that when one reads the literature and statements that come from the Sunni areas or from insurgency sources, they are often as much anti-Shiite as anti-American. The statements don't necessarily say, "We hate the Shiites," but they use expressions like the "Safavid Shiites," which amounts to an insult (it is a reference to the dynasty that brutally imposed Shiism in Persia in the sixteenth century). Or if they are Islamic fundamentalist Sunnis, they would use the term "Rafida" (meaning the "rejecters," those who rejected the legitimate Caliphate), which is also considered pejorative, to describe the Shiites. And they would say they are fighting two occupations: the U.S. occupation and the Iranian occupation.

CHOMSKY: Did the Badr Brigade take part with the Iranian army in the Iran-Iraq war?

ACHCAR: They were not embedded in the Iranian army, apparently. But they tried to force their way through Kurdistan, and this is one reason why the SCIRI has a friendly relationship with the Kurdish forces. On the other hand, after 1991, the Patriotic Union of Kurdistan (PUK), the group led by Jalal Talabani, is known to have developed close links with Iran.

CHOMSKY: Also with Syria?

ACHCAR: Yes, of course, all the Kurdish groups have connections with Syria. They were there as refugees, given political asylum as a result of the conflict between the Syrian Baath and the Iraqi Baath.

So, to sum up, the situation now is that the United States is facing big trouble. It is trying to form enough of a blocking force composed of Allawi and the Kurdish Alliance, along with the Arab Sunni parliamentary forces. Allawi's main concern and Washington's main hope are to win over the former Baathists, trying to detach them from Saddamist loyalism, and to convince them that they could recover their privileges by collaborating with the occupation. The former Baathist Allawi is the right man for that.

The Iraqi Insurgency

SHALOM: To focus a little more on the question of the insurgency, how would you characterize the insurgency? Is it a bunch of terrorists or a national liberation movement?

CHOMSKY: Gilbert can talk about this much more knowledgeably than I can, but my impression is that it's very disparate. There's a genuine national resistance movement, for all sorts of reasons, which apparently has a lot of popular support. There was a secret poll commissioned by the British Ministry of Defense that was leaked to the press in Britain;[32] it's barely been reported here. According to that poll, 82 percent of the population want the withdrawal of "coalition" troops. Fewer than 1 percent think the occupation brings security and 45 percent believe that attacks against the occupying forces are justified. The report in the British press was a little ambiguous. It says 45 percent of *all Iraqis,* but that seems implausible to me; I think they're probably talking about *Arab Iraqis,* because the Kurds don't agree, which means that if it really is all of Iraq, it's an incredible proportion of Arab Iraq, where the occupation forces actually are; they're not in the Kurdish areas. So whatever it is, the national resistance seems to have a lot of popular support. Then, on the other hand, there is a straight terrorist group, the kind who blows up funerals and so on. That's a different strain altogether, whatever they are. I don't think you can put them together and call them all the insurgency. Gilbert, I'm sure you can give a more nuanced picture of it.

ACHCAR: Actually, the 45 percent figure is plausible: It would mean a significant majority, but not an overwhelming one, of the Arabs. If we consider the Kurds as constituting 20 percent of the population of Iraq, as is widely believed, and if we assume that almost no Kurd supports armed resistance against the occupation, that would mean that a 56 percent majority of non-Kurds do. The question asked in the poll seems to have been "Are armed actions against U.S. and British troops justified?" You can be sure that there is an overwhelming majority among Sunni Arabs who would say yes. And it is likely that an important segment of the Shiites would also say yes, although, because there are groups claiming responsibility both for attacks against U.S. troops and for sectarian mass murders of Shiites, the insurgency as a whole is seen negatively by a majority of the Shiite population. We can learn some more by considering the latest Oxford Research International poll conducted for ABC, BBC, and others.[33] This poll shows that an overwhelming majority of Iraqis, 65 percent, oppose the presence of "Coalition Forces." We know that there are problems with polls in general, and that this is all the more the case in a country like Iraq. Nevertheless, the poll shows that a plurality—47 percent—want the foreign troops to leave when the Iraqi state is capable of taking hold of security, compared to 26 percent who want them to leave immediately. But if you add to those the 19 percent wanting the foreign troops to leave right after the formation of the next government—which is very soon in their mind—you get an astonishingly high proportion of 45 percent, almost equal to the proportion of those who link withdrawal to security. In light of these figures, I think we can safely assume that there is a very broad consensus in the country for a timetable for the withdrawal of foreign troops. That was part of the program of the UIA before the January 2005 election. The United States required that this be dropped from any government program. And the Kurdish Alliance required the same, when they concluded their governmental agreement, by a sort of contract, with the UIA.

SHALOM: This was back in 2005?

ACHCAR: Yes, in April, when the negotiations were concluded that led to the formation of the government headed by Jaafari. And since then, the UIA leadership—and Jaafari himself—has said repeatedly, we can't demand a timetable because that would be artificial and dangerous, using the same argument the Bush administration has been using. In Jaafari's case, I think it was in good faith, not a pretext covering a desire to prolong the occupation indefinitely. Jaafari kept saying, we will gradually take over in region after region, as soon as we can, and when we believe we can manage alone, the foreign troops will be asked to leave. But from now on, the UIA will be under much increased pressure from the Sadrists. The Sadrists had already gotten various currents that are likely to be in the next government, including all components of the UIA, to agree on a pact of honor before the recent election, where the demand for a timetable for the withdrawal of foreign troops was prominent.

CHOMSKY: How seriously do you take the UIA's commitment?

ACHCAR: That remains to be seen. From various statements by UIA figures, officials and others, you get the impression that they believe that the year 2006 will be the last one for the occupation—that, before the end of the year, they could manage to do without the U.S. presence. And that is also reflected in the provisos they demanded be included in the UN Security Council resolution extending the mandate of the occupation. They are convinced—and even Muqtada al-Sadr can understand that argument—that they need to be sure that they can control the situation.

CHOMSKY: Control it against whom?

ACHCAR: Against the Baathists, mainly, and Abu Musab al-Zarqawi's al-Qaeda branch, "Al-Qaeda's Organization in the Land of the Two Rivers." These two are considered terrible enemies by the Sadrists, too.

CHOMSKY: But what organized form do the Baathists have at this point?

ACHCAR: There we get to the issue of the insurgency.

First of all, it seems that, especially in the first period of the occupation, when the armed insurgency started to become a noteworthy phenomenon, and then a major one, most of the resistance actions were local actions by local groups appalled by the behavior of U.S. troops and resenting the occupation. But these local groups were acting strictly against the occupation, many of them in areas where you hardly have Shiites. They didn't resort to sectarian actions. But then you started having assassinations, or mass murders through car bombs or suicide attacks, of a sectarian nature, including the assassination in August 2003 of Ayatollah Mohammed Baqir al-Hakim, the head of the SCIRI, who was replaced by his brother, Abdul-Aziz. The assassination was claimed by Zarqawi, but whether it was organized by Zarqawi on his own or for the Baathists is unclear, because although the alleged pre-invasion, or pre-9/11, link between al-Qaeda and the Iraqi Baath is a pure fabrication, we can be sure that there are now connections between the underground armed networks. The Baathist apparatus, having already been through the experience of 1991, when they had an army three times the size they had in 2003, knew perfectly well that they would be no match for U.S. troops. They are not so stupid as to ignore that, and they prepared themselves accordingly for the occupation. We can draw here an analogy with the Nazis, which is not too far-fetched actually, because the Baathist regime under Saddam Hussein was indeed a semi-fascist type of government—I don't hesitate to call it that, and the "semi" is just because they didn't have the benefit of the same broad mass support that traditional fascism had. The analogy is that the Baathist apparatus prepared something similar to the "Werewolf," the stay-behind force that the Nazis designed for the fight against the Allies in those regions of Germany that they started losing in 1945. Similarly, the Baathists had put away and hidden lots of money, in cash, and weapons—huge resources. It took them a while to reorganize after the invasion, of course, but then they started acting.

CHOMSKY: Would you attribute the sectarian killings to them?

ACHCAR: Of course. I believe that much of the politically oriented sectarian killings, at least, could be attributed to them, like those indirectly sectarian attacks on army recruitment centers or police recruitment centers or policemen.

CHOMSKY: What about plain civilian targets? Like the funerals and the mosques?

ACHCAR: Indiscriminate attacks, most of them suicide attacks, on plain civilian targets, I think, are more likely to be the work of hard-line Islamic fundamentalists, of the Wahhabi (or Salafi as they call themselves) kind, who consider the Shiites as heretics who should be fought. Zarqawi's famous speech, declaring war on the Shiites, was thoroughly chilling in its tone and in the terms and very violent metaphors that he used.

So you have a mixture of all sorts of actions and groups, but I think one can safely assume that the bulk of those involved in armed actions are more inspired by nationalistic feelings than by sectarian feelings. Actually, one gets a distorted image from the mass media, because they give much more coverage to the most brutal sectarian killings than to the daily attacks, the IEDs (improvised explosive devices), and other actions that happen commonly and are spread all over the Arab Sunni areas.

A sense of the political balance of forces has been given by the last two rounds of elections: the October 15, 2005, referendum and the December 15, 2005, election. Some of the major groups claiming armed operations decided that the boycott of the January 2005 election that they had ordered and imposed in the Arab Sunni areas was a mistake because, they said, they were losing the leverage they could have on the political future of the country. They understood that, and they decided therefore to call for participation in the electoral process, with a no vote against the draft constitution, on October 15, and a vote for Arab Sunni slates in the parliamentary elections.

CHOMSKY: That was not supported by the Baath?

ACHCAR: No, it wasn't. Although Saddam Hussein's henchmen had prepared the network, it's not at all sure that they could keep control of it, since they have lost the key levers of power. So there are apparently chunks of the former Baathist apparatus who are working on their own, who are no longer "Saddam loyalists." But the "Saddam loyalist" faction is still there and they have a lot of resources, including several websites. Their position was very sharply against any participation in the electoral process, for good reason. They knew that they had no chance whatsoever of ruling the country again through elections, unless they were fake elections like they used to organize. And, in any event, their very conception of power doesn't include real or free elections. So they had a very clear attitude against any participation in the elections, as did Zarqawi, who rejects the very idea of elections. Nevertheless, we saw that the two election days went quite well by Iraqi standards, quite peacefully. That was certainly not due to any measures taken by the occupation; it was due to the change in attitude of the major insurgent groups. It gives a sense of the balance of forces because it shows that the more, so to say, sensible factions of the insurgency could impose the safe completion of the elections on the rest. Now of course, in light of the results of the elections, which were very disappointing for the Arab Sunnis, the Baathists have produced a statement saying, "We warned you, and these elections are just void, and you have served the occupation, legitimizing it by taking part in the votes."

CHOMSKY: That's what you see on Baathist websites? Are they identified as Baathist websites?

ACHCAR: Of course. They are websites with pictures of Saddam Hussein, very official Baathist websites, and there are several of them. They post official Baath Party statements, statements also by Izzat Ibrahim al-Douri, the senior member of the Baathist command who is still at large. (He was reported dead recently, and then the report was retracted.)

The last elections, with massive participation from the whole spectrum of the Iraqi population, gave a clear idea of the political as well as ethnic-sectarian balance of forces. Many of the Sunni Arabs in Iraq believe in the myth that their community is much larger than the 20 percent that they are commonly believed to be. The fact that you had a 58 percent participa-tion rate in the January 2005 election, which they—unlike the Shiites and the Kurds—boycotted massively, led them to conclude that they represent some 40 percent of the population, putting them on a par with the Shiites among Iraqi Arabs; and since the 20 percent of the Iraqis who are Kurds are also Sunnis, Sunni Arabs claimed therefore that there was a 60 percent Sunni majority in Iraq. Consequently, the fact that this was not confirmed by the outcome of the last elections is one of the main reasons why they mounted a protest against the balloting, denouncing the results as rigged, which was not very convincing. While there were naturally flaws and prob-lems of all sorts in the elections, which were certainly very far from being perfect, there was a consensus among observers that they were a true reflec-tion of the balance of forces in the country. Although they contested the results, I believe the Arab Sunni leaders are not so stupid as to subscribe to the myths accepted as true by their constituents. They have just tried to use this protest and their questioning of the results of the elections as a bargaining card to get what they want on the level of the government, threatening otherwise to refuse to grant legitimacy to the new Assembly or to allow a new government to be formed.

CHOMSKY: What's the Saudi attitude toward the elections?

ACHCAR: The Saudis supported the Arab Sunni participation in the election.

CHOMSKY: And they accept the outcome?

ACHCAR: They support the major Arab Sunni force that contested the elec-tions, especially the Islamic Party, which is the Iraqi branch of the Muslim Brotherhood. But how could the Saudis say that the elections were flawed when they don't even have a parliament of their own?

CHOMSKY: But did they give strong support or just keep quiet?

ACHCAR: On the face of it, they didn't interfere in the elections.

CHOMSKY: I would think they would be pretty concerned.

ACHCAR: They are, of course. In their public statements, the furthest they went were the statements by their minister of foreign affairs, Saud al-Faisal, in New York and elsewhere, saying that the United States clumsily brought the Shiites to power in Iraq and empowered Iran.

CHOMSKY: Officially?

ACHCAR: Yes, he said that publicly before the Council on Foreign Relations in New York.[34] And this led to angry Shiite reactions in Iraq, protesting against his interference. The Iraqi minister of the interior, a prominent SCIRI leader, had very harsh words against the Saudi minister and the Saudi ruling family, saying they are backward camel herders and so on. This was a moment of high tension between the two countries.

SHALOM: This was after December?

ACHCAR: Much earlier, it was in September 2005, even before the October referendum. That was not the first time the Saudis publicly expressed their worries about Iraq; the surprise was the public expression of concern about the fact that the United States is completely failing.

To return to the Iraqi elections outcome, we should note that those disputing it were not just the Arab Sunni political groups but also Allawi's coalition, a fact which shows that the United States was very much behind the protest. The UIA is trying to prevent any alliance against them among Allawi, the Arab Sunni groups, and the Kurds. The Sadrists, who represent a kind of Arab nationalist sensitivity among the Shiites, are trying to privilege a deal with the Arab Sunnis, because they consider the Kurds too closely linked to the United States, and they don't like them much anyway.

But the Sadrists have a big divergence with most of the Arab Sunni forces about the Baathists, since the Sadrists are very radically anti-Baathist. As I noted, their burning of the puppet of Saddam Hussein, along with those of Bush and Blair, during the huge demonstration of April 9, 2005, was quite telling in this regard. It's a complex situation, because the Sadrists who are harshly against the U.S. occupation are at the same time fully in favor of the de-Baathification procedure, which was launched by Chalabi. And that's their only area of agreement with Chalabi—smash the Baath! Recall the story of the al-Sadr family: Muqtada's father and two of his brothers were assassinated by the Baathists, and others among his relatives were atrociously tortured and killed by the Baathist regime. So it is easy to understand why Muqtada al-Sadr himself, and of course his constituency—the downtrodden sections of the Iraqi population that suffered most under Saddam Hussein's regime—hold such a deep hatred for the Baathists.

Given that, the Sadrists are selective in their Sunni alliances. They try to build friendly relations mainly with Arab Sunnis who cannot be suspected of Baathism. And that's the case mainly of the Muslim Brotherhood, who were persecuted under Saddam Hussein, and the Association of Muslim Scholars. There are dissonances within the UIA between the Sadrists; who want to ally with these people, and the SCIRI, which cozies up to the Kurdish Alliance, with which it has old ties. But it is unlikely that there could be a new government that is not based on a tripartite coalition. What remains to be seen is whether Allawi will be on board, and the United States is itself exerting all kinds of pressure in that regard. The U.S. ambassador, Khalilzad, has metamorphosed into a local player, like T. E. Lawrence before him in colonial history. He holds meetings with Allawi, and then joint meetings with Allawi and the Kurdish faction, plotting with some of the political forces against the others in a completely visible way—visible, that is, for the Iraqis, but not so visible abroad because the available media reporting is so superficial.

CHOMSKY: Khalilzad is presented as a neutral figure, trying to bring peace.

ACHCAR: And of course, he's not that at all. The UIA spokesmen pointed several times to the fact—they say it quite openly—that the United States is trying to impose its choices on them. This fact is public knowledge in Iraq. That's why Melvin Laird, who was the U.S. secretary of defense at the height of the Vietnam War from 1969 to 1973, was absolutely correct in writing, "Those who call the new Iraqi government [under Jaafari] Washington's 'puppet' don't know what a real puppet government is."[35] Laird knows; he knows very well indeed!

U.S. Policy in Iraq Today

SHALOM: You've touched on this, but what is the United States up to now in Iraq?

CHOMSKY: I think that's clear from first principles, even without knowing the details. From the point of view of U.S. policymakers it is highly imperative to impose something like the East European satellites or the Central American satellites. If they don't do that, it's catastrophe for the United States, for the reasons we talked about previously. They have to impose a real client government, maybe with some degree of internal autonomy, but that was true too of the East European satellites of Moscow. Actually, it was even true of occupied Europe under the Nazis. Vichy ran its own affairs;

the Nazis didn't run it. Vichy had plenty of popular support. The security forces were their own, the political forces were their own, and a lot of the intellectuals supported them, contrary to fantasies that were concocted later. Or in Central America: Once the United States crushed any popular forces, they could hand it over to traditional elites linked to the United States. Actually, with all the talk about postwar Germany and Japan, that's mostly fantasy, too. The United States literally crushed the resistance in Europe and Japan, and reimposed traditional structures, including fascist collaborators. In Germany, they didn't have that much control, but they did do it. In fact, it's not well-known, but it was George Kennan who in 1946 called for "walling [West Germany] off against Eastern penetration."[36] U.S. policymakers were afraid of the German labor movement, and they were afraid of the resistance. The resistance had plenty of prestige after the Second World War. And it was radical democratic, socialist, and communist and so on, and the United States had to crush it. They did that with great brutality in Italy and Greece and in various other ways in Germany, France, Belgium, and elsewhere. The United States continued to be involved in large-scale subversion of Italian democracy at least until the 1970s. We don't know after that because the record runs dry, but I presume it is still going on.

In Japan, General Douglas MacArthur, whose conception of democracy was probably what he learned in eighth grade civics, initially allowed the Japanese to actually begin to construct democratic institutions. The liberals in Washington were furious; they instituted what was called the "reverse course" in 1947, to undermine the labor movement, to restore the traditional elites, and basically to restore something like the traditional order. They succeeded in this, and it's been a one-party state ever since.[37]

And in Latin America, we don't have to go through the story, which is well-known, or should be. In the Reagan years, which is the origin of the current administration, it was just vicious brutality, far worse than anything that was happening in the East European satellites. But once they managed to crush domestic popular forces, then they put into power what's called a "legitimate government."

So we can expect the same in Iraq. Well-educated intellectuals, of course, will point to a paradox. Earlier we mentioned Thomas Carothers, the former official who found that all U.S. administrations—whose "sincerity," he assures us, remains beyond challenge—promote democracy only when to do so promotes U.S. strategic and economic interests. In his 2004 book on "democracy promotion" after the Cold War,[38] he says that he is afraid that in Iraq there'll be the same policy, despite the sincerity of the administration. Big surprise. Yes, we're sincere; even though we consistently do the opposite of what we say, it doesn't change the sincerity. So U.S. officials tried to prevent and then subvert the Iraqi elections, as Gilbert pointed out.

And it's still going on. And what they have to do is continue the strong line of continuity, somehow imposing a Salvador-like or Poland-under-the-Russians-like, or Vichy-like regime, in Iraq. But it won't be easy; Iraq is not El Salvador.

ACHCAR: I quite agree. The United States is in very, very deep trouble in Iraq presently. If you consider the situation in light of statements like "Defeat is no option"—because of the importance of what is at stake, for the reasons we explained—you get a sense of the depth of the trouble in which Washington finds itself. As Noam just said, they went there with blueprints inspired by Japan and Germany in 1945. Tellingly, Italy was not part of the picture, even though the situation in Iraq bears more resemblance to postwar Italy, in that in both countries there is a mass-based force—the Communist Party in Italy in 1945 and the UIA in Iraq today—that is not controlled by the United States and that is linked to an enemy state of the United States. In the case of Italy, it was the Soviet Union; in the case of Iraq, it's Iran. Yet, the balance of forces in Iraq is much worse than what they faced in Italy: In Italy, they could push the Communist Party aside, whereas it will be much more difficult to push the UIA aside in Iraq. Although U.S. officials deployed every possible stratagem in the last year, they have been unsuccessful. Khalilzad could not perform miracles. So the problem for Washington is, if things continue like this, what can be done? There are now worries expressed in Iraq, in articles and web postings, about the fact that the United States is contemplating a coup d'état. There was recently a scandal in Iraq—I don't know if it was reported here—when the minister of defense arranged for Allawi, who is no more than a member of the parliament, to review an army detachment as if he were the head of state. The Iraqi defense minister in the Jaafari government formed after the January 2005 elections had been designated by the United States. The UIA—the SCIRI, in that case—managed to secure for themselves the Interior Ministry after a lot of wrangling with the United States and its proxies. But the U.S. civilian and military occupation authorities insisted on keeping the Ministry of Defense under their control—they put their own nominee at the helm—and they tried to keep the army itself under their control, at least the officer corps. They reinstated a lot of former Baathists; this began when Allawi headed the interim government, and it has continued. The fact that the army is thus the preserve of the United States explains the rumors about a possible coup d'état by the Iraqi military.

The whole recent propaganda campaign waged by the United States about the acts of repression and torture by the minister of the interior, a member of the UIA and the SCIRI, is completely hypocritical, of course—real chutzpah. As when Allawi declared recently that human rights abuses, which he restricted to abuses by the Ministry of the Interior, are "worse" now than under Saddam Hussein[39]—coming from him! Aside from the obvious overexaggeration, this is an astonishing claim. I was bewildered to see how all sorts of commentators, from mainstream to antiwar sources, were happy to quote him uncritically; yet everyone should know that when Allawi headed the interim government with full U.S. support, he is the one who, with the help of U.S. "advisors," some of them trained in El Salvador or similar places, set up special police commandos and secret detention centers, and it's under him that torture by Iraqi forces, in the presence of U.S. advisors, started. So this is sheer hypocrisy again, trying to play to the Sunni Arab sectarian sentiments against the Shiites, and trying to give Western and U.S. public opinion a hint at how "bad" the Shiite forces are. That's where worries are justified, actually. Remember that Rumsfeld has been saying since 2003 that the United States would never allow an Iran-style government to rule Iraq. This is the U.S. equivalent of the Brezhnev doctrine of "limited sovereignty":[40] You have the sovereign right to do as you wish—as long as we approve.

The problem for the Bush administration is that even a coup is not really an option. True, they could probably rely on their control of many of the officers, but a large majority of the soldiers are Shiites and Kurds—whole Kurdish "Peshmerga" units have been integrated into the army. It's very unlikely that Shiite soldiers would abide by the orders of a U.S.-dominated command against their own people. And the Kurds won't fight alongside the Sunnis because the Kurdish Alliance is mainly concerned with getting hold of the city of Kirkuk with its oil, and their rivals there are not Shiites but mainly Sunni Arabs and Turkmen.

And that's why this whole situation is so very complex. The United States is used to black-and-white situations, relatively easy to handle. But the complexities of Middle Eastern society are such that it takes much cleverer people than the gang you've got in Washington presently dealing with the region.

They have a real problem, and the question is, what is U.S. strategy now? All they have is a very short-term strategy. They are intervening in the wheeling-and-dealing around the formation of the next government, trying to secure their positions. But do they have a long-term strategy? I really doubt it, because everything has collapsed. (CHOMSKY: They have a long-term goal.) Of course. As we've discussed, they want to control the energy resources of the region. The problem is, what means can they use to accomplish that goal? And I think they are in a state of real disarray about what to do. When you follow closely what they do on the ground, you have a sense of shifting policies; they are pragmatically trying to react to adversity, but the fact is, they have no good long-term strategy.

The problem is that all of this is truly worrying: The Iraqi vox populi is certainly right in being worried about U.S. plans, because the wounded beast could be terribly dangerous.

CHOMSKY: Did the Shiite population of Iraq view the torture allegations as an anti-Shiite move?

ACHCAR: Yes, the overwhelming majority of the Shiites considered that extremely hypocritical, and when they hear Allawi making these charges, they get especially irritated, because they really hate him, especially the Sadrists, who at the same time are the most anti-U.S. The SCIRI pretends that those people who were tortured, or "mistreated" as they would say, are actually "terrorists"; they see it as quite legitimate, all the more so that the U.S. military showed them the way. We are talking about a part of the world where there is unfortunately no real culture of human rights, where torture is quite common. And if the Bush administration, the self-proclaimed representative of Western civilization, considers torture legitimate in certain circumstances, why would you blame Iraqi Shiites or anybody there for thinking the same? So Washington's campaign against the Interior Ministry has been resented and very much perceived as a U.S. maneuver against the UIA. It is a fact that the armed forces of the Interior Ministry are full of organized partisans of the UIA factions—but not as a result of any "infiltration," since there is nothing secret about it. They very openly merged the militias into the armed forces, as was the official policy backed by the United States—except that instead of these militias coming thus under control, they have seized control of the Interior Ministry forces. The presence of SCIRI and Sadrist partisans, in particular, is very visible within these forces. Reporters will tell you that police cars often carry portraits either of Muqtada al-Sadr or of SCIRI leaders, so that, even visually, one can see how far the situation has gotten out of control for the United States.

What Should the Antiwar Movement Be Calling For?

SHALOM: What stance should the antiwar movement take on Iraq? What should it be calling for?

CHOMSKY: An occupying army or an invading force, which is what U.S. troops are, of course, has only two responsibilities. One is to provide reparations for the damage it has caused. And the other is to just let the people have their way. So we should follow the lead of the people of Iraq, whatever it is. And it's pretty clear what their view is. Unless there is overwhelming evidence of substantial support for a military occupation, it should just withdraw, and that should be the position of everybody here, in fact. And also—and you shouldn't overlook this—there should also be an effort to educate people as to what's at stake. People have to understand the stakes that are involved for the United States in maintaining some kind of client regime in Iraq. That's an enormously high-priority, completely bipartisan concern, with no difference between the Democrats and Republicans. Until that is understood by the antiwar forces, they're not going to be engaged significantly.

ACHCAR: I agree with the way Noam just defined responsibilities. But I think it is important to warn against another way of defining responsibilities in this case. There is a horrendous rule in certain societies that if a man rapes an unmarried woman, he's got to marry her. By analogy, that's what we are hearing from some circles in the United States: We've raped Iraq, we've got to marry her, "we've got to stay there, we have a responsibility." This view of responsibility should be fought very staunchly. It should be clear that if the Iraqis needed military help in stabilizing their country and building its institutions, the worst possible source for that help would be the United States and its troops. And so I would say, in the case of Iraq, the responsibility of the United States is mainly reparations, and to give any help needed, but not by being occupiers. Had Washington a real sense of responsibility and concern for Iraq, it should have withdrawn its troops long ago and provided the necessary logistics for UN troops or the like, if the Iraqi majority asked for them.

CHOMSKY: If I can just add something: That actually has been the majority view of the American public. According to polls, ever since the occupation of Iraq in April 2003, a large majority of the American population said, "Look, it's not our business; responsibility should be handed over to the United Nations for reconstruction, security, political transition, and so on." In fact, it tells you something about American democracy that these poll data weren't reported, even though there have been several such studies by well-established institutions. This was also the position Spanish voters took, in March 2004, when they were bitterly condemned for appeasement. They didn't call for pulling out troops; they said they have to be under UN supervision. That was the same position held by a large majority of Americans. Note two differences between Spain and the United States. One, although Spain is hardly a perfect democracy, its people knew what public opinion was. Here they don't, because it's not reported. And two, in Spain you could vote on the issue. Here, it's inconceivable. No such thing can come up in elections, which tells you something quite significant about the democratic deficit, so called, in the United States. But here's something that the popular movements in the United States *can* do. They already have popular opinion on their side. So they have to organize the public so that the gap between public policy and public opinion is reduced, so that public opinion has some influence on policy.

SHALOM: The United States, I think, would be quite happy if it could now hand off Iraq to UN troops, with Washington maintaining control through the Security Council.

CHOMSKY: That's the next point. It would have to be through the UN General Assembly. The Security Council is discredited by the veto.[41] And despite the talk, vetoes have been cast overwhelmingly by the United States. Since the mid-1960s, when Washington kind of lost control of the United Nations, the United States is far in the lead in vetoes, Britain is second, nobody else is even within shouting distance. So, yes, as long as the United States and Britain can veto freely, the Security Council is essentially meaningless. But they can't do that in the General Assembly.

ACHCAR: It's true; but at the same time, other countries also have vetoes. That's why Washington doesn't like to go through the UN Security Council, because it doesn't have the monopoly of the veto.

In any event, however, it's too late now. If the Bush administration had really cared about the Iraqi people—a big "if"—it would have done this from the start. After toppling the Baathist regime, it would have withdrawn U.S. troops and gotten them replaced with troops that the Iraqi population considered neutral—not troops of a country strongly suspected of competing for influence over Iraq and the region. It is the very presence of U.S. troops in Iraq that has led to the current situation, and the longer they stay there, the more chaotic the situation gets. As the U.S. military commander in Iraq, General George W. Casey, himself said at a hearing before the Senate Armed Services Committee, the very presence of U.S. troops "as an occupying force" is "one of the elements that fuel[s] the insurgency."[42] And that's a fact, because whatever the overall numbers in any polls concerning Iraq, one thing is certain: The overwhelming majority of one important component of the population, the Sunni Arabs, is violently against the occupation, and the fact is that it is precisely in their areas that the occupation is mostly concentrated and most busy killing people. The demand for the withdrawal of U.S. troops is based on this consideration; it's not out of some egoistic, selfish, uncaring, cut-and-run type of view. It is out of a true concern for the fate of Iraqis, because we know what the United States is trying to do in Iraq—as we've discussed at length here—and on the other hand, we know that the very presence of U.S. troops is inflaming the situation.

Of course, there was probably a majority of Iraqis who thought that they were in need of some help to build new institutions, otherwise former power networks with access to weapons and resources could threaten them; you could certainly find such a view among a majority of the Shiites. This is one thing, but it is entirely another to believe that they wanted the *United States specifically* to be that force. If so many of them demand a timetable for the withdrawal of foreign troops, rather than an immediate withdrawal, it is because they were given no choice other than what they consider, at best, to be the lesser evil. So I believe that what we as progressives have been doing from the start—building the antiwar movement—is exactly what should have been done and what still has to be done. Building up the antiwar movement around the demand of "Out Now!" puts pressure on Washington, and that will become decisive when the demand for withdrawal is expressed openly and publicly in Iraq by representatives of the majority. The pressure of the antiwar movement in the United States will be absolutely decisive then, whether as direct pressure through demonstrations and the rest, or as indirect pressure through public opinion polls, which is also taken into consideration by U.S. elites, of course.

Will Withdrawal Lead to Civil War?

SHALOM: How do you address the claim that a withdrawal will lead to a civil war on the Lebanon scale?

CHOMSKY: It's the wrong burden of proof. The burden of proof lies on those who want to maintain a military occupation. Anyone who wants to use force, in any situation, has a burden of proof. You don't have to prove that the failure to use force will be a disaster. You could say the same about the smallest social units—say, a family. Suppose a patriarchal, abusive father says, "Unless I beat my wife and my children, they'll be terrible." Well, it's not the burden of proof for people to prove this *won't* be the case; he has the burden of proof to show it *will* be. There's no further argument needed. And the same is true of any use of force, any form of violence, including military occupation, which is an extreme form of violence. There's a burden of proof on those who claim that it's necessary. Unless they can meet the heavy burden of proof to demonstrate that their use of violence, like occupation, is necessary, they just have to stop. There's nothing else to discuss. You don't have to get into an argument against it, any more than you do with an abusive parent.

ACHCAR: And to that we can add that it's very easy to prove, on the other hand, that the presence of the occupation troops is harmful. No one can give any guarantee whatsoever regarding the future of Iraq, whether U.S. troops stay in or get out. There is no certainty about what will happen next. There are different scenarios, different possibilities, from the worst-case scenario to the best-case scenario. But one thing is certain: The occupation has led Iraq to a very dangerous situation, and the longer the occupation continues, the worse it gets.

The November 2005 Cairo Conference of Iraqi political forces[43] has shown that, when brought together, Iraqi political forces across the spectrum can reach a consensus—when the U.S. ambassador, Zalmay

Khalilzad, is not there to "divide and rule" and manipulate. It's not a coincidence that the consensus reached at this conference was, in part, indirectly phrased against the United States, by making a distinction between legitimate resistance against an occupation in general and terrorist acts, thus reflecting a very common view in Iraq. Generally, people there refer to "the honorable resistance," by which they mean armed actions against U.S. and other occupation troops, as contrasted with "terrorism," which is all other violent actions. Surprisingly, though this is not the kind of news that is commonly reported here, even Jalal Talabani, the Kurdish leader who in 2005 was elected Iraqi president, has used this distinction. He has said on more than one occasion that we should be ready to have talks with the "honorable resistance." Thus the president of Iraq, who is supposed to be a staunch U.S. ally, says that those who confine their actions to attacking U.S. troops are honorable people. So there are enough indications of the possibility of some degree of consensus arising in the country.

It is worth thinking about the claim of General Casey that the presence of U.S. troops fuels the insurgency. Why would this be so? There is strong resentment against these troops, of course, but in addition it is the very presence of the U.S. forces that legitimizes the so-called insurgency. If the troops were withdrawn, there would be two likely consequences: First, the major source of legitimacy of the armed actions would vanish; and second, the Arab Sunni population would see itself faced with the prospect of a civil war. In fact, it is they, the Arab Sunnis, who have the most reason to fear a civil war, because they are no match in number to the Shiites, particularly the Shiites supported by Iran. Therefore, there is good reason to believe that the incentive would be very great for them to stop armed action if the occupation withdrew. And actually, the most influential Sunni group, the Association of Muslim Scholars, has repeatedly said just that: If the occupation announces a timetable for withdrawal—not even, if occupation troops *withdraw*—they will call on all groups to stop armed action.[44]

So, if you take all that into consideration and balance it against the actual results of the occupation, I think the case for the immediate withdrawal of U.S. troops is compelling. Let me repeat one more time that no one can be certain of how the situation will unfold, because it depends on so many variables: for example, on whether sensible, reasonable people, or fanatical ones, take over. Everything is possible. But why build a hypothetical worst-case scenario for withdrawal and consider it the most likely one, and conclude that U.S. troops should stay in, ignoring the actual worst-case scenario resulting from the ongoing occupation? This is, of course, an attempt at justifying the occupation, but it holds no water.

The Kurds in Iraq

SHALOM: What about the Kurds? How have they been treated in Iraq?

CHOMSKY: That's a horrible story. Under Saddam Hussein, it was a monstrosity—the 1988 Al-Anfal Campaign massacres, the gassing, and so on.[45] It is rather striking to bear in mind that, although these atrocities have been brought up as reasons for overthrowing Saddam Hussein, a terrible criminal, the United States and Britain did nothing about them at the time they occurred. In the United States, there were congressional efforts to condemn Iraq at the time of the massacres and the gassing, but the Reagan administration blocked them. They would not permit condemnation. Furthermore, the Reagan and Bush Sr. administrations continued to provide very significant armaments to Iraq after that, including means to develop weapons of mass destruction—missiles, biological weapons, and so on.[46] The Pentagon came up with a story about how it wasn't Saddam Hussein who carried out the gassing, it was the Iranians.[47] As far as Britain is concerned, the government of Prime Minister Margaret Thatcher basically ignored it—at the most, it might have said a few words. There were some parliamentary protests, but what's interesting is that the core of what is now "New Labour"—Tony Blair, Jack Straw, Geoff Hoon, and the rest[48]—didn't join the protests, apparently because they didn't really care that much about Saddam Hussein's crimes against the Kurds. Actually, that continued in a most amazing way. Jack Straw was the home secretary before he became foreign secretary and in the year 2001 he was in charge of asylum requests; an Iraqi who had been tortured in Saddam Hussein's prisons applied for asylum in Britain, but was rejected by Straw on the grounds that Iraqis "could expect to receive a fair trial under an independent and properly constituted judiciary."[49] I happened to be in England when this story appeared, and I thought for sure the government was going to collapse the next day. But there was not a whisper of reaction. I significantly underestimated the loyalty of the British educated classes.

But going back to the Kurds, U.S. and British officials just didn't care. That was the peak of the atrocities, but there's more.

Let me go back to the 1970s, when the United States was exploiting the Kurds as a weapon in their manipulations between Iraq and Iran. Washington supported a Kurdish rebellion against Iraq in 1974. But then Iraq made a deal with Iran the year after, at which point Iraq was free to massacre the Kurds, and the United States just stepped back. That's when Secretary of State Henry Kissinger is reported to have made his famous statement when he was criticized—that "covert action should not be confused with missionary work."[50] And the Kurds are taking a serious risk today if they rely on the United States or any other great power. They have consistently been sold out, right through their history. The great powers will use them for their purposes; but if the Kurds turn out to be opposed to their purposes, they'll pull the rug out from under them, and they'll get massacred again. It's a very risky course.

ACHCAR: Indeed. Kurdish history is full of such betrayals. The most prominent one was the way the shah of Iran stabbed them in the back in 1975 in order to get what he wanted from Saddam Hussein; the shah just abandoned them, and let Saddam Hussein crush them, with the United States standing by. People refer often to the gassing that Noam mentioned; Halabja, the city that was the main target of the chemical weapons attack, has become a kind of symbol—the Guernica of the Kurdish movement, one could say—but we also shouldn't forget 1991. (CHOMSKY: Absolutely.) In 1991, following the Gulf War, the United States gave a very clear green light to Saddam Hussein to crush the Kurdish rebellion, after the Shiite rebellion, after having encouraged both of them.

CHOMSKY: I can't believe the Kurds have forgotten that.

ACHCAR: They can't have forgotten, but the United States "redeemed" itself shortly after it allowed Saddam Hussein to very bloodily suppress the 1991 insurrection. You had an outcry in the West about the plight of Kurdish refugees held in camps on the Turkish side of the border. For the public, the outcry was for humanitarian reasons, but for the governments the worries were more about having to accept these refugees as immigrants, and grant them political asylum. (CHOMSKY: Because Turkey didn't want them.) Exactly, and then they would inevitably come to Europe. So the Turkish government and the European governments, obsessed with fighting immigration, told Washington, "You should do something about that, you should roll them back into Iraq." But the only way to get the refugees to go back to Iraq was by doing what was done then—that is, providing them with a kind of sanctuary, turning the Kurdistan part of Iraq into a sanctuary.

And this led to the fact that the Kurds, after 1991, have been the most privileged section of the Iraqi people, relatively speaking. They did not suffer the consequences of the embargo—they were even profiting from the transit over their territory of all kinds of trade and traffic into and out of Iraq, including illegal sales of oil. It's well-known that part of the Kurdish leadership, especially Massoud Barzani, head of the Kurdistan Democratic Party, got into dealings with the sons of Saddam Hussein, who were the great organizers of the "black market" and illicit trafficking in Iraq. And this also explains, incidentally, why the Kurdish leadership is much less dedicated to de-Baathification than the Shiite leaders are.

CHOMSKY: Do the Kurds maintain these old alliances with the former Baath networks?

ACHCAR: I don't think so; but the Kurdish leadership in general, and Barzani in particular, have a much more moderate position on the issue of the Baath and de-Baathification than do the Shiite leaders. That's why they can very easily adapt to Washington's present turn and cozy up to Arab Sunnis, including the former Baathists. They have no major problem with that. The people who are very insistent on de-Baathification are the Shiite Islamic leaders, especially Muqtada al-Sadr, but also the SCIRI.

CHOMSKY: I was watching the television news during the 1991 massacres, and my impression was that there was quite a difference in the coverage of the massacre of the Shiites and the driving out of the Kurds. The massacre of the Shiites, it seemed, could pass without such commentary, but not the Kurds. I remember watching television reports and the correspondent would say, "Look at these children, blue-eyed just like ours, how could this happen to them?" It seemed to me a straight racist difference, regarding Shiites and Kurds.

ACHCAR: Yes. There have been such comments—about Bosnian Muslims, too, by the way; really racist comments. But the media were prepared to show sympathy for the Kurds in any event because the Kurds are considered allies of the West, while the Shiites are identified with Iran. The insurrection in the south of Iraq was presented, very hypocritically, as being Iranian-inspired. In the West, you found the same claims of an Iranian role that the Baathists spread about the Shiite uprising, although it wasn't Iranian-inspired, much less Iranian-led.

CHOMSKY: Apart from these hideous moments, such as al-Anfal and so on, in the long term the Kurds' treatment in Turkey has been worse than in Iraq. I don't know if you would agree with that, Gilbert?

The Kurds in Turkey

ACHCAR: Aside from the very intensive war periods, yes. With regard to cultural rights and legal status, the Kurds fared better in Iraq than in Turkey. Not because the Iraqi Arabs are more democratically minded than the Turks; it's just a matter of the balance of forces. Iraq is the country where the balance of forces is most favorable for the Kurds, in terms of their size relative to the population. Their condition was better over time, and even the Baathist government, for tactical reasons, granted them autonomy rights in 1970, far more advanced than anything they have in Turkey. They also had greater cultural and linguistic rights in Iraq than in Turkey, where, until quite recently, you could not even mention the existence of Kurds— they were called "Mountain Turks." It's like former Israeli prime minister Golda Meir's statement on the Palestinians in 1969—that there was no such thing as Palestinians.[51] So, in that sense, the practical treatment, the harsh oppression and repression you had in Turkey, was a permanent feature; it was not something with ups and downs, as it was in Iraq, where you had periods where the situation in Kurdistan was even less repressive than in the rest of the country, and periods of war and of very harsh repression. In Turkey, this was a permanent feature until recently, when concessions were made by the Turkish government and the Turkish military under pressure from the European Union. And it's still, of course, very far from a condition of freedom for the Kurds in Turkey, not to mention self-determination.

CHOMSKY: I had a personal experience with that just a few years ago. I was giving talks in Diyarbakir in 2002—the unofficial Kurdish capital in southeastern Turkey. Turkish security forces were all over the place, not hidden, taking pictures. It was still pretty brutal then, not as bad as a couple of years earlier, but remnants of the 1990s terror were still there. After the talk that I gave, three young men came up and handed me a Kurdish-English dictionary, which was an act of just incredible bravery at that time, right in front of the Turkish security forces. It had an inscription that was rather moving, about how their wish was to be able to express their thoughts in their own language. It was a real police state. Actually, I was myself under investigation by the state security forces at the time, for the talk that I gave there, which they claimed fostered separatism. And I had just come from Istanbul where I had insisted on being codefendant in a trial with a Turkish publisher. He had published a translation of a book of mine that happened to have a couple of pages in it on the U.S.-backed atrocities against the Kurds in the 1990s, so he was put on trial for defaming the Turkish state. His lawyer and other lawyers urged me to insist on being a codefendant, which they figured would kill the trial, which indeed it did (though he was later back on trial for essentially the same charges).

The repression was still severe in 2002, but it was not like the 1990s. There is a very good index of the level of repression: It's the level of U.S. weapons transfers to Turkey. U.S. arms correlated very closely with the scale of the Turkish repression of the Kurds, so in the period of the counterinsurgency campaign, there were more U.S. weapons deliveries to Turkey than in the entire Cold War period, up until the onset of the insurgency in 1984. In fact, the single year of 1997 was the peak of the atrocities and also of Clinton's support. In that one year alone Clinton sent more arms to Turkey than it had received from 1950 to 1983.[52] Under the Clinton years, until 1997, Turkey was the leading recipient of U.S. military aid, outside of Israel and Egypt, which are in a separate category. By 1999, Turkey was essentially replaced by Colombia. The reason is that by 1999 the Turkish military had pretty well repressed the insurgency in southeastern Turkey, so they didn't need it that much. But the Colombian government, which is a hideous, atrocious, murderous government, had not yet repressed the insurgency in Colombia, so therefore they became the world's third-largest recipient (again, after Israel and Egypt) of U.S. security assistance grants in 1999.[53]

In the 1990s, the United States was providing 80 percent of Turkey's arms, including heavy equipment, while major atrocities were taking place. Large parts of southeastern Turkey were just wiped out, thousands of villages destroyed, the population driven out; nobody counts actually, but according to Kurdish sources, which are pretty careful, there were maybe up to 3 million refugees. The person who is now the mayor of Diyarbakir was the head of a Kurdish human rights group which estimated that there were 50,000 killed. You don't count your own atrocities, so these are all guesses; it's not like Srebrenica, where you try to find every bone you can and do forensic analysis because the killings were committed by someone else.

Recently, there was an article in the *New York Review of Books* by Stephen Kinzer, which was pretty accurate, about Turkish repression of the Kurds.[54] He was the *New York Times* reporter in Turkey while the atrocities were going on, yet he published virtually no reports on these crimes at the time. There was an occasional report now and then, maybe an op-ed by somebody from Human Rights Watch or something, but essentially no coverage. This changed, however, after what we were discussing before: After Turkey refused to go along with U.S. orders on the invasion of Iraq, articles suddenly started appearing in the *Boston Globe* and the *New York Times* and so on about the terrible Turkish repression of the Kurds, not mentioning the fact that their hero, Bill Clinton, had been paying for it and giving diplomatic support, and their own reporters weren't reporting it. Now all of a sudden, it became appropriate to condemn the Turks for these atrocities against the Kurds. It was shameful.

I should note that dissident Turks are extremely courageous. In fact, I have to laugh when I am in Europe and I hear people say the Turks aren't civilized enough to join the European Union. Turkish intellectuals—not marginal people, but the main writers, artists, journalists, academics, publishers, and so on—throughout this whole period were not only protesting the crimes against the Kurds and the draconian laws, but they were constantly engaged in civil disobedience, facing serious consequences. It's not much fun to be put in a Turkish prison, as many were.

To go back to the situation of the Kurds, some friends were able to take me to the slums in Istanbul where Kurdish refugees are living. It's really indescribable. We visited one family living in horrendous conditions where the family had been driven out of their village; the Turkish government said they'd permit them to go back if the father signed a statement saying that it was the Kurdish Workers Party (the PKK), the Kurdish guerilla movement, that burned down his village. He wouldn't sign because it was the Turkish army that did it, so his family was stuck there. And if you go to the Diyar-bakir area, people are living in caves they dug into the ancient city wall. In terms of the repression, things have improved. There was a time in an area of Turkey when they changed the traffic lights, because red/orange/green happen to be the Kurdish colors, which were prohibited. Since 1991 you can talk Kurdish without punishment, but you can't teach it yet in public schools. Quite recently, private newspapers, radio, and TV stations have been allowed to use the Kurdish language, but on public TV and radio, it's still very limited, like a half-hour a week of music.

The Kurds in Turkey have been treated hideously. This has improved under European Union pressure, and I should say the United States also wants them to clean up their act, so it isn't so violent, because Washington is very eager to have them enter the European Union for cynical reasons. But as Europe began to back off from support for the inclusion of Turkey in the EU, my impression is that conditions got harsher, maybe in reaction, the feeling being—well, if we're not going to be allowed into the European Union, why should we play their human rights game? And I think in Turkey, there is a feeling—and in my opinion it's not inaccurate—that the opposition to admitting Turkey into the EU is not because of its human rights record, but because of racism in Europe. They don't want Turks walking around on the streets. There's a real racist element in several European countries that just doesn't want Turks around and they'll use human rights if that's the way to keep them out.

ACHCAR: The Turkish government is very much under control of the Turkish military, which is very much worried by what is taking place in Iraq. And of course it is very unhappy that the de facto autonomy of Iraqi Kurdistan, which used to be considered a temporary condition due to exceptional circumstances between 1991 and 2003, is now becoming an institutionalized fact, even a constitutional fact. That's a major source of worry for the Turkish military and government, and the United States of course is very much taking Turkey's concerns into consideration.

In Iraqi Kurdistan there is an overwhelming majority, almost unanimity, in favor of independence, beyond the kind of constitutional status that they have already won. The Kurdish leaders, however, are telling their constituents that it's irresponsible to seek this goal, because the environment is such that the best option they have right now is to enjoy a de facto independence within the Iraqi state. And when they say the environment, they mean Turkey above all. But the truth is that, had they any kind of U.S. support for their national aspirations and legitimate right to self-determination, they could fulfill their people's aspiration. The Kurdish nation, like any other nation, should be allowed to exert its right to self-determination, including the right to secede and form its own state—secede from Iraq as well as from Turkey, Iran, and Syria, and create a unified Kurdish national state, which is the dearest aspiration of the Kurdish people (CHOMSKY: They constitute some 25 million people.) That's a nation carved up into oppressed minorities within larger states.

The problem is that Washington, of course, won't back the Kurds against Turkey, as the Turkish state is one of the pillars of NATO, a major ally at the time of the Cold War, and now a major part of U.S. strategy in the Middle East and the Caspian Sea Basin. And we come back therefore to what we mentioned earlier, that the Kurdish leaders keep betting on completely unreliable forces; and the United States is definitely a very unreliable source of protection for the Kurds.

CHOMSKY: Unfortunately the same is true of the Turkish Kurds. For all the very recent bitter, brutal, violent repression, which they know was backed by the United States, they're now putting their faith in the United States to somehow help them gain—not autonomy; they've given up hope for that, though they still probably want it—but just some recognition of Kurdish rights.

ACHCAR: But don't they pin more hopes on Europe, which makes more sense?

CHOMSKY: The ones who are more realistic know that U.S. power is overwhelming, and it's got to be the United States over Europe. Yet, they are happy that Europe is putting some pressure on Turkey, with the Copenhagen criteria on human rights[55] and so on.

Secession, Self-Determination, and Justice

SHALOM: Whenever you talk about a question of secession, it's simple enough if a nationality is the only group in a particular area. But obviously in part because of population transfers during the Saddam Hussein years, there are many contested areas with mixed populations.

CHOMSKY: Kirkuk is the main one.

SHALOM: Yes. So what would be a just solution to this kind of problem?

CHOMSKY: My own feeling, frankly, and the thing that aroused the antagonism of the Turkish state security system, is that the best solution would have some of the elements of the old Ottoman Empire. To say that is just anathema anywhere. Now of course no one wants to reconstruct the Ottoman Empire—it was brutal, corrupt, and everything else. But they had the right idea about how to treat the region: People were left alone. In the Ottoman Empire, to go from Cairo to Istanbul to Baghdad, you didn't have to pass any borders. The Greeks in the town ran the Greek areas, the Armenians ran the Armenian areas. It was a very complex mosaic anywhere you look in that region, essentially leaving people alone. One of the good things about the Ottoman Empire was that it *was* corrupt; it was too corrupt to figure out what was going on and do much about it. So yes, they were brutal, and occasionally they'd carry out some atrocity, but most of the time it worked; they just kind of left people alone. It's the right kind of solution for a complex mosaic of populations. In fact, I think the same is true in Europe; to impose the nation-state system in Europe required centuries of extreme violence. It's a very unnatural system—where do you draw the borders? Take Germany, Italy, or France. Not too long ago, there were lots of people who didn't know the national language, and you had to teach the national language in school. It's only very recently, at different rates in different countries, that there is general comprehension. But to try and impose a national state system on complex societies, which have all kinds of local, regional, ethnic, religious, and other cultural commitments, is just a brutal phenomenon. That's one of the reasons why Europe was one of the most savage places in the world for several hundred years. When the Europeans conquered the rest of the world, they tried to impose the same system—also insanity from the point of view of the populations.

Many of the most horrendous conflicts going on around the world now are reflections of the imposition of the nation-state system on complex societies where it just doesn't fit. If you put people who have nothing to do with each other in the same state, and some of them have to gain control, then they may massacre the others. Some of the major conflicts in the world are in areas that the British Empire alone controlled—like India-Pakistan, or Palestine, for that matter. These are largely residues of efforts to impose a crazed nation-state system on complex mosaics of societies, where it doesn't fit.

One good thing that's happening in Europe now is that, along with the centralizing tendencies of the European Union, there's a lot of devolution. I was in Barcelona a couple of years after Franco's dictatorship was overthrown, and walking through the streets, you couldn't hear a word of Catalan. You wouldn't have known that it was the language of the people; I knew only from the literature. I went back a couple of years later, however, and all you could hear was Catalan. It came out, it was in the woodwork; now there's substantial Catalan autonomy, and the same in the Basque country, to an extent in Asturias, and there's pressure for it in Galicia and so on. It's even happening in Britain, where there's a limited devolution to Wales and Scotland, which I think is a good thing. It's probably much the same throughout most of Europe. So if you ask, what's the *best* system for Kurdistan? I think it would be something like that: Erode the nation-state system altogether and allow more regional and local autonomy, even within the same city. It can work, and it can work in an amicable way, much more so than the nation-state system.

ACHCAR: Ideally, I agree with Noam. Of course, however, the present situation is not ideal, and we should consider it perfectly legitimate that the Kurds aspire to a nation-state, all the more so given that it is an aspiration for the reunification of a nation divided among other states. But in a sense, the Iraqi Kurdish leaders are right to believe that for Iraqi Kurdistan, under present conditions, the best option is very extended autonomy within a federal state. Otherwise, you would get a Kurdish enclave that would be dependent on foreign protection. (CHOMSKY: It's landlocked, after all; there's no access to the water.) Indeed. And that would be a very dangerous situation for the Iraqi Kurdish people and certainly would not be the best option for them.

The problem of Kirkuk is probably the most explosive question in Iraq, at least potentially. People are focused on the Sunni-Shiite issue, but that's actually easier to settle than the question of Kirkuk, which is very volatile and quite complex. Kirkuk is a city that, a few decades ago, was an ethnic melting pot, with Arabs, Kurds, and a large Turkmen community, some say a majority. That's why Turkey threatens to intervene and treats Kirkuk as if it were a Turkish protectorate. But it's true that the development of the oil industry led to a massive immigration of workers from the Kurdish mountainous area into Kirkuk, and Kirkuk then turned into a city with a Kurdish majority. Later on, Saddam Hussein tried to reverse that trend and "Arabize" the city, as indeed he tried to "Arabize" whole parts of Iraqi Kurdistan, by various measures of ethnic cleansing and relocation of populations. So we're left with a very complex situation. The fear is that the Kurdish leaders may behave very aggressively on the issue of Kirkuk, and use their military superiority over the other Iraqi communities in order to try to get full control over the city. That would be very short-sighted: If you try to settle this question by force, you will have a burning problem for decades and that would be quite disastrous. So in that sense, this ideal solution that Noam was pointing to should be implemented, at least in a situation like that of Kirkuk. There should be some compromise, including an agreement on the proper share of the overall Iraqi oil income to be granted to Kurdistan. This principle is inscribed in the constitution that was adopted in October 2005: It stipulates that the oil revenues will be distributed "in a fair manner in proportion to the population distribution in all parts of the country" (article 109),[56] which is a sound principle.

SHALOM: But that's *old* oil income, right?

ACHCAR: It's ambiguous; there have been various interpretations of the phrasing of the constitution on this issue. The principle that the oil income should be distributed over the country in proportion to the population is indeed related to "current fields." But, on the other hand, the constitution states quite unambiguously, "Oil and gas are the ownership of all the people of Iraq in all the regions and governorates" (article 108). That actually favors the Iraqi Kurds, since the bulk of Iraqi oil is in the south. They would gain on balance, if they got a proportionate share of the oil income; that would be better for them than to try to take hold of Kirkuk at a terrible cost. So there should be a way to find a sensible solution and compromise for that burning issue. But it so happens that the United States, which would have been in the position to use its good offices for that purpose, has not been seriously doing anything of the kind, because Washington prefers to keep this issue alive as part of the "divide and rule" strategy that it is now applying as its last resort in Iraq, after having suffered so many setbacks. Let's only hope that reason will prevail in Iraq, and that some peaceful compromise will be reached on this issue, as on the other divisive issues.

Syria

SHALOM: There has been talk of the possibility of U.S. military action against two other Middle Eastern states, Syria and Iran. How do you assess U.S. policy toward Syria?

CHOMSKY: The U.S. position with respect to Syria has always been highly opportunistic. Take Syria and Lebanon. The United States welcomed the Syrians into Lebanon in 1976, as did Israel, tacitly. Because the Syrian task at the time was to massacre Palestinians, that was just fine, and there was no particular opposition to their being there. In 1990, Bush Sr. was very favorable to the Syrians staying in Lebanon, because he wanted to bring Damascus into the anti-Iraq coalition. Over the years, however, Washington has turned to a more natural stand. Syria does not follow U.S. orders. It's a little bit like Serbia was in the 1990s. Strobe Talbott, who was high up in the Clinton administration, agreed that the main reason for the Kosovo war and the bombing of Serbia was, of course, not humanitarian, but that Serbia was the last outpost in Europe not accepting integration into the market system.[57] What he meant is, they're not following orders, they're not joining the neoliberal consensus. And Syria's kind of like that. It's a rotten tooth. In most countries the leadership just bows to the United States. Syria doesn't. It's a horrible leadership and has done all kinds of terrible things, but that's not the reason Washington opposes it.

We can see how serious U.S. criticisms of Syria are, for its human rights violations, just by looking at the history. There is a list of states that support terror, which means mostly states the U.S. doesn't like for some reason, and in 1994, Clinton offered to take Syria off the list of states supporting terror if they accepted the U.S.-Israeli proposals on the Golan Heights that Israel had seized in the 1967 war. Syria wanted to get their territory back, so they didn't accept the deal, and so they stayed on the list of states supporting terror. That tells you all you have to know.

In 2004, there came an opportunity to get rid of this rotten tooth, so together with France, U.S. officials rammed through a UN resolution to get Syrian troops out of Lebanon and now they are pressing hard to overthrow the Syrian regime—which is a good idea, but not for their reasons. Their reasons are the same reasons they bombed Serbia: It was not obedient.

Will the United States do anything? My feeling is that it's more likely to attack Syria than Iran, but I don't really think it is likely to attack either. Syria, however, is more likely than Iran. For one thing, Syria is much weaker. Iran is dangerous to attack, Syria probably isn't. Furthermore, I think Israel might like to do it, and they no doubt have the military force to do it easily; it wouldn't cost them much. So that's a possibility, although I have a feeling it's kind of remote.

The Syrian regime is an awful regime. The Syrians ought to have an opportunity to get rid of it, but outside forces are just going to make matters worse. And the reasons why the United States is anti-Syrian are not attractive. France too, as far as I can tell.

ACHCAR: You're quite right. When one considers the positions of the U.S. government, one should always put them in historical perspective in order to grasp their meaning. And the question is, why did Washington suddenly become so concerned with the Syrian presence in Lebanon in 2004, and not before?

Let's look at the history of this issue: First, the Syrian army entered Lebanon with a green light from the United States and from Israel, in 1976, at a time when the allies of them both, the Christian right-wing forces in Lebanon, were on the verge of defeat at the hands of an alliance of Palestinian forces and the Lebanese left. (The latter was, more accurately speaking, a coalition of left-wing and communal forces, led by Kamal Jumblatt, who combined left-wing pretensions with his status as communal and feudal leader of the Druze sect and peasantry.) This alliance of forces was clashing with the right-wing militias, and was at the point of inflicting a severe defeat on them, when Syria was given a green light to intervene and repress it. The Syrian army engaged in very violent clashes against the Palestinian and Lebanese left forces for several months until a Saudi-sponsored agreement was reached, institutionalizing the Syrian military presence in Lebanon. To be sure, when one says Saudi-sponsored, it also means U.S.-backed. The agreement called for the Syrians along with other Arab forces to reestablish peace and law and order in Lebanon. The honeymoon between Washington and the Syrian regime did not last long, however: In 1977, the right-wing Zionist Likud Party came to power in Israel, and shortly thereafter, Egyptian president Anwar al-Sadat paid his historic visit to Israel, inaugurating a process that would lead ultimately to the Egyptian-Israeli peace agreement. The Syrian regime felt ostracized, and tensions resumed between Damascus and Washington. But at that point, there was no campaign at all for Syrian withdrawal from Lebanon, because Washington still considered the Syrian presence and control in Lebanon as a lesser evil compared with the likely resumption of Palestinian expansion in alliance with Lebanese left-wing and Muslim forces.

It was believed for a while that the Israeli invasion of Lebanon in 1982 had settled the problem, in that the bulk of the Palestine Liberation Organization, the PLO, was expelled from Lebanon, and an Israel-friendly president, first, and then a U.S.-friendly one were put in power. The Israeli invasion reduced the Syrian military presence to a limited part of Lebanon, and the Israeli military presence was depicted, until it ended in 2000, as a direct counterweight to the Syrian one. So it served Israel in some way that the Syrians remained in Lebanon: The two foreign forces could be put on a par. But the whole attempt at building a U.S.-controlled government in Lebanon collapsed in 1984 and, with it, the attempt at concluding a Lebanese-Israeli treaty. There was an uprising in the Muslim-majority parts of the country, and the situation turned sour again, from the point of view of U.S. interests. And again, a green light was given to Syria to reestablish the kind of control over the situation that existed previously by deploying its troops to parts of Lebanon from which it had been driven out by the Israeli invasion, including the capital, Beirut.

This situation continued until Iraq's 1990 invasion of Kuwait, when Syria joined the U.S.-dominated coalition in the war against Iraq. This is often forgotten now, but Syria under the dictatorship of Hafez al-Assad became one of those Arab allies in the 1991 Gulf War about whom the United States boasted. And the reason why suddenly in 2004, the United States—through UN Security Council Resolution 1559,[58] cosponsored with France—became very much concerned with kicking Syria out of Lebanon was the fact that the Syrian regime did not join the second war against Iraq in 2003 and took, on the contrary, a hostile position toward that war, in both cases matching the position of its big brothers in Moscow. In sharp contrast with what it did in 1990–91, Damascus this time not only did not join the U.S.-led coalition but, in vehemently denouncing the invasion of Iraq, went way beyond the semi-neutral attitude that other Arab regimes took. And that's why the United States decided to punish the Syrian government. To that should be added the fact that the United States started using the Lebanese situation as a means to exert pressure on Syria to get Damascus to help U.S. forces control the Iraqi-Syrian border and prevent the infiltration of Arab fighters.

So basically, Washington's attitude is purely instrumental. It doesn't stem from any real concern for the Lebanese population.

CHOMSKY: Why is France involved?

ACHCAR: That's a more complex issue, connected with French disappointment with Syria. They have made some requests—including economic
ones—that were not accepted by the Syrians. Another factor was the
very close—and, some would say, very profitable—relationship between
French president Jacques Chirac and former Lebanese prime minister and
multibillionaire Rafic Hariri, who had broken with Damascus after many
years of close collaboration and was assassinated on February 14, 2005.
And behind Hariri stood his patrons—the Saudi kingdom, of course, with
whom France has a much greater interest than with Lebanon. So Paris's
attitude, too, was not out of any real concern for the Lebanese population.

Washington has used Lebanon and the Hariri assassination as a bargaining card to obtain specific behavior or collaboration from Damascus
concerning Iraq, and also concerning one of Israel's chief concerns: the
Lebanese Hezbollah, which the United States is demanding must disarm.
The truth of the matter is that it was not Washington's pressure that was
decisive in getting Syrian troops out of Lebanon but, rather, the mass
demonstrations and mass mobilization that followed the assassination
of Hariri.[59] That's quite clear. UN Security Council Resolution 1559 was
adopted well before that and was just rejected by both the Lebanese and
the Syrian governments.

I believe that the United States is not considering, to any significant
degree, military action against Syria. The incentive for an attack is very
limited. Nothing like the invasion of Iraq is possible against Syria in any
event. The United States—bogged down as it is in the Iraqi quagmire—is
simply unable to do anything of the kind presently. That would be an act of
sheer madness. The pressure that they are maintaining on Damascus is in
order to obtain what they want: collaboration on both Iraq and Hezbollah.

Nor do I think that Israel has an incentive for military action against
Syria. On the contrary. There were actually worries expressed in Israel
over U.S. action against the Syrian regime, essentially saying, calm it down,
we're not interested in an overthrow of this regime, because we don't want
to have an Iraq on our borders. The Israelis prefer the Assad regime, which
controls the situation. They know pretty well that the Syrian-Israeli demar-
cation line is Israel's safest border. They definitely want the Syrian government to stop supporting Hezbollah, of course, or to exert pressure on
Hezbollah in order to get it to relinquish its arms, but they are not interested in toppling the Syrian government. And the fact is that even less than
in Iraq, Washington commands no minimally credible alternative to the
Syrian regime. In the case of Iraq, you had at least the whole coalition of
the opposition organized by Chalabi. Some of them were not to the taste
of Washington, but nevertheless the Bush administration could still buy

into what Chalabi told them about his clout in Iraq. But the U.S.-backed Syrian equivalent of Chalabi that you see in the U.S. media is even more a nonentity in Syria than Chalabi was and is in Iraq.

CHOMSKY: What about this former Syrian official in Paris—is he appealing to anybody real?

ACHCAR: You are right to point to that. What Washington could have hoped for was a split within the Syrian regime. And as a matter of fact, the regime has lost two prominent members: the former vice president, Abdul Halim Khaddam, now living as a defector in Paris, and the minister of interior and former commander of Syrian troops and intelligence in Lebanon, Ghazi Kanaan, who allegedly committed suicide. Both of these people are known to have had close links with Hariri. And close links with Hariri were always very profitable, whether for Chirac or whomever. The United States and the Saudis might have banked on these people taking over from within, but the key guy "committed suicide," and the other is out of power and out of the country. Unless there is a surprise that cannot be foreseen, at least from what I know, I believe that the United States has no serious alternative in Syria. I think that Washington shares the Israeli concern that if Syria became a chaotic country, that would very much worsen the overall situation created in Iraq.

Iran

SHALOM: What about U.S. policy toward Iran? What are the prospects for military action there?

CHOMSKY: The case of Iran is more complicated. Iran has to be punished because it broke free of U.S. control in 1979. The U.S. picture of Iran—as portrayed in media commentary and so on—says nothing ever happened in Iran up until 1979. The installation of the shah in 1953, that kind of thing, doesn't matter. In fact, there was recently an amazing review in the *New York Times* of Robert Fisk's new book,[60] by Geoffrey Wheatcroft, a sensible historian-journalist.[61] He wrote a pretty favorable review of the book, but he ended up by saying that Fisk is much too critical of the U.S.-British coup that overthrew the parliamentary government of Iran. He knows that, he says, because his neighbor is a very nice British gentleman who was involved in the coup and assured him it was done for good reasons. It's mind-boggling that that could even appear in a newspaper! Anyway, the history's all gone.

There was a good study of the press coverage of atrocities in Iran.[62] From 1953 to 1979, when Iran was ruled by the pro-U.S. shah, all the torture, massacres, and everything else got essentially no coverage at all. Starting in

1979, after the shah was overthrown in a popular revolution, all of a sudden there was huge coverage of the atrocities in Iran.

In any event, Iran broke ranks with the United States in 1979, and this is a crime for which it has to be punished. And it goes way beyond rational state interests. As with Cuba, it's the Mafia mentality: You can't allow disobedience to exist; it's too dangerous because other people might get the idea that they can be disobedient as well. So Iran's going to have to be punished for that act of disobedience. The United States supported Iraq in the Iran-Iraq war partly because they just wanted both sides to slaughter each other, but they also wanted to make sure that Iraq won. When it looked like perhaps they weren't going to win, the United States just entered the war on Iraq's side: reflagging the ships, shooting down the Iranian airliner, and so on. The U.S. actually supported Iraq to such an extent that Iraq was given a privilege that no other country has, except Israel: They were able to attack an American naval vessel and kill a few dozen American sailors and get away with it.[63] Who can do that? They could get away with it because it was part of the attack on Iran. After that, it just continues.

Now the United States is trying very hard to isolate Iran and to carry out subversion, which is maybe possible in that country. It's a complex, ethnically mixed society with a very repressive government. Maybe the United States can stimulate some kind of internal uprising. And of course they want to isolate it economically.

It's interesting that Washington is having success at this in Europe. Europe is sufficiently intimidated by the United States that major European corporations, such as BP and Krupp-Thyssen, are pulling out of Iran. They just don't want to step on the toes of the United States. China, on the other hand, has not gone along. Part of the reason the United States is so angry at China is that they can't be intimidated. India is a mixed story. As we've mentioned, despite a lot of U.S. pressure, India has maintained a pipeline project from Iran. On the other hand, it went along with the United States in voting against Iran at the International Atomic Energy Agency, at least partly in return for U.S. support of its civilian nuclear energy program.[64] So they're kind of on the fence.

But there is a major effort to isolate Iran. Iran has been under terrific threat. According to U.S.-British standards, Iran should be carrying out terrorist acts in the United States right now, in what they call anticipatory self-defense. People make a fuss about Iranian president Mahmoud Ahmadinejad's grotesque statements about the Nazi Holocaust, but suppose that he were saying—credibly—we're prepared to bomb the United States and Israel and carry out terrorist acts there? Of course, that would be the end of Iran, but that's precisely what the United States and Israel, for years now, have been openly saying about Iran. There are claims that about 10 percent of the Israeli air force is in eastern Turkey at American bases there, flying reconnaissance at, or maybe over, the Iranian border—not to learn anything, just as a threat, saying "we're here."[65] Israel is a nuclear state, everybody knows that. It's actually a little country, but it's a U.S. offshoot. According to the head of research and development for the Israeli Defense Forces, its air force and armored forces are larger and more sophisticated than any NATO power apart from the United States.[66] And to beef it up further in the last year or two, the Bush administration has been sending them over a hundred advanced jet fighter-bombers, equipped with what the Hebrew press in Israel calls "special weaponry"[67]—that's for the ears of Iranian intelligence, meaning probably nuclear weapons or something. I don't know if it's true or not; bunker busters and so on. The dispatch of new aircraft apparently didn't get reported here, but you can be certain that Iranian intelligence hears it—it's in the Israeli press and military journals. It's presumably intended to rattle them, to say yes, you're under serious threat.

Are they *really* under threat of attack? Here one can only speculate. My speculation is, probably not; I think the United States would not attack them, for a number of reasons. For one thing, because they're not defenseless; it's ridiculous to attack anyone if they're not defenseless. Every schoolyard bully knows that. You attack people if they can't defend themselves. And Iran can. It can't defend itself from invasion, but it can respond in various ways. For one thing, it can cause enormous trouble for the United States in Iraq, where the U.S. is in plenty of trouble already. And it can do other things. It probably has missiles. Second, if you're going to attack a country, you don't announce it for three years so that they can scatter their targets and prepare retaliation and so on. It doesn't make a lot of sense.

So why is the United States making all these threats? My suspicion is that the reason is partly to isolate them, as is succeeding with Europe—getting the Europeans to back away—and partly to just rattle the leadership. If you can rattle the leadership, they'll become even harsher, which will mean more internal opposition, more options for internal subversion, and maybe sooner or later they would weaken enough so that you could attack them. And there are plenty of opportunities for subversion—Azeris, Kurds, others, or just young people who don't want the repression anymore, and so on. So my guess is that that's what's going on. It's speculation; we don't know internal planning.

But these speculations are based on the assumption of rational planning. It's possible we have what Gilbert calls the wounded-beast phenomenon. If U.S. policymakers are desperate enough, then talk about rational planning is out the window. And then you don't know what they're going to do.

ACHCAR: Regarding Iran, I would put it in reverse compared with what I said about Syria. The likelihood of military strikes against Iran is far higher in my view. First of all, let me clarify that I am not speaking about any kind of Iraq-like invasion, even though Iran, unlike Syria, definitely has important resources: oil and gas. In addition to the Iraqi quagmire, which prevents the United States from invading any other country in the region, especially one the size of Iran, there is the fact that the Iranian regime has a much more important social base than what Saddam Hussein ever had, and that makes it a much tougher nut to crack than Iraq. When you see all the difficulty the United States is facing in Iraq, by no stretch of the imagination can one think of a U.S. invasion of Iran—that would be sheer madness. So that's not what I'm referring to. But as I see it, the fact that Washington inadvertently ended up empowering Iran-friendly forces in Iraq makes it more urgent for the United States to tame the Iranian regime or get rid of it. The Iranian regime is in a much stronger position now than it was before 2003; it's much more powerful. It's been strengthened by U.S. action, unintentionally. That's a real problem for the Bush administration, so they tend to believe that the key to their own control of Iraq is Tehran. Of course, that's right. In addition, there is genuine concern in Washington, and in Israel, needless to say, about Iran going nuclear.

Israel, as is well-known, is a major nuclear power, while none of its regional opponents possesses nuclear weapons, so it has the monopoly of nuclear deterrence and blackmail. It doesn't want any other state in the area to balance this monopoly. That's quite logical. The same goes for the United States, not in the sense that Washington fears that Tehran would launch a nuclear attack on the United States—this would be purely suicidal for the Iranians, or any other state for that matter. The reason Washington fears the Iranians turning into a nuclear power is that this could give Tehran a very effective deterrent or counterdeterrent in the Gulf area and the Middle East versus Israeli or U.S. forces. Beyond that, Iranian acquisition of the nuclear bomb would greatly enhance the prestige of Tehran as a leader of anti-U.S., anti-Israel, Muslim public opinion. Iran is very much working on that. Noam mentioned the grotesque statements of Ahmadinejad about the Holocaust and Israel: On the face of it, you'd say, this guy is deranged. The truth is, these were calculated statements through which Iran is enhancing its position in the Muslim world and especially toward Sunni public opinion. This happens at a time when the United States is trying to isolate Iran, and Washington's Arab allies are trying to whip up anti-Shiite Sunni feeling. You've had many statements to that effect: Saudi statements, Jordanian statements, the king of Jordan warning of a Shiite crescent, etc. So Ahmadinejad's speeches are part of Tehran's countermaneuver, outbidding all the Arab regimes in the rejection of Israel. And the fact that one of the Iranian president's provocative statements was made from Mecca, where he was attending a conference of Islamic states in December 2005, is very meaningful in this respect. Such statements surely strike a chord with the

Wahhabi religious institution in the Saudi kingdom. More important, the head of Palestinian Hamas went to Tehran and expressed full support for the Iranian regime, and even the leader of the Egyptian Muslim Brotherhood came out in support of Iran's position.

CHOMSKY: On these statements about the Holocaust?

ACHCAR: Yes, on these statements. That constituted a major political gain for Iran. So these statements are calculated as part of the strategy of the Iranian regime to increase its appeal to the Muslim masses, the overwhelming majority of whom are Sunnis. So when you take all that into consideration, the likelihood that either the United States or, more possibly, Israel would launch strikes on Iranian nuclear facilities is quite high. Iranian territory is very closely monitored by all kinds of electronics—and the United States has developed various categories of the "bunker buster" weapons that Noam mentioned.

CHOMSKY: I'm not actually sure that they work. And they actually don't have nuclear bunker busters; they haven't gotten the funding for them. They have some kind of conventional deep-penetration weapons.

ACHCAR: But whipping up this issue of Iran gives them an argument for that.

CHOMSKY: It's interesting; for all this whipping up, they haven't been able to get funding. Congress doesn't want too much proliferation; they know there's going to be a reaction.

ACHCAR: Well, in any case, I think the likelihood of strikes on Iran, whether by the United States or Israel, is quite serious. I am not saying they are certain, but we should not consider them improbable.

CHOMSKY: My guess is different, but it's all speculation.

Let me comment on the issue of Iranian nuclear weapons. I don't know for sure, but I suspect the Iranians are working on nuclear weapons. One of the leading Israeli military historians, Martin Van Creveld, recently had an article in the *International Herald Tribune*,[68] in which he said that of course he didn't want the Iranians to have such weapons, but if they're not developing them, they're insane. Any state that's under that kind of threat would be developing a nuclear deterrent. If they are developing nuclear weapons, it's not for use—they can't use them: They'd be instantly destroyed. But it's a deterrent. They've got U.S. forces on two borders. They're surrounded by nuclear armed states—Israel is a major nuclear power, the United States and Israel are openly threatening them with destruction and attack. So my guess is that they likely are developing a nuclear deterrent.

However, if one is seriously concerned about Iranian nuclear weapons, there are simple ways of increasing the probability that they won't develop them. For one thing, if the pressures against Iran were relaxed, they would have much less incentive to create a deterrent.

There are deeper issues having to do with proliferation. One thing on which I happen to agree with the Bush administration is that the Nuclear Non-Proliferation Treaty[69] does need revision. Article IV of the treaty allows countries to develop civilian nuclear power freely, and so far there isn't any evidence that Iran is going beyond its treaty obligations. However, that provision is too weak. It made sense in 1970 when it was introduced. But with the improvement in technology since, the gap between nuclear power and nuclear weapons has been significantly reduced, so that by now when you develop nuclear power, you're much closer to nuclear weapons than you were in 1970, and that's a serious issue. There are ways of addressing this problem, and they've been on the table for years. The basic problem is the enrichment of fissile materials, materials that can be used for nuclear weapons. If you could stop or control the development of fissile materials, it would essentially end the proliferation problem. It wouldn't end the problem of existing nuclear weapons—all the nuclear states are in violation of the treaty, the United States more than any. In fact, the United States rejects some provisions of the treaty. But putting that aside, if you could control fissile material production, that would end proliferation. There was a proposal a couple of years ago from Mohamed ElBaradei, the director-general of the International Atomic Energy Agency, to put enrichment to the level of nuclear weapons under international control. That would essentially end the proliferation problem. But the proposal was dead in the water because the United States wouldn't hear of it. There was a UN decision, back in 1993 or so, to enact a verifiable fissile material cutoff treaty to just terminate the production of enriched fissile materials up to the level of nuclear weapons, and to have international supervision, verification, and control on that. The United States has blocked negotiating on that treaty for a long time. But it did come up for a vote in November 2004. It's no exaggeration to say that the future of the species depends on this. If this isn't enacted, there's inevitably going to be a nuclear war of some sort. It came to a vote in the First Committee of the General Assembly in November 2004, and the vote was 147 to 1, with 2 abstentions. The United States voted no. Israel abstained, reflexively, since it can't vote against the United States. The other abstention was Britain. The British ambassador at the UN meeting explained that Britain is in favor of the treaty, but this version had "divided the international community."[70] It divides the world 147 to 1, so therefore Britain couldn't go along with it. I never saw a report of this, though it was probably one of the most important votes in history. That means that there is no ban on production of these materials for nuclear weapons. If there really were a concern about proliferation, there's a way to stop it. But the United States won't accept it, because it means that U.S.

facilities are going to have to be monitored, and that they will not accept. And Britain just doesn't disobey the master. The others did disobey, but mainly because they know nothing is going to happen—if there had been a chance of it actually being implemented, they probably wouldn't have voted for it either. As long as the U.S. blocks it, then there's no chance.

ACHCAR: In order for any fight against nuclear proliferation in the Middle East to be really effective, it must address the issue of the Israeli nuclear arsenal. You can't turn a blind eye to it and threaten the neighboring states when they seek to reinstate strategic equilibrium. The only working alternative to proliferation in the region is to turn it all into a nuclear-free zone.

5 The Israel-Palestine Conflict

The Legitimacy of Israel

SHALOM: There has been much debate regarding the legitimacy of the Israeli state. To what extent is Israel a legitimate, or an illegitimate, state?

CHOMSKY: I don't think that the notion of legitimacy of a state means very much. Is the United States a legitimate state? It's based on genocide; it conquered half of Mexico. What makes it legitimate? The way the international system is set up, states have certain rights; that has nothing to do with their legitimacy. Every state you can think of is based on violence, repression, expulsion, and all sorts of crimes. And the state system itself has no inherent legitimacy. It's just an institutional form that developed and that was imposed with plenty of violence. The question of legitimacy just doesn't arise. There is an international order in which it is essentially agreed that states have certain rights, but that provides them with no legitimacy, Israel or anyone else.

ACHCAR: We could put the question in another way. If one tries to define the origins of the Israeli state, the formula that comes to mind is the title of a famous piece by Maxime Rodinson, *Israel: A Colonial-Settler State?*[1] It points to a fact that is built into the history of the state; of course, one could say the same of many states. (CHOMSKY: Most.) But then you have the factor of time: Israel is a very recent colonial-settler state, and it is based on the expulsion of the original inhabitants of Palestine, not on genocide like the United States. Ironically, states based on genocide are in a more comfortable position. Not from the moral point of view, of course, but from the political point of view, in terms of the existence of a challenge to their legitimacy. In the case of expulsion, those expelled continue to challenge the state's legitimacy; in the case of genocide, those who might be challengers have been wiped out. And to be sure, all states are based on violence, but cases like the apartheid state in South Africa, or Algeria at the time of

DOI: 10.4324/9781003531753-5

French domination, cannot be put in the same category as, let's say, states that are not or are no longer contested in their legitimacy. So the fact is that Israel is confronted with vehement questioning of its legitimacy, of its "right to exist": Most Arabs are ready to recognize it *de facto*, as a fact, but not *de jure*, by right.

CHOMSKY: The notion of "right to exist" appears to have been invented by advocates of U.S.-Israeli rejectionism. And it's interesting the way it has spread. This notion doesn't exist in international law. No state has a right to exist. So Mexicans don't accept the right of the United States to exist, sitting on half of Mexico. They recognize the United States, they recognize the right of the United States to live in peace and security within recognized borders, but they don't recognize the right of the United States to exist, nor should they. Nor do the Hopi Indians. They recognize the United States, but not its right to exist. I have never seen a careful study, but as far as I can tell, the notion of "right to exist" was developed in the 1970s, at the point where the major Arab states, with the tacit support of the PLO, accepted that Israel had a "right to live in peace within secure and recognized boundaries"—the wording of UN Security Council Resolution 242 adopted in the aftermath of the June 1967 war, incorporated in a UN Security Council resolution vetoed by the United States in January 1976.[2] In order to raise the barriers, to prevent negotiation and settlement from proceeding, U.S. and Israeli propaganda elevated the demand, from a right that holds for all states—"to live in peace within secure and recognized boundaries"—to the "right to exist." So the new barrier was that unless Palestinians accepted the right of Israel to exist—that is, the legitimacy of their dispossession and expulsion—then they couldn't be accepted as negotiating partners. As far as I can tell, that was just a way to prevent negotiations, at a time when the United States and Israel were becoming almost totally isolated internationally in their refusal to proceed with implementing a very broad international consensus on a two-state settlement. I don't think we should accept that notion; that's a propaganda notion. No state has a right to exist, and no one has any reason to accept the right to exist. States are what they are. None of them have any inherent legitimacy. You're right, they differ; they have many different dimensions. So apartheid South Africa was illegitimate in a particular ugly sense. Is it legitimate now? Apartheid is over, but for the same 80 percent of the Black population, maybe the situation is worse than it was before, after the neoliberal measures were instituted in South Africa. Is that a legitimate state?

You're quite right that Israel is close to unique in one sense—namely that it was established *after* the contemporary international order was formed in 1945. Israel became a state in 1948, like India and Pakistan, so it's one of those few states that was established after the current international order was established. That imposes an extra problematic element—the same with India. Why should India be sitting on Kashmir, for example? Kashmiris don't want it; it was because the Maharaja happened to make that decision against the will of the population, and they're holding it by violence. They won't allow a referendum, which the United Nations demanded. The Indian special forces, the Rashtriya Rifles, carry out terrible atrocities. They faked the elections, which led to a lot of violence that still goes on. There's an element of illegitimacy.

ACHCAR: I think there are different levels that are being mixed here. Of course, no state on earth is a state where you have social equality. That's entirely obvious. So what you said about South Africa could apply to the United States or any other state. (CHOMSKY: But there are extremes.) There are extremes, of course, but we are speaking here of a different level. You have states that, for the overwhelming majority of their population, are considered to be their state, and you don't have a problem. But then you have situations that are part of the colonial legacy, created by force and rejected by majorities of the populations concerned. Kashmir, Kurdistan, and the rest are situations that are illegitimate in that sense, where the majority concerned do not consider themselves represented in the existing state structure.

CHOMSKY: We can go on. Take Turkey, after the expulsion of Greeks. The Greeks don't accept that, even to this day. There's no legitimacy to it; it's just been settled by various arrangements of force. Israel is unusual in that it was established a little later than the others, but it's very similar in character. And the United States is maybe the most extreme example. Almost the entire population was either exterminated or driven out of their lands. And then it's sitting on half of another country. The only reason it didn't conquer Canada was because the British deterrent was too strong. I simply don't think that the question of legitimacy of a state can seriously be raised. They're all illegitimate.

ACHCAR: Yes, but once again, it depends on what you mean by that. In the case of Israel, you have a situation where the overwhelming majority— more than 80 percent—of the original Arab Palestinian population of that territory had been expelled in 1948.

CHOMSKY: What would the original population of the current United States think?

ACHCAR: I said from the start that states based on effective genocide are, in a way, in a more comfortable situation, because they don't have any massive population contesting their existence or legitimacy. In the case of the Israeli state, on the other hand, you have a population that is at least as numerous as the settler-dominant one, and is claiming a right to the same territory, which it sees as having been usurped. As long as there is no solution that is acceptable to this population, you have a problem with legitimacy. If this population agrees that the state, although stemming from historical injustice and oppression, should nevertheless be accepted as an established fact, in the context of some settlement, then the problem is solved. But, as long as you don't have that, you have a problem of legitimacy—in the very formal democratic sense of the term.

CHOMSKY: As long as something is contested, it's contested, I agree. So Sri Lanka is seriously contested. India is seriously contested. Alsace-Lorraine is no longer contested because both sides recognize that the next time they contest it, they'll wipe out the world. In the case of Israel, it's mostly accepted even by the Palestinians. But until it's totally accepted, yes, it'll be contested. That's a different dimension than the question of legitimacy. The fact that some people have given up doesn't make it legitimate.

ACHCAR: No. Legitimacy is based on consent. Legitimacy is the consent of the majority. And the consent of the majority defines legitimacy, at least in political philosophy and democratic constitutional law. And a state is legitimate when it is based on the consent of the majority of its rightful population. Now, again, the problem of the Israeli state is that the bulk of the Palestinian population has been expelled and deprived of rights since 1948. So if we consider that these people have rights on the territory from which they have been expelled, then one cannot say that the Israeli state is based on the consent of the majority of its rightful population.

CHOMSKY: Let's drop the word "legitimacy." "Legitimacy" has quite a different meaning in international affairs. You should just say, straight out, that the original indigenous population of the land on which Israel was established does not accept the legitimacy of their expulsion. That's true. But that has nothing to do with whether the state is legitimate. You could say the same about many other states. People may accept it, but they don't accept its legitimacy. I don't know what would happen if you took a poll in Alsace-Lorraine, for example, about whether people would accept the legitimacy of the solution. They'd say, okay, that's the way it worked out. They may think it's legitimate; they may not. If you went to a Native American Hopi reservation, they certainly wouldn't regard the United States as legitimate, but they accept it.

ACHCAR: If even they accept it, then it is legitimate.

CHOMSKY: Fine. But insofar as the Palestinians have any *organized* voice, they accepted Israel a long time ago. They backed the 1976 UN resolution (vetoed by the United States) that called for a two-state settlement.[3] In 1988, the Palestinian National Council *formally* accepted such a settlement.[4] But

I don't think that confers any legitimacy on Israel, any more than any other arrangement confers legitimacy on a state. But as far as acceptance is concerned, yes, they accepted it, though of course there are things that are contested, like the right of return, or the borders and so on.

Take the negotiations at Taba, for example, in January 2001.[5] They didn't reach an agreement, but they came very close. As a matter of fact, at the final press conference the negotiators said, we have never been this close to an agreement, and if we could continue a little longer, we'd probably reach an agreement.[6] That agreement, had it been reached, would have amounted to acceptance by the only organized administrative structure within the Palestinian world. Would that have made Israel legitimate? No. Any more than the United States, or France, or India, or Sri Lanka—go through the list—is legitimate.

ACHCAR: I think we cannot apply double standards here. We cannot blame European governments, the U.S. government, and others for disregarding the opinion of their populations on the issue of the Iraq war, and approve as the authoritative voice of the Palestinian people the decision by what is the equivalent of a government of the Palestinians, disregarding the opinion of the people.

CHOMSKY: So you're now saying the Palestinian Authority is illegitimate?

ACHCAR: No, what I'm saying is that no agreement could be considered legitimate if it is not based on consultation with the Palestinian population by some kind of referendum. It needs to be approved by the majority of the oppressed Palestinian population.

Palestinian Say in Any Settlement

CHOMSKY: Including the refugees in Lebanon and elsewhere?

ACHCAR: Of course.

CHOMSKY: That's a certain way of ensuring permanent war and permanent destruction of the Palestinians. If one insists that there be no settlement unless the Palestinians in the refugee camps accept it, you're giving the greatest gift that could be imagined to the Israeli right wing. In the real world, you have to ask what things are feasible. And people's rights unfortunately are constantly compromised by the fact of feasibility. I think we have to make a crucial distinction here between proposing something and actually advocating it. It's a crucial distinction, often overlooked. You can propose that everyone should beat their swords into plowshares and live in peace with one another; but that's not advocacy until you show us how we're going to get from here to there. Then it becomes advocacy. In the case of the Israel-Palestine problem, we can propose that there be a solution in which the Palestinians gain all their rights. But that's not advocacy; it's a death sentence for Palestinians in the real world. You can propose it as a long-term goal—but if you want to advocate something, you have to show how we get to it.

In fact, there is a way to get to a settlement, and the Palestinians have by and large accepted it, at least as far as their own institutions are concerned, and as far as even polls show. They accept it—they may think it's unjust, but they accept the two-state settlement. And they've moved toward it, and in fact they've been demanding it. I don't know of any polls in the refugee camps of Jordan, Lebanon, and Syria, but the polls in the Occupied Territories show general acceptance of a two-state settlement, if it can be reached. Is that a just solution? Of course not. Could it preserve something for the Palestinians? Yes, it could. Could it be a step toward moving on to something better? Yes, it could. That's advocacy. But to say nothing is any good unless it is a just solution is to simply condemn the Palestinians to a life of misery and destruction.

ACHCAR: You can't say that you want to save the Palestinians from a life of misery while depriving those who live in the worst misery, the refugees, especially those in Lebanon, from any right of expressing themselves on their fate.

CHOMSKY: So what do you advocate?

ACHCAR: These are victims of oppression and of expulsion from their land and they have a right to self-determination, and no one has the right to divide the Palestinian people. This is actually the Israeli policy: to deal with the people in the West Bank and Gaza, while the rest are denied any rights. This policy is rejected by the overwhelming majority of the Palestinians. They consider themselves to be one people, and not various factions some of which can be dispensed with. And therefore, I think, the formula for permanent war is precisely to try to implement deals and settlements without making sure to get the majority of the whole Palestinian population to accept them. If you want a permanent settlement, you need to make sure that you get a clear majority of the overall Palestinian population to accept it. Doing so is no recipe for permanent war, as you're saying, Noam; on the contrary.

CHOMSKY: What are you advocating? Give me the series of steps that you're suggesting.

ACHCAR: I'm advocating a negotiated settlement that would be submitted to referendums of the concerned populations. That goes for the Israelis as well as for the Palestinians.

CHOMSKY: What will the referendum show for the Palestinians?

ACHCAR: It depends on what you are voting on.

CHOMSKY: So what is the settlement on which you will ask them to vote in the referendum?

ACHCAR: It's not up to you or me to say what the settlement should be. You and I could say what we believe the conditions are for a just or acceptable settlement: It has to address the problems and rights of all populations concerned, including those of the Palestinian refugee population. You mentioned the 2001 Taba negotiations. The fact that the negotiators there discussed a detailed blueprint about the fate of the Palestinian refugees supports what I am saying. They were aware—and you can be sure that the Palestinian leadership is perfectly aware—that there is no possible stable settlement that does not get the approval of the majority. Of course it would never be unanimous, but it has to be accepted by at least a majority of the Palestinian population. This is a democratic position.

CHOMSKY: Let's be clear about the position of the Palestinian leadership at Taba. They accepted what the negotiators on all sides called a "pragmatic" settlement, meaning some arrangement regarding the rights of refugees, which would not change the "demographic character" of the state of Israel.[7] That's what the Palestinians—Yasir Arafat, Mahmoud Abbas,[8] the rest of them—accepted. You may say it's wrong, but that's what they accepted.

ACHCAR: There's a problem of democracy here. People should accept a settlement democratically, and if that's not the case, then it's not a settlement, it's a *diktat*. The Oslo agreement[9] was such a *diktat*. What I'm saying then, before entering into a discussion on the conditions of a settlement, is that no settlement will be definitive unless it is agreed to by the majority of the populations concerned.

CHOMSKY: That's a truism, so we don't have to discuss it.

ACHCAR: But that was our starting point. You said the refugees should have no say on that.

CHOMSKY: I didn't say that. What I said is, it's certainly true that no settlement will be acceptable unless it's acceptable. OK. Unless everyone accepts things, there'll be problems. Tautology. Now let's go beyond the level of tautology to actual advocacy. We agree on the tautology; we agree on the principles—people should have a right to make choices about themselves. Now let's go to the real world and say what we are advocating.

ACHCAR: No, it's not a tautology, Noam. When I said there should be an agreement of the whole Palestinian population, you retorted that this is a recipe for war.

CHOMSKY: I said, if there's no agreement until we've reached something that is considered legitimate and just by the Palestinian population, that's a recipe for their destruction.

SHALOM: Maybe one way to think about this is: Imagine if there is a settlement that is accepted by the Palestinians in the Territories, and their elected leadership—

ACHCAR: And rejected by the majority of the refugees?

CHOMSKY: It would be rejected, there's no doubt.

ACHCAR: Not at all. On that, Noam, I don't agree with you.

CHOMSKY: Do you think the people in the refugee camps are going to agree?

ACHCAR: Of course! People want a settlement that puts an end to the precariousness of their existence.

CHOMSKY: It's not going to put an end to it.

ACHCAR: Look at what they agreed to at Taba. Even the Israeli negotiators there understood the need to give something to all the Palestinians. They suggested that a certain number of the refugees would be allowed to return to the pre-1967 Israeli territory; and another number, to pre-1967 Israeli territories that would be conceded by Israel to the Palestinian state in exchange for the territories on which the concentration of settlements has been built and which would be annexed to the Israeli state. (CHOMSKY: Now we're agreeing.) And that all those who want to go to the Palestinian state in the West Bank and Gaza would have the right to do so, and those who want to settle definitely and be rehabilitated in the territories where they presently live—that is, where they have been living for decades as refugees—could do so. And doors would be open even for immigration of those who want to settle overseas. All that combined with rehabilitation assistance and compensation programs cofunded by the "international community" and the state of Israel.[10]

CHOMSKY: We're in total agreement. That's exactly what I proposed at the beginning.

ACHCAR: No, the starting point of our discussion was about democracy: That it is not enough for an agreement on the fate of the Palestinian people to be signed by the Palestinian Authority alone, especially given how corrupt this Authority is, and how much pressure it is under from Israel and the United States. The Oslo agreement is a case in point. People like you and I were very lucid about the problems of the Oslo deal from the start; we knew it wouldn't work, that it was a *diktat*.[11]

CHOMSKY: Why don't we start from the point of agreement? The point of agreement is, first, about the tautologies and, second, about the principles; everyone agrees. We now have reached the point where we should have started. We're agreeing on the actual details. We can take the Taba negotiations as a start; they weren't perfect. With regard to the refugees, it's as you described. Both sides tentatively agreed that (1) there should be some symbolic return of Palestinian refugees, but with the demographic character of Israel left unchanged, to what will be the state of Israel in its pre-1967 international borders, with some mutual adjustments; and (2) the rest will have the right to go to the Palestinian state. It wasn't discussed, but it was agreed that there should be measures taken, and we can talk about the range of measures, for those who don't fit into those two categories. I don't think the Taba negotiations were adequate; there were still serious problems. But the unsettled problems were not with regard to the refugees (that one was basically settled) but with regard to (1) the salients—the Ma'ale Adumim salient, the Ariel salient, and so on,[12] and (2) the land swaps: Should it be three to one, one to one, and so on?[13] OK, so where do we disagree?

SHALOM: One disagreement concerns whether a settlement along the lines of the Taba approach would be acceptable to a majority of Palestinians.

CHOMSKY: I assume if you put this to a vote in Ain al-Hilweh, or Sabra and Shatila,[14] or any of the Palestinian refugee camps, they wouldn't accept a symbolic return to Israel and a free return to the Palestinian state.

ACHCAR: Of course they would accept it. To believe that the Palestinian refugees of Lebanon, Jordan, and Syria are all there—waiting to get back to Haifa, to the depths of the territory from which they were expelled in 1948, and that they couldn't accept any other kind of settlement—is to believe they are crazy people. I don't think they are crazy people. But they are people still bearing the direct consequences of historical injustice and oppression. So their concern, their problem, needs to be addressed. If it is addressed properly, they would accept any settlement that would put an end to their condition of being pariah populations, and would create economic and other conditions for a better life. One very important aspect of the Israeli draft in Taba—although of course that was just a proposal made by a few negotiators, and not an official offer from the Israeli state—is that it had Israel recognize the historical injustice that was done to the Palestinians and express its "sorrow for [their] tragedy, their suffering and losses." That's very important. You shouldn't underestimate the moral impact that such an acknowledgment would have. When the Palestinian refugees stick to the right of return, they stick to a right that for them is the major, if not the only, bargaining card that they have regarding their fate, and one should not dismiss that. It should be addressed, and it can be addressed, through Israel's official recognition of the historical injustice that it has done them, and therefore that this leads to responsibilities. These responsibilities entail finding a proper settlement for these populations. And yes, part of what was suggested at Taba goes in the right direction. I believe that if there were a full-fledged agreement of that kind proposed and explained to the Palestinian population, a majority, even a very large majority, of them would accept it.

CHOMSKY: OK, I'm perfectly willing to drop my judgment about the refugees. If I understand you correctly, you're advocating something on the order of the Taba negotiations. The problem that you keep bringing up is the problem of principle: Should there be *words* that say there was a historical injustice? There should be words.

ACHCAR: I believe that for the refugees, the recognition by Israel of the historical injustice made to them is of a tremendous moral importance.

CHOMSKY: Let's agree with that. We now agree that the Taba negotiations dealt properly with the issue of refugees, so we can put the refugee issue aside.

ACHCAR: The Taba negotiations indicated the right direction for dealing with that, but they didn't settle the *whole* thing. For instance, they left blanks for the numbers.

CHOMSKY: OK, then let's take the later Geneva Accord, where the numbers were filled in.[15] Now suppose that the Palestinians in the Territories and the Israelis accept a settlement along the lines of the Geneva Accord, and the refugees in the refugee camps don't. Then what?

ACHCAR: I'm not advocating split votes. I'm saying that it should be accepted by the majority of the Palestinian population, and not by the majority of every section of the Palestinian population taken separately. If a settlement is rejected by a majority of the Palestinian population, that means—I'm sorry, Noam—that it wouldn't succeed in any case.

CHOMSKY: It doesn't mean that at all. Unfortunately the world works by force, it doesn't work by agreement. That's just a fact about the world. But I'm asking a concrete question. Suppose your judgment about the refugees is incorrect. If your judgment about the refugees is correct, if a settlement can be reached along the Geneva Accord/Taba lines, then there's no issue. But the question arises: Suppose your judgment is wrong? Suppose that a Taba/Geneva Accord-style settlement is reached, between Israel and the Palestinians in the Territories, and the refugees reject it. Then what?

SHALOM: Say that we have a referendum, and that a majority of the Palestinians in the Territories accept and a majority of the Palestinians outside the Territories don't accept, and that when you add the votes together, the total majority of Palestinians reject.

ACHCAR: Then in that case, you can't have a settlement of the refugee question.

CHOMSKY: What are you suggesting in that case?

ACHCAR: In that case, it would be up to the Palestinian leaders to consult with their own people to determine what to do. What is the alternative? If an agreement is not accepted by the majority of the people concerned, it won't be a valid settlement. To be valid, settlements must be accepted by majorities. It's a question of the basic right of self-determination. You can't impose anything on a majority of the people and consider it to be valid. You can tell me force is everywhere in history. But in order for the outcome of force to become an undisputed fait accompli, it takes centuries. In the short run, it doesn't work.

I'm formulating a very basic democratic principle here. (CHOMSKY: And everyone agrees.) When it comes to the practical conditions of a settlement, I indicated what I believe to be the right direction. I am not a representative of the Palestinian people, I am not even a Palestinian, and I can't speak for the Palestinians. So I won't get into a detailed blueprint. I can just indicate what I believe to be the kind of settlement that would work. We were discussing the issue of the refugees. The factual problems that you are bringing into the discussion are on a different level, the Ma'ale Adumim salient and other issues; these are territorial matters. We'll come to that.

CHOMSKY: The only difference between us is a question of judgment—namely: What will the refugees think about it? We have a different judgment about that; yours is obviously better. But a question remains. What if your judgment is wrong? It's a possibility, after all.

ACHCAR: I have answered that: In order for a settlement to be valid, it has to be accepted by the majority. If it is rejected by a majority, then it has to be renegotiated. That's all! That's my answer.

CHOMSKY: Fine, then that means leaving them to fight it out.

ACHCAR: No. As long as people are negotiating, they don't fight.

CHOMSKY: That means things stay the way they are.

ACHCAR: You can move progressively—you know, as long as negotiations are occurring, there should not be violence.

CHOMSKY: You are advocating that we should *not* have a settlement that is acceptable to the Palestinians in the Territories, unless it is also acceptable to the refugees. If that's the case, it's a recipe for permanent devastation.

ACHCAR: But trying to impose a settlement that is rejected by the majority of the population means continued violence! A settlement rejected by the majority must be renegotiated.

SHALOM: Given that Palestinians have been a dispersed population, who speaks for the Palestinians in Palestine?

ACHCAR: Let me remind you of one thing. Israel negotiated the Oslo agreement with the PLO, not with the representatives of the West Bank and Gaza. The talks that started after the Madrid conference in 1991 were talks with direct representatives of the Palestinians of the 1967 Occupied Territories—people like Faisal al-Husseini, despite the technicalities of the Jerusalem issue; Hanan Ashrawi; and Dr. Haidar Abdel-Shafi from Gaza. Of course, everyone knew the PLO stood behind the Palestinian delegation, but Israel then insisted that it could engage in discussions only with people from the Occupied Territories. Later, however, the Israeli government of Yitzhak Rabin and Shimon Peres found it easier to get the kind of agreement they wanted from the PLO leadership, rather than from these people. They got the PLO leadership to essentially stab the Palestinian negotiators in the back, conducting secret negotiations that led to the Oslo agreement. Now the fact is that the PLO is not representative of the West Bank and Gaza alone. It's actually more representative of the refugee population outside Palestinian territory than of the population inside. It considers itself to be speaking for the whole Palestinian people, and, indisputably, it had the legitimacy of being recognized at that time by the majority of Palestinians—whether in the 1967 Occupied Territories or in the Diaspora—as their representative. So even this Oslo precedent points to the fact that a settlement needs to be accepted by a majority of the Palestinian population as a whole in order to get legitimacy in their eyes. And that's very important. It is one of the major conditions. And it's not an issue of empty principle, but a basic democratic principle: If you don't have consent, then you have coercion—it's an either/or situation.

CHOMSKY: We're talking about a particular hypothetical situation: The large majority of the population in the Occupied Territories accepts a settlement and the majority of the total population rejects it. The question is, what attitude do we take toward it? One attitude is to say, if the Palestinians in the Territories accept it, I may not like it, but I'll go along with it. The other possibility is to say, if the Palestinians accept it in the Territories but the majority doesn't, I reject it and insist on continued negotiations—which, as you agree, means continuation of the status quo, which in fact means destruction of the Palestinians.

ACHCAR: No, that doesn't follow. If there's no majority support, then that part of the settlement concerning the refugees should be renegotiated.

CHOMSKY: And should the other parts be implemented?

ACHCAR: If the local representatives want to go ahead provisionally with the part of the deal that concerns the territory where they live, and if the Israeli side agrees on splitting the issues like that, then sure.

CHOMSKY: In that case, we're in agreement. If there is a settlement, between whoever represents the Palestinians in the Territories and Israel, then we should say, OK: I may not like it, but I think it's okay as a temporary settlement. And if the issue of the refugees has still not been settled, then fine. We'll separate the two, implement this one, with whatever the territorial arrangements are, land swaps and so on, implement that, and keep negotiating the refugee problem.

ACHCAR: On the possibility of such a temporary settlement, we do indeed agree.

Going from a Settlement to Lasting Peace

CHOMSKY: Let me make another point. Suppose a Taba-style, Geneva-style settlement is agreed on; and let's say you're right that the Palestinians in the Diaspora agree to the Taba framework for refugees. I don't think that should be the end; I think that should be the first step.

ACHCAR: We agree here again. Of course, such a settlement should open the way to a lasting peace. You then move onward in peaceful conditions, not through war, toward final and lasting conditions of regional coexistence.

CHOMSKY: Let's talk about what we think ought to come after the initial temporary settlement. In my opinion—and I've written about this for thirty-five years—there's no way to draw a line in cis-Jordan—that is, in the territory west of the Jordan River—that meets the needs of the two populations. So I don't think a two-state settlement makes any long-term sense. I think that instead the two-state settlement should be a first step toward a federation of some kind, a single unity, with federated autonomous areas; that is something similar to what the Spanish state is moving toward, or what Belgium is roughly like, and so on. That's the next step. And a further step, as circumstances make possible, should be toward closer integration, that isn't based solely on ethnic lines, but is based on other forms of interaction. Like working-class cooperation for example. And that should be a further step, and a better solution in the long term would be a "no state" solution of roughly Ottoman style that I've mentioned previously.

So there is no "lasting" settlement; there is just a series of steps. It seems to me we're in a process in which there can be further steps toward closer integration, as the populations find it appropriate, breaking down, as I think can happen, the ethnic barriers that exist within Israel and within Palestinian society.

ACHCAR: I quite agree that we are talking about a process. When you get into what the next steps could be, I have always held to the idea that the West Bank, the 1967 Occupied Territories, should be merged with a democratic Jordan. By "a democratic Jordan," I mean a Jordan of the majority of its people, and not an absolute monarchy, based on an ethnic minority of the population. Because otherwise, the Palestinian statelet—the rump state that is being offered—won't have any real effective existence, particularly if Israel imposes all kinds of military conditions and controls over it. In the latter case there would never be a lasting peace. That's why settling the issue of the Palestinians should also involve Jordan; after all, the West Bank has a lot of links with Jordan. It was part of Jordan between 1949 and 1967, and we know that a majority of the population in Jordan is Palestinian. Of course, all the states in the area were artificially carved up by the colonial powers, so a federation makes good sense. And, beyond that, a federal structure at the regional level, which one wishes the Israelis would join, would be great, to be sure. But that would require—and I know we agree on this—a different economic and social structure, some sort of democratic socialism.

CHOMSKY: I agree. That's what I mean about breaking down the ethnic barriers.

Palestinians Within Israel

ACHCAR: There is another problem that should be addressed. It is the problem of the Palestinian population within the pre-1967 borders of Israel, who are presently in a situation of second-class citizenship, suffering oppression and harassment. I believe that a democratic settlement should also involve the possibility for these people in the territories where they are concentrated—in Galilee, the "Triangle," and the Negev—to be able to enjoy autonomy, of the kind they would like; in addition, they should be able to decide whether their territories would remain part of the Israeli state or join the Palestinian or Jordanian/Palestinian state.

CHOMSKY: I agree with that in principle, but here we get into some difficulties. There are extreme hawks in Israel who are concerned about what they call the "demographic problem." They are suggesting that Umm el-Fahem and other Arab areas of pre-1967 Israel be signed over to the Palestinian state as a way of reducing the non-Jewish population of the Jewish state. We know that the Palestinians in Israel, because Israel is a pretty open society, are vigorously opposed to that. They want to stay within Israel; they don't want to be transferred over to the Palestinian state. But if they did want to, that would be fine, and nobody would object, and in fact the Israeli hawks would love it; it would improve their demographic problem, as they call it—their racist problem. But in any event, Palestinians should certainly have rights within Israel.

ACHCAR: Let me clarify the issue of Palestinians holding Israeli citizenship inside the current Israeli state. I was just saying that they should be granted the right to self-determination. If they favor national autonomy within the Israeli state, as I believe they do at present, they should be granted that.

CHOMSKY: It's a tiny little state; national autonomy, they don't even want it. They want equal rights.

ACHCAR: You mentioned previously the example of the Ottoman Empire. This is a situation where communities rule themselves with a large degree of autonomy.

CHOMSKY: There's no disagreement here. That should be true of everyone.

ACHCAR: So I'm not just speaking of "cultural autonomy"; that's unsatisfactory because it's too restrictive. I'm speaking of a more general "autonomy," though not a separate state.

CHOMSKY: Fine. I think that is true for the entire world, and it should be true of Israel as well. But there is a much more immediate question at issue: Should they get authentic *civil* rights?

ACHCAR: Of course!

CHOMSKY: On the question of cultural autonomy, I don't think you'd even have a debate in Israel. Maybe some debate. In Umm el-Fahem, should they be able to write their own textbooks? But for the people in Umm el-Fahem and elsewhere, it's a minor demand. What they want is equal distribution of resources: Fix the sewage, build schools, drop the idea that the state belongs to the Jews and not to other citizens; that's a principle in Israel that is profoundly wrong. The High Court established that Israel is the sovereign state of the Jewish people in Israel and the Diaspora, but not the state of its citizens; that should be dropped.

Another extraordinarily important issue of equal rights involves the land laws, an issue I've been writing about for thirty years.[16] Land belonging to the government or to the Jewish National Fund had been reserved for the exclusive use of Jews—

SHALOM: Hasn't that changed somewhat?

CHOMSKY: It's interesting what's been happening. Ironically, it's the *right* wing that wants to change the situation, not for our reasons, but because they regard the nationalized lands as a socialist move. The right wing wants to privatize the lands, which means that the rich will be able to pick them up.

It's a very complicated story. Take, say, the kibbutzim, the agricultural cooperatives. By now they are mostly rich suburbs. They're on Jewish National Fund land, reserved for the Jewish people. Suppose they were privatized, the way the right wing wants: They'll buy the lands; they'll keep out anybody they want; it will be a gated community for Jews. These are the realities. So the right wing wants to get rid of the land laws.

SHALOM: What about Supreme Court rulings relating to the issue of landownership?

CHOMSKY: There has been one case before the Israeli High Court of Justice affecting the land laws: Katzir. This involved an Israeli Arab couple who wanted the right to settle in Katzir, a Jewish community. The Association for Civil Rights in Israel brought it to court, and finally the High Court in March 2000 did decide formally that you can't exclude them from settling in Katzir.[17] Then we go to the next stage: A series of barriers was imposed and the couple is still not in Katzir. It's been six years now since the court ruling and more than ten years since the case was first brought. So that one case has been *formally* resolved, but not *factually* resolved.[18] That's something we're very familiar with in the United States.

My wife and I, thirty years ago, had this sort of experience here in the liberal city of Boston. We couldn't afford the rents in Cambridge anymore; we had young kids and had to move somewhere cheaper. So we were looking around and drove through the suburb of Winchester. It looked nice, so we talked to the real estate agent and asked, how about Winchester? And he looked at us and said, you wouldn't be happy there, meaning: you're Jewish. That was in the 1960s; by now the situation has changed. But at that time, although Jews were not an oppressed population, nevertheless they could be kept out of places where they weren't wanted. And in Israel it's similar now.

Actually, when I was a kid in the 1930s, living in Philadelphia, when my father got enough money together to buy a secondhand car, we would drive out to the Pocono mountains for a weekend. We had to search for a motel, because most of them had signs on them saying "Restricted." Restricted meant "No Jews." The question of Blacks was not even raised at the time here. There was no *law* against it, and there's no law against Jews being in a motel, but you just accepted it: That's life. You don't like it, and you try to overcome it, but those problems in Israel are much worse.

As far as the Palestinians in Israel go, they should have whatever kind of autonomy they want, which, as far as I read them, is primarily a matter of civil rights—for example, the right to settle in Katzir.

ACHCAR: Including, for example, the right to organize their own schools, their own curricula, and so on. All these aspects of autonomy are basic democratic rights in binational states.

CHOMSKY: About fifteen years ago, a very anti-Zionist Israeli graduate student who got his Ph.D. here came into my office absolutely fuming. He had just received a booklet in Hebrew from the Israeli embassy trying to convince Israeli Ph.D.s to go back to Israel and not stay here—there was something of a brain drain from Israel. The glossy booklet described all the benefits that would accrue to his returning to Israel. What he was angry about was the way it was framed. It said these benefits apply to people who, if they were not Israelis, would be able to immigrate to Israel. That's a formula which means it's only for Jews, because only Jews are allowed to automatically immigrate to Israel. The booklet didn't say, these benefits are for Israelis, because then the benefits would apply to Israeli Palestinians who happen to be here. Now that's a formula that Israel uses everywhere. It is using the formula for the so-called seam—the area between the Separation Wall[19] and the Green Line.[20] There is a complex series of laws that have the same property. They don't say, Jews who live here have certain rights; they say, there are rights here for people who, if they were not Israelis, would be allowed to immigrate to Israel. The whole country is littered with this type of thing, like the restricted zones in the United States. These are methods for suppressing the rights of the Palestinian population. These need to be overcome.

Mizrahim

CHOMSKY: There's another problem we should consider if we're discussing the situation within Israel, and that's the problem of the Mizrahim, the "Oriental Jews." The majority of the population in Israel is from the Arab world, and they're very harshly oppressed. Recently, when Amir Peretz, a Jew who was born in Morocco, was appointed the head of the Israeli Labor Party, there was a bitter attack on him by Shimon Peres's younger brother, warning of "Levantinization": The Labor Party is being taken over by Arabs, just as General Francisco Franco attacked the Spanish republic with Moroccans, a "fifth column" who "shot [the Spanish Republic] in the back."[21] That's a sign of the racism that exists against Jews who are not of Ashkenazi (European) background, though a few have made it to elite sectors.

In many ways they're more repressed than the Palestinian Arab citizens of Israel—literally. In fact, the kind of resentment developing in Israel is similar to what happened in Eastern Europe, where the peasants resented the Jews, because the Jews were one step above them in the hideous hierarchy. And that led to pogroms; the peasants took it out on the Jews, not on the czar. In many ways in Israel, the Palestinians are living by their wits, as a repressed population does, as the Jews did in Eastern Europe. The Mizrahim are poor members of the working class. And sometimes the Palestinians get ahead; they probably have more doctors and other professionals. And the Oriental Jews resent the Palestinians, pretty much the same way the peasants in the Ukraine, where my grandparents lived, resented the Jews. They were all repressed. It's a standard pattern. Those who were beaten down badly focus their hostility one inch above them; they don't focus on the higher authorities. It's not too close an analogy; I don't want to press it too hard, but that phenomenon is showing up, and that's a real problem in Israel.

Some of the Mizrahim who came to Israel were relatively well off, such as the Iraqi Jews. But the Moroccans and others were poor people. After 1948, some Moroccans went to France and some went to Israel. The ones who went to France are today doctors, lawyers, college-educated. The ones who went to Israel are manual laborers, or unemployed.

My wife Carol and I lived in a kibbutz for a while in 1953, when Israel was a poor country, not like it is now. It was a left-wing kibbutz, kind of Buberite,[22] and the center of Arab activities for Mapam, the left Zionist United Workers Party. We lived near some Moroccan kids who had been brought into the country. It was a double-edged story. On the one hand, they were being helped; it was humanitarian. But, on the other hand, they were being told to forget their heritage; they were going to become poor Jews, and not be Arabs anymore. Anyway, the kibbutz members—who were regarded, and regarded themselves, as very pro-Arab—kept telling us that we had to lock our doors because of the Moroccan kids, that they were all criminals, that because they came from the Arab world you had to walk around carefully—which was all total nonsense; they were perfectly nice kids.

One day there was an altercation between some teenagers, and I later asked the kibbutz person in charge what had happened. She told me that the kibbutz kids had thought that those with whom they had been fighting were Moroccan Jews; but she explained to them that the other teenagers were visiting Arabs, invited as part of our outreach program to the Arab community, and therefore they'd have to be nice to them. That really expressed the attitude: The Moroccan Jews were considered worse than Arabs. It was very striking.

ACHCAR: There can only be total agreement between us on the issue of civil rights; I'm sure that there is also total agreement that the fight for these rights is not conditioned at all by any overall settlement of the Israeli-Palestinian conflict. These are issues on which the fight goes on daily and should go on daily, whether regarding the civil rights of the Palestinians within the 1967 Israeli border or regarding the equality of all Israeli citizens including Mizrahim and Ashkenazim.

The Palestinian Refugees

ACHCAR: But then I would add that it is also necessary to address the issues of civic equality and of social and economic betterment for the Palestinian refugees in the countries where they live. In my view, one of the major failings of the Palestinian leadership is that it hasn't addressed this question properly and seriously.

Compare the three main countries of the Palestinian Diaspora—Jordan, Syria, and Lebanon. At least formally speaking, in Syria and Jordan, Palestinians have local citizenship or equality of rights. In Lebanon, where I come from, there is a kind of apartheid situation for the Palestinians and they are deprived of basic rights: They actually have many fewer rights than alien migrant workers in Western countries. This is a major injustice. Progressive movements in the region should be upholding these rights and fighting for them: for full equality of the Palestinians, for their right to get local citizenship if they wish. Citizens or not, they are entitled to full equality of rights and an end to the horrendous social and economic conditions under which they live in the refugee camps, especially in Lebanon. These issues should be addressed and not ignored in the name of the "right of return"—an excuse for inaction that one often hears from some Palestinian leaders in Lebanon. Any steps on the road toward addressing and solving these issues would also facilitate reaching an overall settlement.

CHOMSKY: And the West should be putting in extensive resources for that. After all, the problem was basically caused by the West, so they have responsibilities.

ACHCAR: Yes, of course. Germany paid reparations to Israel. But then Germany owes reparations to the Palestinians, too. (CHOMSKY: Yes, of course.) Because after all, Hitlerism has been the source of all this tragedy, in a major sense.

SHALOM: You mentioned before some kind of federation with Jordan. For a long time it was the slogan of the Zionist right wing that "Jordan is Palestine." What is the difference between what you're suggesting and that view?

ACHCAR: I never adhered to the logic that says: If the enemy side says something, then you shouldn't say anything resembling it, even when you give it a totally different meaning. When Zionists say, "The Palestinians have a state, it's Jordan," they mean that the Palestinians should relinquish sovereignty over the West Bank. What I say is completely different: that the Palestinian West Bank should be able to merge with Jordan again, as the two banks were merged up to 1967, and this, in one democratically ruled entity, not under the Jordanian monarchy. So this is completely different.

CHOMSKY: It was the official position of the Israeli government as late as 1989 that Jordan *is* the Palestinian state. That's one position. But there's another position that is actually a traditional Zionist slogan; translated from the Hebrew it says: "There are two banks to the Jordan River; this one is ours and that one is ours." In other words, both sides of the Jordan are the traditional land of Israel. This was the position of the right wing, of Herut,[23] but it was also the view of the left wing. It's not too well-known, but the majority of the kibbutz movement—which was the left wing—took that position as well. The kibbutz movement had two basic components, and the main one was Ahdut Avodah (Unity of Labor). Their stand, at least until the 1980s, was the same: Maybe we'll give it up because we have to, but, as a matter of principle, both sides of the Jordan are ours. That's the core base of the Labor Party. They don't talk a lot about it, and they never thought it was going to be implemented, but the slogan was there as far as I know at least formally into the 1980s. This slogan involved Israel taking over part of Jordan, which is quite different from the idea of a democratic federation that Gilbert was talking about.

ACHCAR: This question is relevant to what I was saying about the argument used against fighting for equality in Lebanon. When you would ask the PLO leadership, "Why don't you address the problem of power in Jordan?" they would reply that it would fit into Zionist plans, because then the Palestinians would have a state and thereby undermine their claim on the Occupied Territories. It is, of course, a pretext in order to avoid addressing the issue and confronting the Jordanian monarchy. Saying that Jordan should become a state ruled democratically by the majority of its population doesn't mean that you have to abandon your claim to the West Bank or Gaza. This is a complete non sequitur. It is actually only a pretext for abiding by the principle of "noninterference in Arab affairs," in the name of which the Fatah[24] leadership of the PLO defended its desire to build friendly relations with all the reactionary Arab governments. This is not something that the majority of the Palestinians in Jordan approve of. They feel oppressed, they are harassed by the security forces, and they are naturally very much concerned with the political conditions of the state in which they live. They consider Jordan to be their country, an extension of the Palestinian territory in the sense that the population which originated on the West Bank of the Jordan River populated the East Bank too.

Efforts to Achieve Peace

SHALOM: What role have the United States and Israel played over the years in promoting or blocking a settlement of the Israeli-Palestinian-Arab conflict?

CHOMSKY: In June 1967, Israel crossed the Green Line, its borders along the 1949 cease-fire line, and conquered the West Bank, including East Jerusalem, Gaza, the Egyptian Sinai, and the Syrian Golan Heights. The first attempt to say something about this was UN Security Council Resolution 242 of November 1967, which everyone takes to be the basic diplomatic document.[25] Its preamble stated the framework: There can be no acquisition of territory by force. Then it loosely spelled out the terms of a settlement. It called for a settlement along the Green Line. The basic U.S. interpretation of this was that the Green Line should be the final border of a settlement, with minor and mutual adjustments. Since the Green Line was a cease-fire line, a lot of it just didn't make any sense; it depended on where forces were at the time the fighting stopped in 1949. Like cease-fire lines generally, it was somewhat arbitrary. So when one talked about minor and mutual adjustments, one meant overcoming the arbitrariness of the cease-fire line: Straighten out the borders. That was the official U.S. interpretation. Resolution 242 further stated that all states in the region have the right to live in peace and security, within secure and recognized borders. Strikingly, the resolution was totally rejectionist in the sense that it did not acknowledge Palestinian rights. The only thing it said about the Palestinians was that a just solution to the Palestinian refugee problem was needed, but nothing about their right to self-determination.

For the next few years there were various maneuverings, with both sides more or less accepting Resolution 242, but with qualifications. This continued until 1971 when there was a crucial event, which has been pretty much wiped out of history here. In February 1971, Anwar Sadat, who had just become president of Egypt the previous September, offered Israel a full peace settlement, according to the terms of Resolution 242. Sadat also said nothing about the Palestinians.

There was a UN negotiator, Gunnar Jarring, who presented a proposal to both sides and Egypt accepted the proposal, which was essentially Resolution 242, meaning total peace in return for total withdrawal. Now what concerned Sadat was not so much the West Bank but Egypt. Israel at the time, under a Labor Party government, was carrying out a major settlement program in the northeast Sinai, part of the Sinai Peninsula that Israel had conquered from Egypt in 1967. Israeli general Ariel Sharon drove out the people who lived there—they were technically Bedouins, but also farmers and peasants—and uprooted farms, towns, mosques, and cemeteries. He just drove thousands of them into the desert, put them behind barbed wire, razed everything, and then began to establish Jewish settlements there. The main settlement was to be an all-Jewish city, Yamit, but there were also a bunch of other settlements and kibbutzim. Of course, Egypt was never going to accept that, and that was the core issue in 1971.

Israel had a crucial choice at that point. Israeli officials—as we know from Cabinet records and other internal discussions—recognized that they were being presented with a peace offer, and they had to decide whether to accept it or reject it. They rejected it. They said we will not withdraw to the borders, which, at the time, meant we will not eliminate the northeast Sinai settlements. Incidentally, the next year Jordan came along with a very similar offer, but Israel didn't even respond to that. So there was an opportunity for peace along the lines of Resolution 242, offering nothing for the Palestinians but an international peace among the Arab states and Israel—and Israel rejected it.

The crucial question, as always, was what the United States would do. We don't have internal U.S. records from that period yet, but it's pretty clear what happened. There apparently was a dispute between the State Department, which wanted to accept it, and Henry Kissinger, who was national security advisor, who wanted to reject it. I suspect his motives were mostly that he was trying to take over the State Department, which he later did, so it was probably bureaucratic maneuvering. But Kissinger's *position* we know, because he wrote about it in his memoirs; it was what he called "stalemate"[26]—there was no reason for Washington to do anything, since the United States has the military force. It was a view that assumed Arabs didn't know which end of a gun to hold, and so the United States could just do what it wanted by force. Kissinger's position won the internal U.S. policy debate. And this was critical, because Israel at that point made a fateful decision in favor of expansion instead of real security.

If Israel had agreed to Sadat's offer, that effectively would have settled the international aspect of the conflict. There was no pressure for Palestinian rights from the Arab states; the Palestinians were calling for their rights, but no one was paying attention to them—in fact, they'd just been crushed in Jordan.[27] Israel made the choice of expansion rather than security, which meant dependence on the United States, because as long as there's an international conflict, Israel will be dependent on the United States for arms and diplomatic support, and so on.

I think that's probably the crucial decision that was made in the post-1967 period, and everything since then has flowed from it. Sadat kept saying, openly, publicly: If you don't accept the settlement, we'll have to go to war. His formula was "Yamit means war." He expelled Russian advisors in an attempt to get the attention of the United States, and did other things, but was just dismissed. No one paid attention. And finally in October 1973,

Egypt, together with Syria, went to war. It was a very close call for Israel. They were taken by surprise and were almost defeated. They were close to using nuclear weapons. And actually, the United States called a nuclear alert. It was a very serious matter.

In Israel it led to a lot of soul-searching. It's called *mechdal*, the failure.[28] There was a lot of reevaluation of the racist attitudes toward Arabs and of the unwillingness to deal with them. Kissinger also understood. He may not have understood much, but he understood force. He realized you can't just dismiss Egypt as a basket case—Syria too, but it was mainly Egypt—so you've got to deal with them somehow. Then came a long period of negotiations, including Kissinger's shuttle diplomacy, finally ending up with the Camp David Accords[29] in 1978 and with an Egyptian-Israeli peace treaty[30] in 1979. In the United States, this was described as a great diplomatic triumph for the United States. Actually, it was a total diplomatic disaster for the United States. What they agreed to in 1978–79 was Sadat's 1971 proposal, but in a harsher form from the U.S. and Israeli point of view, because now it included a Palestinian state. The situation had changed in the 1970s; Palestinian national rights had come onto the international agenda. So during Sadat's famous trip to Jerusalem in 1977, he called for a Palestinian state. And the Camp David agreements, with all their vagueness—the further negotiations with the Palestinians that the accords envisaged[31] never took place—were based on that demand on the Egyptian side.

ACHCAR: The phrase was "full autonomy" in the Camp David agreements, a "self-governing authority."[32]

CHOMSKY: Israel tried to brush aside these aspects of the accords. It decided to interpret them as meaning it could increase settlements, but not in Egypt, so it pulled out of Yamit.

And it's striking that the way Israel pulled out of Yamit was very much like the Gaza disengagement of September 2005. It was a staged, carefully orchestrated trauma. The general in charge explained that it had all been completely worked out with the settlers, that this would be a dramatic event in which Israeli soldiers with tears coming from their eyes would remove the poor settlers from their homes, and that this should never happen to Jews again, recalling the famous slogan "Never again." Never again would Jews be removed from their homes. There was a lot of ridicule of this staged event in the Hebrew press at the time. In fact the *Ha'aretz* headline said, "Operation National Trauma, '82."[33] And the 2005 Gaza disengagement was just a replay—a very carefully staged national trauma to send the same message: Never again must this happen to Jews, the West Bank is ours; that's the message.

As I mentioned, by 1979 the whole framework of discussion had changed, because Palestinian national rights had come to the international agenda. In 1976, there was a Security Council draft resolution calling for a two-state settlement on the Green Line. The resolution was supported by Syria, Jordan, Egypt, and most of the Arab states and, in fact, tacitly supported by the PLO.[34] The United States vetoed it. This happened again in 1980: the same resolution basically, and the United States vetoed it.[35] If you take a look at the records and search back through the documents, you find that even the scholarly work barely deals with it.

There was a change in 1988 when the Palestinian National Council *formally*, not just tacitly, accepted the international consensus, the two-state settlement.[36] The United States flatly rejected it and, in fact, refused to allow Yasir Arafat to show up at the United Nations, forcing the international organization to switch its meeting to Geneva. The United States was becoming an object of global ridicule at this point for pretending that it didn't hear the Palestinians saying that they accepted negotiations, accepted Resolution 242, accepted a two-state settlement, and condemned terrorism. But finally, after repeated statements by Arafat, Washington indicated that it was willing to talk to the PLO.[37]

The Israeli reaction came in 1989, a couple of months later, and it was very explicit. There was a coalition government in Israel at the time, with Likud's Yitzhak Shamir as prime minister and Labor's Shimon Peres as finance minister, so-called right and left. They came out with a formal statement of the Israeli position on May 14, 1989.[38] Among its principles was what we were talking about before: that there could be no *additional* Palestinian state west of Jordan—"additional" meaning Jordan already is a Palestinian state. Another principle was that Israel would not conduct negotiations with the PLO. A third principle stated that the status of the Occupied Territories would have to be settled according to the guidelines of the state of Israel. And then the document declared that the Palestinians could have free elections. We're in the world of George Orwell at this point. The Palestinians were supposed to have free elections, under Israeli military occupation, with a lot of the educated sector in prison without charge, probably undergoing torture. If you take a look at the American reporting of that, there was a lot of applause for Israel because they were allowing free elections, but the actual principles were never reported. Several months later, the Bush Sr. administration, which was considered critical of Israel, endorsed the Israeli proposals unchanged. That's what's called the Baker Plan, after James Baker, the secretary of state.[39] So the official U.S. position was: No additional Palestinian state west of the Jordan, and resolve the question of the Occupied Territories in accord with Israeli guidelines. Baker did say Palestinian negotiators would be admitted into the discussion, *if* they adhered to these Israeli terms. That was considered very forthcoming, without saying what it meant.

Then came the Gulf War, after which the United States realized it had the situation under control. It ruled the region, so it could do what it liked. George Bush Sr. announced the New World Order: "What we say goes!" were his words.[40] Washington then convened the Madrid negotiations. The United States had been opposed to any international negotiations before, because it couldn't control them. In 1991, however, it could control them. Bush invited the Soviet Union to be a fig leaf—you know how weak the Soviet Union was in 1991—to give it international cover, and Washington simply imposed its conditions. The Palestinians in the West Bank and Gaza, as Gilbert indicated, had a leadership. Their main negotiator was Haidar Abdel-Shafi, a physician and veteran politician from Gaza, probably the most respected person in the Territories. He insisted that any political settlement must stop Israeli expansion into the Territories. That was his primary condition; otherwise, he said, no settlement was possible. The United States and Israel, however, wouldn't accept that. At this point, the PLO, then based in Tunis, made an end run around the Palestinians—and that's the Oslo agreement. The PLO worked out a deal in Oslo that gave them the power, bypassing the domestic Palestinians such as Abdel-Shafi. He was so infuriated that he didn't even attend the famous handshake on the White House lawn. He stayed out of it. This led to a big problem inside the Palestinian leadership that continues to the present: Who is going to lead the Palestinians—the Tunis Palestinians, as they called them, or the indigenous ones such as Abdel-Shafi, Hanan Ashrawi, and the others? Israel and the United States made sure that the Tunis leadership essentially became the official leadership.

The Oslo agreement of September 1993 was just a sellout. The Oslo Declaration of Principles did not even mention Palestinian rights. Literally. It said a lot about Israeli rights, but nothing about Palestinian rights. Interestingly, the Palestinians in the Territories rejoiced. I remember that, a month or two after the signing, my friend Azmi Bishara was here, and there was a meeting arranged at MIT on the Oslo agreement, and we were the two speakers. And I said, what I just said, that it was a sellout, and he talked a little more diplomatically. And we went out for a cup of coffee afterward, and he said, only half as a joke, that if I had said that on the streets of Ramallah, I'd be lynched. There was such euphoria and total delusion.

ACHCAR: That's much exaggerated. Many Palestinian factions denounced the Oslo agreement, including Hamas—

CHOMSKY: But Azmi was talking about the popular mood. What did they think in the streets of Ramallah?

ACHCAR: They wouldn't have "lynched" anyone criticizing the agreement. That's very much exaggerated. There was a lot of skepticism about the agreement even among those who supported it.

CHOMSKY: Azmi was speaking figuratively, of course. I noticed that when I was talking to Palestinian groups, they were just totally deluded. Over the next few years came a series of Oslo interim agreements,[41] which were just outrageous, as I've written in detail elsewhere.[42]

This brings us to the first reference to a Palestinian state in the Israeli discourse, which, as far as I can determine, was made by the ultra-right government of Benjamin Netanyahu. In 1996 the minister of information, David Bar-Illan, was asked by a reporter whether the fragments of the West Bank that were going to be left to the Palestinians could be a Palestinian state. He said, yes, they can call it a state if they want, or they can call it "fried chicken."[43] That expressed the attitude.

And then in May 1997 the Labor Party platform declared, apparently for the first time, that it "does not rule out . . . the establishment of a Palestinian state with limited sovereignty."[44] These were the first references, in Israeli mainstream discourse.

This, in turn, brings us to the Camp David negotiations in July 2000 between Yasir Arafat and Israeli prime minister Ehud Barak, hosted by U.S. president Clinton. If you look at the maps, it is evident that the Israeli proposals couldn't possibly have been accepted. By now there's a lot of material on Camp David. The most important source, I think, is the Israeli scholarship; a lot of it is in Hebrew, but some is in English. The main work on it is by Ron Pundak, who was involved in the Oslo talks and in the background of later negotiations. He's the director-general of the Peres Center for Peace, which is right in the center of Israeli respectable scholarship. He wrote a long joint article in Hebrew and shorter ones in English, including maps.[45] And it's clear that the Palestinian objections made perfect sense. The official story here is that the Palestinians refused peace, that all they want is violence, and so on. But, in fact, no Palestinian could have accepted the Barak offer; even Mahmoud Abbas—the U.S. favorite—rejected it. What it basically did was break the territory into three cantons, mostly divided from one another, with an escape route around the east, pretty much separated from whatever parts of East Jerusalem would go to the Palestinians. That's the center of Palestinian commercial, educational, and cultural life. The Palestinians couldn't accept that. And actually, Clinton agreed: A couple of months after the breakdown in negotiations, he issued his parameters, which were vague, but they were more forthcoming than the Camp David proposals.[46] Again the standard story in the United

States coming from Dennis Ross,[47] Clinton's negotiator, and others, is that Barak—Israel—accepted the parameters and that Arafat rejected them, showing himself to be a man of violence who couldn't be dealt with. That's not what happened. Clinton a few days later made a statement saying that both sides accepted the parameters and both sides expressed reservations.[48] And in fact the Israeli reservations were quite substantial. The two sides then went on to address the reservations in meetings held in Taba, Egypt, from January 21 to 27, 2001. And they made some progress. We have a detailed account of it from a European Union observer, Miguel Moratinos, who wrote a long memorandum about it, which both sides agreed was accurate. It was reported prominently in Israel but ignored in the mainstream press here.[49] The Israeli commentators said that substantial progress was made. On January 27, the last day of negotiations, there was a joint press conference in which the two sides said: We've made substantial progress, we're close to an agreement, if the negotiations could continue we might be able to reach an agreement.[50]

Barak had called off the negotiations earlier that day on January 27. The pretext here was, they couldn't go on because of the impending Israeli elections; that's not true, it was ten days before the elections, and before the planned termination of the talks.[51] He just called them off; he didn't want them. By then George W. Bush had taken over from Bill Clinton, and shortly thereafter Ariel Sharon defeated Barak in the Israeli election. The chance for a settlement was dead.

The Bush administration is extreme. It is the first to officially recognize the effective annexation of what are called the settlement blocks. Take a look at what is meant: It's a large part of the West Bank. The Bush administration is the first one to have backed away from opposition to the annexation of Jerusalem. Ever since Israel conquered East Jerusalem in 1967, the UN General Assembly and Security Council have called the annexation of the city illegal and declared all measures changing the city's legal status to be null and void. The United States sometimes voted yes, but apart from a single no vote in 1981, generally abstained on these resolutions, until December 2002 when the Bush administration began voting no along with Israel. To endorse the annexation of Jerusalem just terminates any hope for political settlement. For Israel it's not just a matter of taking over the former East Jerusalem; Greater Jerusalem extends way beyond. The settlement of Ma'ale Adumim, which the press regularly calls a neighborhood of Jerusalem, reaches almost to the approaches of Jericho; it was built mainly in order to bisect the West Bank. So if the Bush administration really means that it now favors the annexation of Jerusalem, then that's the end of any political discussion.

The Bush administration has also endorsed the Separation Wall. The World Court (the International Court of Justice) unanimously declared that all Israeli settlements are illegal. The U.S. judge dissented from the overall judgment, but he had a separate declaration in which he agreed that all the settlements violate Paragraph 6 of Article 49 of the Fourth Geneva Convention,[52] and therefore that any parts of the Separation Wall that are "being built by Israel to protect the settlements are *ipso facto* in violation of international humanitarian law."[53] The characterization "being built . . . to protect the settlements" applies to about 80 percent of the whole Separation Wall; but Israel pretends it's for the security of Israel, which is nonsense.

That one week at Taba in January 2001 was the one break in thirty-five years of U.S./Israeli rejectionism. The Taba negotiations had serious problems, but the Israeli and Palestinian negotiators were not unrealistic in their final press conference. Probably the differences were resolvable. But the negotiations were called off by Israel, so we don't know. However, informal negotiations went on, also at a pretty high level, between Palestinians and Israelis, and they led to several outcomes; they're all more or less alike. But the most detailed one is the Geneva Accord, which again, in my view, has plenty of problems, but it offers the lines of a potential settlement; it could be the basis for going on. When it was presented in Geneva in December 2003, the major European countries and others sent either representatives or strong statements of support, but the United States refused to attend, and Israel just rejected it. It wasn't endorsed by the Palestinian leadership, so it was left hanging. But if the United States and Israel had accepted it, I think it could have proceeded. But then we get to the other stumbling blocks: the Separation Wall and the Israeli settlement expansion.

ACHCAR: I just want to bring some complements to Noam's narrative, mostly focusing on the Israeli side; we'll get later to the Palestinian side. The first point is that in 1948, as we know, the overwhelming majority of the Palestinian inhabitants of the territory seized by the newly born Israeli state left. I think the discussion about whether they were expelled, or fled, or were duped into fleeing, or whatever other version, is to a certain degree irrelevant, because the key point is that *they were not allowed to return.* That's the major point. If you leave your home even of your own free will, you still have the right to return to it as long as you haven't sold it over. That's the starting point for thinking about this issue. Ever since 1948, Israel has denied these people the right to return to their homes in the territory that Israel seized, accepting only the principle of compensation—by somebody else. However, in 1967, when Israel seized the rest of the Palestinian territory, there was a major difference relative to 1948; this time the Palestinian population, having learned the lesson of 1948, did not leave their land and homes. They did not flee, and it would have been much more difficult to terrorize them into leaving than was the case in 1948, because they now understood that if they left, they wouldn't be allowed to get back and would end up as "refugees" living in "camps." They also understood from the 1948 precedent that if they stuck to their land, they would not be slaughtered. So this created a very different situation, whereby Israel seized new territories, but with the majority of the original population still there.

This issue was addressed very early after the June 1967 war by the Allon Plan, formulated by Yigal Allon, a leading member of the Israeli government at that time. This plan tried to address the problem from what might be called an "enlightened Zionist" perspective—this was also Ben-Gurion's[54] perspective—which maintains that the Israeli state should be both a "Jewish state" and a democratic state. And how do you solve this, how can a "Jewish state" be democratic? Obviously, it can be democratic only if it has a substantial Jewish majority so that democracy is no threat to its "Jewish" character, which meant that Israel had to avoid acquiring large numbers of Palestinians. So the inhabitants of the newly conquered territories posed a problem. And Allon's solution was that Israel should create established facts—military and other settlements—in order to strategically control the West Bank, especially along the Jordan River, and give back to Jordanian control the areas where the Palestinian population was concentrated. This was the Allon Plan, and this has been pursued by Israel ever since 1967.[55] Of course, not all Israeli settlements were established for the purpose of securing strategic control over the West Bank. From early on there was also an ideological and religious settlers' movement led by the Gush Emunim—the Bloc of the Faithful—motivated by more than purely strategic considerations. Overall, however, the Allon Plan was the main framework of policy.

In order to be implemented in full, this plan required the defeat of the Palestinian guerilla movement. That's what Israel tried to achieve in 1982, when it invaded Lebanon in an effort to deal the PLO a decisive blow. PLO fighters were expelled from most of the country and forced to evacuate Beirut. With the PLO seemingly very much weakened, the United States endorsed the framework of the Allon Plan in the form of the so-called Reagan Plan of September 1982.[56] Reagan advocated Palestinian "self-government," meaning not an independent state—that was explicitly excluded—but some sort of Palestinian entity, short of a state, in the West Bank and Gaza "in association with Jordan." Reagan also specified that Israel would not be asked to return to its pre-1967 borders. This was a view with which the Labor Party in Israel could readily agree because it fit in perfectly with the core of the Allon Plan.

Another decisive moment in changing perceptions was the Palestinian Intifada. The Palestinian Intifada in 1987–88 demonstrated, first of all, that the West Bank population was neither resigned nor docile; Israel found that it had a problem not only with the Palestinian refugees in adjacent countries but also with the Palestinians under occupation. And, second, the Intifada led the Jordanian monarchy to officially abandon its claim to the West Bank in 1988, and to announce that the Palestinians were solely responsible for their territory. This led the Israeli side, at least the Labor wing of Zionism, to realize that the previous conception of returning the densely populated Palestinian enclaves to Jordan was no longer workable. That's when Labor Party leader Shimon Peres began to take the view that Israel should be willing to negotiate with the PLO if certain conditions were met—in place of the official Israeli position that barred talks with the PLO under any circumstances. We know the rest of the story. Noam has told it; I have nothing to add, except to mention the fact that the Oslo agreement was actually the realization of the Allon Plan. What it provided for actually was a redeployment of the Israeli army—redeployment and not withdrawal—from the densely populated Palestinian areas of the West Bank, in conformity with the Allon Plan. The difference was that they were not given back to Jordan, but put under the control of the PLO, which agreed to enter this game, probably with a certain degree of illusions. Arafat kept saying that this was but the first step toward an independent and sovereign Palestinian state; he may well have naively believed that, by relying on international pressure and cozying up to Washington, the Palestinian leadership could achieve such a result.

The Palestinian View of a Settlement

ACHCAR: Let me now turn to the Palestinian and Arab side of this long story. Here, the point of departure was total rejection of the Israeli state as a thoroughly alien and colonial implant in the Middle East, which had to be eradicated. At the beginning, the dominant view was that Israel should be wiped off the map as a state, and then, depending on the particular ideological current involved, there were various possible outcomes. The traditional Arab nationalist view used to make a distinction between indigenous Jews—that is, Palestinian Jews—and those who had come from other lands. The most nationalistic version used to say that the immigrants should be sent back to where they came from, or at any rate leave Palestine like the European settlers left Algeria when it achieved independence; the more progressive or democratic version maintained that all Jewish inhabitants who so wished could stay and live as a minority with equal civil rights in the framework of an Arab state.

After 1967, when the Palestinian guerillas took control of the PLO, the organization's official program used the formula of the "secular democratic state of Palestine." This formula was never really adopted on the popular level, and there was never real education around it. One could say that to a certain extent, in the early years at least, it was mainly designed for external consumption, so that the PLO could present some kind of progressive-sounding formula. But the formula itself has a major flaw that is quite obvious. It addressed the question of the Israelis as if they were only a religious community—hence the term "secular"—as if you could solve the problem just by setting up a secular Palestinian state. This ignored a basic dimension of the problem—namely that the Israelis had become a national entity, not only a religious community. This aspect was addressed by some in the Palestinian left, who spoke in terms of a socialist, binational framework. They favored a secular state as well, of course, but the term "secular" addressed only the religious issue, whereas "binational" acknowledges the fact that there are two national communities. At any rate, the project of a state that would replace the Israeli state, a larger Palestinian state, whether in the secular option or the binational one, was no more than a programmatic utopia. It became quickly obvious that, in terms of practical politics, there had to be some achievable or attainable goals. So the Palestinian resistance moved from what I define as "maximalism"—liberate Palestine and change the whole setting into a different kind of state as a single goal—to understanding the necessity of defining goals of an immediate or transitional nature. It appeared quickly to the Palestinian movement that it would have much more leverage in addressing first the issue of the territories occupied in 1967 than in addressing that of the whole of Palestine at once. After the 1973 war, the Palestinian movement made moves toward accepting, in formulas of more or less ambiguity, what amounts to, and everybody interpreted as, the idea of setting up a Palestinian state in the 1967 Occupied Territories. That was defined, of course, as a step toward the liberation of all of Palestine in the official documents and discourse. As time has gone on, Palestinian and Arab popular opinion has become accustomed to the idea of a compromise settlement with the Israeli state. Except for some still-existing nationalistic or Islamic fundamentalist minority currents, a compromise settlement is acceptable to a clear majority of public opinion, *provided* that it addresses the concerns of the Palestinians along the lines of what we have discussed—namely that Israel relinquishes all the territories occupied in 1967 except for small changes that would be compensated by ceding pre-1967 Israeli territory, and that the fate of all components of the Palestinian population be addressed in a way that respects their inalienable right to self-determination. The PLO, or its Arafat leadership, when it accepted the Oslo agreement, was betting, very naively or stupidly, that U.S. support could be obtained through Arab—and especially Saudi—pressure on Washington, leading to a settlement that the PLO believed would be acceptable to the majority of the Palestinian population. But, of course, we know that this bet was very illusory. And because of their illusions, they allowed many time bombs into the Oslo agreement. The fact that the accords did not even address the issue of the settlements, not to mention that of the refugees, made the whole framework of Oslo a deception, and we know what actually happened. The Oslo agreement, through the illusions it created and that Noam mentioned, and also through the role played by the PLO—as an Israeli police force by proxy, in controlling the Palestinian population—created the possibility for the Israeli state during the first post-Oslo years to move forward in implementing an updated version of the Allon Plan. Israel was able to intensify the settlement process and build the infrastructure for strategic military control—roads and the rest—over the West Bank much faster, more intensively, and with much less resistance than would have been the case without the agreement. There was a continuous expansion of the settlements, and the number of settlers doubled in a few years. As we've noted, the Palestinian negotiators from *within* the Occupied Territories had insisted upon an Israeli pledge to freeze the settlements as a precondition for any agreement. The Oslo agreement, however, did not include anything like that, and was therefore sharply criticized by them, some of them rejecting it. Actually, the Oslo deal was even rejected by a majority of the PLO Executive Committee members. The way Arafat got it through was a perfect example of autocratic dictate.

Zionism and the Palestinians

CHOMSKY: I could add that if you look at the growth of the settlements in the West Bank after Oslo, it's been pretty steady. But the peak year was actually Clinton's last year—Clinton-Barak's last year—2000.[57] But that has just been swept under the rug.

There is a long history in Zionist ideology relating to settling on Palestinian land. The Zionist movement recognized from the very beginning, back in the early part of the last century, that they were facing a hostile population. There were some illusions about it being "a land without people," but those quickly dissipated. The general principle that was followed was called "dunam after dunam,[58] goat after goat." This meant don't let the goyim—the non-Jews—know what we're doing, but just take a little bit more, establish a fact, get another dunam of land, and gradually we'll just take it. That's been the deeply rooted principle all along. It's just a conception of how one proceeds: Let *them* talk, meanwhile *we'll* take. Ben-Gurion is reported to have said, "It doesn't matter what the goyim think, it matters what the Jews do." And we shouldn't delude ourselves into thinking there's much of a division on this. In the Peres government in 1995–96, for example, which was supposed to be the doves, the housing minister, Binyamin "Fuad" Ben-Eliezer, who has been in subsequent governments, said, "Fuad does everything quietly." "My goal is to build and not to encourage opposition to my efforts. . . ."[59] He builds quietly so the goyim don't hear it, or at least pretend they don't hear it, because of course they, the United States, know it, since in fact they're funding it. In 1992, there was a series of proposals—the Sharon Plan, a Labor proposal, a couple of others—but they were all basically the same: just various modifications of the Allon Plan, which is: We take it step by step. Moshe Dayan—who among the Israeli leadership has probably been the one most sympathetic to the Palestinians—recognized that the Palestinians were right in charging that Israel had been stealing everything from them. He was in charge of the occupation under the Labor government, from 1967 to 1974. And his opinion was very explicit in describing the same policy: We'll take little bits at a time; Israel was going to be the "permanent government" in the Occupied Territories.[60] We'll take it piece by piece, quietly; we will tell the Palestinians, "We have no solution, you shall continue to live like dogs, and whoever wishes may leave, and we will see where this process leads."[61] The military administrator of the Territories, General Shlomo Gazit, wrote his memoirs a couple of years ago, and they've recently come out in English.[62] Gazit says that shortly after 1967, what they call the Palestinian notables started making proposals to the military government for some kind of autonomy: Let us elect our own mayors, give us some cultural autonomy, and so on. He says the military command and Israeli intelligence transmitted these proposals to the higher political echelons of the ruling Labor Party sympathetically; he thought this was a good idea. But the political leaders just wouldn't hear it; they refused to permit any Palestinian political activity, however innocuous, or to contemplate anything that might lead to a border change. That was the doves: Prime Minister Golda Meir and the Labor government. Gazit—who's a hawk, incidentally, not a dove—says that in his view the failure of the Labor political leadership to allow some kind of limited autonomy to develop was really catastrophic. That led to the Gush Emunim, these religious fanatics, half of them from Brooklyn, who made it an ideological issue with the backing of the government, and it led as well to what was from his point of view the catastrophe of the First Intifada. Gazit says that this would never have happened if the Palestinians had been allowed to take control of their own affairs to some extent.

What this suggests is that in 1971, when Sadat and later Jordan offered to end the international conflict, Israel *might* have ended the internal conflict as well by granting autonomy, maybe moving toward federalism, or some such proposal, inside the West Bank and Gaza—even toward a form of binationalism, in fact, which has roots in the Zionist tradition. In the 1940s I was a Zionist youth leader, but opposed to a Jewish state; such a view was at that time considered part of the Zionist movement. It called for a socialist binational community with working-class cooperation crossing ethnic lines. It wasn't the mainstream of Zionism, but it was within it. I didn't stop being a Zionist youth leader because I believed and advocated it. It probably could have been revived in the 1967–1973 period, but it was rejected with near fanaticism every time it was proposed, even by the extreme Israeli doves—people like Simha Flapan of the *New Outlook*[63] group, who were very angry about it. There was no support for it in Israel apart from *Matzpen*, a little group of left intellectuals.[64]

ACHCAR: And the latest huge illustration of the policy of established facts is of course the Separation Wall.

CHOMSKY: Exactly. "Oh, it's temporary," claim Israeli apologists. Take Alan Dershowitz: He says, oh well, we'll put it on wheels, and as Palestinians perform better, we'll move it a little bit. Literally![65] The pretense is that it's all temporary, that's all for the goyim, it's temporary, we're not doing anything, but meanwhile we'd just take it over piece by piece. Even the annexation of Jerusalem; if you look at the way it was formulated, you could claim legalistically that it wasn't literally an annexation. There's an interesting article on this in the *Journal of Palestine Studies* by Ian Lustick, who's quite good, and very much opposed to the takeover.[66] He points out that *technically* they can say it wasn't a literal annexation; it's just that they expanded the borders, and it's now Greater Jerusalem, going halfway to Jericho.

This approach goes back to the 1920s at least. Zionist leaders quickly overcame the illusion that it was an empty land and that the population wasn't going to care; Ben-Gurion and the rest said, they can go to Iraq, or somewhere; it's just Arab land, they're not going to care. It's not really "transfer"; it's just like moving from one part of the city to another part, because it's all Arab land. So what do they care if they stay here? And that was considered a moral position.

The most left wing of the Zionist leaders, people like Berl Katznelson, Marxists, socialists, and so on, regarded it as a moral position. It's what they called "voluntary transfer," distinguishing between those who favored forcible transfer and those who wanted voluntary transfer. Advocates of the latter said, we'll explain to the Palestinians that they're maybe better off in Arab lands and that Iraq has all this land, and we'll pay off the landowners who are happy to sell, because they're mostly crooks. And then we can say, we didn't take anything, we bought it, and the Palestinians all voluntarily left because they never had any real attachment to this place anyway. And then you get the real extremists like Joan Peters,[67] who said the Palestinians were never there anyway.

SHALOM: The Palestinians who were uprooted were replaced with Jewish immigrants, many of them survivors of the Holocaust. Why did these immigrants go to Israel?

ACHCAR: These are people the majority of whom wanted to go to North America, the United States or Canada.

CHOMSKY: There's quite a scandal that's documented in a book by Yosef Grodzinski.[68] I may have helped get him started on it. About twenty years ago I was having dinner with a friend who was working at the YIVO Institute for Jewish Research, in New York, the leading center for the study of East European Jewry and Yiddish. I asked her a question that had always bothered me: Why did the Jews from the concentration camps end up in Palestine, later Israel? Half of Europe would have come to the United States if they could. Surely the Jews in the DP [displaced persons] camps would have wanted to come here. My friend said she had been translating letters from people in the camps and most of them in fact wanted to come to the United States. The camps were being run by Zionists, who, by withholding food and other means, were forcing them to go to Israel/Palestine, to be cannon fodder, which they didn't want to do. I asked her why she didn't write something about it, and she said YIVO had transferred all the archives to Israel. I later mentioned this to Grodzinski, an Israeli friend and colleague. He knows Yiddish, and he checked and found the archives were open. All these famous Holocaust historians had never bothered to look at them, so he was the first person to use them.

And what he found was just as my friend had described. The Zionists had sent in agents right away to run the camps. His book in Hebrew is called "Good Human Material"—there's a different title in English—because the Zionists wanted "good, human material" to be forced to go to Palestine, and that meant all able-bodied men and women between seventeen and thirty-five—they didn't really care about the rest of them—to be cannon fodder in the war that they knew was coming. The others they used as hostages to coerce the British. For example, they put them on ships that they knew the British were going to have to stop, so they could then say that the British were forcing Holocaust victims back to Europe—the *Exodus* story[69]—and all that sort of thing. The cynicism was just unbelievable. Grodzinski wrote the book in Hebrew and it got pretty good reviews in Israel from fairly mainstream people. The Holocaust historians, however— Yehuda Bauer and the rest—went crazy, because it exposed things they had kept hidden. But Grodzinski's findings were solid, and in Israel, when people made a criticism, he was able to answer it. He finally got it translated here and it's a very interesting book.

The United States was very anti-immigrant at the time, very anti-Semitic, and very racist. But there was an immigration bill in 1947 that was going to let in some small number of people. In the Jewish community the only group that lobbied for it, as far as I can recall, was the (anti-Zionist) American Council for Judaism, not the Zionists. (ACHCAR: The Zionist leadership in Palestine was asking them not to.) The Zionists wanted them to go to Palestine. And also—I remember that period—American Zionists didn't want these dirty Polish Jews around, giving Jews a bad image.

ACHCAR: There is a famous allegory used by Isaac Deutscher,[70] about a house that is on fire and a person jumps from the window and falls by accident on a passerby, meaning the Jewish refugees fleeing Nazism were tragically and accidentally landing in Palestinian territory. But the analogy is not completely accurate, because it wasn't just an unfortunate coincidence; European Jews were *channeled* toward Israel despite the will of their overwhelming majority. The majority did not want to go to a land they imagined to be like a desert with camels; the promised land of their dreams was not Palestine, it was North America. The same goes for the recent wave of Russian immigration to Israel; the Begin government arranged with Moscow that Jewish emigrants would be given only one choice of destination—that is, Israel through Austria.

CHOMSKY: It was Vienna for a while, or Berlin. Israel actually started a campaign against Germany and Austria using the Holocaust weapon—saying, first you carried out the Holocaust, now you won't let the Jews go free. This actually meant, you're letting some of them go free to someplace other than Israel. The cynicism!

ACHCAR: How would you, Noam, assess the story of the Falasha, the Black Ethiopian Jews? Is it the expression of an Israeli desire to look more like the United States?

CHOMSKY: Israel didn't want the Falasha in the worst way, and for a long time they just refused to allow them in. But there were some Jewish groups in the United States that were both Zionist and civil libertarian, and they started a big campaign, with a lot of publicity on the issue. And Israel really began to look bad. When people didn't know about it, people didn't care, but when it got to be known that Israel was blocking Black Jews—this was after the Civil Rights movement—this was too ugly for them, so Israel had no choice but to take them in. But most of them are in development towns.

ACHCAR: Right. And that was used in turn as a propaganda tool: We resemble the United States so much—we are twin societies.

CHOMSKY: Yes, but after they had their arms twisted. What they wanted was the Russians.

Israeli Politics

SHALOM: What differences do you see between the two main Israeli political formations, Labor and Likud?

CHOMSKY: It's kind of like Democrats and Republicans: There are differences if you look really closely. And sometimes those differences matter. Small differences in a big system of power can make a difference. But the basic framework of thinking is not very different. Actually the triumph of Likud in 1977, which broke the Labor monopoly over the government, didn't have much to do with these differences; rather, it had to do with the Mizrahim. Somehow Likud leader Menachem Begin managed to present himself as the representative of the poor Mizrahi Jews. In fact, a lot of them thought he was a Moroccan—he was a Polish Jew, of course, but there was a feeling that really he was a Moroccan, otherwise he wouldn't be this nice to them. And Likud swept Labor out of office on that.

The result was kind of a mixed bag. Begin himself was very right-wing, but pretty legalistic. So the first two or three years of Begin, from 1977, was the only period when torture stopped. Then Sharon joined the government and it started again. Practically every Palestinian prisoner was tortured. The High Court pretended they didn't know, but later they conceded it was true. (One of the High Court justices, Moshe Etzioni, when asked by Amnesty International why Arab prisoners always seemed to confess, explained that "it's part of their nature."[71]) In fact, the whole of Israeli society opened up after 1977 to a large extent, like the press by now: It's pretty lively, we all read it. There's a lot of good material in it. But that's post-Begin mostly. Prior to that, there was a kind of Bolshevik character to the state. In fact, they used the word. It was a very disciplined, conformist, Bolshevik-style state; it wasn't Russia, but with that kind of mentality. After 1977, when Begin came in, a lot opened up.

ACHCAR: Not thanks to Begin, of course, but thanks to the fact that the Labor Party became the opposition.

CHOMSKY: Yes. Labor no longer ran the place, so that did have the effect of opening things up.

ACHCAR: I agree with Noam's general characterization. But if one speaks not of leaders but of party rank and file and basic constituency, the Labor Party, or at least a segment of it, consists of people who would be willing to move or to make the necessary real "concessions," in order to achieve a lasting peace. Within Likud, it is much harder to find such people. And although this is a quantitative difference, it could turn into a qualitative difference when you consider the fact that negotiators from Labor Party circles and from Meretz, the left allies of the Labor Party incorporating the former Mapam, came close to accepting a formula whereby Israel would relinquish 94 percent of the West Bank and provide partial compensation for the remaining 6 percent, whereas we know that Sharon's plan is to relinquish only 42 percent of the West Bank. This difference cannot be dismissed.

CHOMSKY: But remember, it was Barak who called off the Taba negotiations.

ACHCAR: Of course, that's why I made the distinction between the leaders—this or that leader of the Labor Party—and the membership, the constituency, and its ideological orientation. So here there is a difference. As a matter of sociological fact, until very recently the segment of the Labor Party's constituency that was most open to the kind of peace settlement we were discussing was privileged Ashkenazim. The Mizrahim, not to mention the more recent immigrants, Russians and others, would rather be supporters of the Likud or the religious right. And that's the real importance of the recent election of Amir Peretz to head the Labor Party. In the history of Israel, that's a kind of earthquake. Who could have imagined some years ago that a Moroccan Jew from poor social origin and a nonmilitary background—

CHOMSKY: That's the first time—

SHALOM: Other than Golda Meir.

CHOMSKY: Yes. But she was surrounded by generals; the only general who seems close to Peretz is Ami Ayalon.

ACHCAR: So a Moroccan Jew, not closely tied to the military, and a trade union leader moreover, gets to the head of the Labor Party. This is absolutely amazing. Had it been a Mizrahi with a hawkish program, I would have said that doesn't mean much. But it so happens that he has expressed a relatively moderate vision of the relation to the Palestinians, making statements in favor of a settlement entailing a Palestinian state. So I think there is ground for some measured optimism, on two conditions: first, that Amir Peretz sticks to that kind of view instead of the classic move-to-the-center syndrome, which leads people coming from somewhat progressive stances to move to the right, believing that that's the way to secure a majority; and second, of course, provided he manages to get a majority in Israel without shifting sides. This, I believe, would be quite difficult because of how the institutions function. Take as an example the character assassination to which Howard Dean was submitted in the U.S. 2004 presidential campaign. It was amazing how the mass media in the United States assassinated this guy on the basis of some trivial and meaningless yelling. He was treated like that because he was considered a kind of maverick, an unpredictable guy who worried the establishment. Amir Peretz is already being treated similarly by part of the media in Israel; there is already a denigratory campaign going on against him. But he's the head of the Labor Party, so if he doesn't move to the right, as they want him to do, I'm pretty sure he will face a very aggressive and hostile ideological campaign, and that could of course shoot him down.

SHALOM: In January 2006, Prime Minister Ariel Sharon had a massive stroke. How does his absence now change the political dynamic in Israel?

CHOMSKY: Before his stroke, Sharon founded the new party Kadima by splitting Likud. Back in November 2005, before Sharon formed Kadima, I had an interview with *Ha'aretz*[72] in which I guessed that Sharon would form a centrist party, which would be pursuing the Sharon Plan of taking over the Occupied Territories. All this business about Sharon being interested in peace and so on is just preposterous.

I should stress that the appeal of Peretz is primarily that he wants to halt and reverse the disintegration of the social system. That's his appeal to the Mizrahim, who suffer from this situation, and, as Gilbert said, Peretz is going to lose the elites on this, so there's a funny split. It is true that the Ashkenazi elites are the ones who are formally for peace, Meretz and the rest, but they're in favor of the neoliberal system and tend to support the breakdown of the social system, which doesn't harm them, but of course is very harmful to a large majority of the population, most of whom are Mizrahim. The Russian Jews are a separate component; I think there are about a million of them now; and with very few exceptions, they're extremely hawkish and very much opposed to any of the social democratic policies. Most of them are pretty well placed to move themselves into the professions; most of them, particularly the ones who came from Russia itself and not Georgia, are fairly well educated. And they're extremely militant and hawkish. Actually a lot of them aren't Jews. The Rabbinate, which is very corrupt, is willing to accept them as Jews—mostly because they're blond and blue-eyed, figuratively speaking. They don't look like Arabs, they look more like Northern Europeans. So that helps stem the Levantinization. The typical model of the Sabra, an Israeli Jew born in Israel, is supposed to be red-haired and strong, rather like a movie hero in the West. The Russian so-called Jews help with that. I think some of the estimates were that maybe half did not fit the strict criteria for being Jewish. In any event, they're a very hawkish element, and they're politically very significant.

The Ashkenazi elite tend to be dovish, but also tend to be neoliberal, and hopefully Peretz will go along with their dovishness, but not with their commitment to dismantle what's left of the social system, the health care system, and that sort of thing. The real question, which I don't think anybody can predict, is whether he can appeal to the poor Mizrahim. They have a political party, Shas, which is a sort of Jewish religious fundamentalist party. A lot of them are ultra-religious; they go to the local rabbi, who tells them what to do, it's very much out of the feudal system. The rabbi has been willing to make deals with the government in which his followers support the government in return for large government-funded benefits, kind of like a payoff. A lot of them just aren't part of the society—many of the men are studying Talmud and they don't serve in the armed forces; they have their own educational and social systems. It's a little bit like the Islamic fundamentalists. They may be crazy, but they're honest and provide services, and they get appeal out of that. They're a big enough party so their votes matter. The question is whether Peretz can make inroads into that, which would wean them away from their religious attachment to the rabbis, who are often pretty awful, and make them pay some attention to their lives, the social conditions in which they live. It's a little bit like in the United States, the famous *What's the Matter with Kansas?*[73] story: Can you get people away from religious extremism to pay some attention to the fact that the folks they're supporting are kicking them in the face? Not an easy problem, as you see right in the United States.

ACHCAR: I think the only way Peretz could achieve that would be by sticking to a progressive program on both the social issue and the peace issue. Any move to the right in order to accommodate the so-called centrist vote would make him squander this possibility.

Palestinian Politics

SHALOM: On the Palestinian side, what are the different political forces? What is Hamas's position within Palestinian society? What are the other groups?

ACHCAR: Hamas is a consequence of the socially and politically corrupt character of the traditional Palestinian leadership, the PLO leadership. It is an expression of mass resentment against this fact, and at the same time the expression of a radicalization, though in an unfortunate direction, of a segment of the Palestinian population since the time of the First Intifada, which sharpened the confrontation between the Palestinians of the West Bank and Gaza and the Israeli state. Now, Hamas of course built itself on an Islamic fundamentalist program, which, on the issue of Palestine, is an Islamic version of the maximalist program that Arab nationalism and Palestinian nationalism used to uphold in the 1950s—that is, an Islamic Palestinian state on the whole of Palestine, from which nonindigenous Jews should leave.

CHOMSKY: Have they taken that official position—that the nonindigenous Jews should leave?

ACHCAR: That's the kind of discourse their leaders used to maintain. There has been an evolution in the attitude of Hamas with regard to participation in the political process. They moved from an extremist position rejecting participation in any political process, like elections, under the occupation to a much cleverer one—as it proves now in light of the success they are achieving—of getting involved in the political process. I believe that it is a very positive development, because once they get into the political process, they will have to think politically and not only in terms of violent confrontation.

As long as you have corrupt leaders in control of the Palestinian Territories, you will have room for the increasing development of Islamic fundamentalist organizations, like Hamas or the Islamic Jihad. (The Islamic Jihad still rejects any participation in the elections, by the way.) The Islamic fundamentalists are able to contrast the fact that they are "honest" and "clean" with the corruption of the Palestinian Authority (PA) and PLO circles; they contrast their dedication to providing their constituency with social services, in a spirit of serving the population, with the kind of very mafia-like developments that are occurring at the level of the Palestinian authorities—factions of Fatah and of the PA apparatus even started shooting at each other recently. So this is a tragic story, the local illustration of the more general phenomenon we discussed, which is the bankruptcy of leaders originating in the nationalist movement or the left, leaving a wide space open for Islamic fundamentalism in various forms.

SHALOM: What about Marwan Barghouti,[74] for example, who's in jail? Does he represent another, more positive, secular pole?

ACHCAR: Frankly, it's difficult to tell, and one recent development does not go in a promising direction, which is the fact that he has entered an alliance with Mohammed Dahlan,[75] one of the most corrupt and most repressive-minded figures of the Palestinian Authority.

CHOMSKY: Do you think there's any resonance to his statement apologizing for past corruption, declaring that "now we're going to be honest" and so on?

ACHCAR: How could that be credible when he enters into a slate with someone like Dahlan, who is the embodiment of corruption, and who is also considered a kind of U.S./Israeli agent or stooge? There's something deeply rotten in this kingdom, unfortunately.

CHOMSKY: What about the professionals around Mustafa Barghouti?[76]

ACHCAR: Mustafa Barghouti is based in the NGO[77] movement—what nasty people call "the NGO industry"—and he can appeal to educated or relatively privileged segments of the population, but he could certainly not appeal to the large majority of the Palestinians, whether those in refugee camps or the general downtrodden people. These are much more likely to be attracted by an organization combining social activities with a radical nationalist discourse, in Islamic guise, like Hamas. Unfortunately, that's the way it is. There's a lack of credible progressive popular leadership within Palestinian society.

CHOMSKY: What do you think Mahmoud Abbas represents in Palestinian society?

ACHCAR: He represents a big chunk of the PLO–turned–into–Palestinian Authority apparatus, aspiring to set conditions through which they could govern the Palestinian state in a relatively stable way. Long ago I defined the PLO as a state apparatus without a territory of its own, seeking such a territory at the least cost.[78] The adoption by the PLO apparatus of the goal of a Palestinian state in the West Bank and Gaza was thus determined by their social aspiration to enjoy the full privileges of a state apparatus in control of a territory, and Mahmoud Abbas very much expresses that aspiration. He is also a symbol of the bureaucratic corruption of the Palestinian Authority; he is a representative of the bunch of "leaders" who own lavish villas in Gaza overlooking the misery of a Gaza Strip that is the equivalent of a big South African township. And this corruption did not start with the establishment of the Palestinian Authority in the wake of the Oslo Accords. It has much older roots in the corruption of the Palestinian guerilla movement that surged after the Arab defeat in June 1967, mainly in Jordan at first. It was a corruption nurtured, very consciously and deliberately, by the impressive amounts of petrodollars showered on the guerillas by all the major Arab oil-exporting states, each government seeking to secure the guerillas' dependence by addicting them to the external funding. The corruption peaked in Lebanon, especially in Beirut, propelled by several factors: the extermination of a major chunk of the most dedicated and radical Palestinian fighters in the 1970–71 massacres in Jordan; the much more extensive supply of the means and temptations of luxury in Beirut, compared with the Jordanian capital of Amman; and the fiefdoms that the PLO guerillas established for themselves in Lebanon after the start of the civil war there in 1975. This bureaucratic background determined the way the PLO looked for a negotiated settlement, through the kind of reasoning that Yasir Arafat expressed—namely the idea that since we can't beat Israel militarily, we have to settle for the diplomatic road. Of course, corrupt bureaucrats won't think of fighting Israel by means of popular mobilization and struggle. As you know, the Intifada, the first one that peaked in 1988, the one that had a real popular dynamic, started actually as a spontaneous explosion in December 1987 and then led to forms of self-organization at the level of grassroots Palestinian society. The PLO leadership in exile managed only later on, in 1988, to take control of the movement, and what helped them achieve that was the fact that Israeli repression smashed the self-organization of the Palestinians of the interior.

The PLO apparatus, the Palestinian bureaucracy, had come long ago to the view that the only path leading to the state they wished to get goes through the United States, and that means you have to cozy up to Washington. It fit perfectly with the very close links they used to have with the Saudi kingdom—which they lost for a while at the time of Iraq's invasion of Kuwait in 1990, but which were later reestablished. The shared view of the PLO leadership and the Saudi kingdom is, we should fight Israel in the United States; we should win over U.S. sympathy. This is fine if you mean the U.S. public, but they actually mean the U.S. government, and for that they believe that they should outbid Israel in proving useful to the United States—and you know where this leads.

How Can We Support Justice in Israel/Palestine?

SHALOM: What can people in the West, outside the region, do to support justice in Israel/Palestine?

CHOMSKY: My feeling is that the main target ought to be the United States. What the United States decides is conclusive; there's no other power in the world that can come close. The U.S. government has, with the very brief exception of a week in Taba, just blocked any steps toward a sensible political settlement, almost unilaterally. Israel has too, but Israel is limited in what it can do; it can't go much beyond the conditions that the United States establishes. And as long as Washington continues to give colossal military, diplomatic, ideological, media, and other support for Israeli expansion, I don't think anything's going to happen.

It's not an impossible task to change U.S. policy. U.S. public opinion is quite strongly against this. Some poll results are quite mind-boggling. Polls have found that a majority of the American population thinks there should be a negotiated settlement based on the international borders (pre–June 1967); people probably don't know exactly what that means, but that's what they said they want. PIPA, the Program on International Policy Attitudes, which does very serious work, found that two-thirds roughly said that the United States should withhold aid to Israel if it builds or expands its settlements or fails to withdraw its troops from the Occupied Territories. And another question was, suppose both sides agree to terms, then what? Approximately the same two-thirds said, in that case the United States should *equalize* aid to Israel and the Palestinians.[79]

SHALOM: Should these be the positions that the peace movement takes?

CHOMSKY: Yes, I think these are pretty reasonable positions, though they have to be sharpened considerably. Actually on a great range of issues, the stand of the majority of the American population is pretty reasonable. And this is one. You don't have to accept the details, but the general idea seems right to me.

U.S. aid to Israel is illegal because it violates congressional legislation that says "security assistance" cannot be given to countries that systematically violate human rights—a category that includes torture.[80] Israel claims that after many years of committing torture, it no longer does so, but a still secret section of a report by an Israeli government panel, the Landau Commission, authorizes interrogation procedures that human rights organizations agree constitute torture.[81]

So yes, these are all very plausible conditions, and probably the American population agrees with them already. It's again like those other polls. People take these positions without ever having heard the issue discussed in the press, the radio, or the journals of opinion. Nevertheless, that's just what people think on their own; it's common sense. If you could ever turn it into an issue of discussion, it would get enormous support, and that could compel the United States to back away from extreme rejectionism. In that case Israel would have to go along, and probably the majority of the population in Israel would accept it. They wouldn't love it, but they'd accept it because they want peace, too, as do most people. They don't want to live in insecurity. My guess is the Palestinians would accept it too, and then you could move forward to the type of settlements we were talking about before. The main barrier to that is the U.S. government, but that's the one thing we can influence, so that's a hopeful sign. It takes organization and activism, and picking tactics properly and carefully, but it seems to be basically an educational program, which can be carried out.

I should say that one of the major failings of the PLO was their complete unwillingness to try to reach out for some support among the American population—betting instead on their relations with the American government, as Gilbert said. My friends Ed Said[82] and Eqbal Ahmed[83] continually tried to convince them that the way to move forward was not to have a backroom deal with Kissinger and be invited to breakfast somewhere, but to gain some popular support among the American population. I was in on some of the private meetings that Ed set up when the PLO big shots would come to the United Nations; it was surreal. Ed and Eqbal were just tearing their hair out; they could not get them to do it or even understand it. Not only were PLO leaders not helping to organize support, they were making it difficult to do so. Every time Arafat showed up with a Kalashnikov and revolutionary slogans he didn't believe in, he made it harder to reach the American population. If they had come and told the truth—we're conservative nationalists, we'd like to elect our own mayors, we'll be your lackeys or something like that, which was the truth basically—they would at least have made it possible to organize support for them. But they could never understand that point. That was a really serious error. It's now being overcome. The younger Palestinians are different and they're helping, but there's a long way to go. In my own view, educating the American public is the main thing to be done. Europe is important, and it can help, but the main problem is in the United States.

ACHCAR: The Palestinian leadership understood correctly and quite rationally that the United States, as the godfather of the Israeli state, would be a crucial factor in their achieving a satisfactory settlement. And understanding that, they were much more advanced on this issue than advocates of the far-fetched view we already discussed: those who believe the Israeli tail wags the U.S. dog. They understood that the United States is not steered by the Israeli state but is its main sponsor, and if the United States changed course, it could exert tremendous pressure on the Israeli state in order to change its course. Naturally, what Noam meant, and what I am saying, does not at all imply that the Palestinians should try to outbid Israel in cozying up to Washington and try to convince the U.S. government that they could be better servants of U.S. imperial designs, which is basically what the Saudis advocate for the Arab states. Pressure on the United States— for Palestinian progressives or, for that matter, Israeli progressives or Arab progressives—should be accomplished by addressing public opinion in the United States, but addressing it in a manner that is very critical of the U.S. government (CHOMSKY: Exactly.) and linking up with those in the United States who are fighting against the imperial behavior of their government, which means the antiwar movement and other progressive movements. That would be the priority. (CHOMSKY: And in this case, I think they could do it right in the mainstream.) Right!

The same applies actually to how Palestinians can move toward a settlement with the Israeli state that would be acceptable to them: Is it by trying to get friendly with the Israeli rulers, or is it by addressing the Israeli public and trying to link up with and favor those forces in Israel that are sincerely committed to a lasting peace? The same logic applies here. Now to go back to the issue of pressure on Israel: What is the leverage of the United States on Israel? It is, of course, the fact that Israel depends on the United States for subsidizing its military economy. Israel can exist only as a kind of Sparta, a militarized society, because of U.S. funding. Therefore, the demand for the cessation of this funding, the military aid and all this privileging of the state of Israel, is perfectly legitimate. And that means exerting pressure on the Israeli state in order to push it toward the concessions that are necessary for a lasting peace in the region.

We can enlarge this perspective to Europe: For the movement concerned with the fate of the Palestinians, and with the whole Middle East issue, the legitimate approach is to fight against all the privileges that Israel gets from the rich countries. Israel receives all sorts of economic and other advantages from the European states, but when you look at these privileges in the light of Israel's behavior, there is no justification for them. They are rewarding a state that has been carrying out criminal policies and shamelessly violating international law. That is purely outrageous. So the demand to cease granting privileges to the Israeli state, and to attach conditions to any aid that is given to that state, is quite legitimate. But it should not be done—and this is very important—in a way that makes the Israeli *population* feel that it is being ostracized. That would be completely counterproductive. Any campaign on this issue should make great efforts to link up with those Israelis who are fighting the oppressive policies of their government, and that's crucial. So it is not a matter of boycotting Israeli society; it is a matter of boycotting Israeli reactionaries and criminals, those who advocate and put into practice criminal policies that we condemn.

CHOMSKY: I think that's absolutely correct, I think that really has to be emphasized. It's just the right approach, and I think it could work.

Boycotts, Divestment, and Other Tactics

SHALOM: Could you comment specifically on a few of the tactics that have been proposed as a way that people in the West can help to change Israeli policy? Some have proposed an academic boycott of Israeli academics, and then there are various calls for divestment.

CHOMSKY: Personally, I think the academic boycott is a very bad idea. For one thing, the public doesn't understand it. A tactic has to be judged not on the basis of what you think of it as a matter of principle but on what it's effect is going to be. Take, say, South Africa, which is always brought up. The boycotts against South Africa were ultimately significant—they actually didn't work, the Reagan administration evaded them, but they were significant. But that's after decades of educational and organizational work, so people understood what they were about; the boycotts were called at a time when they had mayors carrying out civil disobedience. They had corporations agreeing to the Sullivan conditions,[84] and so on. After a substantial period of education, when people know what you're doing, at that point you can begin to talk about boycotts. But to carry them out when it just looks like some anti-Semitic effort or something, because nobody understands it, that's a very bad tactic. And in fact it's a gift to the hardliners, who will say, you just want to throw us all into gas chambers.

As for divestment, it depends on what you mean. Following the Israeli military incursion into Jenin in April 2002,[85] there were various divestment proposals, mostly initiated by very good people who were just really upset by what was going on. The original versions of the proposals—this was going on all over the country—called for universities to "divest from Israel." But divestment from Israel is meaningless. Universities don't invest in Israel, so they can't divest from Israel. It's just a logical impossibility. So the call for the universities to divest from Israel was just going to lead to accusations of anti-Semitism, and it doesn't mean anything anyway. My feeling has always been that this language should be cut out. Then comes the question of divesting from corporations that invest in Israel. Then I think you have to make it nuanced—arms producers, Caterpillar,[86] and so on, yes. Then it makes sense, because they're actually involved in criminal acts. One shouldn't support corporations that are involved in criminal acts, whether it's in Israel or any other place you mention. But anything that looks like, as Gilbert said, just an attack on Israeli society, that's counterproductive.

SHALOM: What about Israeli government bonds?

CHOMSKY: There's a major scandal that somebody ought to look into. There are labor unions where the working class is mostly Black and Puerto Rican and so on, but the leadership is made up of old-time social democratic Jews. For years they were investing union pension funds into Israeli bonds. I think that that's illegal under U.S. law, because they're required, as part of their fiduciary responsibility, to get the safest and maximal return for their workers. My feeling is they were able to get away with it only because they kept it rather quiet. It wasn't literally secret—pro-Zionist books and organizations boasted about it, so it was public—but if their own workforce had known about it, I think they would have been hanged from the nearest tree. They're sacrificing the interests of their own workforce to support Israel, probably illegally. But the issue was never raised. That's one of the big failures; it should have been pressed with the American working class by saying, "Look what the leadership is doing to you." I doubt that American universities have Israeli bonds, but if they do, it would certainly be right to call for divestment. The major issue regarding Israeli bonds that I know of, however, concerns the unions.

I think the main sort of divestment pressure ought to be pressure on the U.S. government to stop providing military aid to Israel as long as it does not satisfy minimal conditions, like observing the Geneva conventions, or observing international law in other respects, or ceasing its use of torture or its building of settlements. As long as it is doing any of those things in violation of what is almost universally regarded as an application of direct international humanitarian and other law, the U.S. government should stop providing Israel with any kind of military aid. And economic aid also, but there isn't much. And also stop providing them with diplomatic support. As far as divesting from corporations is concerned, I think it has to be focused, if it's going to be meaningful. It's symbolic anyway, so make it a symbolic point that when a corporation is directly involved in criminal activities, as with Caterpillar, or any arms manufacturer, yes, divest from them. And in fact that's a very conservative position. That means: Observe American law. American law says you're not allowed to do any of these things, so observe it and divest from companies that won't do it. That would be a sensible position.

Unfortunately, the divestment petitions were not always entirely sensible. Let's take MIT and Harvard, which I know about because I was right in the middle of it. The MIT/Harvard petition initially had this general formulation, "Divest from Israel"—a blanket statement, which is meaningless. After a lot of discussion, they finally made it specific. You can take a look at the petition; it's on the web.[87] It ended up being mostly quite sensible, saying we "call on the U.S. government to make military aid and arms sales to Israel conditional on immediate initiation and rapid progress in implementing the conditions listed below," and then comes a series of elementary conditions: the Geneva conventions and so on. And we "call on MIT and Harvard to divest from . . . U.S. companies that sell arms to Israel, until these conditions are met." But then, over my strong objection, they insisted on adding the words, and "to divest from Israel." Well, I agreed to sign it, the way you usually sign petitions, even if you don't entirely agree with them, because the spirit is right. But I knew it was a terrible mistake. The whole petition went down the tube. You immediately had Larry Summers, the president of Harvard, and Alan Dershowitz saying, "Oh, they want to divest from Israel," which is that meaningless phrase. Universities can't divest from Israel, but the petition organizers insisted on putting it in. Furthermore, *I* got the flack, because immediately I was deemed the person who was initiating this: you know, the arch criminal who is trying to destroy Israel. I had to deal with all the fallout, while the people who were involved in it, well meaning but often politically inexperienced, mostly went back to their labs. That's the kind of tactical mistake you can make. It is a gift to the extreme hawks. You think you're acting on principle, but you're actually giving a gift to your worst enemies.

Those are the kind of questions that have to be thought about when you carry out some tactic. You just don't give an opening to your worst enemies, an opening that in a sense they have some kind of justification for. You have to prepare the ground for anything you do, and then what you do has to be calibrated so that it is not alienating the people you want to be associated with, like a lot of people in Israel, for example. And so that it's not offering a weapon to your worst enemies. Those are choices that have to be made regarding any action. The same with demonstrations and the Weathermen, and any of these issues: You've got to think of what the consequences are going to be.

ACHCAR: On the issue of academic boycott, one should be precise about what is meant by it. If boycotting Israeli academics is what's meant, it strikes me as completely counterproductive. On the contrary, Israeli academics should be given exposure to the outside world, instead of promoting the kind of siege mentality that Zionism, especially right-wing Zionism, has very much used. But on the other hand, you have the issue of institutional collaboration between universities abroad and Israeli universities. And that should be linked to conditions. For instance, at some point when you had the closure of Palestinian universities,[88] institutional collaboration with Israeli universities should have been conditioned by the possibility of having the same with Palestinian universities, which should be allowed to function. And of course, you have also some academic institutions in Israel that make a direct contribution to the military effort of the Israeli state. And here there is a legitimate point to demand the cessation of any collaboration with such institutions. As a general rule, I would say that the legitimate kind of pressure that can be accepted and understood, and that is productive and useful, consists not in measures giving the impression that you are boycotting the Israeli society, as such, but in measures dealing with the aid and privileges that Israel gets in its relation with Western countries—demanding any such aid be linked to conditions, at least. The most effective conditionality to be put forward is, in my view, that which points to the colonization of Palestinian land: Stop and reverse the colonization policy!

For the rest, I agree completely with Noam, but I should note a problem when one asks the United States to put pressure on Israel to stop torture, since Israeli practice is not worse than U.S. practice in this regard. Where's the morality? (CHOMSKY: That's true of the whole boycott—why don't we boycott the United States?) The point where there is a difference between Israeli and U.S. policy is on the matter of colonization. This is one of the issues that, I'm sure, is well understood by the public. The Israeli settlements in the Occupied Territories are illegal by international law standards; even the U.S. government has long taken the view that they are illegal, and has repeatedly asked for a settlement freeze. Israel has always refused any such freeze, so there's a strong case here that can be readily understood: that any kind of economic aid to Israel should be conditioned on a cessation of settlement activity. It means putting pressure on Israel to move toward what are very basic and elementary prerequisites of any peaceful resolution of the conflict.

CHOMSKY: Now there's another very concrete case that you can focus on, and that's the Separation Wall. No aid until the Wall is dismantled.

ACHCAR: Stop colonization and dismantle the settlements, stop building the Wall and destroy it.

CHOMSKY: If you want a wall, build it on Israeli territory.

Anti-Semitism

SHALOM: You mentioned anti-Semitism. How serious a problem is anti-Semitism in the world today?

CHOMSKY: In the ranking of problems, I think maybe it comes up to a thousandth, or something like that. It differs in different places. For example, what they call anti-Semitism in France is, I think, mostly whatever is going on in the Muslim communities. But there, they're reacting to real things—what's happening to the Palestinians and so on—though probably there's some anti-Semitism in it. Let me talk not about France, however, but about the United States, which is what I know best.

If you go back to the 1930s, there was real anti-Semitism in the United States. It was very striking. I grew up in an Irish and German Catholic neighborhood of Philadelphia where we happened to be the only Jewish family most of the time. The kids on the street were extremely anti-Semitic. It's not like these days—we didn't get shot or knifed, but I'd get beat up, and stuff like that. When the Irish kids came out of the Jesuit school, they were raving anti-Semites. Maybe they'd calm down later and I'd play with them. The families were clearly pro-Nazi: the Irish, because they were anti-British; the Germans, because they were German. The anti-Semitism was just in the streets everywhere; you lived with it.

The situation changed after World War II, and it was the effect of the Holocaust. When I got to Harvard in the early 1950s, however, anti-Semitism was still pervasive. There were almost no Jewish faculty members. In fact, one of the reasons MIT became a great university is because Jewish faculty couldn't get appointed at Harvard, people like Norbert Weiner or I suppose Paul Samuelson. So they went to the engineering school down the street. It was mostly a class issue; MIT didn't have the class prejudice, so it became an important university. Harvard was very clubby and that sort of thing, and people like me didn't even know about it; I was just not in that world, not that I care, obviously. There were a few Jewish professors at Harvard; there was Harry Wolfson, a distinguished scholar who had the official Jewish Studies chair, like some universities might have an official women's chair for the one woman professor. There were a couple of other Jewish faculty, but some were like what Black people often call "white blacks"—they were more Anglo-Saxon than the Anglo-Saxons in their style and manner, their dress, and everything else.

Throughout the 1950s that changed, and changed radically. Anti-Semitism declined in the whole society, enormously, and then you could see it at Harvard. By 1960, there were plenty of Jewish faculty, many of the deans were Jewish, and in 2001 a Jew was made president. That reflects what's going on in the whole society—anti-Semitism has just declined. It's probably still there somewhere, but among prejudices, it ranks very low. And Jews are a very privileged group. If you compare them with other minorities, by any measure you want—income, status, everything else—they're just off the chart.

In fact, the attitude toward Jews reversed. I remember seeing a 1951 movie called *The Enforcer*. It was about "Murder, Incorporated"—which was almost entirely a Jewish operation. Jews were running criminal gangs in the 1920s, as other immigrant groups did in their turn. It later became an Italian operation. But Hollywood is heavily Jewish, so they didn't want Jewish criminals running Murder, Incorporated; Italians were okay, though. So the movie portrayed all these guys who looked Sicilian carrying out operations that in reality Jews were carrying out. It's the kind of thing that was happening. Jews became a privileged group. And it goes on like that—movies, literature, the media, everything else. By now anti-Semitism is almost nonexistent. But there are those who try to build it up. For example, after the divestment proposal that I mentioned, there was a huge campaign around here that involved the president of Harvard University saying, there's a wave of anti-Semitism, and the proof is that there are people calling for divestment from Israel, among other things. This became a major issue in Cambridge, Massachusetts, and now it's going on all over the country, promoted by the David Project[89] and others, trying to show that the universities are anti-Semitic. You don't even know how to talk about it, it's so outlandish.

Just to give you an example: After the Larry Summers–Dershowitz hysteria about anti-Semitism at Harvard and MIT, the head of the anthropology department at Harvard, a progressive African American, asked me to give a talk on anti-Semitism to his race seminar at Harvard. I laughed and asked, what are we talking about? The president is Jewish, many of the faculty are Jewish, many students are Jewish, what's the issue? It's a joke, I said. He said, yes, it was a joke, but it was a very contentious issue on campus. So I agreed to go. I gave a talk, approximately along the lines of my remarks above: I said, yes, there was anti-Semitism, and I went through the background, and how it had changed. At the end of the talk, I came up with something I thought was going to be a great punch line, but it fell totally flat. I concluded by saying you no longer read things like the following written by distinguished and respected Harvard professors; then I gave a bunch of actual quotes from people like Michael Walzer, Ruth Wisse, and Martin Peretz[90]—but they had been talking about Arabs, and at this point in the talk I replaced the word "Arab" in their quotes with "Jew." The quotes sounded like they came out of the Nazi archives, about Jews, and there were gasps from the audience: How could Harvard professors ever have done this? And then I said, well, I misled you, those quotes weren't really about Jews, they were about Arabs. And, interestingly, there was a sigh of relief in the audience. I hadn't anticipated this reaction; apparently, as long as extreme racist comments of the kind that sound like Nazis are about Palestinians and Arabs, then it's fine. But if you were to say anything like that about Jews, the place would blow up.

I think that's basically the answer to the question about the extent of anti-Semitism. There's manufactured anti-Semitism. It's manufactured by the Jewish organizations, very consciously.

Take the Anti-Defamation League. It's hard to believe, but years ago it used to be an authentic civil rights organization. Now it's a kind of Stalinist-style apologetics-for-Israel organization. In 1982 they got worried about the lack of anti-Semitism in the country, because that's their business. So they published a book by their national director called *The Real Anti-Semitism in America*—with the word "Real" italicized.[91] The book says there is old-fashioned anti-Semitism—Holocaust denial, calls to kill the Jews, and so on—but that's marginal and boring. There's a new kind of anti-Semitism, however, that is much more serious than the old kind. The new kind of anti-Semitism consists of peacemakers of Vietnam vintage who want to undermine and attack the Pentagon budget or people who join the nuclear freeze campaign, and the book goes on like that. Why is that the new anti-Semitism? Because they're undermining the power and violence of the U.S. government, and Israel relies on that. So therefore, indirectly, they're undermining Israel; so therefore, they're *real* anti-Semites. It's really quite incredible.

There are major attacks on the universities coming from the far right, from the David Project, from David Horowitz's outfit,[92] and so on, that are significant, not because of their intellectual content but because there's plenty of money behind them. They're going after the university as hotbeds of anti-Semitism and anti-Israel sentiment. The evidence that's given is anecdotal, and most of it is ridiculous. There's an easy way of testing their claims, but they're very careful not to do it: Just run a poll of university faculty and students, asking how many think Israel should have the rights of any state in the international system. They won't run that poll because they know that close to 100 percent would answer affirmatively—actually, to be precise, it would probably be 50 percent, because the other 50 percent would say Israel ought to have *more* rights than any state in the system. This would settle the matter, but since it wouldn't support their claims of anti-Semitic domination of academia, that's a poll we'll never see, and instead come these anecdotes. Dershowitz goes down and makes a speech, Elie Wiesel sheds some tears, and so on and so forth, and by now there are more than a dozen state legislatures that are considering legislation to require monitoring of the universities to make sure that they're not anti-American, anti-Semitic, or anti-Israel, and that they don't punish conservative students for opening their mouths.[93] When was the last time you saw that happen in an American university? There are people who are punished, but it's not conservative students. But this is going through various state legislatures and it's a significant phenomenon. It's intimidating universities—especially state universities, which get their money from the legislature.

The alleged anti-Semitism is a core part of the right-wing attack, because it's a good propaganda weapon: If you can imply in some fashion that anyone is anti-Semitic, you bring out what Norman Finkelstein accurately called the Holocaust Industry.[94] He's been bitterly denounced for telling the truth about it, but he's correct. It's an industry, a carefully planned, programmed, and orchestrated industry. It has nothing to do with the Holocaust; it has everything to do with exploiting it in an extremely ugly way. Exploiting the victims of the Holocaust in order to justify oppression and atrocities is the ultimate insult to their memories, but that doesn't bother these people at all. And the whole industry, as Finkelstein points out accurately, picked up after 1967. Before 1967 there were no Holocaust museums, there was none of the later adulation of Elie Wiesel, none of this stuff. It all picked up as a means of justifying the Israeli occupation; it became a huge business. Every city in the United States has to have a Holocaust museum, not a slavery museum, not a Native American museum, but a Holocaust museum. Why? Is it because of concern about the Holocaust? If it was, why wasn't something done for the victims in the 1940s? One could argue about what was actually possible during the war, but after the war there was no issue, so why wasn't anything done for them? Why was nothing done in the 1950s? It wasn't an issue. After 1967, however, it became a huge phenomenon, and an extremely ugly one; it's simply been used as a weapon to beat people over the heads.

Some of it was really grotesque. Consider the way they went after Dan Berrigan. He was a radical pacifist priest, one of those who were spilling blood on draft centers, in and out of jail, and so on—but in 1973 he made a fairly moderate speech[95] in which he said that Palestinians should have some rights too, they're not just the scum of the earth, and so on. It was an embarrassingly mild speech, but did they go after him! Irving Howe, Seymour Martin Lipset,[96] and others denounced him. I have a discussion of it in a chapter of *Peace in the Middle East*,[97] where I go through a lot of this material. One of the most disgusting was Irving Howe, who had an Op Ed in the *New York Times*, which he thought was so great he even made it the final article in a volume he edited in the early 1970s on democratic socialist views on Israel.[98] He absolutely despised the New Left—mainly, I think, because they weren't paying any attention to him. He thought he should be their leader, having held up the flag all those difficult years, and they didn't really care very much. Part of his line was that the New Left was anti-Israel; as a matter of fact, the New Left was dovish Zionist, to the extent that they cared about the issue at all. Howe starts off his Op Ed by asking how can Israel ever win back the favor of the New Left? He says, here's a way to do it: Israel can establish a fascist dictatorship, with blood flowing in the streets, and then the New Left, from "Scarsdale, Evanston, and Palo Alto"—you have to get the imagery, that's different from the working-class blokes in the *Dissent* office[99]—will all flock to celebrate Israel; Sartre will go there and write a thousand-page book in which he gets the street names wrong; and Howe goes on and on like this. Howe surely knew that Sartre was quite pro-Israel, but no matter. Anti-Semitism is a terrific weapon for justifying Israeli atrocities and for attacking your enemies. If it's not there, you manufacture it. That's anti-Semitism in the United States. Yes, you could probably find some pocket of it here or there, but it's so meaningless it's not worth discussing.

Anti-Semitism in Western Europe

ACHCAR: Regarding Western Europe, one could say that anti-Semitism, in the classic sense of the term, is a residual and marginal phenomenon. If we put aside some of the Muslim communities of immigrant origin that you've got in Europe, for the rest it's relatively minor. The new rise of the far right since the late 1970s and 1980s has not been built around anti-Semitism, although you find anti-Semitic utterances and statements from sections of the European far right. It is clear enough that this is not at all the main appeal of the far right to their constituency, and it's not at all their main ideological argument. Their main ideological argument actually is anti-immigrant. And the immigrants are not Jewish immigrants any longer. Previous waves of anti-Semitism were at their peak when you had Jewish immigration from Eastern Europe—that's a well-known historical fact. But currently immigration is mostly from Muslim countries to Germany, France, Britain, and other West European countries. In that sense, the old anti-Semitism has been progressively reduced to the margins since World War II, and one expression of this change in mentality was the May 1968 mass student movement in France, one of the leaders of which was Daniel Cohn-Bendit, a German Jew. One of the most popular slogans of the student movement, shouted in mass demonstrations, was "We are all German

Jews." For French youngsters, to shout "We are all German Jews" meant a rejection of two features of a century-old historical legacy: anti-German attitudes and anti-Semitic attitudes.

This is one thing, but quite another is the public sentiment in France about Israel and the Israeli state. In that last respect, one could say that throughout the years an increasing proportion of French public opinion has turned critical toward the Israeli state. That went through stages.

One major shift occurred in 1967, when the image of Israel changed from that of a state of people escaping from oppression, people toward whom there was sympathy as victims of European anti-Semitism, to that of an aggressive, expansionist military state, very proud of its prowess at war. And the shift in perception at that time was illustrated by a famous statement by French president Charles de Gaulle, in which he referred to Jews as "an elite people, sure of themselves and domineering."[100] The statement verged on anti-Semitism, but it expressed the new perception of the Israeli state as a domineering state. In a sense, the very boastful Israeli propaganda at the time was harmful to the sympathy that Israel enjoyed, because people normally feel stronger sympathy with victims, especially victims toward whom they have a feeling of guilt, than with boastful victors. And then a second, very important stage followed the Israeli invasion of Lebanon in 1982 with all its consequences, including the Sabra and Shatila massacre. Here were scenes of an Israeli army besieging a section of a city—and even reports of poignant statements by Israelis disgusted at the fact that this reminded them of the Warsaw Ghetto uprising! And then the outcry against Israel's collusion in and responsibility for the Sabra and Shatila massacre was overwhelming. All this did a lot of harm to Israel's image in European public opinion. And the 1987–88 Intifada of course was also very important, the third stage in the shift. Now the Israeli soldiers were shooting at unarmed children, who couldn't possibly be mistaken for terrorists, and breaking the limbs of unarmed Palestinians, with then Minister of so-called Defense Rabin infamously inciting them to do so.[101] I remember how moved I was when I read in the *International Herald Tribune* a statement by an Israeli woman disgusted by an article published in the *Jerusalem Post* about a blood-splattered wall in the West Bank where Israeli soldiers had taken Palestinians to beat them, and likening it to what was done in Nazi camps.[102]

Now when the image of Israel worsens, deservedly, because of the very aggressive and oppressive behavior of the Israeli state, if people who pretend to speak in the name of all the Jews, of the "Jewish community," identify totally, unconditionally, and uncritically with the Israeli army and government, then of course this can only feed resentment and add to confusion. I mentioned the 1968 slogan "We are all German Jews"; there was a clumsy attempt at imitating that kind of slogan thirty years later, in 1999. That took place after thirteen Iranian Jews had been arrested in Iran and accused of being agents of the Israeli equivalent of the CIA, the Mossad. The French branch of the Zionist far-right youth organization, Betar, bought billboards and newspaper ads carrying the sentence "We are all Mossad agents."

Of course, with such ads, you can expect at the very least—since the Mossad does not exactly have the reputation of being a humanitarian organization, any more than the CIA does—that you will arouse a certain degree of hostility toward those in whose name you pretend to speak among all those who sympathize with the countless victims of Mossad. This will especially be the case among those populations who, for reasons of geographical, cultural, or religious origin, as well as because of their feeling that they too are part of "the wretched of the earth," have the most reason to identify strongly with the Palestinians. And that explains the so-called resurgence of anti-Semitism, which bears little relation to what has been called anti-Semitism in recent history, but relates much more to the kind of resentment that is quite common among oppressed populations, as with the "anti-White racism" that was common among the Black majority in South Africa. Since Israel is perceived as the sharpest embodiment of Western domination over the Muslim world, those who boastfully identify with Israel will become natural targets of the same resentment, which more or less degenerates into racist expressions. All this, of course, was very much related to the violence of the repression of the so-called Second Intifada from 2000 onward. That's the time at which there was the sharpest increase in anti-Jewish acts in France, and in anti-Jewish feelings among the Muslim populations of immigrant origin. But, aside from putting this in context, one should stress that, at any rate, the social groups most associated with such feelings are definitely not in a position to represent any threat to the Jews comparable in any way to interwar German anti-Semitism, or interwar French anti-Semitism for that matter, because today the "anti-Semitic" groups are themselves the main victims of racism from the larger society. This latter racism is far more dangerous and threatening than anti-Semitism. Of course, progressives—whether those belonging to these immigrant communities or progressives in general—must fight energetically against any kind of anti-Jewish ethnic hatred, not to mention anti-Semitism, and against any assumption that French Jews are responsible for Israel's acts.

In this fight, French progressives of Jewish descent play a very important role by proclaiming: Not in my name. For instance, when Israel launched its violent repression of the Second Intifada in 2000, there was a statement published in the French daily *Le Monde*, signed by many progressives of

Jewish descent, under the title "En tant que Juifs"—"As Jews."[103] They started by saying that it was not usual for them to express themselves as Jews because they don't want to be stuck into any kind of ethnic or religious identity. But faced with the rulers of a state, Israel, pretending to speak in the name of all the Jews of the world, and implementing in that name actions they deem horrendous, they wanted to say that, "as Jews," they reject all that and condemn the acts of the Israeli state, while fighting, of course, all forms of racism and anti-Semitism.

CHOMSKY: It seems to me that the attitude toward Jews in Europe is very favorable, by and large; it's the opposite of anti-Semitism: They're privileged and respected among minorities.

ACHCAR: Or at the very least I would say that for the vast majority, anti-Semitism is rejected as one acquires education. People have integrated this education that anti-Semitism and any discourse of hatred against the Jews are something to be condemned. It is associated with Hitlerism and fascism. This is something that people have learned; it is integrated into the schools' curriculum, and that's a very welcome development. In Europe, the theater of the Holocaust, and especially in Germany, there is a natural sense of guilt and, accordingly, a positive attitude toward Jews, sometimes bordering on a caricatured philo-Semitism that turns into unconditional pro-Zionist or pro-Israel stances. For instance, the so-called Antideutsch current in Germany grew out of an ultra-left rejection of Germany as a nation; however, members of this current are at the same time unconditional supporters of Israel, sometimes falling into anti-Muslim, anti-immigrant attitudes; but these are fringe phenomena, actually.

Now, all that doesn't mean that there is no threat of, and potential for, anti-Semitism—especially in countries like Germany and Austria, or Poland. Because of that, I think progressives should take great care to combine their condemnation of the policies of the Israeli state with denunciation of anti-Semitism and racism. I think that's very important. Progressive critiques of Israel and/or Zionism should be combined with the clear-cut rejection of all manifestations of racism and anti-Semitism.

CHOMSKY: My feeling is that this would be more critical in Europe than in the United States; here, anti-Semitism is so marginal, sensible people wouldn't even know what you're criticizing. I think it might seem very affected here.

ACHCAR: You know better than I about the United States. In Europe, however, this is a concern that should remain present. Progressives should advocate and work for the common struggle of Jews and Muslims against racism and anti-Semitism. They must explain that the racist frame of mind is the problem, whether it's directed against Jews, Muslims, Blacks, other minorities, or all of them combined, and all the minorities actually have a clear interest in joining together against any kind of ethnic hatred in alliance with the antiracist movement.

CHOMSKY: It was once true in the United States; there were Black-Jewish alliances against racism. But unfortunately that's turned into the opposite.

SHALOM: Previously, when we were talking about fundamentalism, you mentioned the anti-Semitism among pro-Israeli Christian fundamentalists.

CHOMSKY: They don't call it anti-Semitism, but their position is that when the Second Coming takes place, those who accept Christ are saved—and everyone else is damned. That means all the Jews. How can you be more anti-Semitic than that?

SHALOM: What does the Anti-Defamation League say about that?

CHOMSKY: They're quiet about it, because the Christian fundamentalists are a big pro-Israel group. So that's what they call the old, antique, and obsolete anti-Semitism—not the real kind, such as opposing the Pentagon budget. That's literally their line.

ACHCAR: But televangelist Pat Robertson went a step too far with his statement about Sharon.[104] He dumped on Sharon for wanting to divide the land of Israel!

CHOMSKY: So God struck him down!

ACHCAR: I want to pick up where I stopped, when I was saying it's necessary to combine critiques of Zionism and Israel with a clear-cut rejection of anti-Semitism, and add that this is all the more important in the Arab world, where for obvious reasons the hatred of the Israeli state is greater than anywhere else and can easily turn into anti-Jewish hatred. And that has increasingly been the case actually at the level of the most militant forms of anti-Israeli expression, because of the huge ideological regression in that part of the world: from early on, when you had progressive Arab nationalism and other brands of even more progressive left-wing forces prominent in the mass movement, to the present time when the most active, most militant forces in opposition to the whole system, unfortunately, are Islamic fundamentalists. It's very important that there be a thorough education in the Arab world and among the Palestinians against any confusion between Zionism and the Jews in general, or even the Israelis in general.

This is very important not only for principled reasons, because any kind of racism or ethnic hatred is basically reactionary, even when it is the racism of the weak against the strong. Of course, one should make a distinction between the racism of the weak and the racism of the strong—the anti-White racism of Black South Africans under apartheid cannot be equated with White anti-Black racism. This being said, however, any kind of racism is essentially reactionary. But moreover, as I said before, one of the preconditions for moving toward implementation of the rights of the Palestinian people is to have a major segment of the Israeli population breaking from the present policies of the Israeli state. Otherwise it's strictly impossible. And the more that discourse of an anti-Semitic character prevails on the Arab side, the less there will be any inclination among the Israelis to compromise. Therefore, anti-Semitism is actually self-defeating for the Palestinian struggle. Unfortunately you have such a level of ideological regression and idiocy nowadays that this basic fact is obscured.

CHOMSKY: Are you aware of any initiatives in the Arab world to address anti-Semitism?

ACHCAR: There are some Arab intellectuals and small groups who have done so.

CHOMSKY: Were they outspoken?

ACHCAR: There was some criticism of Ahmadinejad's Holocaust denial statements in the Arab world. The problem is that the criticism comes more from liberal and pro-Western circles than from left-wing circles. That's a pity.

CHOMSKY: The left was silent on this?

ACHCAR: What remains of the Arab left is overwhelmed by narrow-minded regressive nationalism. That's also true in Egypt. There's been a real regression when we compare the current situation with the 1970s or the late 1960s—a massive ideological regression. Of course, you have many prominent intellectuals, whether inside or outside the Arab world—Edward Said was one of them—who warn against that and condemn it strongly; but unfortunately the opposite trend is gaining ground nowadays. And this despite the fact that, as I said, it is completely self-defeating on top of all the principled considerations. Just take as an example Ahmadinejad's speeches. If this guy had just said, why should the Palestinian people have paid the price for European anti-Semitism? that would have been OK. But he added Holocaust denial statements. That's not only false but completely contradictory: One cannot say that those responsible for the Holocaust should be the ones to pay for it, not the Palestinian people, and then put into question the reality of the Holocaust in the most stupid manner. That's a contradictory argument that plays into the hand of unconditional, pro-Israeli forces.

CHOMSKY: How does it play in Iran?

ACHCAR: Same thing: It has been criticized by the most Westernized or liberal circles. But at the level of the popular movement, not only in Iran but in the Arab world and probably the Muslim world in general, Ahmadinejad's statements struck a chord. They cater to some popular feeling that derives from a combination of ignorance and exasperation with Israeli policies and Western endorsement of them. Of course this sort of reaction to Israel's oppressive policies is incredibly stupid, playing into the hands of Zionist propaganda.

Anti-Arab Racism and Islamophobia

SHALOM: What are the significance and extent of anti-Arab racism?

CHOMSKY: In the United States, it's really the last legitimate form of racism. You don't have to try to cover it up. You may be racist toward other groups, but you have to pretend you aren't. In the case of anti-Arab racism, there's no pretense required. The things I mentioned before are a perfect example: Distinguished Harvard professors produce statements that you would regard as hideously racist if they were aimed at any other target—Jews: impossible; Blacks, Italians, any of them: unacceptable—but if you say them about Arabs, it's fine. Jack Shaheen is one scholar who's done a lot of research on images of Arabs in the cinema.[105] It's grotesque, right up to the present day. There's not even much to say about it; it's open, it's considered natural and normal that you should be an anti-Arab racist. Nobody will use that term for it, but it's the kind of attitude and discourse that we would regard as hideously racist if it was directed at any other target. It's all over the place.

ACHCAR: And anti-Arab racism is probably the sharpest form of even something more general, Islamophobia.

CHOMSKY: Well, nobody makes that distinction—Arabs, Iranians, Islam, it's all the same thing.

ACHCAR: Exactly. Try to put yourself in the shoes of a Muslim and monitor the mass media. It's appalling. You get a feeling of being assaulted permanently. I am not speaking of actual acts of racist aggression, discrimination, and all that. I am speaking just about the media. Edward Said touched upon that in *Covering Islam*.[106] The situation has worsened a lot since that book was first published in 1981, and it reached a peak after 9/11. The sheer quantity of anti-Islam insanities and racist categorizations being hurled by people who are in most cases totally ignorant is absolutely horrible. I can't measure the difference between Europe and the United States, but in any case, in Europe, this Islamophobia is a huge and very worrying phenomenon. Sometimes it is expressed unwittingly with those good intentions with which the road to hell is paved, in the name of secularism or opposition to women's oppression, or whatever, but with a blatant lack of sensitivity for the feelings of the most downtrodden sections of the resident population, who are of Muslim descent. At the very least, if one is sincerely expressing a view in the name of progressive values such as secularism or women's liberation, one should at the same time take into consideration the obvious fact that discourse hostile to Islam is overwhelmingly racist—and not just for progressive reasons that would hence apply to all major religions. Here again, what one could call the "anti-Semitic test" is very useful: Replace "Islam" with "Judaism" in the statements and you get a measure for Westerners of what Muslims may feel. You even find best-selling authors attacking "Islam" as a whole, not this or that peculiar interpretation of Islam. Of course, measured by present-day criteria, a lot of what you find in Islamic scriptures—especially about women—looks terribly backward, but the fact is that many Muslim believers reject a literalist fundamentalist interpretation of the scriptures and believe, instead, in the necessity of taking heed of their spirit, their progressive character at the time of their first appearance, and of adapting religion to modern times. The same is very much true for Judaism: The original scriptures are horribly backward on the issue of women, to consider just that touchstone— definitely not better than anything you find in Islamic scriptures, if not worse, actually. And there is an ocean of difference on such issues between Jewish fundamentalism and reformed Judaism. So most people in Western countries would not stomach a pamphlet attacking Judaism per se, by singling it out and without qualification. But unfortunately even many well-intentioned people don't pay enough attention to that when it comes to Islam and end up reinforcing the general and very worrying trend of Islamophobia. So if you compare the levels of anti-Semitism and of Islamophobia in Europe today, not to mention the United States, it is clear that Islamophobia is far more pervasive and far more intense than anything that could properly be labeled anti-Semitism.

CHOMSKY: One pretty dramatic illustration of such racism is the difference in the reactions to Sharon's life-threatening stroke and to Arafat's death. The former was treated as if one of the great figures of modern history was in danger, a man who was the hope for peace, and so on, whereas Arafat's death was treated with a mixture of relief and contempt. Relief that finally this monster is gone, and utter contempt; that was the way it was dealt with. The difference is just dramatic. Whatever one thinks of Arafat, his record doesn't come close to Sharon's record of crimes and atrocities. It's a very dramatic illustration of this difference.

ACHCAR: Absolutely. And one could give innumerable examples pointing likewise to the fact that Islam and the Muslims have become the most "natural" targets of the diffuse racism really existing in Western countries. The so-called culturalist view of the rise of Islamic fundamentalism, attributing it to some ingrained features pertaining to the very essence of the Islamic religion, is pervasive—aggravated by the fact that Islamic fundamentalism was relabeled by some as "Islamism," thus introducing confusion in the general public between Islamic fundamentalism and Islam as such. Modern-day "Orientalism," in the pejorative sense of this expression that was made famous by the late Edward Said[107]—that is, the practice of explaining the state of Islamic countries or the fate of Muslims not by history but by some alleged ahistorical, immutable essence of Islam—has become one of the most common and widespread entries in the contemporary version of Gustave Flaubert's dictionary of "accepted ideas." Many people in the West don't understand that there is nothing "natural" or ahistorical in the fact that Islamic fundamentalism is nowadays the most visible political current among Muslim peoples. They ignore or forget that the picture was completely different in other historical periods of our contemporary history—that, for instance, a few decades ago the largest nongoverning communist party in the world, a party officially referring therefore to an atheistic doctrine, was in the country with the largest Muslim population: Indonesia—of course, until the party was crushed in a bloodbath at the hands of the U.S.-backed Indonesian military starting in 1965. They ignore or forget, to give another example of the same kind, that in the late 1950s and early 1960s, the most massive political organization in Iraq, especially among the Shiites in southern Iraq, was not led by some cleric but was here, too, the Communist Party.

And, needless to say, they overlook the fact that even nowadays the overwhelming majority of Muslim believers bear no relation to that religious fundamentalism that has been on the rise in most major religions in the last few decades. But still, they consider that the only good Muslim is a non-Muslim—a nonbeliever, that is—who eats pork and drinks alcohol. Not that they apply this view to all religions out of some fierce atheism, but they reserve it to Islam as if the problem was inherent to this religion specifically.

Islamophobia is based on fear, as the etymology of the term indicates.[108] It grows in a specific and complex manure: the many anxieties created by neoliberal social and economic deregulation, seeking scapegoats through a well-known psychological phenomenon, compounded by the fear instilled in Western public opinion by governments unwilling to give the true answer to the much-asked question: Why do "they" hate us?

We have addressed this question at length and offered our own answers throughout our three days of discussion. I hope we have contributed to alerting public opinion to what is at stake and what the real issues are, a task that Noam has been undertaking more than anyone else for several decades. Unless the people of the United States understand these matters, there can't be a change in the present course of U.S. foreign policy in the Middle East—a course that is leading us all inexorably toward the abyss.

Epilogue

The preceding text reflects a conversation that took place on January 4–6, 2006. Six months later, several questions were directed to Gilbert Achcar and Noam Chomsky to enable them to comment on recent developments and to update their analyses as necessary. We set July 20, 2006, as the closing date for their responses.

Gilbert Achcar

The Situation in Iraq

SHALOM: The past few months in Iraq have seen widespread sectarian attacks. How do you assess the evolution of the situation? In particular, do you believe that a civil war is going on? Is the sectarian turmoil a reason to extend the stay of U.S. troops?

ACHCAR: In the six months that have elapsed since we had our three days of exchange, the situation in Iraq has deteriorated in a truly frightening manner, proceeding inexorably toward the actualization of the worst-case scenario—the worst for Iraq, that is, which is not necessarily the worst for Washington, as I shall explain.

Remember where things stood in January: We already knew that the outcome of the December 2005 parliamentary election was quite bad for U.S. plans in Iraq, although we hadn't yet gotten the official results. These confirmed later that the United Iraqi Alliance (UIA) once again secured a major voting bloc in the parliament (128 seats out of 275), although it did not get the majority that it enjoyed in the previous assembly. That was foreseen, however, as the January 2005 election had been boycotted by most Arab Sunnis and its outcome was accordingly quite exceptional. Nevertheless, the loss of 12 seats by the UIA was rather less than the 22-seat loss by the Kurdish Alliance, while the coalition list headed by Washington's

DOI: 10.4324/9781003531753-6

henchman, Iyad Allawi, suffered a very serious decline, falling to 25 seats from 40, which had already been a poor showing.

These results meant that, had any of the "Sunni" coalitions—whether the Iraqi Accord Front (44 seats), which is a coalition between the Islamic Party (i.e., the Iraqi "moderate" branch of the Muslim Brotherhood [the Association of Muslim Scholars being the "hard-liners" originating in the same tradition]) and traditionalist Arab Sunni tribal forces; or the Iraqi National Dialogue Front alone (11 seats), a motley Arab nationalist coalition including present or former Baathists who disavow Saddam Hussein's leadership—agreed to join an alliance with the UIA, they would have secured together an absolute majority in the parliament. For that, the UIA needed only 10 more votes, or even fewer if one takes into account the 2 seats won by a small Shiite grouping close to the Sadrists, which joined the UIA. Such an extended cross-sectarian bloc would thus have been able to counter political pressure exerted by Washington through its Kurdish allies and Allawi's group and whoever else might have joined with them.

Yet, both "Sunni" coalitions proved more interested in doing business with Washington, believing that getting U.S. support against the Shiite UIA would put them in a better overall position than allying with the latter. They were thus keener on playing a petty sectarian political game than on speeding national liberation from the occupation. On the other hand, many Arab Sunnis consider Iran's hegemony—of which, they believe, the UIA is but a tool—to be a greater threat than U.S. hegemony, thus justifying politically that kind of behavior. The Arab Sunni parliamentary coalitions entered into an alliance with Allawi to dispute the electoral results. During my discussion of this matter last January, I commented that their objections to the election results were not sincere, but aimed only at exerting political blackmail on the UIA.[1] What happened afterward proved this assessment correct: When they—and U.S. proconsul Zalmay Khalilzad—got what they wanted with regard to the government, they just ended all their clamoring about "rigged elections."

In the meantime, intensive tugs-of-war took place in Iraq between several forces. The main contest pitted, on one side, the UIA, backed by Iran, and on the other side, a broad coalition of the Kurdish Alliance, the "Sunni" electoral parties, and Allawi, backed by Khalilzad and by regular statements and high-ranking visitors from Washington insisting hypocritically on the need to give Arab Sunnis an important share of power. As after the January 2005 election, the Bush administration tried to dictate not only its own conditions on the UIA but also Allawi's participation in the government, despite Iran's and the UIA's red line. Washington finally conceded this last point, but only after it managed to get rid of the candidate designated by the UIA to head the first "regular" Iraqi government under the new constitution—the same man who headed the provisional government based on the Constituent Assembly: Ibrahim al-Jaafari.

The other major contest took place within the UIA itself, pitting against one another the two major blocs: the SCIRI and the followers of Muqtada al-Sadr. The SCIRI wanted the premiership for their own man, Adel Abdel-Mahdi, an ex-Maoist turned fundamentalist in both Islamic and neoliberal religions. Despite the fact that the SCIRI is the closest of all Iraqi groups to Iran and despite its advocacy of a super-federal state in southern Iraq, an idea that is resented by the United States (and rejected by all other Arab Iraqi forces, including Muqtada al-Sadr's followers), Washington backed Abdel-Mahdi, hoping that he would help the United States lay its hands on Iraq's oil in the name of free marketeering. Khalilzad, chiefly obsessed with reducing Muqtada al-Sadr's clout, was also trying in this way to fan the dissension within the UIA. For his part, Sadr strongly backed his friend and leader of the Dawa Party, Jaafari, whom he deemed closer to his political stance (Jaafari had subscribed without reservation to the "Pact of Honor" that Sadr tried to get all major Iraqi forces independent of Washington to sign)[2] and more open to his pressure.

Tension might have arisen between the two factions, but Tehran—which invited Muqtada al-Sadr for a visit after the December election—was certainly instrumental in preventing the UIA from splitting and urging the SCIRI to consider the UIA's unity as a priority. The issue of the UIA's candidate for premiership was thus decided democratically by a vote within the alliance, which gave a narrow majority to Jaafari. Washington's "democracy promoters" did their best thereafter to prevent the constitutional mechanism from getting under way: Normally, the Assembly would have convened and elected among others a president who would have been required to designate the candidate put forward by the largest bloc in parliament—Jaafari, in this case—to try to form a government. This position would have enabled Jaafari to maneuver between the other blocs and try to win over enough Arab Sunni representatives to secure a parliamentary majority, thus forcing the Kurdish Alliance to join lest it be excluded from the government.

Obviously, such a scenario was out of the question for Washington: The result was a very tense and highly dangerous standoff, until a compromise was reached whereby Jaafari agreed to be replaced with his second-in-command in the Dawa Party, Nouri al-Maliki. The latter was presented as being less sympathetic to Iran and more flexible and amenable than Jaafari. As a matter of fact, Maliki seems more compliant than Jaafari in his relations with the United States. The difference between the two men, leaders of the same party, was nonetheless not such as to warrant Washington's and London's indecent self-congratulation after Maliki's designation, as if Allawi himself had been anointed again prime minister of Iraq.

The whole situation was clearly a setback for Sadr, however. As I mentioned earlier, he had tried hard to convince the Sunni Arab parliamentary and extra-parliamentary groups to join in an anti-occupation alliance. He failed totally in that respect: The Arab Sunni parliamentary groups rejected his advances and stuck to their alliance with the Kurdish parties and Washington's proconsul. In addition, the Association of Muslim Scholars, which is very close to the Arab Sunni insurgency, disappointed Sadr bitterly: He couldn't get them to condemn Zarqawi and his al-Qaeda branch in strong terms (Sadr even wanted them to excommunicate Zarqawi's group), and his radical anti-Baathist attitude was equally a stumbling block in his relations with Sunni Arab nationalists. He has complained that of the Sunni groups he approached before the December election and asked to adhere to his "Pact of Honor," none have signed it.

The next major blow to Sadr's strategy of trying to build an anti-U.S. alliance with anti-occupation Arab Sunni forces was the single event that contributed most to fueling the sectarian tension between Arab Shiites and Sunnis in Iraq—I mean, of course, the attack against the Al-Askari Mosque in Samarra on February 22, 2006. This sectarian attack unleashed reprisals on a large scale by Shiite militants infuriated by the unending series of murderous sectarian attacks to which their community had been subjected ever since the occupation started. In these reprisals, Sadr's ragtag "Mahdi Army" was apparently very much involved. Not that Sadr gave a green light for this—on the contrary, like most other Shiite leaders, he tried his best to cool things down—but since his militias are much less centralized than the quasi-military SCIRI Badr militia, Sadrist militiamen obeyed their impulses before considering any other option and before getting to listen to the voice of political rationality.

At any rate, these unfortunate events were hugely exploited by an odd array of forces—including U.S. friends, pro-Zarqawi Sunni fundamentalists, and pro-Saddam Baathists—in order to discredit Muqtada al-Sadr among Arab Sunnis and to destroy any appeal he might have had for both his uncompromising anti-occupation stance and his reputation for being very much independent of Iran. All that Sadr had achieved politically in the previous period, in terms of building his influence on a pan-Arab (Sunnis and Shiites) Iraqi basis, was thus shattered along with the dome of the Al-Askari Mosque. To be sure, he retains formidable clout among the Shiites—above all, among the downtrodden layers of the Shiite community, a clout that very likely has been enhanced by the role of his "army" in embodying the armed wing of the community more than any other group. But the fact remains that he is further from imposing himself as a leader of both Arab nationalist Shiites and Sunnis than he has ever been since he clashed with occupation troops in 2004.

Despite these developments, Iraq has not yet reached a state of full-fledged civil war. Indeed, what I characterized a year ago as a "low-intensity civil war"[3] had not ceased increasing in intensity throughout 2005 and early 2006, even before the sudden and most serious flare-up provoked by the Samarra attack. Nevertheless, drawing on my own Lebanese experience, I would say that there are two elements that at this moment still stand between the present situation in Iraq and a full-scale civil war. The first is the persistence of a unified Iraqi government and the existence of still-unified Iraqi armed forces: In Lebanon, it was the split-up of the government in early 1976 and the disintegration of the Lebanese army that signaled the shift to a full-fledged civil war. The second element is the existence of foreign armed forces playing the role of deterrent and arbiter, like the role that the Syrian army used to play—but only intermittently—in Lebanon from 1976 onward.

To say this is to point to what I hinted at already, namely that the slide of Iraq toward the worst-case scenario for its population does not necessarily represent the worst-case scenario for Washington. Actually, most of what has happened in recent months in Iraq, except for the publicity surrounding U.S. troops' criminal behavior, has suited Washington's designs. The sharp increase in sectarian tensions as well as the defeat of Muqtada al-Sadr's project played blatantly into Washington's hands. Along with many others, I have warned for quite a long time that, when all is said and done, Washington's only trump card in Iraq is going to be the sectarian and ethnic divisions among Iraqis, which the Bush administration is exploiting in the most cynical way according to the most classical of all imperial recipes: "Divide and rule." This is what Washington's proconsuls in Baghdad, from L. Paul Bremer to Khalilzad, have tried their best to put in place and take advantage of.

Seen in this light, the present flare-up in sectarian tensions is a godsend for Washington, to the point that many Iraqis suspect that U.S. and Israeli intelligence agencies stand behind the worst sectarian attacks. Note how the occupation seems now "legitimized" by the fact that many Arab Sunnis in mixed areas, who feel threatened, request the presence of foreign troops to guarantee their safety as they have no confidence in Iraqi armed forces.[4] What a paradox, when you think of the fact that Arab Sunnis were and are still the main constituency of the anti-occupation armed insurgency—though surely not the only one: There has been a growing pattern of anti-occupation armed actions in southern Iraq that is hardly reported, if at all, in the Western media, or even in the Arab media for that matter.

However, Washington is playing with fire: The sectarian feud suits its designs, but only provided that it is kept within limits. It is not in the United States' interests for Iraq to be carved up into three separate parts, as has been advocated cynically in the U.S. media by self-proclaimed "experts" and as neocons and friends believe is the second-best outcome, short of safe U.S. control over a unified Iraq. Not only would that actually be a recipe for a protracted civil war, but it would make U.S. control over the bulk of Iraqi oil that is located in the Shiite-majority South even more uncertain. Washington's best interest is therefore to foster the sectarian feud at a controllable level that suits its "divide and rule" policy, without letting it get out of control and turn into a most perilous civil war. A federal Iraq, with a loose central government, could fit neatly with this design, provided it were accepted by all major Iraqi actors (which is quite difficult), but an Iraq torn apart could be a disaster—all the more so that it could trigger a dangerous regional dynamic. (Think of the Shiite-populated eastern province of the Saudi kingdom where the bulk of oil reserves is concentrated.)

Now, if U.S. forces in Iraq are to be compared to a firefighting force, the truth of the matter is that they are led by highly dangerous arsonists! Ever since the occupation started, the situation in Iraq has steadily and relentlessly deteriorated: This is the undeniable truth, which only blatant liars like those in Washington can deny, insisting that the situation is improving in the face of glaring evidence to the contrary. Iraq is caught in a vicious circle: The occupation fuels the insurgency, which stirs up the sectarian tension that Washington's proconsul strives to fan by political means, which in turn is used to justify the continuing occupation. The latest major way in which U.S. occupation authorities are throwing oil on the Iraqi fire, according to Shiite sources, is by helping the Islamic Party—the Iraqi Arab Sunni group closest to Washington and to the Saudis—build an armed wing that is already taking part in the sectarian feud.

There is no way out of this burning circle but one: Only by announcing immediately the total and unconditional withdrawal of U.S. troops can a decisive step be taken toward putting out the fire. This would cool down the Sunni insurgency that the Association of Muslim Scholars has repeatedly pledged to call to a halt as soon as a timetable for the withdrawal of occupation troops is announced. It would dampen as well the sectarian tension, as Iraqis will then look squarely at their future and feel compelled to reach a way to coexist peacefully. And if ever they came to the conclusion that they needed a foreign presence for awhile to help them restore order and start real reconstruction, it should definitely not be one composed of troops from countries that harbor hegemonic ambitions over Iraq, but one that is welcomed by all segments of the Iraqi people as friendly and disinterested help.

Hamas in Power

SHALOM: The background you provided in January made the electoral victory of Hamas not so surprising. But what do you see as the impact of this victory on Palestinian society generally, and on the prospects for peace in particular, especially in light of the recent Israeli offensive?

ACHCAR: The electoral victory of Hamas was indeed not so surprising when seen in the general framework of our comments of last January before the election. What must be stressed is that the general trend whereby the failure and corruption of leaders originating in the nationalist movement or the left—the Fatah PLO/PA leaders in the Palestinian case, personified by the likes of Mahmoud Abbas and Mohammed Dahlan—lead to Islamic fundamentalism filling the void in mass leadership thus created, is a trend that manifests itself in quite varied ways.

"Islamicization," in the sense of a reversal in social secularization and the progression of a strict adherence to the Islamic religion, is not a uniform process. Let me note, first of all, that those who voted for Hamas were only a 44.45 percent plurality of Palestinian voters, whereas a majority voted either for Fatah or for secular left-wing or liberal slates. (Hamas got a majority of the seats in parliament due to an electoral system based partly on district constituencies and partly on proportional representation.) Second, many of those who did vote for Hamas did so less out of adherence to Islamic fundamentalism than out of exasperation with both Israel and the Fatah PA leadership. Hamas—whose name is based on the Arab acronym of Islamic Resistance Movement—built itself historically as the main enemy of both its opponents, as an "Islamic" substitute for Fatah in the resistance against Israel. It forged its image as the staunchest and most radical foe of the "Jewish state," sharply contrasting its steadfastness against Israel and its U.S. godfather with Fatah leaders' endless compromises on principles and capitulations. It did that, of course, out of a religious fundamentalist vision of the world, with a charter representing a regression toward anti-Semitic views that the PLO had carefully kept out of its official discourse. This laid the ground for resorting to the indiscriminate anti-Israeli suicide attacks that became Hamas's trademark from the 1990s on, with the increasing violence of Israel's oppression giving these attacks legitimacy in the eyes of many Palestinians. Hamas also promoted itself as the most radical critic of Fatah's utterly corrupt mafia-like rule, contrasting it with the apparent selflessness of its system of Muslim charities and social services and the modest way of life of its leaders.

To be sure, in parallel with Hamas's rising clout, a wave of "Islamicization" developed over the years and was chiefly visible, in Palestine as elsewhere, through the infallible symptom of women's way of dressing. But contrary to what we've seen in other circumstances, such as the Iranian revolution, Hamas's accession to power was not followed by a sweeping campaign of compulsory or voluntary submission to religious injunctions. That was definitely not the movement's priority. The fact is that Hamas seemed clearly embarrassed by its electoral victory, not having expected to get a majority of the seats for itself alone (it won a stunning majority of 45 out of the 66 seats allocated on a district basis, giving it a total of 74 seats out of 132). In January, I considered its involvement in the political process to be most welcome as it would compel Hamas to think in more political terms.[5] Its accession to power dramatically intensified this same compulsion.

Like any beginners in power following a radical change of government, the leaders of Hamas were quite insecure and clumsy in the way they dealt with things, all the more so having immediately been confronted with devious maneuvers from Fatah and Mahmoud Abbas—the latter using against them the very same autocratic presidential powers Yasir Arafat had designed for himself and used against Abbas when Washington imposed the latter at the head of the Palestinian Cabinet in 2003. Hamas leaders were further destabilized when Israel and the Western powers, led by the United States, started to gradually strangulate the whole Palestinian polity and society, proving once again that they cannot bear the results of truly democratic elections and that they support democracy only when it brings their friends and lackeys to power—as Noam and I stressed in January. The leaders of Hamas managed nevertheless to learn very quickly from this crash course in realistic politics. They understood that they were caught between the hammer of Fatah and the anvil of Israeli and Western pressure. They realized that their opponents wanted them to act in such a way as to be discredited and facilitate their own overthrow either by political means or by some kind of putsch.[6]

Torn between their own hard-liners and their realists, the leaders of Hamas took nevertheless an important step toward adopting a political stance more in tune with the aspirations of the vast majority of the Palestinian people. This was chiefly achieved through what has come to be known as the "prisoners' document"—that is, the platform discussed and adopted by Palestinian prisoners in Israeli jails belonging to the whole spectrum of Palestinian organizations from Fatah to Hamas, with the exception of the Islamic Jihad. There was first an attempt by Mahmoud Abbas to use the document as a means to delegitimize the Hamas government, as the latter was reluctant, under the pressure of its hard-liners, to approve the document—this despite the fact that the document's line reproduces the fundamentals of Palestinian nationalism and is thus actually closer to Hamas's stance than to Abbas's. He tried nevertheless to use it in a demagogic way but Hamas succeeded in turning the situation to its advantage by getting an agreement on a new version of the document, amended so as to be more palatable to its taste.

This constituted a major turning point, resulting in the adoption of an overwhelmingly consensual Palestinian political program based on an independent state in the territories that Israel occupied in 1967. The first clause of the amended document declared that

> the Palestinian people in the homeland and in the Diaspora seek and struggle to liberate their land; dismantle the settlements and evacuate the settlers; remove the wall of racist segregation and annexation; achieve their right to freedom, return and independence and their right to self-determination, including the right to establish their fully sovereign independent state on all the territories occupied in 1967, with Jerusalem as its capital; secure the right of the refugees to return to their homes and properties from which they were expelled and to get compensated; and liberate all prisoners and detainees without exception or discrimination—basing themselves for all that on the historical right of our people on the land of the fathers and grandfathers and on the UN Charter and international law and what has been guaranteed by international legitimacy without reducing our people's rights.[7]

The second clause provided for a radical restructuring of the PLO on a democratic basis, through the formation of a new National Council (the PLO's equivalent of a legislative body) on a proportionate basis—through election by all segments of the Palestinian people wherever it is possible to organize elections, and agreement between the major organizations for the representation of the rest. Clause 7 stated that

> the conduct of negotiations is a prerogative of the PLO and the President of the Palestinian National Authority on the basis of clinging to Palestinian national goals as they are formulated in this document, on condition that any agreement in this respect be submitted to the new Palestinian National Council to approve and ratify it, or hold a general referendum in the homeland and the Diaspora by a law organizing it.

This agreement was reached on June 27, 2006, but went almost unnoticed. The very next day—just as the Palestinians had concluded a historic programmatic accord among themselves, the most encompassing ever, providing for negotiations with Israel aimed at reaching a political settlement—Israel launched its horribly brutal military offensive in Gaza. Israel was reacting in the most violent way to the abduction on June 25 of one of its soldiers in retaliation for its abduction of Palestinian civilians, with the aim of exchanging the kidnapped soldier for Palestinians held in Israeli custody. Israel could have tried to obtain the release of the soldier by giving Palestinian officials time to work things out. But it decided instead to escalate dramatically its policy of holding the whole Palestinian population hostage in order to impose its unilateral will on their government, in a way that corresponds entirely to the canons of mass state terrorism, including resorting to collective punishment inspired by the notion of collective guilt.

In his steering of the Israeli government, Ehud Olmert thus proved that he is the legitimate heir of Ariel Sharon. And, very disappointingly, Amir Peretz tried to imitate the ruthlessness of his military predecessors at the head of the Labor Party, but succeeded only in looking like a pitiful caricature. Not only did he betray the programmatic platform upon which he waged his electoral campaign, but he entered a coalition government under the premiership of Olmert, a man dedicated to a unilateral "settlement" that means, in fact, annexation and permanent violence, taking the "defense" portfolio that is not only the furthest from his own competence but also the least related to the social program that he advocated—not to mention the peace program. As a result of all this, the prospects for peace in the region are at their bleakest, for the present, and only further descent into barbarism looms on the horizon.

The Israel-Hezbollah-Lebanon Conflict

SHALOM: What about the sudden and ongoing flare-up on the Lebanese front? How do you assess the actions of Hezbollah and Israel?

ACHCAR: The abduction by a Palestinian group in Gaza of an Israeli soldier was a legitimate reaction to the systematic abduction by Israel of numerous Palestinian civilians—provided that the soldier is kept for an exchange of detainees and not executed as a scapegoat. This was certainly not the most appropriate answer to the Israeli aggression: The whole history of the Palestinian struggle shows clearly that it is not by resorting to violent means that the Palestinians can achieve their goals, given that Israel enjoys an overwhelming and crushing military superiority over them. But it was, all the same, a legitimate retaliation to a full-fledged aggression, rightfully targeting the Israeli military instead of Israeli civilians.

Now, although Hezbollah, too, launched an attack on Israeli soldiers, not civilians, killing several of them and abducting two, this action is certainly more questionable. To be sure, Israel has been constantly harassing Hezbollah, encroaching aggressively on Lebanese sovereignty, ever since the Israeli army was compelled in the year 2000 to withdraw from the part of Lebanese territory that it had been occupying since 1982—a withdrawal that Hezbollah had played a key role in inducing. In that sense, the July 12 action against the Israeli military could certainly be deemed legitimate. But, on the other hand, it was utterly clear that, coming not as direct retaliation against an ongoing or very recent Israeli offensive on Lebanese territory, the attack was going to be regarded internationally as an "aggression" and used by Israel as a pretext in order to launch a massive military campaign aimed at crushing Hezbollah—a campaign that was certainly going to seriously harm the Lebanese population in the well-known tradition of "collateral damage." In that sense, Hezbollah's action was both adventuristic and irresponsible.

Of course, one can perfectly understand the satisfaction felt by many people in the region when they heard of Hezbollah's operation, interpreting it as an act of solidarity with the people of Gaza subjected to the most inhumane and unlawful repression. But actions should not be evaluated only through an ethical prism: They should be measured as well by their likely consequences and their appropriateness to the goals pursued. Seen in that light, Hezbollah's attack was indeed quite ill-considered. Instead of relieving the people of Gaza—if that was its goal (Hezbollah's chief, Hassan Nasrallah, stated that his group's attack had been planned for several months, long before the onslaught on Gaza)— it put in jeopardy the lives, security, and livelihood of another and larger population.

But the adventurism and irresponsibility of Hezbollah's attack, however one rates them, are completely dwarfed by Israel's adventurism and irresponsibility. With its arrogance and brutality, Israel bears by far the major blame for the violence and persists in inflaming the whole area by its permanent aggression and contemptuous carelessness about the lives and rights of the Palestinians—and, now again, the Lebanese. In short, Israel retaliated in the most disproportionate and cowardly manner against a much weaker country, inflicting a collective punishment on the Lebanese population and holding it hostage, as it did with the still weaker Palestinian people. It launched a military action that, in the first nine days alone, killed many more than the 300 reported Lebanese casualties (since this figure doesn't take into account those buried under the rubble of the impressive number of flattened buildings), wounded countless others, destroyed substantial parts of Lebanon's infrastructure, and imposed a blockade on the entire country. Those among the Lebanese who had believed Washington's proclaimed concern for the Lebanese people and their democracy could see revealed the full measure of Washington's hypocrisy, as the United States prevented the UN Security Council even from issuing a call for a cease-fire. Washington in fact shares the responsibility—or rather the irresponsibility—for Israel's aggression on the Lebanese people, as everybody knows that the United States and the United States alone had the power to impose its immediate cessation.

The very scale of the aggression proved that Hezbollah's attack was seized upon by Washington and Israel as a pretext for trying to achieve a goal they have been pursuing for several years and in a particularly intensive manner since 2004. That was the year the United States, with France's enthusiastic support, had the UN Security Council adopt Resolution 1559, which called not only for the withdrawal of Syrian troops from Lebanon but also for the disarmament of armed groups in the country, meaning chiefly Hezbollah and secondarily Palestinians with weapons in refugee camps. The arrogant, brutal, and unrestricted predatory behavior of the Israeli state, backed by Washington, follows a familiar pattern that aims this time at compelling the Lebanese governmental majority to confront Hezbollah at the cost of a new civil war in the country. At the time of this writing, such obviously premeditated aggression actually seems to have backfired, in terms of unifying most Lebanese in a deep resentment over Israel's brutality and reinstating Hezbollah as the main embodiment of the country's national resistance, beyond the Shiite community where it was always considered as such.

The present Lebanese government, which resulted from the elections held in the spring of 2005, had started addressing the issue of Hezbollah's armament: To that end, it had requested that Israel return to Lebanon the last stretch of territory that it occupies in southern Lebanon, the Shebaa farms,[8] and free the two prisoners officially held in Israeli custody, one of them since 1978. It had also asked that Israel cease its interference and harassment against Hezbollah, a plainly legitimate actor on the Lebanese political scene, participating in parliament and the government.

As long as it is under threat, it is perfectly legitimate for Hezbollah to keep its armament in order to defend itself, as the Lebanese state is unable to protect it against Israel. True, Lebanon's means of defending its sovereignty is another matter altogether that should be decided democratically by the Lebanese people as a whole, not unilaterally by any of its political forces. But at any rate, the issue of Hezbollah's armament should be settled by the Lebanese themselves through political means. What Israel, backed by Washington, Paris, and their allies, is trying to impose on Lebanon is a violent internal confrontation, a new civil war in a country that has already been bled by fifteen years of war. Israel is telling the Lebanese what it keeps telling the Palestinians: Destroy each other or we shall destroy you all!

As for the motivation of the United States in backing—nay, inciting—Israel in this new aggression, it goes beyond Lebanon, of course, and aims principally at Iran. This is part of Washington's obsession with the so-called Shiite crescent that stretches from Iran to Hezbollah in Lebanon, through Iran's allies in Iraq and the Syrian regime. Seen in the context of the Cold War-like mentality that prevails in Washington, Iran is the main regional enemy, as the Soviet Union once was on the global level, and every clash with a force backed by the main enemy is viewed as part of the confrontation with the main enemy itself. Now, Iran's very close relation with Hezbollah is a secret to nobody. Iran has supported since its inception this organization that shares its Islamic fundamentalist ideology: funding it, training it, and arming it. And Hezbollah would have been foolish to launch such a bold attack as the one it launched on July 12, abducting Israeli soldiers, without coordinating with its backers in Damascus and Tehran. The question then is: So what?

Washington's claim that states are not entitled to back forces fighting against their enemies in other countries reeks of hypocrisy, given the U.S. record: Take, for example, Washington's backing of the Nicaraguan contras against the Sandinista government, or the Afghan Mujahideen against the Soviet occupation of their country. And much more important, hasn't the United States been the backer, funder, sponsor, and weapons-provider of the Israeli state in its many acts of aggression? Moreover, the fact that Hezbollah is supported by Iran, Syria, or any other state no more signifies that it is not waging a legitimate fight for the liberation of its country than did Russian or Chinese support to the Vietnamese communists mean that the latter were not waging a war of national liberation against the occupiers of their land and seen as such by the overwhelming majority of the Vietnamese population. Washington's chutzpah has no limits: It condemns "foreign interference" in countries that it itself occupies—Vietnam yesterday, Iraq today—or that its allies invade!

Israel's new aggression against Lebanon, along with the onslaught on Gaza, bodes ill for the future of the region, just as Israel's unrestricted use of overwhelming brutality, along with the similar behavior of the United States and its allies, feeds various kinds of fanaticism that inevitably backfire on the perpetrators and their own countries—New York's September 11, 2001, Madrid's March 11, 2004, and London's July 7, 2005, are gruesome testimonies to that. It is important to stress one more time that a tremendous responsibility falls on the people of the United States in this regard, for it is only by changing the course of Washington's policy toward the Middle East that it will be possible to stop the descent into barbarism and the spiral of violence and death that affect the region and spill over into the rest of the world.

Noam Chomsky

The Israel Lobby

SHALOM: In the last few months there has been a great deal of attention paid to the issue of the Israel lobby, precipitated by a study by Mearsheimer and Walt.[9] What is your response to the study and to the ensuing controversy?

CHOMSKY: It is a serious study, which merits attention. I am not sure the word "controversy" is appropriate for what followed. There were serious reactions, including those from Norman Finkelstein, Joseph Massad, and Stephen Zunes, who gave a detailed review of what is at stake.[10] But a good deal was bluster and irrationality, even ludicrous accusations of anti-Semitism.

No one doubts that there is a significant Israel lobby, which influences policy—though, as we discussed earlier, I think that Mearsheimer and Walt (like many others) ignore what may be its most important component. Their work also seems to me to suffer from a general inadequacy of the "realist" approach to international relations: It is based on a dubious concept of "national interest" that is largely divorced from the domestic distribution of authentic power, hence from factors that substantially determine the operative "national interest"; in our society, concentrated economic power, uncontroversially.

As a matter of simple logic, we cannot conclude that policy conflicts with the operative "national interest" if the policy fails. Thus if the Rumsfeld-Cheney-etc. invasion of Iraq ends up as a disaster for the state-corporate interests they serve, we cannot conclude that the policy conflicted with those interests in intention or motivation. As we discussed, the policies—however criminal—were not irrational in their terms.

Also as a matter of logic, we can evaluate the power of the lobby only by investigating the cases where its goals conflict with perceived state-corporate interests. A review of history reveals that these factors largely converge in areas that matter much to domestic power concentrations, state and private. We then face the academic question of sorting out the relative weight of two factors that largely converge.

The question would be more than academic if it had implications for action. It actually does. If the power of the lobby is as great as many believe, then the proper tactics for critics of U.S. support for Israeli policies are clear: They should go to the corporate headquarters of Lockheed-Martin, Intel, Goldman-Sachs, Warren Buffett, ExxonMobil, etc., and patiently explain to them that their interests are being harmed by a lobby that they overwhelm in political influence and economic power. I'd like to believe it. It would greatly simplify my life: No more need to devote great time and energy to efforts to mobilize public opposition to long-standing state policy. But no one follows this advice.

It seems hard to avoid Gilbert's earlier observation that "[a]ttributing decisive influence to the pro-Israel lobby is a phantasmagoric view of politics, which is quite widespread."[11] And I cannot refrain from adding that concentration of energy and attention on the rather abstract academic problem of sorting out the effects of largely convergent factors seems to me distasteful, to say the least, while Palestine is being destroyed before our eyes by U.S.-backed Israeli policies.

The United States and Iran

SHALOM: Back in January, you rated the likelihood of a U.S. attack (or an Israeli attack by proxy) on Iran as rather low. Given the events of the past few months, how would you update your assessment?

CHOMSKY: Evidently, that was speculation—and, as we discussed, speculation based on the assumption of rational planning, not taking into account what Gilbert called "the wounded-beast phenomenon."[12] Bush planners have created remarkable catastrophes for themselves in the Middle East and in much of the rest of the world. And it is conceivable that they might strike out in desperation, hitting the system with a sledgehammer to see if somehow the results will come out in their favor.

There have been relevant developments since our discussion in early January. More evidence has accumulated about the broad opposition to U.S. military actions in Iran. That includes even the "international community," a technical term referring to a small clique in Washington that has amassed tremendous power and whoever else joins them: Blair almost reflexively, the French government consistent with whatever cynical motives happen to be uppermost, sometimes a few others. On military action against Iran, even the usual accomplices are opposed. The "international community" did go along with the United States in demanding that Iran halt uranium enrichment as a precondition for negotiations, but China and Russia ambiguously rejected that call.[13] Going beyond the "international community," we find that the nonaligned movement supports Iran's "inalienable right" to develop nuclear energy and called for negotiations without preconditions. It also opposed any threat of attack against Iran, demanded that Israel join the non-proliferation treaty, and called for a nuclear-free zone in the Middle East, a long-standing goal of the authentic international community, blocked by Washington. Polls by Terror Free Tomorrow, an organization dedicated to eroding popular support for terror, found that "[d]espite a deep historical enmity between Iran's Persian Shiite population and the predominantly Sunni population of its ethnically diverse Arab, Turkish, and Pakistani neighbors, the largest percentage of people in these countries favor accepting a nuclear-armed Iran over any American military action."[14] The Weapons of Mass Destruction Commission established by the Swedish government at the suggestion of the United Nations, chaired by Hans Blix, issued a general report on the urgent matter of reducing the dangers of weapons of mass destruction (WMD) and also called for "assurances against attacks and subversion aiming at regime change" in Iran.[15] Military action is also strongly opposed by Mohammed ElBaradei, the respected head of the International Atomic Energy Commission. The limited information available suggests that the U.S. military and U.S. intelligence are opposed to military action as well.

Nevertheless, policymakers may once again ignore overwhelming world opinion. It is not a novel stance, but the statist reactionaries at the helm in Washington have set new records in flaunting their credentials as international outlaws.

A good deal has also been learned about Bush administration efforts to bar a diplomatic resolution. Flynt Leverett, former Bush administration adviser to the National Security Council on Middle East issues, reported that in May 2003 Iran's reformist Khatami government, with the support of the hard-line "supreme leader" Ayatollah Khamenei, "sent Washington a detailed proposal for comprehensive negotiations to resolve bilateral differences." That included WMD, ending support for anti-Israel organizations, and a two-state solution to the Israel-Palestine conflict. Washington's response was to censure the Swiss diplomat who conveyed the offer. In October 2003, "the Europeans got Iran to agree to suspend enrichment in order to pursue talks that might lead to an economic, nuclear and strategic deal," Leverett added; "[b]ut the Bush administration refused to join the European initiative, ensuring that the talks failed." This "stonewalling" by the United States "left many in Tehran with the impression that no Iranian concession would be sufficient to please Washington, even if they changed their position on Israel"; it also strengthened the hand of President Mahmoud Ahmadinejad, according to Trita Parsi, a Middle East specialist at Johns Hopkins University. In May 2006, a senior Iranian official who was involved in the 2003 offer informed the London *Financial Times* that "Iran was still ready for wide-ranging talks provided the U.S. was serious about being ready to address Iranian concerns and did not see the negotiating table as just another component of attempted 'regime change.'"[16]

In June 2006, Ayatollah Khamenei "stated that Iran poses no threat to other countries, including its neighboring states, and that it shares a common view with Arab countries on the most important Islamic-Arabic issue, namely the issue of Palestine." Khamenei is therefore stating that Iran accepts the position of the Arab League, which in 2002 called for full normalization of relations with Israel if Israel withdraws to the international border and allows a two-state settlement, in accord with the international consensus that has been blocked by the United States (and rejected by Israel) for thirty years. Khamenei's statement may have been a response to the widely condemned declarations of his subordinate Ahmadinejad on "wiping Israel off the map"—declarations that may well have been mistranslated, and may refer to a long-term goal of "regime change."[17]

Ahmadinejad's statements, some undoubtedly outrageous, received wide coverage and condemnation in the West, but I noticed no report of the far more important statement of his superior, Ayatollah Khamenei. Also remaining in oblivion are other gestures by the Iranian government—how significant they are, we do not know, since they are ignored. To mention a few, according to Trita Parsi, Iran "offered the Europeans on January 30th [2006] to suspend their enrichment program. That proposal was dismissed by the Europeans," perhaps in an effort to conform to Washington's demands. Two weeks later, Iran accepted the very important and comprehensive proposal of Mohammed ElBaradei that we discussed earlier: that all weapons-usable fissile materials be placed under international control. Iranian senior negotiator Dr. Ali Larijani stated that "[s]hould a credible international system for providing nuclear fuel be in place, the Islamic Republic of Iran would be ready to procure its nuclear fuel from that system." To my knowledge, Iran is alone in accepting ElBaradei's proposal, a matter of very great importance, extending far beyond Iranian nuclear activities, as we have already discussed.[18]

The EU-Iran negotiations to which Leverett referred were based on a bargain: Iran would suspend uranium enrichment, and Europe would provide "firm commitments on security issues." Iran lived up to its side of the bargain. The EU did not—under U.S. pressure, according to Selig Harrison, a respected expert.[19] Iran finally resumed uranium enrichment. The standard version is that Iran violated its commitments, not quite the full story.

We might also recall that while Iran was ruled by the shah, the tyrant the United States and Britain had installed, Washington strongly supported Iranian nuclear programs similar to those it now condemns. During the Ford administration, Rumsfeld, Cheney, and Wolfowitz not only "endorsed Iranian plans to build a massive nuclear energy industry," the *Washington Post* reported, "but also worked hard to complete a multibillion-dollar deal that would have given Tehran control of large quantities of plutonium and enriched uranium—the two pathways to a nuclear bomb. Either can be shaped into the core of a nuclear warhead, and obtaining one or the other is generally considered the most significant obstacle to would-be weapons builders." Justifying these policies in a National Security Memorandum, Secretary of State Kissinger explained that "introduction of nuclear power will both provide for the growing needs of Iran's economy and free remaining oil reserves for export or conversion to petrochemicals." Today Kissinger writes that "for a major oil producer such as Iran, nuclear energy is a wasteful use of resources," a position echoed by Cheney and others.[20] Iranians may perhaps be pardoned if they detect an element of cynicism in the Western stance, underscored by the United States' unremitting torment of the people of Iran for over fifty years, which they remember but the West prefers to forget.

It appears that Washington is virtually alone in maintaining the threat of military action, and that it has systematically blocked a diplomatic path, which might have prospects for success in resolving not only the issue of

Iranian nuclear weapons but also the alleged threat to Israel. Despite rhetorical gestures, Washington still is undermining these prospects. A proposal for negotiations at the point of a gun, and with the desired outcome a precondition, plainly means very little—putting aside the fact that the threat itself is a serious violation of international law. Washington refuses to withdraw the threat and insists on the precondition, thus virtually guaranteeing that meaningful negotiations will not proceed.

The capture of two Israeli soldiers by Hezbollah in July elicited new Washington denunciations of Iran. It became "the received wisdom in the U.S. that Iran was directing Hezbollah to deflect international pressure on Tehran's nuclear programme," the *Financial Times* reported, adding that experts disagree, citing prominent Iranian dissidents and scholars who hold that "Iran has taken a pragmatic approach in its foreign policy and does not want to get into a serious confrontation with Israel" (dissident academic Fatemeh Haghighatjoo) and that "Hezbollah's leaders are not the types to take orders from elsewhere" (Ervand Abrahamian). Concurring, an Iranian expert "close to Tehran's thinking" concluded: "It was inconceivable that Iran had ordered Hezbollah to take Israeli soldiers prisoner." Amal Saad-Ghorayeb, a Lebanese academic specialist on Hezbollah, writes that "[t]o suggest Hezbullah attacked on the orders of Tehran and Damascus is to grossly oversimplify a strong strategic and ideological relationship." Though "they form a strategic axis" that "confronts U.S.-Israeli designs to redraw the map of the region, [Hezbollah] has never allowed any foreign power to dictate its military strategy." Her general analysis is supported by Dilip Hiro, another specialist on the region. Evidently, nothing definite can be known, but the confident claims are at best dubious.[21]

Will Washington extremists proceed to attack Iran directly? I still doubt it, and suspect that they will prefer economic strangulation and subversion, possibly support for secessionist movements that they can then "defend" by bombing Iran.

Hezbollah

SHALOM: You visited Lebanon for the first time in May 2006. Your meeting on this occasion with Hezbollah leader Hassan Nasrallah caused a lot of static, with pro-Israeli sources vehemently attacking you. Why did you meet with him despite the obvious major differences between you and Hezbollah?

CHOMSKY: It's an interesting question; and understandable, given the coverage. Another question is why I spent even more time visiting the home of the prominent Lebanese political figure who is perhaps the most outspoken opponent of Hezbollah, the Druze leader Walid Jumblatt. And why I met many others over a broad spectrum, while trying to gain as broad a picture as I could of the reality of this complex, vibrant, conflicted, sad, and remarkably attractive country. The real question is why only one of these meetings aroused "static" and "attacks." No need to tarry on that.

Hezbollah is a significant political organization in Lebanon. It has substantial popular support because it played the major role in driving out the Israeli invaders after a long and brutal occupation in defiance of UN Security Council orders, and because, like other Islamic movements, it provides social services for the poor. In the last parliamentary elections, Hezbollah won nearly half the votes assigned to the Shia bloc in the confessional system; the other half went to Amal, a party closely allied with Hezbollah.

I won't review the days I spent in Lebanon, because this is already being done by others who accompanied me throughout and know far more about Lebanon than I do—personal friends of mine (and Gilbert's).[22] With regard to Nasrallah, I believe they will confirm my impression that he was articulate and knowledgeable, someone whose views—whatever one thinks of them—should not be ignored by those who hope to understand Lebanese reality or the Shiite movements of the region.

Perhaps Hezbollah's most controversial stand is its refusal to give up its arms in accord with Security Council Resolution 1559. That is a problem for the Lebanese to deal with. The government has not called for implementation of this part of the resolution, and Hezbollah's rejection of it has substantial support within Lebanon. Prime Minister Fouad Siniora describes Hezbollah's military wing as "resistance rather than as a militia, and thus exempt from" Resolution 1559.[23]

The argument for retention of arms is based on the premise that Lebanon should have a deterrent against another Israeli invasion, and that the only deterrent is a capacity for guerrilla warfare, which finally led to Israeli withdrawal in 2000. Excluding the current crisis, Israel has invaded Lebanon four times during the past three decades: in 1978, in 1982, and (north of the piece of Lebanon that Israel continued to occupy—its "security zone," in U.S.-Israeli parlance) under the Rabin and Peres governments in 1993 and 1996, respectively. Throughout, Israel acted with U.S. support, though both Reagan and Clinton ordered Israel to halt the invasions (1982, 1996) when Israeli atrocities became damaging to the United States. In none of these cases was there a credible pretext: In 1982 the goal, pretty much acknowledged, was to terminate PLO diplomatic initiatives and to impose a client regime in Lebanon; in 1993 the official reason was that Hezbollah violated Israel's "rules of the game," namely that Israel is entitled to carry out terrorist acts in Lebanon north of its "security zone" but Lebanese may retaliate only within occupied Lebanon; 1996 was similar. It is easy to imagine scenarios for another invasion.

The United States and Israel, of course, reject the basic premise: No one has the right to a deterrent to their righteous violence. If we accept this premise, then what can a deterrent be? Not the Lebanese army, or meaningless words from Europe. The United States could provide a credible guarantee that Israel will not attack, undercutting the argument for retention of arms. But there are no signs of that.

I raised this question with the most outspoken opponents of Hezbollah I met in Lebanon. Though all oppose its retention of arms, none had a convincing response. The presence of armed forces independent of the state within a country is, doubtless, a very dangerous situation. The same can be said about the arms kept by Palestinians in miserable refugee camps, for self-defense. But the basic questions merit answers.

The issues are more general. Veteran Middle East correspondent Rami Khouri writes that "[t]he Lebanese and Palestinians have responded to Israel's persistent and increasingly savage attacks against entire civilian populations by creating parallel or alternative leaderships that can protect them and deliver essential services." Another experienced analyst, Patrick Seale, agrees: "You have the rise of essentially non-state actors like Hezbollah and Hamas because of the vacuum created by the impotence of Arab states to contain or deter Israel. These actors are basically taking issue with Israel's 'deterrence,' which posits that Israel can strike but no one can strike at it." Until the basic questions are dealt with, it is likely that "the Middle East will sink further into violence and despair," as Khouri predicts.[24]

Confrontation with Hamas and Hezbollah

SHALOM: How would you assess the Israeli and U.S. responses to the election of Hamas, and to the ensuing conflicts in Gaza and Lebanon?

CHOMSKY: The U.S. response reveals, once again, that the United States supports democracy if and only if it conforms to U.S. strategic and economic objectives.[25]

Perhaps it would be useful to review some highlights since Hamas was elected in late January 2006.

On February 12, the statements of Osama bin Laden were reviewed in the *New York Times* by NYU law professor Noah Feldman. He described bin Laden's descent into utter barbarism, reaching the depths when he advanced "the perverse claim that since the United States is a democracy, all citizens bear responsibility for its government's actions, and civilians are therefore fair targets." Utter depravity, no doubt. Two days later, the lead story in the *Times* casually reported that the United States and Israel are joining bin Laden in the lower depths of depravity. Palestinians offended the masters by voting the wrong way in a free election. The population must therefore be punished for this crime. The "intention," the correspondent observed, "is to starve the Palestinian Authority of money and international connections" so that President Mahmoud Abbas will be "compelled to call a new election. The hope is that Palestinians will be so unhappy with life under Hamas that they will return to office a reformed and chastened Fatah movement." Mechanisms of punishment of the population are outlined. The article also reports that Condoleezza Rice will visit the oil producers to ensure that they do not relieve the torture of the Palestinians. In short, bin Laden's "perverse claim"; but when the United States advances the claim, it is not ultimate evil but rather righteous dedication to "democracy promotion."[26]

These paired articles elicited no comment that I could discover. Also overlooked was the fact that bin Laden's "perverse claim" is standard operating procedure. Familiar examples are "making the economy scream" when Chileans had the effrontery to elect Salvador Allende—the "soft track"; the "hard track" brought Pinochet. Another pertinent illustration is the U.S.-UK sanctions regime that murdered hundreds of thousands of Iraqis, devastated the country, and probably saved Saddam Hussein from the fate of other monsters like him (often supported by the United States and Britain to the very end). Not quite bin Laden's doctrine; rather, much more perverse, not only in terms of scale but also because Iraqis could not by any stretch of the imagination be held responsible for Saddam Hussein.

The most venerable illustration is Washington's forty-seven-year campaign of terror and economic strangulation against Cuba. From the internal record, we learn that the Eisenhower and Kennedy administrations determined that "[t]he Cuban people are responsible for the regime," so they must be punished with the expectation that "[r]ising discomfort among hungry Cubans" will cause them to throw Castro out (JFK). The State Department advised that "[e]very possible means should be undertaken promptly to weaken the economic life of Cuba [in order to] bring about hunger, desperation, and overthrow of the government."[27] The doctrine remains in force.

Without continuing, we find ample evidence that it is no departure from the norm to adopt bin Laden's most perverse claim in order to punish Palestinians for their democratic misdeeds.

The United States and Israel then proceeded to implement their "intention" with scrupulous care. Thus, for example, an EU proposal to provide some desperately needed aid for health care was stalled when U.S. "officials expressed concerns that some of this money might end up paying nurses, doctors, teachers, and others previously on the government payroll, thereby helping to finance Hamas." Another achievement of the "war on terror." With U.S. backing, Israel also continued its terrorist atrocities and other crimes in Gaza and the West Bank—in some cases, perhaps, in an attempt to induce Hamas to violate its embarrassing cease-fire, so that Israel could respond in "self-defense," another familiar pattern.[28]

In May 2006, Israeli Prime Minister Olmert announced his plan to formalize Sharon's West Bank expansion programs, which were announced along with the "Gaza disengagement." Olmert chose the term "convergence" ("hitkansut") as a euphemism for annexation of valuable land and resources (including water) of the West Bank, programs designed to break the continually shrinking Palestinian areas into separated cantons, virtually isolated from one another and from whatever corner of Jerusalem will be left to Palestinians, all imprisoned as Israel takes over the Jordan valley and controls air space and any external access. In a stunning public relations triumph, Olmert won praise for his courage in "withdrawing" from the West Bank as he put the finishing touches on the project of destroying any hope for recognition of Palestinian national rights. We were enjoined to lament the "anguish" of the residents of scattered settlements that would be abandoned as they "converge" into the territories illegally annexed behind the cruel and illegal "Separation Wall." All of this proceeds, as usual, with a kindly nod from Washington, which is expected to fork out the billions of dollars needed to carry out the plans, though there are occasional admonitions that the destruction of Palestine should not be "unilateral": It would be preferable for President Mahmoud Abbas to sign a surrender declaration, in which case everything would be just fine.

The people of Gaza and the West Bank are supposed to observe all of this submissively, rotting in their virtual prisons. Otherwise they are sadistic terrorists.

The latest phase began on June 24, when the Israeli army kidnapped two civilians, a doctor and his brother, from their home in Gaza. They were "detained" according to brief notes in the British press. The U.S. media mostly preferred silence.[29] They will presumably join the 9,000 other Palestinian prisoners in Israeli jails, 1,000 reportedly in prison without charges, hence kidnapped—as were many of the rest, in that they were sentenced by Israeli courts, which are a disgrace, harshly condemned by legal commentators in Israel. Among them are hundreds of women and children, their numbers and fate of little interest. Also of little interest are Israel's secret prisons. The Israeli press reported that these have been "the entry gate to Israel for Lebanese, especially those who were suspected of membership in Hezbollah, who were transferred to the southern side of the border," some captured in battle in Lebanon, others "abducted at Israel's initiative" and sometimes held as hostages, with torture under interrogation. The secret Camp 1391, possibly one of several, was discovered accidentally in 2003, since forgotten.[30]

The next day, June 25, Palestinians kidnapped an Israeli soldier just across the border from Gaza. That did happen, very definitely. Every literate reader also knows the name of Corporal Gilad Shalit, and wants him released. The nameless kidnapped Gaza civilians are ignored; international law, while rightly insisting that captured soldiers be treated humanely, absolutely prohibits the extrajudicial seizure of civilians. Israel responded by "bombing and shelling, darkening and destroying, imposing a siege and kidnapping like the worst of terrorists and nobody breaks the silence to ask, what the hell for, and according to what right?" as the fine Israeli journalist Gideon Levy wrote, adding that "[a] state that takes such steps is no longer distinguishable from a terror organization." Israel also kidnapped a large part of the Palestinian government, destroyed most of the Gaza electrical and water systems, and committed numerous other crimes. These acts of collective punishment, condemned by Amnesty International as "war crimes," compounded the punishment of Palestinians for having voted the wrong way. Within a few days, UN agencies working in Gaza warned of a "public health disaster" as a result of developments "which have seen innocent civilians, including children, killed, brought increased misery to hundreds of thousands of people and which will wreak far-reaching harm on Palestinian society. An already alarming situation in Gaza, with poverty rates at nearly eighty per cent and unemployment at nearly forty per cent, is likely to deteriorate rapidly, unless immediate and urgent action is taken."[31]

The pretext for punishing Palestinians is that Hamas refuses to accept three demands: to recognize Israel, cease all acts of violence, and accept earlier agreements. The editors of the *New York Times* instruct Hamas leaders that they must accept the "ground rules that have already been accepted by Egypt and Jordan and by the Arab League as a whole in its 2002 Beirut peace initiative" and, furthermore, that they must do so "not as some kind of ideological concession" but "as an admission ticket to the real world, a necessary rite of passage in the progression from a lawless opposition to a lawful government"—like us.[32]

Unmentioned is that Israel and the United States flatly reject all of these conditions. They do not recognize Palestine; they refused to end their violence even when Hamas observed a unilateral truce for a year and a half and called for a long-term truce while negotiations proceed for a two-state settlement; and they dismissed with utter contempt the 2002 Arab League call for normalization of relations, along with all other proposals for a meaningful diplomatic settlement, as we have already discussed. Even when it accepted the "Road Map" that is supposed to define U.S. policy, Israel added fourteen "reservations" that rendered it entirely meaningless, eliciting the usual tacit approval in Washington and silence in commentary.[33]

The Hamas electoral victory was eagerly exploited by the United States and Israel. Previously, they had to pretend that there was "no partner" for negotiations, so they had no choice but to continue their project of taking over the West Bank, as they had been doing systematically since the Oslo Accords were signed (extending earlier actions). As we noted previously,[34] the pace of settlement peaked in 2000, the last year of Clinton and Israeli Prime Minister Ehud Barak, then escalated under Bush-Sharon. With Hamas in office, Olmert and his cohorts can lament that there is "no partner." Therefore, they must proceed with annexation and destruction of Palestine, counting on articulate Western opinion to applaud politely, perhaps with mild reservations about unilateral "convergence," and to suppress the fact that while Hamas's programs are in many respects entirely unacceptable, their own are comparable or much worse, and are not just rhetoric: They are systematically implementing their denial of any meaningful Palestinian rights, a crucial difference.

The next act in this hideous drama opened on July 12, when Hezbollah launched a raid in which it captured two Israeli soldiers and killed several others, leading to an all-out Israeli attack, killing hundreds and destroying much of what Lebanon has painfully reconstructed from the wreckage of its civil wars and the Israeli invasions. Whatever its motives, Hezbollah took a frightful gamble, for which Lebanon would surely pay dearly. Again, we see the danger of processes that have led to the rise of "parallel or alternative leaderships that can protect [civilian populations] and deliver essential services" with their own military wings, as Rami Khouri discussed above.

On the motives, analysts differ. "Hezbollah's official line," the *Financial Times* reports, "was that the capture was aimed at winning the release of the few remaining Lebanese prisoners in Israeli jails. But the timing and scale of its attack suggest it was partly intended to reduce the pressure on the Palestinians by forcing Israel to fight on two fronts simultaneously." Many agree, recalling Hezbollah's reaction to the outbreak of the al-Aqsa Intifada in September 2000—when it seized soldiers in a cross-border raid that led to a prisoner exchange—as well as its response to Israel's devastating attacks in the West Bank in 2002 (Amos Harel).[35] Others highlight the prisoner motive, which is also suggested by the exchange in 2000, by the fact that Hezbollah had attempted capture of soldiers before the recent crisis, and by the matter of Israel's secret prisons, mentioned earlier. Amal Saad-Ghorayeb regards the Gaza connection as primary, but argues that one should not ignore "the domestic significance of these hostages."[36]

Still others regard Iran and/or Syria as the main actors. As noted earlier, many experts and Iranian dissidents disagree, though few doubt that Iran and Syria authorized Hezbollah's actions. Most Arab rulers place the blame on Iran. At an emergency Arab League summit, they were willing "to openly defy Arab public opinion" because of their concerns about Iranian influence. One Dubai military specialist commented that the Iranians, by means of Hezbollah, "are embarrassing the hell out of the Arab governments," who are doing nothing while "[t]he peace process has collapsed, the Palestinians are being killed . . . . And here comes Hezbollah, which is actually scoring hits against Israel." The criticism of Hezbollah was opposed by Syria, Yemen, Algeria, and Lebanon; the Iraqi parliament, "in a rare show of unity," condemned the Israeli attack as "criminal aggression," and Prime Minister Nouri al-Maliki, whose designation Washington applauded, "call[ed] on the world to take quick stands to stop the Israeli aggression." The fact that most Arab leaders, however, are willing to "defy public opinion" may have large-scale regional implications, strengthening radical Islamist groups. It is noteworthy that the "Supreme Guide" of the Egyptian Muslim Brotherhood, Mahdi Akef, sharply condemned the Arab states. "The Brotherhood would win a comfortable majority" in a free election in Egypt, according to Middle East scholar Fawaz Gerges, and has broad influence elsewhere, including with Hamas, one of its offshoots.[37]

A broader analysis is suggested by retired colonel Pat Lang, former head of the Middle East and terrorism desk at the Pentagon's Defense Intelligence Agency: "This is basically tribal warfare. If you have someone who's hostile to you and you're unwilling to accept a temporary truce, as Hamas offered, then you have to destroy them. The Israeli response is so disproportionate to the abduction of the three men it appears it's a rather clever excuse designed to appeal both to their public and to the U.S."[38]

Speculation about motives and conflicting factors should not blind us to the tragedy that is unfolding. Lebanon is being destroyed, Israel's Gaza prison is suffering still more savage blows, and on the West Bank, mostly out of sight, the United States and Israel are consummating their project of the murder of a nation, a grim and rare event in history.

These actions, and the Western response, illustrate all too clearly the amalgam of savage cruelty, self-righteousness, and injured innocence that is so deeply rooted in the imperial mentality as to be beyond awareness. One can easily understand why Gandhi, when asked what he thought of Western civilization, is alleged to have said that he thought it might be a good idea.

Postscript: Two More Years of Crisis

For the paperback edition, several further questions were directed to Gilbert Achcar and Noam Chomsky to enable them to bring their discussion and analysis up to date. Their responses were completed on March 24, 2008.

Gilbert Achcar

The Iraq "Surge"

SHALOM: The last few months have seen a downturn in U.S. military casualties in Iraq and—it is claimed—in Iraqi casualties as well. Does this mean that George Bush's "surge" is working, that the United States is finally winning?

ACHCAR: Well, the two questions are definitely not the same: The "surge" could be said to be working within certain limits and in ways that amount to playing with fire, as I shall explain; but it doesn't mean at all that the United States is winning the war, as George W. Bush boasted so imprudently, one more time, on the occasion of the invasion's fifth anniversary. This man is such a crank that he cannot learn any lesson from even the very near past: There he is, repeating "Mission Accomplished" with the same smile of satisfaction that adorns most of his speeches.

The "surge" was announced by George W. Bush in January 2007, as an attempt to get out of the dire straits into which his administration had steered the U.S. occupation of Iraq at that point. The year before had ended in catastrophe for the administration: The Republican Party had lost both houses of Congress in the November 2006 elections, while the administration's Middle East policies were openly disavowed by the bipartisan Iraq Study Group, leading to the announcement of the resignation of the administration's most prominent hard-liner next to Vice President Dick Cheney himself: former Defense Secretary Donald Rumsfeld.

DOI: 10.4324/9781003531753-7

The Iraq Study Group was formed in March 2006 and co-chaired by James Baker, a veteran of the Bush senior administration of 1989–1992, well known for his close ties with the oil industry and with the Saudi ruling family,[1] and Lee Hamilton, a man who calls for the United States to "better understand Saudi concerns," which he defines as follows: "The reality is that the Saudis see many things differently from the Bush administration. They don't want the Palestinians to descend into civil war, but they do see Hamas as a legitimate player in Palestinian politics. They don't want us to pull out of Iraq immediately, but they do want us to do more to protect Sunni Arabs from Shiite militias. They don't want a nuclear Iran next door, but they are open to engagement with Iran and groups like Hezbollah. The Saudis want to maintain close ties with the U.S. and certainly want our military presence to provide stability in the region, but they also appear to be looking for other ways to advance their interests."[2]

Baker and Hamilton's *The Iraq Study Group Report*,[3] made public in December 2006, unmistakably addressed these Saudi concerns, much to the annoyance of the Bush administration. This is very clear even from the "Executive Summary": "Given the ability of Iran and Syria to influence events within Iraq and their interest in avoiding chaos in Iraq, the United States should try to engage them constructively. . . . There must be a renewed and sustained commitment by the United States to a comprehensive Arab-Israeli peace on all fronts. . . . This commitment must include direct talks with, by, and between Israel, Lebanon, Palestinians (those who accept Israel's right to exist), and Syria."[4]

As for Iraq proper, *The Iraq Study Group Report* made the following key recommendation: "It is clear that the Iraqi government will need assistance from the United States for some time to come, especially in carrying out security responsibilities. Yet the United States must make it clear to the Iraqi government that the United States could carry out its plans, including planned redeployments, even if the Iraqi government did not implement their planned changes. The United States must not make an open-ended commitment to keep large numbers of American troops deployed in Iraq. . . . The United States should work closely with Iraq's leaders to support the achievement of specific objectives—or milestones—on national reconciliation, security, and governance. If the Iraqi government does not make substantial progress toward the achievement of [these milestones], the United States should reduce its political, military, or economic support for the Iraqi government."[5] In other words, the report advocated that the U.S. government threaten to significantly reduce the number of its troops in Iraq in order to compel the Iraqi government to achieve steps on the path to national reconciliation—an indirect vindication of the antiwar movement's long-standing claim that the best possible incentive for the Iraqis to reach a peaceful *modus vivendi* would be the short-term prospect of U.S.

troop withdrawal. This was further acknowledged in Recommendation 34 of the report: "*The question of the future U.S. force presence must be on the table for discussion as the national reconciliation dialogue takes place. Its inclusion will increase the likelihood of participation by insurgents and militia leaders, and thereby increase the possibilities for success.*"[6]

By "national reconciliation" the report meant primarily U.S. and Iraqi governmental overtures to Iraq's Arab Sunnis in order to better fight the "insurgency" as well as to please the Saudis and other Arab allies of Washington. Acknowledging the fact that Washington's original Sunni allies were isolated—"Sunni politicians within the government have a limited level of support and influence among their own population, and questionable influence over the insurgency"[7]—the report actually advocated collaboration with Arab Sunni tribes: "The Iraqi government and Sunni Arab tribes must aggressively pursue al Qaeda."[8] It noted with satisfaction that "Sunni Arab tribal leaders in Anbar province recently took the positive step of agreeing to pursue al Qaeda and foreign fighters in their midst, and have started to take action on those commitments."[9]

The key nonsecurity "milestone" was, of course, related to oil. Recommendation 62 insisted on the necessity of adopting "as soon as possible" an "oil law" in order to create "*a fiscal and legal framework for investment. Legal clarity is essential to attract investment.*"[10] The goal is naturally, according to Recommendation 63, to "*encourage investment in Iraq's oil sector by the international community and by international energy companies*" and to "*reorganize the national oil industry as a commercial enterprise.*"[11] With regard to the security of oil transport too, venal tribes were regarded as a possible adjuvant to the existing combination of forces: "*The U.S. military should work with the Iraqi military and with private security forces to protect oil infrastructure and contractors. Protective measures could include a program to improve pipeline security by paying local tribes solely on the basis of throughput (rather than fixed amounts).*"[12]

When it came to the actual military steps to be undertaken by the United States, the report's real inspiration was quite the opposite of withdrawal. Its authors considered the possibility of a "substantial increase" (100,000 or more) of U.S. troops in Iraq, but rejected it only because the "needed levels" are not available and because "adding more American troops could conceivably worsen those aspects of the security problem that are fed by the view that the U.S. presence is intended to be a long-term 'occupation.'"[13] This latter observation is a further vindication of one of the antiwar movement's key claims: that the occupation itself is the main reason for the "insurgency." The report went on: "We could, however, support a short-term redeployment or *surge of American combat forces to stabilize Baghdad, or to speed up the training and equipping mission,* if the U.S. commander in Iraq determines that such steps would be effective."[14]

Thus not only the idea of the "surge," but the term itself, was present indeed in *The Iraq Study Group Report*—a fact that has been completely overlooked among the plethora of comments describing the announcement by G. W. Bush of a "surge" of 30,000 troops in Iraq in January 2007 as signaling a blatant rejection of the Baker-Hamilton recommendations. This oversight was actually, in most cases, the result of a wishful misreading of the report, as if it had been written by moderate peaceniks. The Bush administration did in fact adopt the main recommendations of *The Iraq Study Group Report* with regard to Iraq—and had no serious other choice, since it was confronted with a bipartisan consensus against the backdrop of deteriorating conditions in Iraq and an electoral debacle domestically. It adopted the report up to the term "surge" itself and to the official title of Bush's new Iraqi strategy announced on January 10, 2007, "The New Way Forward"—a direct echo of the title under which the recommendations were detailed in the report: "The Way Forward—A New Approach."

The regional recommendations with regard to Iran and Syria were adopted most reluctantly as they were the most irreconcilable with the policy prevailing since the start of the "war on terror." The administration engaged nevertheless in negotiations with both Tehran and Damascus, although quite half-heartedly and unconvincingly, offering no real incentives to either regime for a change in its stance. Washington's attitude toward the two states remained on the whole a very thuggish one, based on threat and provocation. However, with regard to Iraq proper, the adoption of the report's key recommendations was much more resolute, and did translate into concrete steps on the ground.

The focus on "stabilizing Baghdad," where the bulk of "surge" troops was deployed, achieved noticeable results after a few months, with a significant ebb in the number of clashes and attacks in the capital. This outcome was greatly facilitated by the fact that the Sadrists decided to opt for a low profile: Muqtada al-Sadr, obviously demoralized by his inability to control his own troops and by the deterioration of his image as a bridge between Arab Shiites and Sunnis in Iraq—a consequence of the outburst of sectarian violence in the wake of the February 2006 attacks in Samarra, as I explained in the epilogue to our first edition—announced a long-term freeze of his "Mahdi Army." He more or less "vanished" from the public scene since then, and went a step further by announcing recently—quite bitterly—his official retirement into religious studies for a while.

Sadr's bitterness surely stems in great part from a series of disappointments: Given his frustration over the exacerbation of sectarian hatred in Iraq and his disillusionment regarding the attitude of those Arab Sunni forces he considered allies, he has been considerably annoyed by the fact that the Iraqi government has turned into an increasingly docile collaborator of the U.S.-British occupiers. In this sense, the shift from Jaafari—whom

Sadr supported and Washington vetoed—to Maliki as a compromise candidate at the head of the cabinet resulted in the Sadrists losing clout on governmental affairs. Clearly more compliant toward Washington than his predecessor ever was, Maliki tilted the intra-Shiite balance of forces in favor of the Sadrists' bitter rivals, the SCIRI (who dropped "Revolution" from their name and became the Supreme Islamic Council of Iraq), prompting a pro-Jaafari split from Dawa after Maliki replaced him as the head of the party in May 2007.

This led to further radicalization of the Sadrists, increasingly imitating Lebanon's Hezbollah and, like them, getting closer to the "radical" Ahmadinejad wing of the Iranian regime, whereas the Supreme Council and Dawa clearly have more affinities with the so-called pragmatic wing represented by Rafsandjani—Ahmadinejad's chief opponent in Iran's 2005 presidential election. The widening political gap between the Sadrists—in this case, not only Muqtada al-Sadr's followers but also the rival "Sadrist" faction, the Islamic Virtue Party (Fadhila)—and the two other main Shiite parties is a source of increasing tension and clashes, which might be seriously aggravated by the "governorate" (provincial) elections due to be held in late 2008. A likely result will be a fierce fight among former members of the same United Iraqi Alliance.

The Bush administration's greater reason for pride is, however, the success of its Sunni tribal policy. Resorting to the old colonial recipe used by the British empire in its involvement in the Middle East, and most directly so in Iraq itself, the U.S. occupation authorities cut deals with the most archaic social formations in Iraq—formations that resisted "modernization" so well because most so-called modernizers in the history of independent Iraq, especially Saddam Hussein himself, made extensive use of tribalism to assert their power. The "blueprint" for a democratic Iraq that would be a model for the whole "Greater Middle East" thus sank in the quicksand of tribalism.

Dealing with Arab Sunni tribal chiefs, most of whom had been staunch supporters and allies of the Baathist regime, U.S. occupation authorities offered them money, military means, and carte blanche in their regions—much to the annoyance of the Shiites. This new collaboration, which led to the creation of the so-called Awakening ("Sahwa" in Arabic) Councils, was facilitated by the Sunni tribes' increasing irritation with al-Qaeda's organization in Iraq, in particular with its disrespect for traditional tribal authority, which it wanted to subordinate to its totalitarian project. This "first large-scale Arab uprising against Osama bin Laden" was the main argument in G. W. Bush's boastful speech on the occasion of the fifth anniversary of the invasion—omitting to say that it was the invasion itself that had allowed the establishment of *al-Qaeda's first large-scale territorial base in the heart of Arab lands!* The way Bush described the achievement is arresting: "In Anbar, Sunni tribal leaders had grown tired of al-Qaeda's brutality and started a popular uprising, called the 'Anbar Awakening.' To take advantage of this opportunity, we sent 4,000 additional Marines to help these brave Iraqis drive al-Qaeda from the province. As this effort succeeded, it inspired other Iraqis to take up the fight. Soon similar uprisings began to spread across the country. Today there are more than 90,000 concerned local citizens who are protecting their communities from the terrorists and insurgents and the extremists."[15]

Note the formula used—"concerned local citizens"—as if Iraqi tribes were applying the Second Amendment of the U.S. Constitution[16] in some kind of Jeffersonian citizen-based democracy. The real value of this great "achievement" is well illustrated by the following report published in the Arabic daily *Al-Hayat* three days after Bush's speech: "Sahwa Councils in Baghdad's periphery have threatened to stop fulfilling their security tasks as a result of the U.S. army's delay in remunerating their members. Colonel Saad Aziz Salman, the leader of the 'Sahwa' of al-Taji region to the north of Baghdad, said that his men are considering the possibility of announcing their collective withdrawal from the Sunni neighborhoods that they control, if the issue of their funding is not settled. He told *Al-Hayat* yesterday that 'Sahwa Councils' deployed in the southern Baghdad area did not receive their salaries (300 to 700 dollars) for two months. . . . He emphasized that if the issue of funding were not settled, Sahwa Councils would go on collective strike in Baghdad. The efforts to impose security in Baghdad depend to a great extent on the combatants who constituted the 'Sahwa Councils' in order to expel al-Qaeda from their regions. But a dispute has arisen between the Iraqi government and U.S. forces over whether these Councils should be funded [by the U.S. forces] or integrated in the [Iraqi] security forces."[17]

The report says it all: These "councils" of "concerned local citizens" are actually acting as mercenaries of the U.S. government. They are as unreliable as soldiers of fortune usually are—indeed, if not quite more so than usual, due to the lack of sympathy for the United States by Arab Iraqis in general, and Sunnis among them in particular. Moreover, by striking a deal with Arab Sunni tribes—who until recently were Saddam Hussein's privileged constituency and therefore resent the empowerment of the Shiites as well as that of the Kurds—and letting them deploy militarily, nay relying on them to impose (their) order in Arab Sunni areas, the U.S. occupation is giving them powerful leverage over the United States itself—a bargaining power, that is—and sowing more seeds of sectarian and ethnic confrontation for the near future in Iraq. Arab-Kurdish tensions are on the rise, with the issue of Kirkuk—the oil-rich northern area claimed by the Kurds—dangerously stalled against a backdrop of Turkish incursions into Iraq's Kurdistan, whose real purpose is to intimidate the Iraqi Kurds on top of their official purpose of fighting the PKK, the guerilla movement of Turkey's Kurdistan. Washington is perilously playing with fire, one more time, and will sooner or later get its fingers burned.

The tribal policy—designed originally to isolate al-Qaeda as well as to circumvent the Shiite governmental parties deemed too close to Iran—has already a serious downside for Washington. It has led to a significant weakening of the government, a weakening aggravated by the withdrawal of the Sadrists and their increasingly oppositional stance. As a result of this, none of the "milestones" defined in the Baker-Hamilton report has been truly achieved, and—most important among them—the government did not manage to get the parliament to approve the "oil law" that it drafted jointly with U.S. institutions. The one clear thing at the onset of this sixth year of the occupation of Iraq is that the United States is far from achieving its designs in that country—it is very far from "winning the war." Yesterday's "Mission Accomplished" is actually a "Mission: Impossible."

Lebanon and Israel

SHALOM: At the time of our last update, Israel and Lebanon were at war. Today, we see both a significant domestic crisis in Lebanon and renewed tensions between Israel and Hezbollah. Can you explain what's going on and how this fits into the larger picture of Middle East politics?

ACHCAR: Obviously, all these issues are narrowly interconnected. Lebanon is still facing the consequences of Israel's aggression in July-August 2006—what has become known since then as the "33-Day War."[18] The starting point for an assessment of today's situation, therefore, should be an assessment of the war's result. In that respect, what is indisputable is that it was a resounding fiasco, a major failure in Israel's military history. More than a full month of intensive and savage bombing, flattening whole urban zones and villages, and killing 1,200 people, according to very moderate estimates, that is, 40 per day, most of them harmless civilians; this, from a position of incommensurable superiority in military means—one of those "postheroic" wars[19] that characterize the dominant powers' warfare in this electronic/informational age—against a guerilla force, equipped with light weapons and blind missiles. And what was the result?

The guerillas, waging a truly heroic war, stood fast to the very last moment and kept firing missiles at Israel—a poor retaliation to Israel's deluge of bombs launched from land, air, and sea, to be sure, but embarrassing enough for Israel in practice and, more so, symbolically. Hezbollah ended up negotiating indirectly a cease-fire with Israel—undeniably the most humiliating in Israel's sixty-year series of cease-fires and truces since the first Arab-Israeli war. Not only was Hezbollah not destroyed or even decapitated, but none of the goals of the Israeli aggression, whether official or unofficial, were achieved. The two Israeli soldiers abducted in July 2006 were not released, and are still being held by Hezbollah at the time of this writing, in March 2008; Hezbollah was not disarmed, but has replenished its arsenal according to its own claims and to Israeli sources; and, far from being exhausted or isolated, the Shiite organization is stronger than ever, more firmly rooted in its popular constituency, and commanding a greater clout within the multi-religious Lebanese opposition to the pro-U.S. Saudi-backed government of Prime Minister Fouad Siniora.

This balance sheet constituted a terrible blow both to Israel's "credibility" in the region, as a state keen on cultivating its image of military supremacy and invincibility, and to U.S. regional strategy. The latter indeed was in dire straits by the fall of 2006: Not only was Iraq more blatantly a tragic quagmire than at any point since the occupation began, but Washington's attempt at extricating itself victoriously from this quagmire—by means of a regional offensive against Iran that would affect the balance of forces within Iraq itself to the advantage of the United States—proved a total failure. Hezbollah in Lebanon had been one target of this offensive; Hamas in Palestine had been the second—both forces being close allies of the Tehran-Damascus axis that cuts through Iraq. The U.S. anti-Iranian regional offensive by means of Israel had backfired. It had to give way to some sort of war of attrition in Lebanon and Palestine—and to a revamped strategy in Iraq proper, as we have seen.

Hezbollah had accepted only reluctantly the cease-fire based on UN Security Council Resolution 1701. What could be called very accurately in this case the "continuation of war by other means" started as soon as the cease-fire was implemented. Among the issues of this "continuation of war," two are still unresolved and lie very much at the heart of the ongoing political crisis in Lebanon. Allow me to quote from what I wrote in the aftermath of the war to describe the stakes: "The issue of Hezbollah's disarmament is, to be sure, the major stumbling block for Resolution 1701, as no country on earth is presently willing to try to disarm Hezbollah by force—a task that even the most formidable modern army in the whole Middle East and one of the world's major military powers has blatantly failed to achieve. This is indeed why Washington's aim is to prepare conditions under which the Lebanese army, commanded by the Lebanese allies of the United States, would be able to take the initiative in a new attempt at disarming Hezbollah, in which case NATO troops would come to its aid as authorized by UNIFIL's [the UN Interim Force in Lebanon] new mandate. . . . The [other] issue, still on the domestic Lebanese level, is the fate of the cabinet. The existing parliamentary majority (the outcome of the elections held in Lebanon in 2005) resulted from elections flawed by a defective and distorting electoral law that the Syrian-dominated regime had enforced in 2000. One major consequence . . . was the distortion of the representation of the Christian constituencies, with great underrepresentation of the movement led by General Michel Aoun, who entered into an alliance with Hezbollah after the elections. And what makes the legitimacy of the present parliamentary majority even more disputable is the profound effect of the recent war on the political mood of the Lebanese population. Of course, any change in Lebanon's government in favor of Hezbollah and its allies would radically alter the interpretation of Resolution 1701, as it depends very much on the Lebanese government's attitude. Hezbollah and Michel Aoun have therefore jointly launched a campaign for political change according to the following timetable: enlargement of the Siniora government with the addition of followers of Aoun; drafting and promulgation of a new and fairer electoral law; organization of early elections; formation of a new government; and election by the new parliament of a new president of the republic. Aoun, of course, is the candidate for this latter office. The March 14 coalition, which currently holds the majority in parliament and government, has flatly refused these demands, thus contributing to the creation of a strong tension in the country—a tension that has increased the country's uncertainty over its future, both in the short and in the long run. Only one thing is certain: The offensive led by Washington in Lebanon since 2004, in line with which the 33-Day War was a particularly devastating episode, is not close to conclusion. . . . Lebanon stands again at a crossroads: A political settlement through the democratic way of holding new elections in the short term is reasonably the best alternative, the other one being a decision by the Aoun-Hezbollah alliance to resort to extra-parliamentary mobilizations that entail the risk of degenerating into new bloody clashes between the Lebanese. The Bush administration's frenzied interference in Lebanese affairs encourages the governmental majority to stiffen its attitude and aims at provoking a new Lebanese civil war with NATO's involvement. However, Iran's deterrence power at the regional level weighs on the attitude of the Saudi kingdom and hence on that of Paris. Riyadh tries therefore to calm things down, jointly with Nabih Berri, the leader of Amal, the Shiite movement allied with Hezbollah. These were the main factors in the Lebanese equation during October 2006."[20]

Let us assess the developments that occurred since then with regard to each issue, starting with the political institutional crisis. In November 2006, the Shiite ministers, members of Hezbollah and Amal, resigned from the government: From then on, the opposition regarded the Siniora government as unconstitutional due to the lack of Shiite representation. Then, at the beginning of December 2006, the opposition started an extra-parliamentary campaign including a sit-in/camping-in in downtown Beirut that is still continuing at the time of this writing, sixteen months later. The risk of bloody clashes materialized in January 2007 with a sudden outburst of sectarian violence pitting Sunnis against Shiites, as well as pro-Aoun against pro-government Maronites. The clashes were able to be contained, fortunately, but tension has remained quite high ever since, with new clashes occurring at intervals.

All Arab mediation efforts have failed to reconcile the two factions, including Saudi attempts in early 2007, at a time when the Saudis—worried about the degradation of the overall regional situation and in light of the considerable weakening of the Bush administration that became obvious in November 2006, as I explained earlier—were engaging in a dialogue with Tehran. They were encouraged to do so, moreover, by the Baker-Hamilton report, which called for negotiations with both Iran and Syria. Washington actually thwarted every such effort, by advising its Lebanese allies to remain intransigent, inciting the hard-liners among them—Druze leader Walid Jumblatt and Maronite leader Samir Geagea—to nip in the bud every conciliatory move by means of provocative public statements.

Damascus, on the other side of the fence, played the same "tension strategy," so as to show that Lebanon could not be stabilized without its direct involvement, and in order to use the Lebanese situation as a bargaining card against the offensive mounted by the Bush administration against it, the main component of which is the international tribunal on the assassination of former Lebanese Prime Minister Rafik Hariri.

In the meantime, the Lebanese army was tested for the first time, to check whether it could serve as a tool in future attempts to disarm Hezbollah. The chosen target was the least controversial possible, so as not to impair at such an early stage the image of "neutrality" between Lebanese factions that the army has been keen on maintaining since Syrian troops evacuated Lebanon in 2005. And nothing could be a more consensual target in Lebanon than a Palestinian-based group related to al-Qaeda, the so-called Fatah al-Islam: The Palestinian refugees are the country's pariahs, and al-Qaeda—the most extremist of all Sunni fundamentalist groups and a foe of both Washington and the Saudi ruling family—is loathed by both the allies of Washington and Riyadh, on the one hand, and by the Shiites, on the other. The Lebanese army's military campaign against Fatah al-Islam, in the Nahr el-Bared refugee camp in northern Lebanon where the group was based, lasted for three months. The Lebanese army took control of the camp only after suffering heavy casualties and inflicting the same on Palestinian civilians—all that against a group numbering only a few hundred combatants besieged in a slum-like camp.

After initially supporting the army's campaign, following suit with all other Lebanese political forces, Hezbollah had second thoughts and took a more reserved attitude. They must have realized that the army's assault could be seen as a first step in implementing U.S.-sponsored UN Security Council Resolution 1559 of 2004, which called for the disarmament of both the Palestinians in Lebanon's camps and Hezbollah. This first test of the army's ability to implement said resolution was, however, far from positively conclusive. If it took the Lebanese army so long to get the better of a few hundred isolated fighters, how could it possibly face several thousand or tens of thousands of Hezbollah's first-rate fighters, deeply popular in their community, the largest of Lebanon's religious communities—indeed, so popular that there is little doubt most Shiite army soldiers would rather desert than clash with their community's flagship. One conclusion Washington drew from this test, coming after the failure of Israel's 2006 aggression, was to encourage the intensive rearming of its Lebanese partners.

The continuing stalemate kept the country in highly dangerous limbo until the tension flared up sharply with the term of Lebanon's pro-Syrian President Emile Lahoud due to end in November 2007. With the heavy risk entailed—a vacancy in the presidency aggravating the constitutional crisis, and thus opening the way to possible conflagration and disintegration—Washington tried to defuse the tension through a stopgap deal cut with Damascus, reversing for a short while its aggressively hostile policy. Syria was invited to the November 2007 Arab-Israeli "peace conference" in Annapolis, Maryland, and accepted the invitation, even though its ally Iran had denounced the endeavor. Washington and Damascus agreed on the president to be elected in Beirut: Michel Suleiman, the head of the Lebanese army, and a man maintaining good relations with the Syrians (he was appointed to his army position when the country was under direct Syrian tutelage) as well as with the Americans, who have supported the Lebanese army over the years.

At first, it was widely believed that the deadlock over the presidency was resolved and that it would be only a matter of days before Suleiman was elected by the Lebanese parliament—after meeting a constitutional requirement through a legal arrangement in order to allow for his election despite his being in military service. But it soon became clear that the crisis was far from over: Eager to become the president of the country, Aoun put forward unacceptable conditions, such as one requiring that the new president be elected only for a very short term until there was a new parliament. Damascus saw in this unexpected obstacle a good means of raising the price of its collaboration, especially since it did not get anything out of the Annapolis conference. And Washington went back to the tug-of-war with Damascus, urging its allies to remain intransigent.

It is against this tense background that Imad Mughniyah, a senior military chief of Hezbollah, closely tied to the Iranian power elite, was assassinated in Damascus on February 12, 2008. He was most probably assassinated by the Israeli Mossad, possibly through agents from within the Syrian services. In any case, this was how the assassination was interpreted by Hezbollah, with its leader Hassan Nasrallah vowing to avenge

Mughniyah's death in an "open war" with Israel. Mughniyah's assassination could very well be a provocation intended to push Hezbollah precisely to such a course of action: A major attack by the Shiite organization would serve as a convenient pretext for a new large-scale Israeli action against it—in the same way that the border clash on July 12, 2006, was used as a pretext to launch Israel's murderous aggression. Remember in that respect what a well-informed Israeli military analyst wrote in the aftermath of the 33-Day War: "A war that has ended in a tie and without an agreement between the sides being signed is destined to flare up again, sooner or later. In the conflict between Israel and Iran, by means of its proxy, Hezbollah, neither side achieved its strategic aim. Therefore, the prime minister was correct in telling the Knesset that it is necessary to ensure that next time 'things will be done better.' How can this be ensured? One must start from the working assumption that the next confrontation will erupt relatively soon; for purposes of the discussion, let us assume two years from the eruption of the previous confrontation and to act in all areas as though this will happen with absolute certainty. Possibly there will be another round in the format of the second Lebanon war, but we must prepare for the possibility of something larger and more dangerous: an all-out war with regular armies, including the army of a regional power."[21]

We are quite close to "two years from the eruption of the previous confrontation." The Israeli army has already refurbished its forces and built on the lessons of the previous round. The Israeli Goliath is definitely looking forward to an opportunity to take revenge on the Lebanese Arab David who dared to taunt him. This at a time when the Bush administration, with only a few remaining months in power and fearing that the next administration might not stand up to the high standard of aggressiveness that it has set, is increasing its threats against Iran.

Palestinian Developments

SHALOM: The internal divisions among Palestinians—with the Hamas seizure of power in Gaza—have become far more intense. What do you think this means for Palestinians and for their relations with Israel?

ACHCAR: Well, as I have stressed on several occasions, the Lebanese and Palestinian situations are twins in Washington's strategy: two societies and polities torn between forces backed by the Washington-Riyadh axis and others backed by Tehran-Damascus, where the "internationally" recognized government is the Western-subservient one, and where Washington pushes for civil war. In my discussion of the Palestinian situation in the epilogue to the first edition of this book, I explained how the national agreement of principles reached almost unanimously by the Palestinian political forces, including both Fatah and Hamas, on June 27, 2006, had been nipped in the bud by the murderous aggression launched by Israel on Gaza the very next day.

Here again, as in Lebanon, Washington's main concern has been to prevent an agreement between the contending factions. The Israeli onslaught on Gaza fit neatly within that frame. It was so brutal, however, that the Palestinian Authority (PA) headed by Mahmoud Abbas could not but condemn it, and faced increasing popular pressure for a rapprochement with Hamas. This created suitable political conditions for Saudi mediation efforts to succeed. As I have explained in my discussions of both the Iraqi and Lebanese situations, the Saudis were in a very conciliatory mood in the first months of 2007 after Bush's electoral debacle and in light of the Baker-Hamilton report. Their renewed and upgraded contacts with Tehran paralleled the conciliatory efforts being made in Lebanon and in Palestine. In the latter case, they had more clout inasmuch as both factions, contrary to the case in Lebanon, have Saudi links: Hamas—the Palestinian branch of the (Sunni) Muslim Brotherhood—having traditionally been supported by the Saudi (Sunni) Islamic fundamentalist regime, although this support was watered down in recent years with Hamas building up its links with Iran.

In February 2007, both major Palestinian factions were convened to a reconciliation meeting in Mecca and an agreement was reached providing for their joint government of the Palestinian territories. Like the June 2006 agreement, this one too did not last long. As was recently described in detail in *Vanity Fair*,[22] Washington plotted with Mohammed Dahlan, the leader of one of the major quasi-mafia "security services" created under Yasir Arafat, in order to subvert the Mecca agreement and any prospect of collaboration between Hamas and Fatah. The plan was to deal Hamas a decisive military blow in its Gaza stronghold, where Dahlan's gang was based: "*Vanity Fair* has obtained confidential documents, since corroborated by sources in the U.S. and Palestine, which lay bare a covert initiative, approved by Bush and implemented by Secretary of State Condoleezza Rice and Deputy National Security Adviser Elliott Abrams, to provoke a Palestinian civil war. The plan was for forces led by Dahlan, and armed with new weapons supplied at America's behest, to give Fatah the muscle it needed to remove the democratically elected Hamas-led government from power. (The State Department declined to comment.) But the secret plan backfired, resulting in a further setback for American foreign policy under Bush. Instead of driving its enemies out of power, the U.S.-backed Fatah fighters inadvertently provoked Hamas to seize total control of Gaza."[23]

The *Vanity Fair* piece—quite accurate on the whole, as far as I can tell— was in substance no scoop for the people of the region. Hamas itself had justified its resort to a coup de force in Gaza as being a preemptive move intended to thwart a U.S.-backed attempt by Dahlan's gang to strike at them and seize control of the strip. The scenario, actually, could be—and was— foreseen from the very beginning after Hamas's electoral victory in January 2006. Compare everything that happened since then to what I wrote just a few days after that victory, on January 27, 2006: "In order to try to rescue the very sensitive Palestinian component of overall U.S. Middle East policy that it managed to steer into dire straits, the Bush administration will very likely consider three possibilities. One would be a major shift in the policies of Hamas, bought by and mediated by the Saudis; this is, however, unlikely . . . and would be long and uncertain. Another would be fomenting tension and political opposition to Hamas in order to provoke new elections in the near future, taking advantage of the vast presidential powers that Arafat had granted himself and that Mahmoud Abbas inherited, or just by having the latter resign, thus forcing a presidential election. For such a move to be successful, or meaningful at all, there is a need for a credible figure that could regain a majority for the traditional Palestinian leadership; but the only figure having the minimum of prestige required for this role is presently Marwan Barghouti, who—from his Israeli jail cell— made an alliance with Dahlan prior to the election. It is therefore likely that Washington will exert pressure on Israel for his release. A third possibility would be the 'Algerian scenario'—referring to the interruption of the electoral process in Algeria by a military junta in January 1992—which is already envisaged, according to reports in the Arab press: the repressive apparatuses of the PA would crack down on Hamas, impose a state of siege and establish a military-police dictatorship. Of course, a combination of the last two scenarios is also possible, postponing the crackdown until political conditions are created that are more suitable for it."[24]

This description of the likely moves of the Bush administration and its Palestinian stooges matches remarkably their actual moves in the eighteen months that followed, with the last one prompting Hamas's preemptive coup in June 2007. The fact that the latter was truly a "preemptive" coup—that is, a move preceding an imminent one prepared by the enemy, rather than a "preventive" strike against a hypothetic future threat as in the argument invoked by the Bush administration for the invasion of Iraq—does not make it a sound move for all that. Hamas behaved quite clumsily: Instead of limiting its action to the disarmament of Dahlan's thugs, it orchestrated a full-fledged coup de force, subverting the PA's institutions in Gaza, thus sanctioning the strip's de facto severance from the West Bank. Far from driving a wedge between collaborationists and anti-Zionists within Fatah, it desecrated all of Fatah's symbols, including the memory of Arafat himself, thus cementing Fatah's unity against it. It therefore gave Mahmoud Abbas an opportunity to dismiss the elected Palestinian Parliamentary majority and government, while laying the blame on Hamas. Worse still, it offered Israel an opportunity to abjectly strangulate the strip to a degree that only the international isolation of Hamas made possible, with the PA itself looking as if it was somewhat acquiescing. Having appointed as his new prime minister Washington's pick, former International Monetary Fund representative to the Palestinian Authority Salam Fayyad, Abbas reached new depths in collaborationist abjection.

Since Hamas seized exclusive control of Gaza, its governance of the strip confirmed that the fact that an organization adheres to religious fundamentalism is not a minor feature bearing no consequences for its behavior. Hamas tried to stifle all other independent forces, not just its foe Fatah, and to impose measures of Islamic moral order. Hamas's ideological nature already determined its type of activities to a large extent: from the suicide attacks that became its specialty within the Palestinian struggle to the "Qassam" rockets launched from Gaza into Israeli territory—both being ineffective means, if not counterproductive ones, not to mention the problem they raise for a struggle that ought to compensate for its military inferiority with moral superiority.

What will come next? For the time being, the de facto partition between Gaza and the West Bank will carry on, as neither Fatah nor Hamas has the means to dislodge the other from its stronghold. This tragic situation of the Palestinian people, whose terrible suffering at Israel's hands is compounded by the nature and behavior of the dominant organizations in its midst, will go on for quite some time and could last for the long haul. It suits Israel well to see the Palestinians divided in this way. The only thing that bothers Israel is the problem of the "Qassam" rockets: Against that, Israel knows only to resort to brutal force, as in the case of its most recent blitz on the strip, which started on February 29, killing more than 120 persons, mostly noncombatants, and wounding scores of others. It is certainly not "an eye for an eye" that Israel practices against its enemies, whether Palestinian or Lebanese: rather, one hundred eyes for an eye!—not to mention the fact that it is the aggressor in the first place.

Moreover, Israel maintains the blockade on Gaza that it imposed supposedly in retaliation for the rocket attacks. This is leading to a truly tragic situation, threatening to kill slowly many more people—harmless civilians most of them—than are killed directly by military fire. In the same way, the twelve-year embargo imposed on Iraq between 1991 and 2003 killed more people than did together the two U.S. wars on Iraq in those two years. The tragic character of the situation was most vividly emphasized in January 2008 when a huge proportion of the strip's population—close to half, according to some estimates—flooded into the breach opened by militants in the border barrier between Gaza and Egypt, near Rafah. The human tidal wave in quest of food visually confirmed what Gaza is, more than ever since Israel occupied the strip in 1967: nothing but a large concentration camp. The situation there is alarming to the point that in early

March 2008 eight of the most respected international NGOs in the fields of aid, development, and human rights published a joint report titled *The Gaza Strip: A Humanitarian Implosion*,[25] which describes the situation there as "worse now than it has ever been since the start of the Israeli military occupation in 1967." As detailed in the report, "In terms of poverty, food aid dependency, humanitarian access, unemployment, access to basic services and medical supplies, we are witnessing an unprecedented humanitarian crisis in Gaza. Though there has been a long-term pattern of deterioration stemming from decades of occupation and, more recently, international sanctions on the Hamas-led Palestinian Authority (PA), the severity of the humanitarian situation has increased exponentially due to the Israeli Government's imposition of the blockade in response to indiscriminate rocket attacks against Israel."[26] This takes place not against a background of indifference from the Western powers, as is usual, but with their direct criminal participation as in the case of Iraq previously. In Gaza, we are witnessing a new instance of what U.S. professors John Mueller and Karl Mueller, referring to Iraq, aptly called in the establishment's prestigious journal, *Foreign Affairs*, "sanctions of mass destruction."[27]

Noam Chomsky

The U.S. Elections and Iraq

SHALOM: Eight long years of the George W. Bush administration are coming to an end. The next U.S. president may well be a Democrat. What difference would a Democratic administration make in U.S. policy toward the Middle East?

CHOMSKY: The short answer is that we do not really know and can only speculate. The reason has to do with the way elections are designed, a topic we discuss earlier in the book (pp. 41f.). Issues are typically marginalized, a reflection of the general elite distaste for democracy and fear of its consequences. The concern is heightened by the fact that on a host of major issues, both parties are to the right of the electorate, which tends to have consistent and coherent positions over time.[28]

The current electoral campaigns conform to the usual pattern, and therefore leave the stands of the candidates on crucial issues unclear. There has been a flow of largely vacuous rhetoric; favorites have been "change," "hope," "unity," "experience," and a few others. One can investigate the websites of the candidates, where there are some statements about plans. They are typically not very specific, and their significance is debatable: What matters more is what the candidates and campaign managers stress prominently and insistently, not words posted on Internet sites that can be variously interpreted or ignored at will. It is not unusual for candidates, once elected, even to back away from explicit and prominent campaign promises. Clinton, for example, "put the call for universal health care at the center of his program," Vicente Navarro recalls. "But, once president, his closeness to Wall Street and his intellectual dependence on Robert Rubin of Wall Street (who became his Secretary of the Treasury) made him leery of antagonizing the insurance industry," so he backed away from a program that has long been strongly favored by a large majority of the population.[29]

On "super-Tuesday" February 5, the day of many crucial primaries, the *Wall Street Journal* ran a lead story with the headline "Issues Recede in '08 Contest as Voters Focus on Character: Candidates Pitch Style, Avoid Big Ideas; 'Folks Are Tired of Partisan Paralysis.'" The story is largely correct, but not entirely. First, issues could hardly "recede" very far since they had been kept in the background to begin with. Second, while it may be that "voters focus on character," they are given little choice when "candidates pitch style, avoid big ideas." And while "folks" are no doubt irritated that the government does not serve their interests (as polls regularly show), that hardly indicates that they have abandoned those interests.[30]

The occasional departures from the pattern reveal a good deal about "really existing democracy," and also give some indication of what might lead to changes in Middle East policy. The most dramatic change from 2004 to 2008 has to do with health care, which for a long time has been a leading domestic concern of the public. Not surprisingly: Per capita expenditures are twice those of other industrial societies, and health outcomes are among the worst in the industrial world, barely above Third World standards in some respects. Forty-seven million people have no health coverage apart from emergency rooms, the most cruel (and expensive) form of guaranteed health care. A great many others have insufficient coverage, a leading cause of bankruptcy. Navarro observes that "nearly 40% of people in the U.S. who are dying because of terminal illness are *worrying about paying for care*—how their families are going to pay the medical bills, now and after they die. No other developed country comes close to these levels of insensitivity and inhumanity."[31]

The public has long favored a government health care system to overcome the huge administrative and marketing costs, intrusion into doctor-patient relations, profits, and other burdens of the privatized system. As discussed above (p. 42), during the 2004 campaign Kerry could not mention any government involvement in health care, the press reported, because it was "politically impossible" and had "so little political support"—only the support of the large majority of the population, as in earlier years. In 2008, by contrast, government involvement does have "political support." Beginning with John Edwards, Democratic candidates have put forth proposals that partially approach what the public has been seeking for decades. What changed between 2004 and 2008? Not public opinion. Rather, a significant element of the functioning political system has become concerned about the health care catastrophe: manufacturing industry. General Motors estimates that it costs over $1,000 more to produce a car in Detroit than in Windsor, Canada, right across the border, because of health care costs. Corporate distress was sufficient to shift policies from "politically impossible" to politically possible.

With regard to Middle East policy, unless there is some comparable shift among sectors of authentic power, it is unlikely that policies will change significantly—assuming, that is, that the public remains marginalized: "spectators" rather than "participants," in accord with prevailing democratic theory.

Nevertheless, some changes are likely. The Bush administration has been far to the radical nationalist and adventurist extreme of the policy spectrum, and has been subjected to unprecedented mainstream criticism for that reason. It is possible that McCain might be similar, but a Democratic candidate is likely to shift more toward the centrist norm. However, the spectrum is narrow. Thus the Bush National Security Strategy of September 2002 was harshly criticized right away, even in the major foreign policy journals, but more because of its brazen style and arrogance than because of its content, as was pointed out by Clinton's Secretary of State Madeleine Albright, who was surely aware of Clinton's fairly similar doctrine.

Looking at the records and statements of the candidates, I see little reason to expect significant changes in policy in the Middle East.

Take the issue of Iraq. It is important to bear in mind that neither Democratic candidate has expressed a principled objection to the invasion. By that I mean the kind of objection that was universally expressed when the Russians invaded Afghanistan or when Saddam Hussein invaded Kuwait: condemnation on the grounds that aggression is a crime—in fact, the "supreme international crime" differing from others in that it encompasses all the evil that follows, as the Nuremberg Tribunal determined. No one criticized those invasions merely as a "strategic blunder" or as involvement in "another country's civil war, a war [we] can't win" (Obama and Clinton, respectively, on the Iraq invasion).

Similarly, there was universal and principled condemnation of Russian criminal atrocities in Chechnya. The crime is not mitigated by the fact that Putin's brutal measures appear to have largely succeeded in restoring order and reconstruction under a Chechen government, with fighting "limited and sporadic" and Grozny in the midst of a "building boom" after having been reduced to rubble by the Russian attack.[32] No one applauds Putin for the grand achievement. The criticism of the Iraq war, in contrast, is on grounds of cost and failure; what are called "pragmatic reasons," a stance that is considered hard-headed, serious, moderate—in the case of

Western crimes. If General Petraeus could approach Putin's achievements in Chechnya, he might be crowned king. For that reason alone a significant change of course is unlikely.

The intentions of the Bush administration, and presumably of McCain, were outlined in a Declaration of Principles released by the White House in November 2007—an agreement between Bush and the U.S.-backed Maliki government of Iraq, which is housed in the heavily protected U.S.-run Green Zone in Baghdad. The Declaration allows U.S. forces to remain in Iraq indefinitely to "deter foreign aggression" (though the only aggression threatened in the region is posed by the United States and Israel, presumably not the intention) and to maintain internal security—though not, of course, internal security for a government that would reject U.S. domination. The Declaration also commits Iraq to facilitate and encourage "the flow of foreign investments to Iraq, especially American investments." This unusually brazen expression of imperial will was underscored when Bush quietly issued yet another of his hundreds of "signing statements," declaring that he will reject crucial provisions of congressional legislation that he had just signed, including the provision that forbids spending taxpayer money "to establish any military installation or base for the purpose of providing for the permanent stationing of United States Armed Forces in Iraq" or "to exercise United States control of the oil resources of Iraq." Shortly before, the *New York Times* had reported that Washington "insists that the Baghdad government give the United States broad authority to conduct combat operations," a demand that "faces a potential buzz saw of opposition from Iraq, with its . . . deep sensitivities about being seen as a dependent state."[33]

In brief, Iraq is to remain a client state, agreeing to allow permanent U.S. military installations (called "enduring" in the preferred Orwellism), granting the United States the right to conduct combat operations freely, and ensuring U.S. investors priority in accessing its huge oil resources—a reasonably clear statement of the goals of the invasion that were evident to anyone not blinded by doctrine.

What are the alternatives of the Democrats? They were clarified in March 2007, when the House and Senate approved Democratic proposals setting deadlines for withdrawal. The proposals were analyzed by General Kevin Ryan (ret.), senior fellow at Harvard University's Belfer Center of International Affairs.[34] He pointed out that the proposals permit the president to waive their restrictions in the interests of "national security," which leaves the door wide open. They permit troops to remain in Iraq "as long as they are performing one of three specific missions: protecting US facilities, citizens, or forces; combating Al Qaeda or international terrorists; and training Iraqi security forces." U.S. facilities include the huge U.S. military bases being built around the country and the U.S. Embassy— actually a self-contained city within a city, unlike any other embassy in the world. None of these major construction projects are under way with the expectation that they will be abandoned. If U.S. troops are in close contact with the Iraqi security forces, they may need plenty of protection, because a majority of Arab Iraqis regard them as a legitimate target of attack. Combating terrorism and training Iraqi military and police are also open-ended and highly flexible commitments. Ryan concludes that the proposals are likely to leave about as many troops as had been in Iraq for several years: "Military experts would rightfully point out that the bills before Congress are more correctly understood as a re-missioning of our troops." Ryan sums up: "Perhaps a good strategy—but not a withdrawal."

It is difficult to see much difference between the Democratic proposals of March 2007 and those of Obama and Clinton. Both of the candidates provide figures for planned troop withdrawal, but as Obama foreign policy advisor Samantha Power commented, these are tentative, a "best case scenario." Power was lambasted for speaking the truth (and later resigned from the campaign following impolite references to Clinton).[35]

The Obama-Clinton proposals not only leave open the continued use of mercenaries ("contractors"), who match U.S. forces in number, but also ignore the issue of logistics and supply, which require huge operations, often traveling from Kuwait through dangerous territory in southern Iraq. And they say nothing about continued bombing. Those who recall the last years of the Indochina wars will recognize that open door—for example, in rural Cambodia, where U.S. bombing exceeded the total bombing in all theaters of World War II and "drove an enraged populace into the arms of an insurgency [the Khmer Rouge] that had enjoyed relatively little support before the bombing began."[36] Current bombing levels are apparently substantial. James Paul of Global Policy Forum, who has followed the war closely, writes that "Balad Airbase, north of Baghdad, is probably the busiest air facility in the world. Now, some of that is supply shipments, but fundamentally, it's attacks—everything from drones to fixed wing [planes], all coming at an enormous cost of human life."[37]

The proposals are also silent about the more advanced forms of state terror available to high-tech outlaw states. Thus when Israeli forces murdered the quadriplegic cleric Sheikh Yassin as he was leaving a mosque in March 2004, along with seven civilians nearby, they appear to have used a helicopter-fired hellfire missile directed by a drone, one of many such cases.[38] The assassination of Yassin, a revered figure who was the spiritual leader of Hamas and considered to be one of its more conciliatory figures, set off massive protests in Iraq and the murder of four U.S. contractors in Fallujah by the previously unknown "Brigades of Martyr Ahmed Yassin," then a murderous reaction by U.S. Marines killing hundreds of people that contributed to a sudden spread of violence throughout much of Iraq, barely contained.

The United States has a much longer reach. In one recent case, "on Oct. 30, 2006, a Hellfire missile hit a madrassah in Bajaur killing . . . 80–85 people, mostly students. Even if those killed were allegedly training to become Al Qaeda militants, and even if a few key Al Qaeda leaders such as Abu Laith al-Libi have been eliminated, the more usual outcome has been flattened houses, dead and maimed children, and a growing local population that seeks revenge against Pakistan and the U.S."[39]

This terrorist incident was hailed as a grand achievement of the "war on terror" because Libi, the presumed target, was "believed to have plotted and executed attacks against U.S. and coalition forces." The 80–85 students, dead and maimed children, and other "collateral damage" passed unnoticed. Other terrorist atrocities are treated quite differently, and not all are permitted to celebrate them. There was, for example, very prominent and vivid coverage of the murder of eight students in the Merkaz HaRav seminary in Jerusalem, the spiritual center of the settler movement, and great outrage over Palestinian support for the atrocity, even though Palestinian endorsement of violence can be attributed to "recent actions by Israel, especially attacks on Gaza that killed nearly 130 people, an undercover operation in Bethlehem that killed four militants and the announced expansion of several West Bank settlements, [which] have led to despair and rage among average Palestinians who thirst for revenge." Similarly, those who denounce Palestinians for heartlessly celebrating deaths of Jews did not seem to mind when "angry students and local residents lined up behind police tapes, chanting, 'Death to Arabs.'"[40]

Overall, it is not easy to find substantial grounds for expecting significant changes in U.S. policy with regard to Iraq with Democrats in the White House and Congress, though it is likely that there would be a softening of the extremist Bush-Cheney (and probably McCain) stance.

Iran

SHALOM: What about the issue of Iran? Is there reason to expect a different U.S. policy if a Democrat wins the election?

CHOMSKY: Obama is considered the more moderate of the two remaining candidates, and his leading slogan is "change." So let us keep to him.

With regard to Iran, Obama calls for more willingness to negotiate, but within the standard doctrinal constraints. His reported position is that he "would offer economic inducements and a possible promise not to seek 'regime change' if Iran stopped meddling in Iraq and cooperated on terrorism and nuclear issues," and stopped "acting irresponsibly" by supporting Shiite militant groups in Iraq.[41]

Some obvious questions come to mind. For example, how would we react if Ahmadinejad said he would offer a possible promise not to seek "regime change" in Israel if it stopped its illegal activities in the occupied territories and cooperated on terrorism and nuclear issues? Or if, in the 1980s, the Kremlin had announced that it might not seek "regime change" in Pakistan (or Saudi Arabia, or the United States) if it stopped "acting irresponsibly" by supporting terrorists in Afghanistan, then under Russian occupation? If the comparisons sound outlandish, that tells us a lot about the reigning doctrinal system.

It is noteworthy that Obama's moderate approach is well to the militant side of public opinion—a fact that passes unnoticed, as is often the case. Like all other viable candidates, Obama has insisted throughout the electoral campaign that the United States must threaten Iran with attack (the standard phrase is "Keep all options open")—a violation of the UN Charter, if anyone cares. But a large majority of Americans have disagreed: 75 percent favor building better relations with Iran, as compared with 22 percent who favor "implied threats."[42] All the surviving candidates, then, are opposed by three-fourths of the public on this issue.

That is not unusual. I have already mentioned a leading domestic issue, health care. To take a case with some similarity to Iran, two-thirds of Americans favor establishing diplomatic relations with Cuba, as has largely been true since polls began to be taken thirty years ago. But as in the past, all candidates reject that option and insist that the United States must continue its efforts to strangle Cuba economically, in splendid isolation, supported only by Israel (which votes with the United States reflexively but violates the U.S. sanctions) and an occasional Pacific island. In this regard, too, Obama is considered the most moderate of the candidates, "hinting that he might be open to changes in US policy if Havana made moves towards openness and democracy"[43]—a stand that might seem forthcoming to a Martian observer who knows nothing about Washington's record, past and present, with regard to tyrannical regimes. Even much of the business world favors entering into normal relations with Cuba. But the state interest in punishing Cubans for "successful defiance" of the master prevails. The disgraceful record of almost a half-century of terror and economic strangulation carries lessons for U.S.-Iran policy today: Iranians must be punished for overthrowing the tyrant whom the United States and Britain imposed when they destroyed Iranian parliamentary democracy in 1953 (to great acclaim in the national press).

In many respects, the conduct of international affairs resembles the Mafia. The Godfather does not tolerate disobedience, even from a small storekeeper who fails to pay protection money. "The rot might spread," as leading statesmen have warned, and the system of control might unravel.

Like the other candidates, Obama is far to the right of the public on resolution of the confrontation with Iran, a matter of no slight importance: British military historian Correlli Barnett hardly exaggerates when he warns that an attack on Iran by the United States (or its Israeli client) "would effectively launch World War III."[44]

American and Iranian opinion on the core issue of nuclear policy has been carefully studied. In both the United States and Iran, a large majority holds that the latter should have the rights of any signer of the Non-Proliferation Treaty: to develop nuclear power but not nuclear weapons. The same large majorities favor establishing a "nuclear-weapons-free zone in the Middle East that would include both Islamic countries and Israel." Over 80 percent of Americans favor eliminating nuclear weapons altogether—a legal obligation of the states with nuclear weapons, officially rejected by the Bush administration. And surely Iranians agree with Americans that Washington should end its military threats and turn toward normal relations. At a forum in Washington when the polls were released in January 2007, Joseph Cirincione, senior vice president for National Security and International Policy at the Center for American Progress (and Obama advisor), said the polls showed "the common sense of both the American people and the Iranian people, [who] seem to be able to rise above the rhetoric of their own leaders to find common sense solutions to some of the most crucial questions" facing the two nations, favoring pragmatic diplomatic solutions to their differences.[45] Establishing a nuclear-weapons-free zone would be particularly important, even apart from the fact that the United States and Britain have a unique commitment to this objective. In their effort to concoct a thin legal justification for their invasion of Iraq, they charged that Iraq was in violation of UN Security Council Resolution 687, which requires Iraq to eliminate weapons of mass destruction. The fate of that charge is well known, but few recall Article 14 of Resolution 687, which affirms "the goal of establishing in the Middle East a zone free from weapons of mass destruction and all missiles for their delivery and the objective of a global ban on chemical weapons," and thus surely commits the initiators and supporters of the resolution to that goal: crucially, the states that appealed to the resolution to justify their aggression.

The polls suggest that if the United States and Iran were functioning democratic societies, in which public opinion was a significant factor in determining policy on crucial issues, the very dangerous U.S.-Iran confrontation might be resolved peaceably. The prospects, however, seem remote. The opinions of the American public are so far beyond what is "politically possible" that these important polls do not even seem to have been reported. They clearly do not enter into the electoral process or discussion in the media and journals. Sophisticates commonly argue that policy cannot be "poll-driven." The premier polling agency, the Program on

International Policy Attitudes at the University of Maryland, reports that "[w]hen ABC News correspondent Martha Raddatz cited polling data showing majority opposition to the Iraq war, [Dick] Cheney responded, 'So?' Asked, 'So—you don't care what the American people think?' he responded, 'No,' and explained, 'I think you cannot be blown off course by the fluctuations in the public opinion polls.'" As she attempted to explain Cheney's comments, White House spokeswoman Dana Perino was asked whether the public should have "input." Her reply was: "You had your input. The American people have input every four years, and that's the way our system is set up."[46]

Correct. Every four years the American people can choose between candidates whose views they reject, and then they should shut up.

Evidently failing to understand democratic theory, the public strongly disagrees. "Eighty-one percent say when making 'an important decision' government leaders 'should pay attention to public opinion polls because this will help them get a sense of the public's views.'" And when asked "whether they think that 'elections are the only time when the views of the people should have influence, or that also between elections leaders should consider the views of the people as they make decisions,' an extraordinary 94 percent say that government leaders should pay attention to the views of the public between elections."[47]

Once again, however, the views of the public "lack political support" and hence can be ignored.

Nevertheless, circumstances may change. Public opinion may not remain marginalized and easily ignored. The concentrations of domestic economic power that largely shape policy may come to recognize that their interests are better served by joining the general public, and the rest of the world, than by accepting Washington's hard line. Though we do not have internal records, there is good reason to believe that the Pentagon is opposed to an attack on Iran. The March 11 resignation of Admiral William Fallon as head of the Central Command, responsible for the Middle East, was widely interpreted as tracing back to his opposition to an attack, probably shared with the military command generally. The December 2007 National Intelligence Estimate (NIE) reporting that Iran had not pursued a nuclear weapons program since 2003, when it sought and failed to reach a comprehensive settlement with the United States (see p. 204), perhaps reflects opposition of the intelligence community to military action.[48]

Israel is a rare exception to global opposition to a U.S. attack on Iran. Israel has long wanted the United States to eliminate the only power in the region it cannot dominate on its own. However, it is also possible, as Trita Parsi has argued, that Israel might come to realize that it could gain from reestablishing its traditional close relations with Iran, continuing through the 1980s after Khomeini took power—a relationship so close that Israel and its U.S. lobby "lobbied the United States *not* to pay attention to Iranian rhetoric" about Israel's destruction.[49]

There are many uncertainties, and one should not underestimate Bush-Cheney adventurism, desperation, and dedication to violence, which would render all speculation moot. But it is hard to see concrete signs that a Democratic presidency would improve the situation very much, let alone bring policy into line with American or world opinion.

Israel-Palestine and the United States

SHALOM: And what about the issue of Israel-Palestine? What differences in policy can we expect here as a result of the forthcoming U.S. election?

CHOMSKY: On Israel-Palestine too, the candidates have provided no reason to expect any constructive change. Keeping again to Obama, the candidate of "change" and "hope," his website states that he "strongly supports the U.S.-Israel relationship, believes that our first and incontrovertible commitment in the Middle East must be to the security of Israel, America's strongest ally in the Middle East." He may have meant "closest ally," but taking the words literally, Israel is indeed the "strongest ally." Transparently, it is the Palestinians who face by far the most severe security problem—in fact, a problem of survival. But the Palestinians are not a "strong ally." At most, they might be a very weak one. Hence their plight merits little concern, in accord with the operative principle that human rights are largely determined by contributions to power, profit, and doctrinal needs.

Obama's website presents him as a superhawk on Israel. "He believes that Israel's right to exist as a Jewish state should never be challenged." He is not on record as demanding that the right of countries to exist as Muslim (Christian, White) states "should never be challenged." During the 2006 Lebanon war, "Obama stood up strongly for Israel's right to defend itself from Hezbollah raids and rocket attacks," but had nothing to say about Lebanon's right to defend itself from the U.S.-backed Israeli aggression that killed over 1,000 people and destroyed much of the country. He "is an original cosponsor of the Senate resolution expressing support for Israel [during its invasion of Lebanon], condemning the [Hezbollah] attacks, and calling for strong action against Iran and Syria," though vastly greater U.S. support for the aggressors is apparently right and just, just as it was during Israel's four previous invasions of Lebanon since 1978. "Throughout the war, Barack Obama made clear that Israel should not be pressured into a cease-fire that did not deal with the threat of Hezbollah missiles." Rather, Israel must be permitted to destroy Lebanese civilian society until it is free from the threat of a deterrent to its assaults: No missiles attributed to Hezbollah had struck Israel after its withdrawal from Lebanon in 2000, until the July 2006 war.

Obama calls for increasing foreign aid "to ensure that [the] funding priorities [for military and economic assistance to Israel] are met." He also insists forcefully that the United States must not "recognize Hamas unless it renounced its fundamental mission to eliminate Israel." No state can recognize Hamas, a political party, so what he must be referring to is the government formed by Hamas after a free election that came out "the wrong way" and is therefore illegitimate, in accord with prevailing elite concepts of "democracy." To leave no ambiguity, Obama's website explains that he was "a cosponsor of the Palestinian Anti-Terrorism Act of 2006. Introduced in the wake of Hamas' victory in the Palestinian elections, this act outlaws direct assistance to any entity of the Palestinian Authority controlled by Hamas." Punishment of the Palestinians for voting the wrong way must continue, Obama holds, until Hamas meets the three conventional conditions: "recognize Israel, abandon violence, and abide by previous agreements made between the Palestinian Authority and Israel."

Obama does not ignore Palestinians: "Obama believes that a better life for Palestinian families is good for both Israelis and Palestinians." He also adds a vacuous statement about two states living side by side, leaving it in a form that has been acceptable to Israel ever since the Israeli ultraright considered a meaningless version of a two-state settlement in 1996, followed in this a few years later by the more dovish parties (see pp. 151f.).

Also conventional is Obama's failure to mention that the United States and Israel continue to reject for themselves the very conditions they have imposed on Hamas: Obviously they do not recognize Palestine or renounce violence, and though the facts are evaded, they also reject previous commitments, including the "Road Map" (p. 211).

Virtually every reference to Hamas identifies it as the Iranian-backed group dedicated to the destruction of Israel as its "fundamental mission." One will search in vain for condemnation of the official Israeli-American commitment to destroy Palestine (the 1989 Shamir-Peres-Baker Plan), a fundamental mission that was not mere words: Shamir, Peres, and Baker were actively implementing that commitment at the time of their 1989 declaration, as before (pp. 149), and their successors continue to do so today, with only rhetorical change. It is irrelevant that Hamas has repeatedly proposed (and unilaterally implemented) a cease-fire to allow negotiations to proceed toward the political settlement approved by the international consensus that the United States and Israel have unilaterally rejected. Similarly, it is irrelevant that Hamas has repeatedly advocated a two-state settlement in terms of this consensus, as when Hamas Prime Minister Ismail Haniyeh called for "statehood for the West Bank and Gaza" or when the most militant Hamas leader Khalid Mish'al, in exile in Damascus, called for "the establishment of a truly sovereign and independent Palestinian state on the territories occupied by Israel in June 1967."[50]

Such facts cannot be facts, virtually by definition, because they conflict with deeply held doctrine. Accordingly, though staring us in the face, they are invisible, as is the U.S.-Israeli leadership of the rejectionist camp tracing back to 1971 and 1976 (pp. 146–149). It must be that the United States is an "honest broker," not the leading barrier to political settlement. Facts cannot be permitted to interfere with such crucial doctrines of the faith.

Operative U.S.-Israeli policy conforms to the Olmert "convergence" program (see pp. 210). The program was withdrawn after the Lebanon war as too forthcoming, but remains the basic guideline for policy. Always with U.S. backing, apart from some mild clucking of tongues, Israel is continuing to construct the Separation Wall, by now very clearly an annexation wall. The authoritative determination by the highest international legal authority (the International Court of Justice, commonly known as the World Court) that the Wall violates international law (pp. 152f.) has joined other unwanted historical facts in the memory hole, cavernous but brimful. It is of no concern that the Court ruled that all settlement activities violate the Geneva conventions, established to formally criminalize Nazi crimes. The Court ruled that "the Fourth Geneva Convention, and international human rights law are applicable to the Occupied Palestinian Territory and must there[fore] be faithfully complied with by Israel," so that populations cannot be transferred there, and the segments of the Separation Wall "being built by Israel to protect the settlements are ipso facto in violation of international humanitarian law" (U.S. Justice Buergenthal, in a separate declaration)—segments that comprise more than 80 percent of the wall. All irrelevant, since George Bush the "decider" has ruled that Israel can permanently keep the illegal settlements that are being protected by the Wall. Also irrelevant is the fact that as a High Contracting Party, the United States is obligated to enforce the Geneva conventions and punish those who violate them: itself, in this case.

The same ICJ ruling, of course, applies to everything to the east of the annexation wall as well, particularly to Israeli settlement programs in the Jordan Valley—an extremely important fact, though barely reported. These programs have been clearly designed to drive Palestinians out of the region in favor of Jewish settlement, thus imprisoning whatever scattered fragments are to be left to Palestinians.

As I write, Israeli troops and bulldozers have just demolished homes in more Jordan Valley villages, leaving sixty-five people homeless, along with another ten whose homes were demolished near the town of Qalqilya, almost entirely surrounded by the Wall so as to render it virtually uninhabitable. To consider another current case, the village of Fasayil in the Jordan Valley is right next door to the flourishing Israel settlement of Tomer. Fasayil, in contrast, is not flourishing. Its drinking water is rationed by the occupying authorities, it is not allowed to construct or repair roads, electricity is scheduled to be cut. There is no school in the village, so children have to walk miles along dangerous paths. The villagers have tried to build a school, but that is banned, because "the area is designated for Israeli farming," according to the Israeli Civil Administration. Nevertheless, the villagers have again been attempting to build a school, despite an injunction from the Israeli authorities to halt work. Since the crimes are masked by silence, we do not know the outcome. But we do know, if we choose to, that there is nothing unusual about Fasayil and Tomer. Rather, the paired towns are a microcosm of the West Bank—the reality of what we should call the U.S.-Israeli occupation, if we are honest.[51]

Israel continues to carry out its settlement programs, announcing, if questioned, that the territories "will remain in Israel's hands."[52] The programs in the Greater Jerusalem area violate Security Council resolutions dating back to 1968. Some of the new settlements surrounding Jerusalem are designated for religious settlers, "who will benefit from new homes at relatively inexpensive prices," thanks to robbery of Palestinian land and government subsidies. The "ultra-Orthodox . . . constitute the fastest-growing portion of the settler population, according to figures from Peace Now and Israel's Central Bureau of Statistics." The United States "reacted by reminding Mr. Olmert that limiting settlement activity is a 'road-map obligation' Israel committed itself to as part of the Annapolis Process," probably eliciting a few chuckles in Tel Aviv and Jerusalem. The settlements have the multiple purposes of benefiting ultraorthodox settlers, extending the bounds of the (unchallengeably) Jewish state, improving Olmert's political prospects, and, crucially, cutting Palestinians off from the traditional center of their cultural, political, social, and economic life in Jerusalem.[53]

Highly visible violations of international law and the "Road Map" are sometimes reported, as are major atrocities. But not the traditional methods of reaching the intended goals, dating back to the origins of the Zionist project: "dunam after dunam," quietly, in the manner frankly explained by the dovish Shimon Peres administration in accord with the principles enunciated decades earlier by Moshe Dayan (pp. 157–158).

The "Annapolis Process" to which Washington's stern admonition referred is the series of peace talks that were planned at Annapolis, Maryland, in November 2007. A common and plausible interpretation is that the dramatic events were staged as part of the effort to line up the "moderate" Arab states, such as the Saudi tyranny, in Washington's crusade against Iran. Presumably there are other meeting places in the Washington area, but only one that is the base for the naval forces that are menacing Iran's coasts—a point that was presumably not lost on the participants and on Iran.

Some argue that, on its present course, Israel will become a pariah state like apartheid South Africa, with a large Palestinian population deprived of rights, laying the basis for a civil rights struggle for a unitary democratic state. That is dubious, however. Rather, the United States and Israel are likely to proceed exactly as they are now doing: quietly establishing the effective takeover of everything of value to them in the West Bank, including the Jordan Valley and the regions within the annexation wall, and carrying out massive infrastructure programs that leave Palestinians in unviable cantons. Gazans will be left to rot in desperation in the prison constructed for them, which Israel can use for target practice, sometimes resorting to violence to respond to—or, often, to incite—mindless criminal acts of rocket firing.[54] The contention of Gaza militants that the rockets are retaliation for continuing Israeli crimes in the West Bank, which Gazans accurately describe as inseparable from Gaza, is not even rejected in the West, because it is incomprehensible: How can anyone retaliate for actions supported by the leader of the Free World? Israel will take no responsibility for Palestinians who may somehow survive in the cantons that dot the West Bank landscape, far from the eyes of Israelis traveling on their segregated superhighways to their well-subsidized West Bank towns and suburbs, controlling the crucial water resources of the region, and benefiting from their ties with U.S. corporations that seem quite satisfied to see a loyal military power at the periphery of such a critical area, with an advanced high-tech economy offering them ample opportunities and benefits and with close links to Washington.

While systematically proceeding to undermine the basis for a viable two-state settlement in the West Bank, Israel can also turn to solving its internal "demographic problem," the presence of non-Jews in a Jewish state. The ultranationalist Knesset member Avigdor Lieberman was harshly condemned as a racist in Israel when he advanced the idea of forcing Israeli Arab citizens in the "triangle"—Wadi Ara—into a "Palestinian state," the population of course not consulted. One sign of the drift to the nationalist right in Israeli culture is that Lieberman's bitterly denounced proposal is slowly being incorporated into the mainstream. Knesset member Otniel Schneller of the governing party Kadima, "considered to be one of the people closest and most loyal to Prime Minister Ehud Olmert," proposed a plan that "appears very similar to one touted by Yisrael Beiteinu leader Avigdor Lieberman," though Schneller says his plan would be "more gradual," and the Arabs affected "will remain citizens of Israel even though their territory will belong to the [Palestinian Authority and] they will not be allowed to resettle in other areas of Israel." In December 2007, Foreign Minister Tzipi Livni, the last hope of many Israeli doves, adopted the same position. An eventual Palestinian state, she suggested, would "be the national answer to the Palestinians" in the territories and those "who live in different refugee camps or in Israel." With efficient PR, the forceful transfer of unwanted Arab citizens to a derisory "Palestinian state" could even be presented to the world as a generous "land swap."[55]

The basic line of argument was laid out decades ago by the respected humanist Michael Walzer, editor of the democratic socialist journal *Dissent*: "[N]ation building in new states is sure to be rough on groups marginal to the nation," he explained, and people of good will should appreciate that "the roughness can only be smoothed out . . . by helping people to leave who have to leave"—in this case, the marginal people who are the remnants of what is now recognized to have been the "ethnic cleansing" of 1948.[56]

Once Israeli Arabs are dispatched to their natural place, Israel would have achieved the long-sought goal of freeing itself from the Arab taint—a stand that is familiar enough in U.S. history, for example in Thomas Jefferson's hope, never realized, that the rising empire of liberty would be free of "blot or mixture," red or black.

Livni is quoted in a rare report that slightly opens the door on why the Walzer-Lieberman-Schneller-Livni concerns are so important. Despite heroic efforts by apologists, it is not easy to conceal the fact that a "democratic Jewish state" is no more consistent with liberal principles than a "democratic" Christian, Muslim, or White state, as long as the blot or mixture is not removed. Such notions could be tolerated if the religious/ethnic identification were mostly symbolic, as when selecting an official day of rest. But in the case of Israel, it goes far beyond that. The most extreme departure from minimal democratic principles is the complex array of laws and bureaucratic arrangements designed to vest control of more than 90 percent of the land, including state land, in the hands of the Jewish National Fund (JNF), an organization committed to using charitable funds in ways that are "directly or indirectly beneficial to persons of Jewish religion, race or origin," so its documents explain: "a public institution recognized by the Government of Israel and the World Zionist Organization as the exclusive instrument for the development of Israel's lands," restricted to Jewish use in perpetuity, and barred to non-Jewish labor (though the principle is often ignored for imported cheap labor, and there are some marginal exceptions).[57]

This radical violation of elementary civil rights, funded by American citizens thanks to the tax-free status of the JNF, finally reached Israel's High Court in 2000, in a case brought by the highly assimilated middle-class Kaadan family, who had been barred from the all-Jewish town of Katzir near the Arab village where they lived (see p. 141). The Court ruled in their favor. After an "11-year battle," and six years after the High Court ruling, the Kaadan family finally succeeded in buying a home in Katzir. They hope that their former home will be bought by a Jew, explaining that "[i]t's a known fact that the State of Israel takes care of every Jew, all over the world. As soon as a Jew moves in they'll give us new asphalt roads without potholes. The electricity network will be replaced too, and even the sewer system will be improved. And maybe, just maybe, they'll build a little synagogue, the light from which will finally enable us to see our way at night."[58]

The narrowly worded Court decision seems to have been barely implemented. Few cases are reported. Seven years later, a young Arab couple was barred from the town of Rakefet, on state land, on grounds of "social incompatibility."[59] Again, none of this is unfamiliar in the United States. After all, it took a century before the Fourteenth Amendment was even formally recognized by the courts, and it still is far from implemented.

Reflecting on recent and probably continuing U.S. policies, Israeli journalist and dovish political leader Yossi Sarid observed that U.S. "moral deterrence has vanished. . . . Any war criminal can scrub and launder his misdeeds with U.S. soap." It is a regular occurrence. Some of the illustrations are surreal. Thus Lithuania issued an arrest warrant for an "enemy combatant," borrowing from the Bush-Cheney-Rumsfeld lexicon, where the term applies to someone believed to be defending his country from foreign aggression. The target in this case was Yitzhak Arad, a partisan hero who went on to become an Israeli general and served for twenty years as head of the Holocaust museum Yad V'shem. Arad had "written openly and proudly of his contribution as a partisan to the liquidation of several ranking Lithuanian Nazi collaborators," Israeli commentator Reuven Kaminer writes, noting that "Lithuania was unique in that most of the Jews murdered in that country were victims of Lithuanian authorities." Lithuania approached Israel through diplomatic channels to get its hands on Arad. A few months later its Foreign Minister was welcomed to Israel on a state visit, meeting with President Shimon Peres and Foreign Minister Tsipi Livni, and was greeted with respect on a visit to Yad V'Shem, while relations remain just fine.[60]

What tomorrow will bring if matters proceed on their present course, one hates to think.

Notes*

Notes to Preface to the 2024 Edition

1 George H. W. Bush, "Address Before a Joint Session of the Congress on the Persian Gulf Crisis and the Federal Budget Deficit, 1990–09–11," at https://bush41library.tamu.edu/archives/public-papers/2217.

2 Barack Obama, "Remarks by the President at Cairo University, 6–04–09," at https://obamawhitehouse.archives.gov/the-press-office/remarks-president-Cairo-university-6–04–09.

3 More on this in Gilbert Achcar, *The People Want: A Radical Exploration of the Arab Uprising* (Berkeley: University of California Press, and London: Saqi Books, 2013; second edition with a new preface, London: Saqi Books, 2022).

4 Hillary Clinton, "America's Pacific Century," *Foreign Policy*, October 11, 2011, at https://foreignpolicy.com/2011/10/11/americas-pacific-century/.

5 For an analysis of this sequence of events, with a special focus on Egypt and Syria, see Gilbert Achcar, *Morbid Symptoms: Relapse in the Arab Uprising* (Stanford, CA: Stanford University Press, and London: Saqi Books, 2016).

6 Robert M. Gates, "The Dysfunctional Superpower: Can a Divided America Deter China and Russia?," *Foreign Affairs* online, September 29, 2023, at https://www.foreignaffairs.com/united-states/robert-gates-america-china-russia-dysfunctional-superpower.

Notes to Preface to the 2007 Edition

1 New York: Vintage, 1974. An expanded edition incorporating this work was published as *Middle East Illusions* (Lanham, MD: Rowman & Littlefield, 2003).

2 Boston: South End Press, 1983. An updated edition was published in 1999.

3 http://www.zcommunications.org/znet.

4 Gilbert Achcar and Stephen R. Shalom, "Getting Out of Iraq," *New Politics* 10, no. 4 (Winter 2006), pp. 5–10. The first part of this article, "On John Murtha's Position," was widely posted on the web, for example on ZNet, November 21, 2005, http://www.zcommunications.org/znet/viewArticle/4973.

5 *La Nouvelle guerre froide. Le Monde après le Kosovo* (Paris: Presses universitaires de France, 1999). An English translation appears in *Masters of the Universe? NATO's Balkan Crusade*, ed. Tariq Ali (London: Verso, 2000), pp. 57–144.

---

* *Note:* All websites were accessed July 2–3, 2008. Arabic transliterations in quotations have been made consistent.

6 New York: Monthly Review Press, 2002; second edition (with a new preface and a new chapter), Boulder, CO: Paradigm Publishers, 2006.

7 *The Israeli Dilemma: A Debate between Two Left-Wing Jews. Letters between Marcel Liebman and Ralph Miliband,* selected, with an introduction and epilogue, by Gilbert Achcar (London: Merlin Press, 2006).

8 New York: Monthly Review Press, 2004.

9 This "letter," written right after the fall of Baghdad, was published wholly or in part in daily papers—*L'Humanité* (Paris), *Liberazione* (Rome), *La Libre Belgique* (Brussels), *Le Courrier* (Geneva)—and posted widely on the web (for example, ZNet, http://www.zcommunications.org/znet/viewArticle/10556. It is reproduced in *Eastern Cauldron* (see note 8 above), pp. 258–264.

Notes to Chapter One

1 See, for example, Edward S. Herman, *The Real Terror Network: Terrorism in Fact and Propaganda* (Boston: South End Press, 1982); Noam Chomsky, *Towards a New Cold War: Essays on the Current Crisis and How We Got There* (New York: Pantheon, 1982, pp. 47–55); Edward S. Herman and Frank Brodhead, *The Rise and Fall of the Bulgarian Connection* (New York: Sheridan Square Publications, 1986); Noam Chomsky, *Pirates and Emperors: International Terrorism in the Real World* (New York: Claremont Research and Publications, 1986; extended version, Cambridge, MA: South End Press, 2002); Noam Chomsky, *The Culture of Terrorism* (Boston: South End Press, 1988); and Edward S. Herman and Noam Chomsky, *Manufacturing Consent: The Political Economy of the Mass Media* (New York: Pantheon, 1988).

2 *US Army Operational Concept for Terrorism Counteraction,* TRADOC Pamphlet No. 525-37, 1984.

3 UN roll call votes are available online at http://unbisnet.un.org:8080/ipac20/ipac.jsp?profile=voting&menu=search.

4 General Assembly Resolution 42/159, December 7, 1987, section 14; available online at http://www.un.org/documents/ga/res/42/a42r159.htm.

5 Two years later the United States and Israel agreed to a similar resolution (General Assembly Resolution 44/29, December 4, 1989, available online at http://www.un.org/documents/ga/res/44/a44r029.htm). By then the United States had accepted a post-apartheid regime, so the South African issue was moot, and the replacement of "foreign occupation" by "alien domination" was apparently considered an acceptable evasion of the right to resist.

6 Council Framework Decision of June 13, 2002, on combating terrorism (2002/475/JHA); available online at http://www.statewatch.org/news/2002/jul/frameter-r622en00030007.pdf.

7 "Proposed Definition of 'Aggression,' Submitted by American Delegation, July 25, 1945," in *International Conference on Military Trials* (London, 1945); available online at http://www.yale.edu/lawweb/avalon/imt/jackson/jack 50.htm.

8 UN General Assembly Resolution 29/3314, December 14, 1974, accessible online from http://www.un.org/documents/ga/res/29/ares29.htm.

9 Ibid., Article 3, section (g) reads as follows: "Any of the following acts, regardless of a declaration of war, shall, subject to and in accordance with the provisions of article 2, qualify as an act of aggression: . . . (g) The sending by or on behalf of a State of armed bands, groups, irregulars or mercenaries, which carry out acts of armed force against another State of such gravity as to amount to the acts listed above, or its substantial involvement therein."

10 Gilbert Achcar, *The Clash of Barbarisms*, 2nd expanded ed. (Boulder, CO: Paradigm Publishers, 2006), p. 91.

11 See, for example, Jonathan B. Tucker (ed.), *Toxic Terror: Assessing Terrorist Use of Chemical and Biological Weapons* (Cambridge, MA: MIT Press, 2000); Philip B. Heymann, *Terrorism and America: A Commonsense Strategy for a Democratic Society* (Cambridge, MA: MIT Press, 1998); and Richard A. Falkenrath, Robert D. Newman, and Bradley A. Thayer, *America's Achilles' Heel: Nuclear, Biological, and Chemical Terrorism and Covert Attack* (Cambridge, MA: MIT Press, 1998).

12 Robert McNamara, "Apocalypse Soon," *Foreign Policy* (May–June 2005); Graham Allison, *Nuclear Terrorism* (New York: Times Books, 2004).

13 "Treasury Office Has Four Agents Investigating Wealth of Bin Laden, Saddam," White House Bulletin, April 29, 2004; Marc Frank and Richard Lapper, "US Squeeze Angers Cubans: Bush Clampdown Is Seen as Blow to Family Ties," *Financial Times*, May 10, 2004, p. 4; Nancy San Martin, "More Focus on Cuba Embargo Than Terror Trail Is Questioned," *Miami Herald*, April 30, 2004, p. 1A.

14 See, for example, 9/11 Public Discourse Project, *Final Report on 9/11 Commission Recommendations*, December 5, 2005; available online at http://www.9-11pdp.org/press/2005–12–05_report.pdf. Other reports can be found on the 9/11 Public Discourse Project website at http://www.9-11pdp.org/.

15 National Intelligence Council, *Global Trends 2015: A Dialogue About the Future with Nongovernment Experts*, NIC 2000–02 (Washington, DC, 2000), p. 10; available online at http://www.dni.gov/nic/PDF_GIF_global/globaltrend2015.pdf.

16 U.S. Space Command, *Vision for 2020*, February 1997; available online at http://www.fas.org/spp/military/docops/usspac/visbook.pdf.

17 Wolfowitz told Sam Tannenhaus of *Vanity Fair* in May 2003: "[W]e can now remove almost all of our forces from Saudi Arabia. Their presence there over the last 12 years has been a source of enormous difficulty for a friendly government. It's been a huge recruiting device for al Qaeda. In fact if you look at bin Laden, one of his principal grievances was the presence of so-called crusader forces on the holy land, Mecca and Medina." Posted on the Department of Defense website at http://www.defenselink.mil/transcripts/2003/tr20030509-depsecdef0223.html.

18 "Operations Security Impact on Declassification Management Within the Department of Defense," February 13, 1998, produced by Booz Allen & Hamilton Inc., Linthicum, MD, available online at http://www.fas.org/sgp/othergov/dod_opsec.html. The document recommends a declassification strategy that includes "Diversion: List of interesting declassified material—i.e. Kennedy assassination data" and later notes that "[t]he use of the Internet could reduce the unrestrained public appetite for 'secrets' by providing good faith distraction material."

19 "[T]he process of transformation [that is needed in order 'to preserve American military preeminence in the coming decades'], even if it brings revolutionary change, is likely to be a long one, absent some catastrophic and catalyzing event—like a new Pearl Harbor." See Thomas Donnelly et al., *Rebuilding America's Defenses: Strategy, Forces and Resources for a New Century* (Washington, DC: PNAC, 2000); archived online at http://www.informationclearinghouse.info/pdf/RebuildingAmericasDefenses.pdf.

20 "U.S. Senators Chat with Saddam," in *The Gulf War Reader*, ed. Micah L. Sifry and Christopher Cerf (New York: Times Books, 1991), pp. 119–121.

21 "In hindsight, Foreign Minister Tariq Aziz disclosed that Iraq originally planned to occupy only the islands and the disputed oilfield. He described taking Kuwait City as Saddam's 'last-moment' decision just before the invasion." See Amatzia Baram, "The Iraqi Invasion of Kuwait: Decision-making in Baghdad," in *Iraq's Road to War,* ed. Amatzia Baram and Barry Rubin (New York: St. Martin's, 1993), p. 23.

22 Tariq Aziz actually added, according to the previous quote in Baram: "Saddam's argument was that 'it would make no difference [to the United States]' how much of Kuwait was conquered."

23 "The Glaspie Transcript: Saddam Meets the U.S. Ambassador," in *The Gulf War Reader,* ed. Micah L. Sifry and Christopher Cerf (New York: Times Books, 1991), pp. 130, 133.

24 Ibid., p. 129.

Notes to Chapter Two

1 "In God We Trust" first appeared on coins in 1864 and was continuously present as of 1909, but it became mandatory on coins and bills and was declared the national motto only in 1955. See Louis Fisher and Nada Mourtada-Sabbah, "Adopting 'In God We Trust' as the U.S. National Motto," *Journal of Church and State* 44, no. 4 (September 2002), pp. 671–692. The phrase "under God" was added to the Pledge of Allegiance in 1954.

2 Rabbi Menachem Mendel Schneerson (1902–1994), referred to by his followers as "The Rebbe," was a prominent Orthodox Jewish rabbi and spiritual leader of the Chabad Lubavitch branch of Hasidic Judaism.

3 See Simha Flapan, *The Birth of Israel: Myths and Realities* (New York: Pantheon, 1987), p. 239.

4 H. Con. Res. 275, December 19, 2005; available online at http://thomas.loc.gov/cgi-bin/query/z?c109:hcon.275.eh:.

5 The Hashemite family, backed by Britain, ruled part of the Arabian peninsula (1917–1924) as well as Syria (1918–1920), Iraq (1921–1958), and since 1921, Jordan. See Study Group on "A New Israeli Strategy Toward 2000," *A Clean Break: A New Strategy for Securing the Realm,* Institute for Advanced Strategic and Political Studies (2000); available online at http://www.israeleconomy.org/strat1.htm. This study group was led by Richard Perle, and it included Douglas Feith, David Wurmser, and Meyrav Wurmser.

6 See, for example, Roger Morris, "A Tyrant 40 Years in the Making," *New York Times,* March 14, 2003, p. A29.

7 Steven R. Weisman, "On Mideast 'Listening Tour,' the Question Is Who's Hearing," *New York Times,* September 30, 2005, p. A1.

8 Lysandra Ohrstrom, "Debate on U.S. Diplomacy in the Middle East at AUB Starts with a Blunder," *Daily Star* (Beirut), October 14, 2005.

9 The 4 E's were also part of Karen Hughes's congressional testimony. See Karen Hughes, "America's Dialogue with the World," Statement before the House International Relations Committee, Washington, DC, November 10, 2005; available online at http://www.state.gov/r/us/2005/56926.htm.

10 Samuel P. Huntington, *The Third Wave: Democratization in the Late 20th Century* (Norman: University of Oklahoma Press, 1993).

11 Gilbert Achcar, "The Arab Despotic Exception," *Eastern Cauldron: Islam, Afghanistan, Palestine and Iraq in a Marxist Mirror* (New York: Monthly Review Press, 2004), pp. 69–74; originally published in *Le Monde diplomatique* (English edition) in June 1997.

12 Samuel P. Huntington, *The Clash of Civilizations and the Remaking of World Order* (New York: Touchstone, 1998), p. 94.

13 "President Bush Discusses Freedom in Iraq and Middle East: Remarks by the President at the 20th Anniversary of the National Endowment for Democracy," Washington, DC, November 23, 2003; available online at http://www.white-house.gov/news/ releases/2003/11/20031106-2.html.

14 Thomas Carothers, *In the Name of Democracy: U.S. Policy Toward Latin America in the Reagan Years* (Berkeley: University of California Press, 1991); Thomas Carothers, "The Reagan Years," in *Exporting Democracy: The United States and Latin America*, ed. Abraham Lowenthal (Baltimore: Johns Hopkins University Press, 1991).

15 Thomas Carothers, *Critical Mission: Essays on Democracy Promotion* (Washington, DC: Carnegie Endowment for International Peace, 2004).

16 Thomas Carothers, "Promoting Democracy and Fighting Terror," *Foreign Affairs* 82, no. 1 (January–February 2003), p. 96. Reprinted in Carothers, *Critical Mission.*

17 See "Our Man in Baku," *Washington Post,* January 25, 2004, p. B6.

18 See Gilbert Achcar, "Greater Middle East: The U.S. Plan," *Le Monde diplomatique,* English edition, April 2004.

19 Program on International Policy Attitudes (PIPA), "Public Perceptions of the Foreign Policy Positions of the Presidential Candidates," September 29, 2004; PIPA, "The Separate Realities of Bush and Kerry Supporters," October 21, 2004 (both available online at http://www.pipa.org/).

20 Gardiner Harris, "In American Health Care, Drug Shortages Are Chronic," *New York Times,* October 31, 2004, p. IV:12.

21 See, for example, Lee Walczak and Richard S. Dunham, " 'I Want My Safety Net': Why So Many Americans Aren't Buying into Bush's Ownership Society," *Business Week,* May 16, 2005, p. 24.

22 See, for example, Latin American Studies Association, *The Electoral Process in Nicaragua: Domestic and International Influences,* the report of the Latin American Studies Association delegation to observe the Nicaraguan general election of November 4, 1984 (Austin, TX: LASA, November 19, 1984); "Report of the British Parliamentary Delegation to Nicaragua to Observe the Presidential and National Assembly Elections" (British Parliament, London, November 1984); and "The Elections in Nicaragua, November 1984" (Irish Parliament, Dublin, November 21, 1984).

23 Robert Satloff, "Assessing the Bush Administration's Policy of 'Constructive Instability' (Part I): Lebanon and Syria," Washington Institute for Near East Policy, PolicyWatch #974, March 15, 2005, available online at http://www. washingtoninstitute. org/templateC05.php?CID=2278.

Notes to Chapter Three

1 Subcommittee on Multinational Corporations, Committee on Foreign Relations, United States Senate, *Multinational Oil Corporations and U.S. Foreign Policy: Report with Individual Views* (Washington, DC: US Government Printing Office, January 2, 1975), p. 38; available online at http://www.mtholyoke. edu/acad/intrel/oil1.htm.

2 Ibid, p. 39.

3 The quotation in full is as follows: "After the Falklands, grateful for US Sidewinders and satellite imagery, Britain focused on the role of compliant ally.

Since 1991 Britain has been seen as a spear carrier for the *pax americana*, a role it adopted without public debate or consideration of possible alternatives." See Michael MccGwire, "The Rise and Fall of the NPT: An Opportunity for Britain," *International Affairs* 81, no. 1 (2005), p. 134.

4 "Transcript of Roundtable Discussion on American Foreign Policy toward China," Oct. 6, 7, 8, 1949, quoted in Bruce Cumings, *The Origins of the Korean War*, vol. II, *The Roaring of the Cataract, 1947–1950* (Princeton: Princeton University Press, 1990), p. 57.

5 Zbigniew Brzezinski, "Hegemonic Quicksand," *The National Interest* 74 (Winter 2003–2004): 8. Available online at http://www.kas.de/upload/dokumente/brzezinski.pdf.

6 See Chapter One, note 15 above.

7 William Stivers, *Supremacy and Oil: Iraq, Turkey, and the Anglo-American World Order, 1918–1930* (Ithaca: Cornell University Press, 1982), pp. 28–29, 34.

8 Quoted in Gordon Connell-Smith, *The Inter-American System* (New York: Oxford University Press, 1966), p. 16.

9 In 1968, the heavily Jewish United Federation of Teachers went on strike against a program of decentralized community control that the union claimed violated due process clauses of their contract. In the eyes of many Black and minority residents, however, community control empowered their districts, including Ocean Hill–Brownsville, for the first time. The strike helped end the previous Black-Jewish political alliance. See Jerald E. Podair, *The Strike That Changed New York: Blacks, Whites, and the Ocean Hill–Brownsville Crisis* (New Haven: Yale University Press, 2003).

10 Tom Regan, "US, Israel Working to Mend Rifts; Israel Arms Sales to China, FBI Investigation into Alleged Spy Affair Sour Relations," *Christian Science Monitor*, July 29, 2005, updated version posted on web, August 2, 2005, http://www.csmonitor.com/2005/0801/dailyUpdate.html. Ze'ev Schiff, "U.S. to Israel: Tighten Arms Exports Supervision," *Ha'aretz*, June 12, 2005; Ze'ev Schiff, "U.S. Insists: Mofaz Must Sign Drone Apology," *Ha'aretz*, July 27, 2005; Ze'ev Schiff, "A Shallow Strategic Dialog," *Ha'aretz*, July 29, 2005.

11 Harvard Law School professor and fervent Israel supporter and Chomsky-hater. For a sample of Dershowitz's views, see his *The Case for Israel* (Hoboken, NJ: Wiley, 2003) and *The Case for Peace: How the Arab-Israeli Conflict Can Be Resolved* (Hoboken, NJ: Wiley, 2005); for a critique, see Norman G. Finkelstein, *Beyond Chutzpah: On the Misuse of Anti-Semitism and the Abuse of History* (Berkeley: University of California Press, 2005).

Notes to Chapter Four

1 John F. Burns, "Pakistan Antiterror Support Avoids Vow of Military Aid," *New York Times*, September 16, 2001, p. I:5.

2 Barry Bearak, "Misery Hangs over Afghanistan After Years of War and Drought," *New York Times*, September 24, 2001, p. B1.

3 See, for example, Alex Duval Smith, "'Cease Air Strikes' So Aid Work Can Go On," *Independent*, October 16, 2001, p. 4; Luke Harding, "Aid Agencies Plead for Pause in Raids," *Guardian* (London), October 18, 2001, p. 4; Jason Burke, "The Ground Attack: UN Set to Appeal for Halt in the Bombing," *Observer*, October 21, 2001, p. 2; Tom Mashberg, "Aid Groups: Stop Bombing; Humanitarian Disaster Feared," *Boston Herald*, October 23, 2001, p. 6; Nuala Haughey, "Aid Agency Calls for US to Cease Bombing to Allow in Food Supplies," *Irish Times*, November 1, 2001, p. 10.

4 John Sifton, "Temporal Vertigo," *New York Times Magazine*, September 30, 2001, pp. 48ff.

5 Michelle Nichols and Paul Gallagher, "Bread Harder to Deliver Than Bombs," *The Scotsman*, October 8, 2001, p. 6; Elisabeth Bumiller and Elizabeth Becker, "Bush Voices Pride in Aid, but Groups List Hurdles," *New York Times*, October 17, 2001, p. B3.

6 See, for example, Jonathan Fowler, "U.N. expert: U.S. Food Drops in Afghanistan Will Harm Future Aid Efforts," Associated Press, October 15, 2001; Bumiller and Becker, "Bush Voices Pride in Aid," p. B3.

7 Abdul Haq, "US Bombs Are Boosting the Taliban," *The Guardian* (London), November 2, 2001, p. 20.

8 John F. Burns, "Afghan Gathering in Pakistan Backs Future Role for King," *New York Times*, October 26, 2001, p. B4; Kathleen Kenna, "Summit of Afghan Exiles Demands End to U.S. Raids," *Toronto Star*, October 26, 2001, p. A8.

9 Samina Ahmed, "The United States and Terrorism in Southwest Asia: September 11 and Beyond," *International Security* 26, no. 3 (Winter 2001–2002), p. 92.

10 Walter Pincus, "Mueller Outlines Origin, Funding of Sept. 11 Plot," *Washington Post*, June 6, 2002, p. A1.

11 Michael R. Gordon, "Allies Preparing for a Long Fight as Taliban Dig In," *New York Times*, October 28, 2001, p. A1.

12 George W. Bush announced the United States' unilateral withdrawal from the 1972 Anti-Ballistic Missile Treaty on December 13, 2001.

13 In July 2005, Uzbekistan demanded that the United States leave the Karshi-Khanabad Air Base, known as K-2, which it had been using since shortly after 9/11, within six months. The last U.S. troops withdrew in November 2005.

14 For discussion and sources, see Noam Chomsky, *9–11* (New York: Seven Stories Press, 2001), pp. 45–54.

15 See Chapter 2, note 12 above.

16 Walter Pincus, "Skepticism about U.S. Deep, Iraq Poll Shows; Motive for Invasion Is Focus of Doubts," *Washington Post*, November 12, 2003, p. A18.

17 George H. W. Bush and Brent Scowcroft, *A World Transformed* (New York: Alfred A. Knopf, 1998), p. 489.

18 Project for the New American Century, Letter to President William J. Clinton, January 26, 1998; archived online at http://www.informationclearinghouse. info/article5527.htm.

19 Thomas L. Friedman, "Baker Finds Doors Open, Minds Sealed," *New York Times*, March 17, 1991, p. IV:1. Friedman also noted: "The same iron fist that Saddam Hussein used to smash Kuwait he used to hold his centrifugal republic together. If the United States hopes to withdraw its troops from the gulf, and preserve all of its military gains from the war, it is essential that Mr. Hussein, or, preferably, a different but equally strong figure, is at the helm in Baghdad."

20 Alan Cowell, "Kurds Assert Few Outside Iraq Wanted Them to Win," *New York Times*, April 11, 1991, p. A11.

21 Douglas Jehl with Dexter Filkins, "U.S. Moved to Undermine Iraqi Military Before War," *New York Times*, August 10, 2003, p. I:1.

22 Agence France Presse, "Majority of Spanish Against War on Iraq," February 22, 2003. According to this article, 2.3 percent supported a war waged by the United States and its allies without UN authorization (the actual war that was waged), 11.8 percent opposed war unless there was UN authorization, and 84.7 percent opposed war in all circumstances.

23 Richard Boudreaux and John Hendren, "U.S. Drops Its Bid to Base Troops in Turkey," *Los Angeles Times*, March 15, 2003, p. A5.

24 David Ignatius, "A War of Choice, and One Who Chose It," *Washington Post*, November 2, 2003, p. B1.

25 Mark Lacey, "Turkey Rejects Criticism by U.S. Official over Iraq," *New York Times*, May 8, 2003, p. A15. Wolfowitz said: "Let's have a Turkey that steps up and says: 'We made a mistake. We should have known how bad things were in Iraq, but we know now. Let's figure out how we can be as helpful as possible to the Americans.'" Wolfowitz "singled out the Turkish military for criticism. 'I think for whatever reason, they did not play the strong leadership role that we would have expected.'" For Turkish poll data, see Philip P. Pan, "Turkey Plans for 62,000 U.S. Troops," *Washington Post*, February 26, 2003, p. A17.

26 This is apart from the allegations that German intelligence helped the American military during its invasion. See, for example, Richard Bernstein, "2 German Roles: Opposing War and Aiding U.S.," *New York Times*, March 3, 2006, p. A12.

27 See Gallup International, Iraq Poll, conducted 2003, available online at http://www.gallup-international.com/ContentFiles/survey.asp?id=10.

28 UN Security Council Resolution 688, April 5, 1991, ordered the Iraqi government to cease its repression against the Iraqi civilian population. The full text of this resolution is accessible online from http://www.un.org/Docs/scres/1991/scres91.htm.

29 Fereydoun Ahmadi, "SAIRI [SCIRI] Official Warns of Saddam Disaster Plan for War," *Tehran Times*, January 26, 2003.

30 UN Security Council Resolution 1637, November 8, 2005, accessible online from http://www.un.org/Docs/sc/unsc_resolutions05.htm.

31 Sadr City is an area of Baghdad populated by poor Shiites; it was renamed after Muqtada al-Sadr's father, who was assassinated by the Baathist regime in 1999.

32 Sean Rayment, "Secret MoD Poll: Iraqis Support Attacks on British troops," *Daily Telegraph*, October 23, 2005, available online at http://www.telegraph.co.uk/news/worldnews/middleeast/iraq/1501319/Secret-MoD-poll-Iraqis-support-attacks-on-Britishtroops.html.

33 Gary Langer and Jon Cohen, "Poll Finds Broad Optimism in Iraq, but Also Deep Divisions Among Groups," ABC News Special Report, December 12, 2005. The full text of the poll and results is available online at http://abcnews.go.com/images/Poli tics/1000a1IraqWhereThingsStand.pdf.

34 Prince Saud al-Faisel, "The Fight Against Extremism and the Search for Peace," New York, Council on Foreign Relations, September 20, 2005, transcript from Federal News Service, available online at http://www.cfr.org/publication/8908/fight_against_ex-tremism_and_the_search_for_peace_rush_transcript_federal_news_service_inc.html.

35 Melvin R. Laird, "Iraq: Learning the Lessons of Vietnam," *Foreign Affairs*, November–December 2005, p. 35; available online at http://www.foreignaffairs.org/20051101faessay84604/melvin-r-laird/iraq-learning-the-lessons-of-vietnam.html.

36 Cited in John H. Backer, *The Decision to Divide Germany* (Durham, NC: Duke University Press, 1978), pp. 155–156.

37 The process is described by historian Michael Schaller (*The American Occupation of Japan: The Origins of the Cold War in Asia* [New York: Oxford University Press, 1985]). He writes that George Kennan, head of the State Department Policy Planning Staff, reflected in later years that "besides the Marshall plan, setting the 'reverse course' in Japan was 'the most significant contribution I was ever able to make in government'." The goal was to impose constraints

on MacArthur (SCAP, Supreme Commander for Asia and the Pacific), and to "assure a conservative political hegemony within Japan" (p. 122). Kennan's view was that "the idealistic reforms of 1945–47 [under MacArthur] had no basis in Japanese life," and "[only] the resilience of traditional conservative groups could protect Japan from an even more radical infection—communism—after the Occupation" (p. 125)—which, he apparently feared, could have a "basis in Japanese life." Effectively, then, the old order must be restored, but now under U.S. control. Under the reverse course, "[p]roduction was to be accelerated by the drastic relaxation of antimonopoly measures, placing severe curbs on organized labor, controlling inflation, fixing the yen's foreign exchange value, and discouraging domestic consumption in favor of exports." Reparations to the victims of Japanese fascism "were to be virtually eliminated" (p. 129). In June 1948, under Kennan's initiative, the National Security Council proposed "to halt further destabilizing reforms, to curb the power of organized labor," and to promote "greater efforts by SCAP and the Japanese government to promote industrial discipline and production for export" (p. 132). The recommendations were approved by Truman. MacArthur adapted, in part with agreement: "despite his rhetoric about holding true to the original Occupation program, during the summer of 1948 he, too, moved forcefully to the Right" in accord with the demands of Washington liberals. "SCAP began to act against left-wing political and labor groups, promoted industrial 'discipline,' and initiated a new purge against 'radicals' within its own organization." Adopting Washington's call "for greater labor discipline, SCAP began its own assault on organized labor, . . . stripping all these workers [in public enterprises] of their right to strike or bargain collectively." Condemnations by other Far Eastern Commission members, including the British, were dismissed with fury (pp. 134–6). The liberal Democrats of the Truman administration succeeded in effectively creating a state under one-party business rule, with labor severely weakened, imposing a "vision of Japan's future, one in which the former enemy would cooperate with the United States in dominating the future of Asia" (p. 140).

38 Thomas Carothers, *Critical Mission: Essays on Democracy Promotion* (Washington, DC: Carnegie Endowment for International Peace, 2004).

39 Peter Beaumont, "Abuse Worse Than Under Saddam, Says Iraqi Leader," *The Observer* (London), November 27, 2005, p. 1.

40 Leonid Brezhnev was the leader of the Soviet Union at the time of its invasion of Czechoslovakia in 1968, which he defended in a speech in November 1968, arguing that the Eastern European countries didn't have the right to decide to leave the "socialist" camp.

41 In the fifteen-member Security Council, a resolution is defeated if there are one or more negative votes from any of the permanent members: the United States, Britain, China, France, and Russia.

42 Hearings, Senate Armed Services Committee, *United States Military Strategy and Operations in Iraq and the Central Command Area*, Washington, DC, September 29, 2005 (transcript from Federal News Service).

43 See Salah Nasrawi, "Iraqi Leaders Call for Timetable for Withdrawal of U.S.-Led Forces," Associated Press, November 22, 2005; Final Statement of the Preparatory Meeting for the Iraqi National Accord Conference of November 19–21, 2005, Cairo, Egypt; available online at http://www.arableagueonline.org/las/english/details_en.jsp?art_ id=3926&level_id=239.

44 See, for example, Steve Negus, "Shia Coalition Split over Choice of Iraq Premier," *Financial Times,* February 7, 2005, p. 8.

45 From 1986 to 1989, but especially in 1988, Saddam Hussein launched brutal
attacks—known as the Al-Anfal Campaign—against Iraq's Kurdish population, leading to a huge number of deaths. The Iraqi government used chemical
weapons against the Kurds, most notably at Halabja. See Middle East Watch,
Genocide in Iraq: The Anfal Campaign Against the Kurds (New York: Human
Rights Watch, July 2003); available online at http://www.hrw.org/reports/1993/
iraqanfal/.

46 See Bruce W. Jentleson, *With Friends Like These: Reagan, Bush, and Saddam,
1982–1990* (New York: W. W. Norton, 1994). See also Irene Gendzier, *Dying
to Forget* (Lanham, MD: Rowman and Littlefield, forthcoming).

47 Joost R. Hiltermann, "Iran's Nuclear Posture and the Scars of War," Middle East
Report Online, January 18, 2005, http://www.merip.org/mero/mero011805.
html.

48 Under the prime ministership of Tony Blair, Straw served as home secretary
from 1997 until June 2001 and then as secretary of state for foreign and com-
monwealth affairs until 2006. Hoon served as secretary of state for defense
from 1999 until 2005 and has been Lord Privy Seal and leader of the House of
Commons since May 2005.

49 Mark Thomas, "Mark Thomas Wonders If Saddam's Men Recycle Paper,"
New Statesman, December 9, 2002.

50 House Select Committee on Intelligence, Pike Report of January 19, 1976, in
Village Voice, February 16, 1976, p. 88–471. The Report attributes the quote
only to a "senior official"; William Safire (*Safire's Washington,* New York:
Times Books, 1980, p. 333) identifies the official as Kissinger.

51 *Sunday Times* (London), June 15, 1969. In both cases, it is not a matter of
denying the existence of the oppressed people as such, but just denying its identity. Here is Meir's full statement: "There were no such thing as Palestinians.
When was there an independent Palestinian people with a Palestinian state? It
was either southern Syria before the First World War, and then it was a Palestine including Jordan. It was not as though there was a Palestinian people in
Palestine considering itself as a Palestinian people and we came and threw them
out and took their country away from them. They did not exist."

52 Tamar Gabelnick, William D. Hartung, and Jennifer Washburn, *Arming Repression: U.S. Arms Sales to Turkey During the Clinton Administration,* World Policy Institute and the Federation of American Scientists, October 1999, table 1;
available online at http://www.fas.org/asmp/library/reports/turkeyrep.htm. The
years given are fiscal years. These weapons transfers represent direct commercial sales and foreign military sales, the two largest U.S. arms export programs.
Additionally, Washington provided Turkey with surplus used weapons (nearly
$2 billion worth in original acquisition cost, three-quarters during the Clinton
administration) and military training (with Turkey being the world's largest
recipient of such training in the 1990s).

53 See Adam Isacson and Joy Olson, *Just the Facts: 1999 Edition, A Civilian's
Guide to U.S. Defense and Security Assistance to Latin America and the Carib-
bean* (Washington, DC: Latin America Working Group and Center for International Policy, 1999), p. 27. Narrative available online at http://ciponline.org/
facts/co99.htm. Security assistance includes both military and police aid, which
increasingly have become intermixed. See Adam Isacson, Joy Olson, and Lisa
Haugaard, *Blurring the Lines: Trends in U.S. Military Programs with Latin
America* (Washington, DC: Latin America Working Group Education Fund,
Center for International Policy, and Washington Office on Latin America, September 2004), available online at http://www.ciponline.org/facts/0410btl.pdf.

54 Stephen Kinzer, "Kurds in Turkey: The Big Change," *New York Review of Books*, January 12, 2006.

55 The reference here is to the set of political and economic reforms set down as requirements for EU membership at a meeting of the European Council in June 1993 in Copenhagen, Denmark.

56 The full text of article 109 is as follows: "First: The federal government with the producing governorates and regional governments shall undertake the management of oil and gas extracted from current fields provided that it distributes oil and gas revenues in a fair manner in proportion to the population distribution in all parts of the country with a set allotment for a set time for the damaged regions that were unjustly deprived by the former regime and the regions that were damaged later on, and in a way that assures balanced development in different areas of the country, and this will be regulated by law. Second: The federal government with the producing regional and governorate governments shall together formulate the necessary strategic policies to develop the oil and gas wealth in a way that achieves the highest benefit to the Iraqi people using the most advanced techniques of the market principles and encourages investment." See Iraqi Constitution, ratified by voters on October 15, 2005, available online at http://portal.unesco.org/ci/en/files/20704/11332732681iraqi_constitution_ en.pdf/iraqi_constitution_en.pdf. There are various translations of the constitution available, with different numbering of the articles.

57 See John Norris, *Collision Course: NATO, Russia, and Kosovo* (Westport, CT: Praeger, 2005), p. xxiii. He writes that "it was Yugoslavia's resistance to the broader trends of political and economic reform—not the plight of Kosovar Albanians—that best explains NATO's war." Norris was director of communications during the war for Deputy Secretary of State Strobe Talbott, who was a leading figure in State Department and Pentagon planning concerning the war. Talbott writes in his foreword that "thanks to John Norris," anyone interested in the war in Kosovo "will know . . . how events looked and felt at the time to those of us who were involved" in the war.

58 UN Security Council Resolution 1559, September 2, 2004, accessible online from http://www.un.org/Docs/sc/unsc_resolutions04.html.

59 Syria formally notified the United Nations on April 26, 2005, that it had withdrawn all of its troops, military assets, and intelligence apparatus from Lebanon.

60 Robert Fisk, *The Great War for Civilisation: The Conquest of the Middle East* (New York: Alfred A. Knopf, 2005).

61 Geoffrey Wheatcroft, "One Man's Arabia," *New York Times Book Review*, December 11, 2005, p. 1.

62 William A. Dorman and Mansour Farhang, *The U.S. Press and Iran: Foreign Policy and the Journalism of Deference* (Berkeley: University of California Press, 1987).

63 In May 1987 during the Iran-Iraq war, the USS *Stark*, a U.S. naval vessel patrolling the Persian Gulf, was struck by two missiles fired from an Iraqi Mirage fighter, killing thirty-seven crew members. Both Washington and Baghdad said the attack was an accident. Iraq had not paid reparations for the attack by the time of the 1991 Gulf War. In 1989, U.S. officials urged that Washington seek closer relations with Saddam Hussein despite his continued development of chemical and biological weapons, his support for terrorism, and his failure to pay the *Stark* reparations. (See Elaine Sciolino, "1989 Memo to Baker Listed Abuses by Iraq but Urged Conciliation," *New York Times*, September 22, 1992, p. A15.) In June 1967, Israeli air and naval forces attacked the USS *Liberty*,

a U.S. electronics intelligence ship, off the coast of Egypt, killing thirty-four Americans. Israel claimed the attack was accidental and Washington officially accepted the apology, though substantial doubts still remain. For different views, see James M. Ennes Jr., *The Assault on the Liberty: The True Story of the Israeli Attack on an American Intelligence Ship* (New York: Random House, 1979; updated Reintree Press Edition published in Gaithersburg, MD: Signature Books, 2002); A. Jay Cristol, *The* Liberty *Incident: The 1967 Israeli Attack on the U.S. Navy Spy Ship* (Dulles, VA: Brassey's, 2002); and David C. Walsh, "Friendless Fire?" *Proceedings of the U.S. Naval Institute,* June 2003, available online at http://www.military.com/NewContent/0,13190,NI_Friendless_0603,00.html.

64 The Press Trust of India, "India, Iran and the U.S.," February 18, 2006; Daniel Dombey, Roula Khalaf and Arkady Ostrovsky, "US Warns India to Back Iran UN Referral or Lose Nuclear Deal," *Financial Times* (London), January 26, 2006, p. 9.

65 Robert Olson, "Turkey-Iran Relations, 2000–2001: The Caspian, Azerbaijan and the Kurds," *Middle East Policy* 9, no. 2 (June 2002), pp. 111–129.

66 Yitzhak ben-Yisrael, *Ha'aretz,* April 16, 2002.

67 Ha'aretz services, *Ha'aretz,* February 10, 2004 (Hebrew).

68 Martin Van Creveld, "Is Israel Planning to Attack Iran? Sharon on the Warpath," *International Herald Tribune,* August 21, 2004, p. 6.

69 The Treaty on the Non-Proliferation of Nuclear Weapons (NPT) came into force in 1970 and is currently accepted by 189 nations; only Israel, India, and Pakistan have not acceded to it. The text of the treaty is available online at http://disarmament.un.org/ wmd/npt/npttext.html.

70 See "Text Urging Negotiations on Fissile Material Treaty Approved by Disarmament Committee," Press Release, GA/DIS/3291, Fifty-ninth General Assembly, First Committee, November 4, 2004, available online at http://www.un.org/News/Press/docs/2004/gadis3291.doc.htm (in the plenary session on December 3, 2004, the vote on Resolution 59/81 was 179–2–2, with the United States and Palau voting no and Britain and Israel abstaining); "General Assembly Adopts 55 Texts Recommended by First Committee on a Wide Range of Disarmament, Security Matters," Press Release, GA/10310, Fifty-ninth General Assembly, Plenary, December 3, 2004, available online at http://www.un.org/News/Press/docs/2004/ga10310.doc.htm.

Notes to Chapter Five

1 Maxime Rodinson, *Israel: A Colonial-Settler State?* (New York: Pathfinder Press, 1973).

2 UN Security Council Resolution 242, November 22, 1967; text accessible online from http://www.un.org/documents/sc/res/1967/scres67.htm. Security Council Draft Resolution S/11940, January 23, 1976; text and vote available online at http://domino.un.org/UNISPAL.NSF/bdd57d15a29f428d85256c3800701fc4/696d540fd7821bce052 5651c00736250!OpenDocument. On support for the resolution by Syria, Egypt, Jordan, and the PLO, and condemnation of Washington's "tyranny of the veto," see the verbatim record of the Security Council meeting of January 26, 1976, S/PV.1879, available online at http://domino.un.org/unispal.nsf/9a798adbf322aff38525617b006d88d7/d0242e9e210d937585256c6e0054df8a!OpenDocument. Israeli President Chaim Herzog, who was Israel's UN ambassador at the time, has written that the PLO not only backed this resolution but, in fact, "prepared" it (*Jerusalem Post,* November 13, 1981).

3 See note 2 above.

4 See Palestine National Council, "Political Communiqué," Algiers, November 15, 1988, printed in *Journal of Palestine Studies* 18, no. 2 (Winter 1989), pp. 216–223. The statement calls for the convening of an international peace conference "on the basis of United Nations Security Council resolutions 242 and 338 and the attainment of the legitimate national rights of the Palestinian people," and for "arrangements for security and peace between all the states concerned in the region, including the Palestinian state"; the National Council also "reiterates its rejection of terrorism in all its forms." For discussion, see Rashid Khalidi, "The Resolutions of the 19th Palestine National Council," *Journal of Palestine Studies*, 19, no. 2 (Winter 1990), pp. 29–42.

5 Delegations from Israel and the Palestinian Authority met at Taba, Egypt, from January 21 to January 27, 2001, making considerable progress, but the discussions were broken off by the Israel side as Israeli elections approached. For a report on the meetings, see Miguel Moratinos, "'Non-Paper' on Taba Negotiations," January 27, 2001, printed in *Journal of Palestine Studies* 31, no. 3 (Spring 2002), pp. 81–89; also available online at http://domino.un.org/UNIS-PAL.NSF/3d14c9e5cdaa296d85256cbf005aa3eb/cea3efd8 c0ab482f85256e37 00670af8!OpenDocument.

6 Israeli-Palestinian Joint Statement at Taba, January 27, 2001, printed in *Journal of Palestine Studies* 31, no. 3 (Spring 2002), pp. 80–81; also available online at http://domino.un.org/UNISPAL.nsf/0/badaa58661cc084f85256e37006fc44d? Open Document.

7 See Ron Pundak, "From Oslo to Taba: What Went Wrong?" *Survival* 43, no. 3 (Autumn 2001), p. 44; available online at http://www.peres-center.org/Media/from%20 oslo%20to%20taba.pdf.

8 A leading official of the PLO, Mahmoud Abbas (1935–), also known as Abu Mazen, was elected president of the Palestinian Authority in January 2005.

9 This is a reference to the Oslo Accords, which, officially known as the Declaration of Principles on Interim Self-Government Arrangements, were negotiated between the Israeli government and the Palestine Liberation Organization in Oslo and officially signed in Washington, DC, on September 13, 1993. Under the accords, the PLO recognized Israel in return for limited autonomy for five years and permanent-status talks that would lead to a final resolution of the Israel-Palestine conflict. The accords did not prohibit increased Israeli settlement in the Occupied Territories. (The text of the accords is available online at http://www.bitterlemons.org/docs/dop.html.)

10 Palestinian Proposal on Palestinian Refugees, January 22, 2001, Taba, ARTICLE XX: REFUGEES, and Israeli private response to the Palestinian refugee proposal of January 22, 2001, "Non-Paper—Draft 2," January 23, 2001, Taba; both are available online at http://www.mideastweb.org/taba.htm.

11 See, for example, Gilbert Achcar, "The Washington Accords: A Retreat Under Pressure," December 1993, reprinted in *Eastern Cauldron* (New York: Monthly Review Press, 2004), pp. 189–204; and Noam Chomsky, "The Israel-Arafat Agreement," *Z Magazine*, October 1993, reprinted in *The Fateful Triangle: The United States, Israel and the Palestinians*, updated ed. (Cambridge, MA: South End Press, 1983, 1999), pp. 533–568.

12 The territorial map proposed by the Israeli side showed protrusions of Israeli territory deep into what was to be the Palestinian state. One of these extended from Jerusalem east to Ma'ale Adumim; another, from the Shomron settlements east to Ariel.

13 The Palestinian side agreed that Israel could retain 3 percent of West Bank territory where there were dense settlements, provided that Israel ceded an equivalent amount of its pre-1967 territory to the Palestinian state; Israel wanted to

retain 6 percent of the West Bank and wanted to cede a much smaller amount of territory to the Palestinian state.

14 Ain al-Hilweh is the largest Palestinian refugee camp in Lebanon, in terms of both land area and population (about 45,000). It is situated near the town of Saida 45 kilometers south of Beirut. (For details, see the UNRWA website at http://www.un.org/unrwa/refugees/lebanon/einelhilweh.html.) Sabra and Shatila are refugee camps in the Beirut area that witnessed horrendous massacres against Palestinian civilians carried out by Phalangist militias with Israeli support.

15 The Geneva Accord (also called the Geneva Initiative and the Geneva Agreement) is a detailed peace agreement worked out by unofficial, though prominent, Israeli and Palestinian negotiators determined to show that a settlement within the parameters of the Taba talk was possible. The accord was presented in Geneva in December 2003. See the official Geneva Accord website at http://www.geneva-accord.org/HomePage.aspx?FolderID=11&lang=en.

16 See Noam Chomsky, *Towards a New Cold War: Essays on the Current Crisis and How We Got There* (New York: Pantheon, 1982), pp. 247–254; originally written in 1975–76.

17 H.C. 6698/95, *Kaadan v Israel Lands Administration*, 54(1) P.D. 258. The summary of this case is posted on the website of the Israeli Ministry of Foreign Affairs ("High Court: Decision on Katzir," March 8, 2000) at http://www.mfa.gov.il/MFA/Government/Communiques/2000/High+Court-+Decision+on+Katzir+-+8-Mar-2000.htm.

18 Alexandre Kedar of Haifa University Law School noted the duality of the Supreme Court's decree, describing it as "proclaiming simultaneously the illegality of the discriminatory procedure, while apparently leaving the respondents with discretion whether to continue this illegal practice." See "'A First Step in a Difficult and Sensitive Road': Preliminary Observations on *Qaadan v. Katzir*," *Israel Studies Bulletin* 16, no. 1 (Fall 2000), pp. 3–11.

19 The Separation Wall is a barrier being built by Israel cutting through the West Bank to mark off Palestinian territory that Israel intends to unilaterally annex. In some places the Wall will consist of wire fences, trenches, and exclusion zones, extending for a width of 200 feet; elsewhere it will be a 25-foot-high concrete structure.

20 The Green Line refers to the border of Israel before its conquests in June 1967—that is, along the 1949 armistice lines.

21 Gil Hoffman and jpost.com staff, "Peres's Brother Says 'Peretz Took Over Labor Like Franco Took Over Spain,'" *Jerusalem Post*, November 27, 2005. For background on the Mizrahim, see Chomsky, *Fateful Triangle*, pp. 118–123.

22 Martin Buber (1878–1965) was a Jewish philosopher and theologian, a "cultural Zionist" committed to Arab-Jewish cooperation, and a member of Ihud, an organization advocating a binational state in Palestine. Among his books are *I and Thou* (1923) and *Paths in Utopia* (1946).

23 Herut was the political party of the right-wing Revisionist Zionist movement, led from 1948 to 1983 by Menachem Begin. It later became part of the right-wing coalition Likud.

24 Founded by Yasir Arafat and others in the late 1950s, Fatah has been the leading component of the PLO since 1969.

25 UN Security Council Resolution 242, November 22, 1967 (see note 2 above). Relevant portions state: "The Security Council, . . . *Emphasizing* the inadmissibility of the acquisition of territory by war and the need to work for a just and lasting peace in which every State in the area can live in security, 1. *Affirms* that

the fulfillment of Charter principles requires the establishment of a just and lasting peace in the Middle East which should include the application of both the following principles: i. Withdrawal of Israeli armed forces from territories occupied in the recent conflict; ii. Termination of all claims or states of belligerency and respect for and acknowledgement of the sovereignty, territorial integrity and political independence of every State in the area and their right to live in peace within secure and recognized boundaries free from threats or acts of force; 2. *Affirms further* the necessity . . . b. For achieving a just settlement of the refugee problem . . ."

26 Henry Kissinger, *The White House Years* (Boston: Little, Brown, 1976), p. 1279.

27 In September 1970, conflict between Jordan's King Hussein and the Palestine Liberation Organization erupted into bloody fighting. The Jordanian army slaughtered thousands of Palestinians and subsequently expelled the PLO from the country.

28 *Mechdal* is a Hebrew term meaning "omission," "nonperformance," or "neglect." Here it refers to the failure of the Israeli intelligence community to predict the Arab attack.

29 The Camp David Accords consisted of two agreements signed on September 17, 1978, by President Anwar Sadat of Egypt and Prime Minister Menachem Begin of Israel, and witnessed by U.S. president Jimmy Carter. For the text of these accords, see "The Framework for Peace in the Middle East" (http://www.jimmycarterlibrary.org/documents/campdavid/accords.phtml) and "Framework for the Conclusion of a Peace Treaty between Egypt and Israel" (http://www.jimmycarterlibrary.org/documents/campdavid/frame.phtml). The agreements were supplemented with an exchange of letters written by Sadat, Begin, and Carter (http://www.jimmycarterlibrary.org/documents/campdavid/ letters.phtml).

30 The text of this treaty is available online at http://www.mfa.gov.il/MFA/Peace+Process/Guide+to+the+Peace+Process/Israel-Egypt+Peace+Treaty.htm.

31 The reference here is to "The Framework for Peace in the Middle East" (see note 29 above), which states: "Egypt, Israel, Jordan and the representatives of the Palestinian people should participate in negotiations on the resolution of the Palestinian problem in all its aspects."

32 See ibid.: "In order to provide full autonomy to the inhabitants [of the West Bank and Gaza], under these arrangements the Israeli military government and its civilian administration will be withdrawn as soon as a self-governing authority has been freely elected by the inhabitants of these areas to replace the existing military government."

33 *Ha'aretz,* April 27, 1982.

34 See note 2 above.

35 UN Security Council S/13911, April 28, 1980, available online at http://domino.un.org/unispal.nsf/9a798adbf322aff38525617b006d88d7/e819629c2575bc3e0525652900793664!OpenDocument&Highlight=2,veto. On April 30, 1980, the draft resolution failed by a vote of 10–1(U.S.)–4.

36 See Palestine National Council, "Political Communiqué" (initially cited in note 4 above).

37 Secretary of State George P. Shultz had written to President Reagan: "In one place Arafat was saying, 'unc, unc, unc' and in another he was saying, 'cle, cle, cle,' but nowhere will he yet bring himself to say, 'Uncle.'" In a press conference on December 14, 1988, however, Shultz concluded that "Arafat finally said 'Uncle.'" See George P. Shultz, *Turmoil and Triumph: My Years as Secretary of State* (New York: Charles Scribner's Sons, 1993), p. 1043.

38 See Israeli Ministry of Foreign Affairs, "Israel's Peace Initiative, May 14, 1989," available online at http://www.mfa.gov.il/MFA/Peace+Process/Guide+to+the+Peace+Process/ Israel-s+Peace+Initiative+-+May+14-+1989.

39 Baker's "Five-Point Framework for an Israeli-Palestinian Dialogue" is dated October 10, 1989, but it was released by the State Department nearly two months later, on December 6, 1989. For the text, see *Journal of Palestine Studies* 19, no. 2 (Winter 1990), pp. 169–170; also printed in Thomas L. Friedman, "Advance Reported on Mideast Talks," *New York Times*, December 7, 1989, p. A11.

40 Rick Atkinson and Ann Devroy, "Bush: Iraq Won't Decide Timing of Ground War," *Washington Post*, February 2, 1991, p. A1.

41 These agreements included "Israeli-Palestinian Interim Agreement on the West Bank and the Gaza Strip," September 28, 1995 (known as Oslo II), available online at http://www.israel-mfa.gov.il/MFA/Peace+Process/Guide+to+the+Peace+Process/ THE+ISRAELI-PALESTINIAN+INTERIM+AGREEMENT.htm; "The Wye River Memorandum," October 23, 1998, available online at http://www.israel-mfa.gov.il/NR/exeres/EE54A289–8F0A-4CDC-93C9–71BD631109AB.htm; and several other agreements and understandings. Oslo II divided the West Bank into three zones: Zone A, under Palestinian control (initially 1–3 percent of the West Bank); Zone B, under Palestinian administration but controlled by Israeli security (about 30 percent); and Zone C, totally controlled by Israel (about 70 percent).

42 Noam Chomsky, *World Orders Old and New* (New York: Columbia University Press, 1996), pp. 277–297; Noam Chomsky, "A Painful Peace," *Z Magazine*, January 1996; reprinted in Chomsky, *The Fateful Triangle*, pp. 540–558.

43 This reply by David Bar-Illan, director of Communications and Policy Planning in the office of the prime minister, was recorded during an interview with Victor Cygielman, "Palestinian Self-Rule, Israeli Security: A Conversation with David Bar Illan," *Palestine-Israel Journal of Politics, Economics, and Culture* 3, no. 3/4 (Summer/Autumn 1996): 14.

44 Labor Party, political platform as approved at the 6th Party Congress, May 1997, available online at http://www.jewishvirtuallibrary.org/jsource/ Politics/labor.html. The platform further stated that "united Jerusalem, the capital of Israel," would remain "under Israeli sovereignty," that the "Jordan river will be Israel's eastern security border and there will be no other army stationed to the west of it," and that "Israel extends its sovereignty over areas that are major Jewish settlement blocs."

45 See Pundak, "From Oslo to Taba: What Went Wrong?" and other articles in English and Hebrew available on the website of the Peres Center for Peace, http://www. peres-center.org/.

46 Clinton's "parameters" (which were also referred to as "bridging proposals") were never officially released. Rather, on December 23, 2000, they were presented orally to Israeli and Palestinian negotiators, who took notes. Various versions of the proposals are available, similar in their essentials. See, for example, *Journal of Palestine Studies* 30, no. 3 (Spring 2001), pp. 171–173; http:// www.fmep.org/documents/clinton_parameters12-23-00.html; and http://www.mideastweb.org/clintonproposal.htm.

47 Dennis Ross, *The Missing Peace: The Inside Story of the Fight for Middle East Peace* (New York: Farrar, Straus and Giroux, 2004). For a critique, see Jerome Slater, "The Missing Pieces in *The Missing Peace*," *Tikkun* 20, no. 3 (May–June 2005), pp. 22–29.

48 "Both Prime Minister Barak and Chairman Arafat have now accepted these parameters as the basis for further efforts. Both have expressed some reservations." See White House, Office of the Press Secretary, January 7, 2001,

Remarks by the President at Israel Policy Forum Gala, The Waldorf Astoria Hotel, New York, New York, January 7, 2001; available online at http://www. clintonfoundation.org/legacy/010701-speech-by-president-at-israel-policy-dinner.htm.

49 Moratinos, "'Non-Paper' on Taba Negotiations" (see note 5 above).

50 Israeli-Palestinian Joint Statement at Taba (see note 6 above).

51 David Matz, 'Trying to Understand the Taba Talks (Part I)," *Palestine-Israel Journal of Politics, Economics, and Culture* 10, no. 3 (2003), pp. 96–105, available online at http://www.pij.org/details.php?id=32; David Matz, "Why Did Taba End? (Part II)," *Palestine-Israel Journal of Politics, Economics, and Culture* 10, no. 4 (2003), pp. 92–98.

52 Geneva Convention Relative to the Protection of Civilian Persons in Time of War, 1949, available online at http://www.unhchr.ch/html/menu3/b/92.htm.

53 See International Court of Justice, Advisory Opinion, "Legal Consequences of the Construction of a Wall in the Occupied Palestinian Territory," July 9, 2004, available online at http://www.icj-cij.org/docket/files/131/1671.pdf; and the Declaration of Judge Buergenthal, available online at http://www.icj-cij. org/docket/files/131/1687.pdf. The quote is from paragraph 9 of Buergenthal's declaration.

54 David Ben-Gurion was the leader of the pre-independence Jewish community in Palestine and the first prime minister of the Israeli state.

55 See Gilbert Achcar, "Zionism and Peace: From the Allon Plan to the Washington Accords," reprinted in *Eastern Cauldron*, pp. 205–222.

56 Ronald Reagan, "Middle East Peace Initiative," September 1, 1982, in U.S. Department of State, *American Foreign Policy: Current Documents, 1982* (Washington, DC: Department of State, 1985), pp. 753–757; available online at http://www.reagan.utexas. edu/archives/speeches/1982/90182d.htm.

57 See Menahem Klein, *The Jerusalem Problem: The Struggle for Permanent Status* (Gainesville: University Press of Florida, 2003), pp. 16–17. He reports a 44 percent increase in construction in the first half of 2000 (up to the Camp David meetings) as compared to the equivalent period in 1999, under the ultra-right Netanyahu government.

58 A *dunam* is an Ottoman unit of land measure, formalized under British rule in Palestine and still used by Israel and the Palestinian Authority, among others; it is equal to 1,000 square meters.

59 "Building Settlements Quietly," *Settlement Report* 6, no. 1 (January 1996), available online at http://www.fmep.org/reports/vol06/no1/07-building_settlements_ quietly.html.

60 Jay Bushinsky, *Christian Science Monitor*, August 21, 1971.

61 Quoted from internal discussions in Yossi Beilin, *Mehiro shel Ihud* (Revivim, 1985), p. 42.

62 Shlomo Gazit, *Trapped Fools: Thirty Years of Israeli Policy in the Territories* (London: Frank Cass, 2003).

63 *New Outlook* was an Israeli monthly with a joint Jewish-Arab editorial board, aiming to "serve as a medium for the clarification of problems concerning peace and co-operation among all the peoples of the Middle East." It was published from 1957 to 1993.

64 The Israeli Socialist Organization, usually known by the name of its Hebrew-language monthly, *Matzpen*, was a small anti-Zionist and anti-imperialist organization of Israeli Jews and Arabs founded in 1962, now defunct. See Arie Bober, ed., *The Other Israel: The Radical Case Against Zionism* (New York: Doubleday Anchor, 1972).

65 In a debate with Chomsky, Dershowitz stated, "I proposed, actually, that the security fence be placed on wheels and constantly be able to be moved consistent with Israeli security needs" (see "Israel and Palestine After Disengagement: Noam Chomsky Debates with Alan Dershowitz," Kennedy School of Government, November 29, 2005, available online at http://www.chomsky. info/debates/20051129.htm). Earlier, Dershowitz had said: "Actually, when I was last in Israel and was at the fence, I recommended that the fence be put on wheels, literally be put on wheels to make it so obvious . . . And a fence on wheels would clearly represent its goal, its function as a defensive structure." See Alan Dershowitz, "The Case for Israel and Palestine," Institute of Politics, Kennedy School of Government, May 3, 2004, available online at available on video at http://www.iop.harvard.edu/Multimedia-Center/All-Videos/The-Case-for-Israel-and-Palestine2 (at 22:34).

66 Ian S. Lustick, "Yerushalayim and Al-Quds: Political Catechism and Political Realities," *Journal of Palestine Studies* 30, no. 1 (Autumn 2000), pp. 5–21.

67 Joan Peters, *From Time Immemorial: The Origins of the Arab-Jewish Conflict over Palestine* (New York: Harper & Row, 1984). For a decisive refutation, see Norman G. Finkelstein, "A Land Without a People: Joan Peters's 'Wilderness Myth,'" in *Image and Reality of the Israel-Palestine Conflict* (New York: Verso, 1995).

68 Yosef Grodzinski, *In the Shadow of the Holocaust: The Struggle Between Jews and Zionists in the Aftermath of World War II* (Monroe, ME: Common Courage, 2004).

69 The Zionist underground organized the voyage of the *Exodus 1947*, a ship full of Jewish refugees from Europe who tried to enter Palestine illegally. The British, to much international criticism, sent the refugees to France and, when the passengers wouldn't get off, to Hamburg where they were forcibly removed. The story was much glorified and distorted in a novel by Leon Uris—*Exodus* (Garden City, NY: Doubleday, 1958, and many later editions)—and in a 1960 motion picture directed by Otto Preminger.

70 Isaac Deutscher, *The Non-Jewish Jew and Other Essays*, ed. Tamara Deutscher (New York: Oxford University Press, 1968), pp. 136–137.

71 Amnesty International, *Newsletter*, September 1977.

72 Noam Chomsky interviewed by Shira Hadad, "Master Mind," *Ha'aretz*, November 10, 2005, available online at http://www.chomsky.info/interviews/ 20051110.htm.

73 See Thomas Frank, *What's the Matter with Kansas? How Conservatives Won the Heart of America* (New York: Metropolitan Books, 2004).

74 Marwan Barghouti, a leader of Fatah on the West Bank, was charged by Israel with involvement in terrorism and in 2004 was sentenced to life in prison.

75 Mohammed Dahlan is head of the Preventive Security Service and the Fatah movement in the Gaza area.

76 Mustafa Barghouti is a medical doctor, secretary of the Palestinian National Initiative, founder and president of the Union of Palestinian Medical Relief Committees, and founder and director of the Health, Development, Information and Policy Institute.

77 Nongovernmental organization.

78 See Achcar, *Eastern Cauldron*, p. 135.

79 Mark Sappenfield, "Americans, Europeans Differ on Mideast Sympathies," *Christian Science Monitor*, April 15, 2002, citing TIPP polls, available online at http://www.tipponline.com/articles/02/csm/c041502.htm; PIPA, "Questionnaire: Americans on the Middle East Road Map, May 14–18, 2003," available

online at http://www.worldpublicopinion.org/pipa/pdf/may03/IsPalMap_
May03_quaire.pdf.

80 "Except under circumstances specified in this section, no security assistance may
be provided to any country the government of which engages in a consistent pattern of gross violations of internationally recognized human rights" (*U.S. Code*,
Title 22, Chapter 32, Subchapter II, Part I, § 2304 (a) (2); available online at
http://www4.law.cornell.edu/uscode/html/uscode22/usc_sec_22_00002304----
000-.html). See also Amnesty International, "Imported Arms Used in Israel and
the Occupied Territories with Excessive Force Resulting in Unlawful Killings
and Unwarranted Injuries," AI Index: MDE/15/65/00, November 17, 2000,
http://web.amnesty.org/library/index/ ENGMDE150652000.

81 See, for example, B'Tselem, *Routine Torture: Interrogation Methods of the
General Security Service* (Jerusalem, February 1998), available online at http://
www.btselem.org/Download/199802_Routine_Torture_Eng.doc; and Human
Rights Watch, *Israel's Record of Occupation: Violations of Civil and Political
Rights* (New York: Human Rights Watch, August 1, 1998), available online at
http://www.hrw.org/reports98/israel/.

82 Edward Said (1935–2003) was a prominent Palestinian-American academic,
political activist, and, from 1977 to 1991, a member of the Palestine National
Council. Among his books are *Orientalism* (1978), *The Question of Palestine*
(1979), and *The End of the Peace Process* (2000).

83 Eqbal Ahmed (1932–1999) was a Pakistani writer and antiwar activist. He
lived for many years in the United States, teaching at Hampshire College from
1982 to 1997. Two books of his interviews are *Confronting Empire* (2000) and
Terrorism: Theirs and Ours (2001), and newly forthcoming is the collection
The Selected Writings of Eqbal Ahmad, ed. Carollee Bengelsdorf, Margaret
Cerullo, and Yogesh Chandrani (New York: Columbia University Press, 2006).

84 The Reverend Leon Sullivan (1923–2001), a Black minister and activist, was
made a member of the Board of Directors of the General Motors Corporation
in 1971, becoming the first African American to be on the board of a major
U.S. corporation. In 1977 he developed a set of principles—such as equal pay
for equal work and nonsegregation of facilities—that any foreign corporation
doing business in apartheid South Africa had to agree to or else face substantial
public pressure.

85 A major city and refugee camp on the West Bank under nominal Palestinian
authority, Jenin was attacked by Israeli military forces in April 2002, incurring
many casualties (including unlawful killings): shooting of peaceful civilians,
uniformed medical personnel tending the wounded, and curfew violators; innocent people bulldozed to death, and so on. See "Report of the Secretary-General
Prepared Pursuant to General Assembly Resolution ES-10/10 (Report on
Jenin)," A/ES-10/186, July 30, 2002, available online at http://www.un.org/
peace/jenin/; Amnesty International, *Shielded from Scrutiny: IDF Violations in
Jenin and Nablus*, AI Index: MDE 15/143/2002, November 4, 2002, available online at http://web.amnesty.org/library/index/ENGMDE151432002; and
Human Rights Watch, *Jenin: IDF Military Operations* 14, no. 3 (F.) (May 2002),
available online at http://hrw.org/reports/2002/israel3/israel0502.pdf.

86 The Caterpillar Corporation produces an armored bulldozer that has been used
by Israel "as its primary weapon to raze Palestinian homes, destroy agriculture
and shred roads in violation of the laws of war." See Human Rights Watch,
"Israel: Caterpillar Should Suspend Bulldozer Sales: Weaponized Bulldozers
Used to Destroy Civilian Property and Infrastructure," November 23, 2004,
available online at http://hrw.org/ english/docs/2004/11/22/isrlpa9711.htm.

87 Joint Harvard-MIT Petition for Divestment from Israel, available online at http://physics.harvard.edu/~wilson/2002_divestment.html.
88 Israeli authorities have at various times closed down Palestinian universities. See, for example, Molly Moore and John Ward Anderson, "Israelis Close Colleges in Hebron," *Washington Post*, January 16, 2003, p. A15.
89 The David Project is an organization founded in 2002 to, in its own words, "defeat the ideological assault on Israel that is taking place on campuses, in high schools, in churches and in the general community" (http://davidproject. org/). For critiques of its activities, see M. Junaid Alam, "Columbia University and the New Anti-Semitism," *Counterpunch*, March 2, 2005, available online at http://www.counterpunch.org/jun-aid03022005.html; and Scott Sherman, "The Mideast Comes to Columbia," *The Nation*, April 4, 2005, available online at http://www.thenation.com/doc/20050404/sherman.
90 Some of these, along with other examples of anti-Arab racism, are cited in Noam Chomsky, *Necessary Illusions: Thought Control in Democratic Societies* (Boston: South End Press, 1989), pp. 214, 315–316.
91 Nathan and Ruth Ann Perlmutter, *The Real Anti-Semitism in America* (New York: Arbor House, 1982). Nathan Perlmutter was the national director of the ADL.
92 David Horowitz is a right-wing ideologue, author of *The Professors: The 101 Most Dangerous Academics in America* (Washington, DC: Regnery, 2006), founder of Frontpagemag.com (http://frontpagemag.com/), and one of the founders (along with Natan Sharansky and Benjamin Netanyahu, among others) of One Jerusalem, an organization committed to "maintaining a united Jerusalem as the undivided capital of Israel" (http://www. onejerusalem.org/faq. asp#answer0_1). Horowitz has also initiated a campaign to get state legislatures to enact his "academic bill of rights" (http://www.studentsforacademicfreedom. org), which, in the words of the American Association of University Professors (AAUP), "infringes academic freedom in the very act of purporting to protect it" (AAUP, "Academic Bill of Rights," Washington, DC, December 2003, available online at http://www.aaup.org/AAUP/comm/rep/A/abor.htm).
93 See, for example, Michael Janofsky, "Professors' Politics Draw Lawmakers into the Fray," *New York Times*, December 25, 2005, p. I:22.
94 Norman Finkelstein, *The Holocaust Industry: Reflections on the Exploitation of Jewish Suffering*, 2nd ed. (London: Verso, 2003).
95 Talk delivered October 19, 1973, to the Association of Arab University Graduates, printed in *American Report*, October 29, 1973.
96 Seymour Martin Lipset (1922–) is a prominent political sociologist, now affiliated with the Hoover Institution. He has served as president of the rabidly pro-Israel American Professors for Peace in the Middle East. Among his many writings is "þThe Socialism of Fools': The Left, the Jews & Israel," in Mordecai S. Chertoff, ed., *The New Left and the Jews* (New York: Pitman, 1971). For a critique, see Noam Chomsky, "The Peace Movement and the Middle East," in his *Peace in the Middle East? Reflections on Justice and Nationhood* (New York: Vintage, 1974), pp. 153–198. Reprinted in Noam Chomsky, *Middle East Illusions* (Lanham, MD: Rowman & Littlefield, 2003), pp. 123–155.
97 Chomsky, "The Peace Movement and the Middle East."
98 Irving Howe, "The Campus Left and Israel," *New York Times*, March 13, 1971, p. 29; reprinted in Irving Howe and Carl Gershman, eds., *Israel, the Arabs, and the Middle East* (New York: Bantam Books, 1972), pp. 428–430.
99 *Dissent* is a quarterly social democratic journal published in New York City, and Irving Howe was one of its editors from its founding in 1954 until his death in 1993.

100 De Gaulle, November 27, 1967, quoted in Gilbert Achcar, ed., *The Israeli Dilemma: A Debate Between Two Left-Wing Jews. Letters Between Marcel Liebman and Ralph Miliband* (London: Merlin Press, 2006), pp. 10–11, n. 18.
101 Yitzhak Rabin later denied in the Knesset having issued "orders to break bones," after a few soldiers were court-martialed for excessive violence. Knesset member Yossi Sarid replied, however, "that even if Rabin did not actually utter the remark 'break their bones,' he must be held responsible for what the soldiers understood him to mean and therefore did. . . . Sarid said that since Rabin was in the territories and personally gave orders to use beatings as punishment, he could now not avoid his own ministerial responsibility." Asher Wallfish, "Rabin Denies He Gave Orders to Break Bones," *Jerusalem Post,* July 12, 1990.
102 *International Herald Tribune,* January 26, 1988. Quoted in Achcar, *Eastern Cauldron,* p. 125.
103 *Le Monde,* October 19, 2000.
104 David Goldiner, "PAT: GOD SMOTE HIM. Gaza upset Lord, says Robertson," *Daily News* (New York), January 6, 2006, p. 4; Larry B. Stammer, "Evangelical Leaders Criticize Pat Robertson," *Los Angeles Times,* January 7, 2006, p. A8.
105 Jack G. Shaheen, *Reel Bad Arabs: How Hollywood Vilifies a People* (New York: Olive Branch Press, 2001).
106 Edward W. Said, *Covering Islam: How the Media and the Experts Determine How We See the Rest of the World,* rev. ed. (New York: Vintage Books, 1997).
107 See his *Orientalism* (New York: Vintage, 1978).
108 The Greek word *phobia* means "fear."

Notes to Epilogue

1 See p. 95 above.
2 See Gilbert Achcar, "A Pan-Iraqi Pact on Muqtada Al-Sadr's Initiative," ZNet, December 9, 2005, http://www.zcommunications.org/znet/viewArticle/4849.
3 "The only hope one could have of avoiding the slide into a full-blown, devastating civil war—if Sistani were to be assassinated—is [not the presence of U.S. troops, but] if the forces involved in the political process, i.e., those not already involved in the low-intensity civil war going on in Iraq, were successful in achieving control over their constituencies after an inevitable first outburst of anger, by emphasizing that the perpetrators are either the Baathists or Zarqawi's followers or the like, that their objective is exactly to ignite a civil war, and that the best reply to that is precisely to pay heed to Sistani's insistence on the necessity of avoiding any kind of sectarian war." See "Achcar on Cole Proposals for Withdrawal of U.S. Ground Troops," posted on August 23, 2005, on Juan Cole's blog, Informed Comment, at http://www.juancole.com/2005/08/achcar-on-cole-proposals-for.html, and on ZNet at http://www.zcommunications.org/znet/viewArticle/5566.
4 This analysis was confirmed by Edward Wong and Dexter Filkins's edifying story published in the *New York Times* on July 17, 2006, under the title "In an About-Face, Sunnis Want U.S. to Remain in Iraq."
5 See pp. 165–166 above.
6 See Achcar, "First Reflections on the Electoral Victory of Hamas," posted on ZNet on January 27, 2006, at http://www.zcommunications.org/znet/viewArticle/4535.

7 Translation from the "prisoners document" here and below is by Gilbert Achcar. The original Arabic document is available online at http://www.arabs48.com/display.x?cid=11&sid=19&id=37631. An English translation, though in need of revision for better accuracy, is available at http://www.jmcc.org/documents/prisoners2.htm.

8 There is a legal quibble over the question of whether this area belongs to Syria or Lebanon, but not over the fact that it has been illegally occupied by Israel since 1967; at any rate, the Syrian government does not dispute the Lebanese government's claim.

9 John J. Mearsheimer and Stephen Walt, "The Israel Lobby and U.S. Foreign Policy," John F. Kennedy School of Government, Harvard University, Working Paper Number RWP06–011, March 13, 2006, available online at http://ksgnotes1.harvard.edu/Research/wpaper.nsf/rwp/RWP06–011/$File/rwp_06_011_walt.pdf. A shorter version of this paper was published as "The Israel Lobby," *London Review of Books* 28, no. 6 (March 23, 2006), available online at http://www.lrb.co.uk/v28/n06/mear01_.html.

10 Norman G. Finkelstein, "The Israel Lobby: It's Not 'Either/Or,'" *Counterpunch*, May 1, 2006, available online at http://www.counterpunch.org/finkelstein05012006.html; Joseph Massad, "Blaming the Lobby," *Al-Ahram Weekly*, March 23–29, 2006, available online at http://weekly.ahram.org.eg/2006/787/op35.htm; Stephen Zunes, "The Israel Lobby: How Powerful Is It Really?" *Foreign Policy in Focus*, May 16, 2006, available online at http://www.fpif.org/fpiftxt/3270.

11 See p. 56 above.

12 See p. 100 above.

13 Agence France Presse, "China, Russia Refuse to Join Iran Sanctions Statement," June 13, 2006.

14 Ministerial Meeting of the Coordinating Bureau of the Non-Aligned Movement, Putrajaya (Malaysia), "Statement on the Islamic Republic of Iran's Nuclear Issue," NAM/MM/COB/9, May 30, 2006, available online at http://www.un.int/malaysia/NAM/MMCOB_StatementIran.pdf; Agence France Presse, "NAM Backs Iran, Condemns Israel's 'Brutal' Occupation," May 30, 2006; Japan Economic Newswire, "Non-Aligned Nations Back Iran's Nuclear Program," May 30, 2006; U.S. Newswire, "First Public Opinion Poll in Iran's Neighboring Countries Reveals Startling Findings on Possibility of Iranian Nuclear Arms," June 12, 2006.

15 Weapons of Mass Destruction Commission, *Weapons of Terror: Freeing the World of Nuclear, Chemical, and Biological Arms* (Stockholm, 2006), p. 72, available online at http://www.wmdcommission.org/files/Weapons_of_Terror.pdf.

16 Flynt Leverett, "The Gulf Between Us," *New York Times*, January 24, 2006, p. A21; Guy Dinmore, "U.S. Allies Urge Direct Dialogue with Iran," *Financial Times*, May 3, 2006, p. 8.

17 "Leader Attends Memorial Ceremony Marking the 17th Departure Anniversary of Imam Khomeini," Institute for Preserving and Publishing Works by Ayatollah Seyyed Ali Khamenei, June 4, 2006, available online at http://english.khamenei.ir//index.php?option=com_content&task=view&id=442&Itemid=30; Jonathan Steele, "Lost in Translation: Experts Confirm That Iran's President Did Not Call for Israel To Be 'Wiped Off the Map.' Reports That He Did Serve to Strengthen Western Hawks," *Guardian* (online comment), June 14, 2006, http://commentisfree.guardian.co.uk/jonathan_steele/2006/06/post_155.html.

18 Trita Parsi, "Iran Unlikely to Halt Nuclear Enrichment Unless the United States Agrees to Direct Talks," interview with Bernard Gwertzman, May 31, 2006,

available online at Council on Foreign Relations website, http://www.cfr.org/publication/10797/; press release, Government of Iran, February 17, 2006, reporting Larijani's presentation of "the latest positions of the Islamic Republic of Iran on the issue of Iran's peaceful nuclear program" in a French radio interview, February 16, 2006. See also p. 124.

19 Selig Harrison, "It Is Time to Put Security Issues on the Table with Iran," *Financial Times*, January 18, 2006, p. 19.

20 Dafna Linzer, "Past Arguments Don't Square with Current Iran Policy," *Washington Post*, March 27, 2005, p. A15.

21 Guy Dinmore, "Experts Challenge White House Line on Iran's Influence," *Financial Times*, July 18, 2006, p. 6, citing also the prominent dissident Arun Ganji; Amal Saad-Ghorayeb; "The Framing of Hizbullah," *Guardian*, July 15, 2006, p. 30; Dilip Hiro, "Hostages and History," *Guardian* (online comment), July 18, 2006, http://commentisfree.guardian.co.uk/dilip_hiro/2006/07/post_232.html.

22 In particular, see Assaf Kfoury, "Noam Chomsky in Beirut," ZNet, July 12, 2006, http://www.zcommunications.org/znet/viewArticle/3577.

23 Orly Halpern and Nicholas Blanford, "A Second Front Opens for Israel," *Christian Science Monitor*, July 13, 2006, p. 1.

24 Rami G. Khouri, "The Mideast Death Dance," *Salon*, July 15, 2006, http://www.salon.com/opinion/feature/2006/07/15/fourpairs/index_np.html; Patrick Seale, Institute for Public Accuracy, July 13, 2006, http://www.accuracy.org/newsrelease.php?articleId=1310.

25 See pp. 38 and 99.

26 Noah Feldman, "Becoming bin Laden" (review of *Messages to the World: The Statements of Osama bin Laden*), *New York Times Book Review*, February 12, 2006, p. 12; Steven Erlanger, "U.S. and Israelis Are Said to Talk of Hamas Ouster," *New York Times*, February 14, 2006, p. A1.

27 Louis Pérez, "Fear and Loathing of Fidel Castro: Sources of U.S. Policy Toward Cuba," *Journal of Latin American Studies* 34, no. 2 (May 2002), pp. 227–254.

28 Steven R. Weisman, "Europe Plan to Aid Palestinians Stalls over U.S. Salary Sanctions," *New York Times*, June 15, 2006, p. A10. See also Tanya Reinhart, "A Week of Israeli Restraint," *Yediot Ahronot*, June 21, 2006. A striking illustration of this pattern is the intense (and failed) effort to elicit Palestinian violence to justify the planned 1982 invasion. Palestinian violence does continue, however, notably in the form of Qassam rocket attacks from Gaza by groups that refused to accept the Hamas truce—actions both criminal and foolish.

29 Jonathan Cook, "The British Media and the Invasion of Gaza," *Medialens* (UK), June 30, 2006, http://www.medialens.org/alerts/06/060630_kidnapped_by_israel.php; Josh Brannon, "IDF Commandos Enter Gaza, Capture Two Hamas Terrorists," *Jerusalem Post*, June 25, 2006; Ken Ellingwood, "2 Palestinians Held in Israel's First Arrest Raid in Gaza Since Pullout," *Los Angeles Times*, June 25, 2006, p. A20. Apart from the *Los Angeles Times*, there were only a few marginal words in the *Baltimore Sun* (June 25) and the *St. Louis Post-Dispatch* (June 25). Moreover, no mainstream media source chose to refer to this event when discussing Shalit's capture. The only serious coverage I know of in the English-language press appeared in the *Turkish Daily News* (June 25). (Database search by David Peterson.)

30 Aviv Lavie, "Inside Israel's Secret Prison," *Ha'aretz*, August 22, 2003; Jonathan Cook, "Facility 1391: Israel's Guantanamo," *Le Monde Diplomatique*, November 2003; Chris McGreal, "Facility 1391: Israel's Secret Prison," *Guardian*, November 14, 2003, p. 2.

31 Gideon Levy, "A Black Flag," *Ha'aretz*, July 2, 2006; Christopher Gunness, "Statement by the United Nations Agencies Working in the Occupied Palestinian Territory," July 8, 2006, available online at http://www.un.org/unrwa/news/UN_agencies_8Jul06.htm; Amnesty International press release, "Israel/Occupied Territories: Deliberate Attacks a War Crime," AI Index: MDE 15/061/2006 (Public), News Service No. 169, June 30, 2006, available online at http://www.amnesty.org/en/library/info/ MDE15/061/2006.

32 Editorial, "A Problem That Can't Be Ignored," *New York Times*, June 17, 2006, p. A12.

33 Israeli Cabinet Statement on Road Map and 14 Reservations by State of Israel, July 9, 2004, originally released on May 25, 2003; available online at http://www.mideastweb.org/roadmapreservations.htm.

34 See p. 157.

35 Roula Khalaf, "Hizbollah's Bold Attack Raises Stakes in Middle East," *Financial Times*, July 13, 2006, p. 5; David Hirst, "Overnight Lebanon Has Been Plunged into a Role It Endured for 25 Years—That of a Hapless Arena for Other People's Wars," *Guardian*, July 14, 2006, p. 29; Megan K. Stack and Rania Abouzeid, "The Nation of Hezbollah," *Los Angeles Times*, July 13, 2006, p. A1; Neil MacFarquhar and Hassan Fattah, "In Hezbollah Mix of Politics and Arms, Arms Win Out," *New York Times*, July 16, 2006, pp. I:1; Amos Harel, "Israel Faces a Wide Military Escalation," *Ha'aretz*, July 12, 2006; Uri Avnery, "The Real Aim," July 15, 2006, Gush Shalom Web site, http://zope.gush-shalom.org/home/en/channels/avnery/1152991173.

36 Mouin Rabbani, *Democracy Now!*, July 14, 2006, transcript available online at http://www.democracynow.org/article.pl?sid=06/07/14/146258; Saad-Ghorayeb, quoted in Halpern and Blanford, "A Second Front Opens for Israel," p. 1. [The number of prisoners is unknown, apart from the one or two officially admitted. In what may be the first mainstream reference, *Ha'aretz* commentator Nehemia Shtrasler writes that in the course of the six years since Israel's withdrawal from Lebanon, "no one found it correct to neutralize the central demand of Hezbollah: freeing the Lebanese prisoners. The head of the Lebanese government, Fuad Siniora, stated two days ago that freeing these prisoners is a central condition for any agreement. In addition to Samir Quntar, Israel holds about 15 Lebanese prisoners, who have been held here for many years. It was possible to free them long before—to the hands of the moderate Siniora." See Shtrasler, "A Path to Strengthen the Extremists," *Ha'aretz*, July 21, 2006 (in Hebrew)]

37 Hassan Fattah, "Militia Rebuked by Some Arab Countries," *New York Times*, July 17, 2006, p. A1; Dan Murphy and Sameh NaGuib, "Hizbullah Winning over Arab Street," *Christian Science Monitor*, July 18, 2006, p. 1; Edward Wong and Michael Slackman, "Iraqi Prime Minister Denounces Israel's Actions," *New York Times*, October 20, 2006, p. A1; Fawaz Gerges, *Journey of the Jihadist: Inside Muslim Militancy* (Orlando, FL: Harcourt, 2006), p. 26.

38 Lang, quoted in Dan Murphy, "Escalation Ripples Through Middle East," *Christian Science Monitor*, July 14, 2006, p. 1.

Notes to Postscript: Two More Years of Crisis

1 On James Baker, see Naomi Klein, "James Baker's Double Life," *Nation*, November 1, 2004, available online at http://www.thenation.com/doc/20041101/klein.

2 Lee Hamilton, "Let's Get to Know the Saudis," Saudi-US Relations Information Service (SURIS), April 16, 2007, available online at http://www.saudi-us-relations.org/articles/2007/ioi/070416-hamilton-relations.html.

3 James A. Baker III and Lee H. Hamilton et al., *The Iraq Study Group Report* (New York: Vintage Books, 2006), available online at http://www.c-span.org/ pdf/ iraq_study_group_report.pdf.

4 Ibid., p. xv.

5 Ibid., pp. xvi–xvii.

6 Ibid., p. 67 (emphasis in original).

7 Ibid., pp. 19–20.

8 Ibid., p. 20.

9 Ibid.

10 Ibid., p. 84 (emphasis in original).

11 Ibid., p. 85 (emphasis in original).

12 Ibid., p. 84 (emphasis in original).

13 Ibid., p. 73.

14 Ibid. (emphasis added).

15 "President Bush Discusses Global War on Terror," Office of the Press Secretary, White House, Washington, DC (March 19, 2008), available online at http:// www.whitehouse.gov/news/releases/2008/03/20080319-2.html.

16 The Second Amendment, which was ratified on December 15, 1791, reads as follows: "A well regulated Militia, being necessary to the security of a free State, the right of the people to keep and bear Arms, shall not be infringed."

17 "'Sahwa Councils' Threaten to Go on General Strike Due to a Two-Month Delay in the Salaries of Their Members," *Al-Hayat*, March 22, 2008.

18 See Gilbert Achcar with Michael Warschawski, *The 33-Day War: Israel's War on Hezbollah in Lebanon and Its Consequences* (Boulder, CO: Paradigm Publishers, 2007).

19 Edward Luttwak, "A Post-Heroic Military Policy," *Foreign Affairs* 75, no. 4 (July–August 1996).

20 Achcar with Warschawski, *33-Day War*, pp. 51–54.

21 Avraham Tal, "Preparing for the Next War Now," *Ha'aretz*, August 17, 2006; cited in Achcar with Warschawski, *33-Day War*, pp. 78–79.

22 David Rose, "The Gaza Bombshell," *Vanity Fair*, April 2008, available online at http://www.vanityfair.com/politics/features/2008/04/gaza200804.

23 Ibid.

24 Gilbert Achcar, "First Reflections on the Electoral Victory of Hamas," *ZNet*, January 27, 2006, http://www.zcommunications.org/znet/viewArticle/4535.

25 Amnesty International U.K., CARE International U.K., CAFOD, Christian Aid, Médecins du Monde U.K., Oxfam, Save the Children U.K. and Trócaire, *The Gaza Strip: A Humanitarian Implosion*, March 6, 2008, available online at http://www.oxfam.org.uk/resources/downloads/oxfam_gaza_lowres.pdf.

26 Ibid., p. 6.

27 John Mueller and Karl Mueller, "Sanctions of Mass Destruction," *Foreign Affairs* 78, no. 3 (May–June 1999).

28 See Benjamin Page with Marshall Bouton, *The Foreign Policy Disconnect* (Chicago: University of Chicago Press, 2006). The same is true of domestic policy. For many examples, see my *Failed States* (New York: Metropolitan Books, 2006).

29 Vicente Navarro, "Yes, We Can! Can We? The Next Failure of Health Care Reform," *Counterpunch Special Report*, March 6, 2008, available online at http://www.counterpunch.org/navarro03062008.html. Professor of Public Policy, Sociology, and Policy Studies at Johns Hopkins University, Navarro is one of the leading specialists on health care reform.

30 For useful analysis, see Mike Davis, *In Praise of Barbarians* (Chicago: Haymarket, 2007), Ch. 8.

271

66666666666666

31 Ibid. (emphasis in original). See also pp. 42f. of this paperback edition.

32 C. J Chivers, "Grozny Journal: Nonstop to Chechnya: As War Ebbs, Flights Return," *New York Times*, September 11, 2007.

33 "Declaration of Principles for a Long-Term Relationship of Cooperation and Friendship Between the Republic of Iraq and the United States of America," signed on August 26, 2007, available online at http://www.whitehouse.gov/news/releases/2007/11/20071126–11.html; Charlie Savage, "In Signing Statement, Bush Looks to Bypass Four Laws," *Boston Globe*, January 29, 2008; Thom Shanker and Steven Lee Myers, "U.S. to Insist Iraq Grant It Wide Mandate in Operations," *New York Times*, January 25, 2008.

34 Kevin Ryan, "The 'Withdrawal' That Isn't," *Boston Globe*, March 29, 2007.

35 On vacillation, see Carolyn Lochhead, "Even If Dems Win, Total Exit Uncertain; Neither Clinton Nor Obama Promises to Pull Out All Troops," *San Francisco Chronicle*, March 17, 2008.

36 Taylor Owen and Ben Kiernan, "Bombs over Cambodia," *Walrus*, October 2006.

37 James Paul, quoted in "Five Years After Invading Iraq," Institute for Public Accuracy News Release, March 19, 2008, available online at http://www.accuracy.org/news-release.php?articleId=1672. For extensive background details, see Global Policy Forum, "War and Occupation in Iraq," June 2007, available online at http://www.globalpolicy.org/security/issues/iraq/occupation/report/index.htm.

38 Akiva Eldar, "Killing Yassin Saved Sharon," *Ha'aretz*, March 23, 2004; Brian Whitaker, "Assassination Method: Surveillance Drone and a Hellfire Missile," *Guardian*, March 23, 2004; and Palestinian Center for Human Rights, March 22, 2004, reporting seven civilians killed along with Yassin. For a review of Israel's assassination policies, see Tanya Reinhart, *The Road to Nowhere: Israel-Palestine Since 2003* (New York: Norton, 2006); and Victoria Brittain, "They Had to Die: Assassination Against Liberation," *Race and Class* 48, no. 1 (2006), p. 60. As Brittain observes, "With the beginning of the twenty-first century, Israeli assassination tactics became more violent, more reckless of the consequences for civilians and heedless of any international censure," thanks to U.S. protection, without which "Israel would long since have become the pariah state that apartheid South Africa became."

39 Pervez Hoodbhoy, "The War of Drones," *Dawn* (Pakistan), March 9, 2008.

40 CNN, February 1, 2008, transcript available online at http://edition.cnn.com/2008/US/01/31/alqaeda.death/index.html; Ethan Bronner, "Poll Shows Most Palestinians Favor Violence over Talks," *New York Times*, March 19, 2008; Steven Erlanger and Isabel Kershner, "Gunman in Jerusalem Attack Identified," *New York Times*, March 7, 2008.

41 Michael R. Gordon and Jeff Zeleny, "If Elected . . . Obama Envisions New Iran Approach," *New York Times*, November 2, 2007.

42 Program on International Policy Attitudes, "A Majority of Americans Reject Military Threats in Favor of Diplomacy with Iran," December 7, 2006, available online at http://www.worldpublicopinion.org/pipa/articles/brunitedstatescanadara/286.php.

43 Peter Grier, "Castro's Exit May Spur U.S. Policy Rethink," *Christian Science Monitor*, February 21, 2008.

44 Correlli Barnett, "Attack Iran and Spark World War," *Daily Mail* (London), March 4, 2007.

45 Cirincione quoted online at PIPA, "Iranians Want Capacity to Enrich Uranium But Accept NPT Rules Against Developing Nuclear Weapons," January 30, 2007, http://www.worldpublicopinion.org/pipa/articles/brmiddleeastnafricara/311.php.

46 PIPA, "American Public Says Government Leaders Should Pay Attention to Polls; Eight in Ten Say Public Should Have Greater Influence on Government," news release, March 21, 2008, available online at http://www.world publicopinion.org/pipa/articles/governance_bt/461.php.

47 Ibid.

48 The published parts of the NIE do not indicate that Iran had a nuclear weapons program prior to 2003. On reasons to question whether they did, see the interview with Iran specialist Ervand Abrahamian in David Barsamian, *Targeting Iran* (San Francisco: City Lights, 2007), pp. 86–87, citing high Iranian military officials. The critique by these officials of a nuclear program bears some similarity to the detailed argument by the prominent Israeli strategic analyst Zeev Maoz that Israel's nuclear weapons program has harmed its security. See *Defending the Holy Land* (Ann Arbor: University of Michigan Press, 2006).

49 Trita Parsi, *Treacherous Alliance: The Secret Dealings of Israel, Iran, and the United States* (New Haven, CT: Yale University Press, 2007).

50 Ismail Haniyeh, "Aggression Under False Pretenses," *Washington Post,* July 11, 2006; Khalid Mish'al, "Our Unity Can Now Pave the Way for Peace and Justice," *Guardian,* February 13, 2007.

51 News bulletin, Stop the Wall Campaign, March 11, 2008, available online at http://stopthewall.org/latestnews/1620.shtml; Rosie Walker, "Another Brick in the Wall: Saving Schools in the West Bank," *Independent* (U.K.), November 22, 2007.

52 Olmert quoted in Ilene Prusher, "Israel's 'Religious Right' Gains Clout, Complicating Peacemaking," *Christian Science Monitor,* March 19, 2008.

53 Prusher, "Israel's 'Religious Right' Gains Clout."

54 One index is provided by a Human Rights Watch report indicating that from September 2005, when Israeli settlers were transferred from Gaza to other occupied territories (called "withdrawal"), to late June 2006 (when Israeli attacks on Gaza sharply intensified), Israel fired more than 7,700 155-mm shells at northern Gaza. See Howard Friel and Richard Falk, *Israel-Palestine on Record* (New York: Verso, 2007).

55 "MK Schneller: Give PA Wadi Ara, 'Triangle,'" Israel National News, April 27, 2007; Livni quoted in Scott Wilson, "For Israel's Arab Citizens, Isolation and Exclusion," *Washington Post,* December 20, 2007.

56 See Michael Walzer, "Nationalism, Internationalism, and the Jews: The Chimera of a Binational State," in *Israel, the Arabs and the Middle East,* ed. Irving Howe and Carl Gershman (New York: Bantam 1972), a collection of democratic socialist essays. See also Benny Morris's interview with Ari Shavit in *Ha'aretz,* January 8, 2004. Morris, who has done some of the most important historical work refuting the traditional Zionist version of the events of 1948 and the subsequent conflict, believes that Ben-Gurion's greatest error in 1948, perhaps a "fatal mistake," was not to have "cleansed the whole country—the whole Land of Israel, as far as the Jordan River." The Hebrew phrase is "tihur etni," which translates literally as "ethnic purification."

57 Wilson, "For Israel's Arab Citizens." On the array of mechanisms, see my *Towards a New Cold War* (New York: Pantheon, 1982), and for more extensive analysis, Walter Lehn and Uri Davis, *The Jewish National Fund* (New York: Kegan Paul International, 1988). Some note that the JNF *owns* about an eighth of Israel's land, but the relevant figure is the amount of land it effectively *controls* and to which its discriminatory policies apply.

58 Yoav Stern, "Three-Story Home in Baka al-Garbiyeh for Sale; Jews Encouraged to Apply," *Ha'aretz,* May 1, 2006.

59 Wilson, "For Israel's Arab Citizens."
60 Yossi Sarid, *Ha'aretz*, November 11, 2006, quoted in Friel and Falk, *Israel-Palestine on Record*, p. 268; Reuven Kaminer, "Concern over Anti-Semitism," March 1, 2008, available online at http://groups.yahoo.com/group/JustPeaceUK/message/22794.

Index

expansion of 83; Kurds and 112;
terrorism and 5
Navarro, Vicente 230
Nazis 3, 6, 93, 97–98, 120, 161, 175,
177, 180, 240, 244
Neoconservatives 21, 27, 46, 78, 79,
194; influence of 38; Saudi kingdom
and 34, 78
Neoliberalism 9, 27, 28, 29, 30, 82,
115, 164, 187; opposition to 83;
pursuing 81, 84
Netanyahu, Benjamin 151
New Deal 29
"New Europe" 80, 84
"New Labour" 106
New Left 179
New Outlook 159, 261n63
"New Way Forward, The" (Bush) 217
New York Review of Books 110
New York Times 79, 110, 211, 232;
on bin Laden/democracy 45, 208;
Friedman and 77; on health care
42; Howe in 178–179; on Hughes
speeches 36; on September 11th/
Afghanistan 63, 64; Wheatcroft
in 119
Nongovernmental actors 229;
terrorism and 5, 8, 24
Non-Proliferation Treaty 236, 256n69
Northern Alliance 39, 69, 70
North, Oliver 67
"No state" solution 139
Nour, Ayman 46
Nouvelle Guerre Froide, La (*The New
Cold War*) (Achcar) xiii
Nuclear issues 234, 235, 236, 237
Nuclear Non-Proliferation Treaty 124
Nuclear weapons 6, 9, 12, 25, 62, 177,
236; elimination of 83; Iran and
122, 123–124, 203, 205–206, 236,
237, 271n48; Israel and 121, 122,
125, 148; proliferation of 124–125;
terror and 6, 12, 14
Nuremberg Tribunal 3, 231

Obama, Barack: Cuba and 235; Iran
and 234, 235, 236; Iraq and 231,
233; Israel and 238, 239
Occupation (Iraq) 4, 21, 79, 85, 88;
dangers of 92, 104; insurgency and
103, 105; opposition to 102, 103;

resistance to 4, 87, 91, 93, 105;
responsibility for 102; security and
91; support for 101, 105; worst-case
scenario 104
Occupied Territories, Palestinian 26,
137, 168, 240; corruption in 166,
167; Jordan merger and 139; Oslo
agreement and 150, 156–157, 211;
Palestinian state in 156; permanent
government in 158; settlement and
137, 138, 139; settlements in 31,
168, 174; Sharon Plan and 164;
status of 149; two-state settlement
and 129, 131
Ocean Hill-Brownsville conflict 54,
250n9
Office of Foreign Assets Control
(OFAC) 7
Oil 25, 33, 34, 37, 47–53; access to 50;
controlling 52, 75; as driving force
49; economic/strategic interests
and 50; foreign policy and 50, 56;
fundamentalists and 52; illegal sales
of 107; income distribution from
115; price of 16, 19, 20, 33, 57, 74;
reserves of/location 10, 74; robbing
Iraq of 74; U.S. military presence
and 22
Oil interests 39, 60, 82, 89; foreign
policy and 50, 56
Oil law 216, 220
"Old Europe" 80, 83, 84; Iraq war
and 84
Olmert, Ehud 198, 210, 212, 240, 241
Omar, Mullah 64
"Operation National Trauma, '82"
(*Ha'aretz*) 148
Organization in the Land of the Two
Rivers 92
Orientalism 187
Orthodoxy, fundamentalism and 30
Oslo Accords 59, 257n9, 260n41;
Allon Plan and 154; criticism of
132, 134, 137, 151, 160; Occupied
Territories and 150, 156–157, 211;
PA and 167; Palestinians and 137;
PLO and 137, 150, 155, 156–157
Ottoman Empire 47, 140; corruption
of 112–113; "no state" solution
and 139
Oxford Research International 91

Printed in the United States
by Baker & Taylor Publisher Services